EARLY MUSIC HISTORY 22

STUDIES IN MEDIEVAL AND EARLY MODERN MUSIC

Edited by
IAIN FENLON
Fellow of King's College, Cambridge

Printed in the United Kingdom at the University Press, The Edinburgh Building, Cambridge CB2 2RU, United Kingdom
40 West 20th Street, New York, NY 10011–4211, USA
477 Williamstown Road, Port Melbourne, VIC 3027, Australia

First Published 2003

Phototypeset in Baskerville by Wyvern 21 Ltd, Bristol
Printed in Great Britain at the University Press, Cambridge

ISSN 0261–1279

ISBN 0 521 83109 1

SUBSCRIPTIONS The subscription price (excluding VAT) of volume 22, which includes postage plus electronic access to istitutional subscribers only, is £75 (US $115 in USA and Canada) for institutions, £40 (US $63 in USA and Canada) for individuals ordering direct from the Press and certifying that the annual is for their personal use. An electronic only price is available to institutional subscribers for £70 (US$105 in USA and Canada). Airmail (orders to Cambridge only) £10.00 extra. Copies of the annual for subscribers in the USA and Canada are sent by air to New York to arrive with minimum delay. Orders, which must be accompanied by payment, may be sent to a book-seller, subscription agent or direct to the publishers: Cambridge University Press, The Edinburgh Building, Shaftesbury Road, Cambridge CB2 2RU. Payment may be made by any of the following methods: cheque (payable to Cambridge University Press), UK postal order, bank draft, Post Office Giro (account no. 571 6055 GB Bootle – advise CUP of payment), international money order, UNESCO coupons, or any credit card bearing the Interbank symbol. EU subscribers (outside the UK) who are not registered for VAT should add VAT at their country's rate. VAT registered subscribers should provide their VAT registration number. Japanese prices for institutions (including ASP delivery) are available from Kinokuniya Company Ltd, P.O. Box 55, Chitose, Tokyo. Orders from the USA and Canada should be sent to Cambridge University Press, 40 West 20th Street, New York, NY 10011–4211, USA.

BACK VOLUMES Volumes 1–8 and 11–21 are available from the publisher at £62 ($102 in USA and Canada).

NOTE Each volume of *Early Music History* is now published in the year in which it is subscribed. Volume 22 is therefore published in 2003. Readers should be aware, however, that some earlier volumes have been subscribed in the year *after* the copyright and publication date given on this imprints page. Thus volume 8, the volume received by 1989 subscribers, is dated 1988 on the imprints page.

INTERNET ACCESS This journal is included in the Cambridge Journals Online service which can be found at www.journals.cambridge.org. For further information on other Press titles access http://www.cambridge.org.

CONTENTS

EDITORIAL BOARD

Early Music History (2003) Volume 22. *© Cambridge University Press*
DOI:10.1017/S0261127903003012 Printed in the United Kingdom

JEANICE BROOKS

O QUELLE ARMONYE: DIALOGUE SINGING IN LATE RENAISSANCE FRANCE

François de Billon's *Fort inexpugnable de l'honneur du sexe feminin* (1555) was among the most extensive contributions to the sixteenth-century polemic on the nature of women known as the *querelle des femmes*. In keeping with the military connotations of its title, Billon's 'impregnable fortress' is an exercise in bellicose rhetoric; his sallies are illustrated with woodcuts of roaring lions and fire-spitting cannons to heighten the effect of bravado. In the section on women's musical gifts, he vaunts the 'angelic sweetness' of the female singing voice, and claims that although male musicians more often win fame, women have always been better singers:

In [singing] nevertheless women have always been the very best. Whatever may be said by Sandrin, Arcadelt or Janequin, the most renowned musicians of Europe in our time, whom I would willingly ask, 'Where is it that one can find sweetness of vocal harmony, in general, if not in the musical throat of Woman, even if she puts forth only a little warbling?' And if they answered that in some men one finds more, could I not rightly reply, 'What is the reason, my friends, that so few men of your profession are married and that you all flee marriage, if not that through propriety [*honnesteté*] you would be forced to bring your wives (instead of choirboys) into princely chambers to sing with you, or without you, which would be found so much sweeter than any childish voice? O what harmony, if you were all married in the normal fashion to beautiful women; if they were well instructed by you in the rules of music; and if in the aforementioned manner, you tuned yourselves well with them. The pleasure of listening to you would be double, the advantage triple, and thus, frequently nothing would be sung except in duo'.[1]

I would like to thank Tim Carter, Francesca Chiarelli, Robert Evans, Thorsten Hindrichs, Leofranc Holford-Strevens, Jonathan Le Cocq, Laurie Stras, Richard Wistreich and anonymous readers for their help and suggestions. Earlier versions of this study were presented at the Université Libre de Bruxelles, the University of Texas at Austin and the Annual Meeting of the American Musicological Society in Toronto, 2000; my thanks to Richard Freedman for stepping in for me on the latter occasion and for his helpful comments on my work.

[1] 'En quoy ce nonobstant les Femmes se sont tousjours trouvées les Superlatives. Quoy qu'en sachent dire Sendrin, Arcadel, ou Jennequin, de ce temps les renomméz Musiciens de l'Eürope, Ausquelz je demanderois volontiers, la où c'est que l'on pourroit trouver

In this passage Billon aims his artillery at more than one masculine stronghold. He implicitly criticises the church, the institutional frame for the careers of most famous musicians of the day. Despite their involvement in secular music-making at court, Sandrin, Arcadelt and Janequin were all clerics, learned their trade as choirboys themselves and spent large portions of their lives holding ecclesiastical appointments that generally involved the supervision of boy singers. Billon's advocacy of marriage for men 'de vostre qualité' is thus disingenous at best, and his use of the notoriously slippery word *honnesteté* in this context lends a moral tinge to his recommendation.[2]

Billon's main target, however, is the princely chamber, which in late medieval France had been an almost exclusively male preserve. The early sixteenth century saw radical changes to this tradition. With Anne de Bretagne's creation of the *maison de la reine* and its troop of ladies-in-waiting, aristocratic women had a permanent place in the court's structure for the first time, and under François I (d. 1547) these women played a vital part in the strategies of sociability through which courtiers impressed their superiors and each other. Courtly manners, a crucial element in the construction of early modern monarchy, relied heavily on the notion of woman as a necessary mirror for male achievement. Through their company and their pleasing attainments – conversation, music-making, dancing – well-born women provided the setting in which the perfect courtier's accomplishments could shine.

suavité de vocalle armonye, en génerale, fors qu'en la Gorge organisée de la Femme, soit qu'elle ne déploye que son petit Ramage. Et s'ilz me respondoient qu'en aucuns Hommes s'en trouve davantage, Pourrois-je pas bien replicquer, Qu'elle est la cause mes Amys, que si peu d'Hommes de votre qualité sont maryéz et que tous fuyéz Mariage, fors pour n'estre Subjets par honnesteté (et au lieu d'Enfans de coeur) de mener voz Femmes es Chambres des Princes, tenir la Partie avec vous, ou sans vous, qui trop plus douce seroit trouvée que de toute autre Voix puérile? O quelle Armonye si vous etiéz tous communement maryéz à belles Femmes: Qu'elles feüssent de vous bien instruytes des Reigles de Musique: Et qu'en la façon dessusdite, vous vous accordissiéz bien avec elles. Le plaisir de vous écouter seroit double, le proufit triple, et si, bien souvent ne seroit chanté qu'en Duo.' F. de Billon, *Le fort inexpugnable de l'honneur du sexe feminin* (Paris, 1555; facs. edn. with introduction by M. A. Screech, Wakefield, NY and The Hague, 1970), fol. 156^{r-v}. Billon explains in the preface that although not published until 1555, the text was written in 1550 while its author was in Rome in the service of Guillaume Du Bellay; its descriptions of court life thus relate primarily to the reign of François I.

2 *Honnesteté* had a range of meanings from 'goodness' or 'loyalty' to more complex concepts of truthfulness, propriety, suitability, dignity, civility or elegance; the *Dictionnaire du moyen français: la Renaissance* (Paris, 1992) supplies no fewer than twelve definitions of the adjective *honneste* from which it is derived.

Backlash against this new role is a central component of the anti-female writing of the *querelle*; in their descriptions of female moral and intellectual inferiority, misogynist contributors to the debate focus almost exclusively on the activities and characters of courtiers.[3] By championing women's cause against those who saw their influence as trivialising or pernicious, Billon aligned himself with the new courtly ideals. He goes much further, however, than simply endorsing the practice of music by aristocratic women as part of a suite of courtly attainments. He advocates the creation of a class of professional female musicians, women who share the social status of their husbands and who perform together with their partners in duos that provide a musical realisation of their relationship. At the same time, he proposes an innovative career path for the king's male singers, leading not through holy orders and the royal chapel but through marriage and the secular environment of the chamber.

It would be good to know what Arcadelt, Sandrin or Janequin thought of Billon's challenge; unfortunately, none responded, at least not in print. Billon's call for the replacement of choirboys in princely chambers with beautiful singing women went unheeded too, at least at the French royal court he frequented: payment records from the late sixteenth century continued to include two to three choirboys among the singers of the king's *musique de chambre*.[4] The traditional career pattern for male musicians remained common, and many of the royal chamber singers of the second half of the century took orders and held positions in the polyphony chapel while simultaneously exercising functions in the secular arm of the court musical establishment.[5] But in the

[3] For a brief review of the *querelle* and its connections to courtly Neoplatonism, see L. D. Kritzman, 'The Neoplatonic Debate', in *A New History of French Literature*, ed. D. Hollier (Cambridge, 1989), pp. 187–9; Nancy Vickers's article 'Manners and Mannerisms at Court' in the same collection (pp. 148–54) traces connections between court etiquette, politics and literature under François I. For a recent evaluation of the vast literature on civility and early modern statehood, see J. Adamson, 'The Making of the Ancien-Régime Court 1500–1750', in id. (ed.), *The Princely Courts of Europe: Ritual, Politics and Culture under the Ancien Régime 1500–1750* (London, 1999), pp. 7–41.

[4] For transcriptions of extant royal *états de maison* (lists of household members) from 1559 to 1589, see J. Brooks, *Courtly Song in Late Sixteenth-Century France* (Chicago, 2000), pp. 393–412.

[5] On career patterns for royal chapel and chamber singers, see *ibid.*, pp. 78–81, and ead., 'From Minstrel to Courtier: The Royal *Musique de Chambre* and Courtly Ideals in Sixteenth-Century France', *Musikalischer Alltag im 15. und 16. Jahrhundert = Trossinger Jahrbuch für Renaissancemusik*, 1 (Kassel, 2001), pp. 39–49.

decades after the appearance of Billon's book, the court also cherished a pair of singers who made a better match with the model he proposed: Girard de Beaulieu and Violante Doria, a married couple who were among the most successful musicians in France during the reigns of the last Valois kings.

Beaulieu and Doria belonged to a generation of singers whose activities are usually said to be instrumental in the development of the characteristic musical language of early seventeenth-century solo song. Though it is generally accepted that Renaissance performers played a vital role in the emergence of styles that were not consistently reflected in print until after 1600, we are only beginning to understand how the process may have worked, and relationships between singers' biographies, performance practice, musical style and cultural setting can be difficult to establish. Recent studies that have begun to redress this situation have focused exclusively on Italian singers and repertories, and the particular case of singing couples has been addressed only in an Italian context.[6] Yet the social and musical currents that shaped the careers of such Italian musicians were at work in other European centres as well. For France, study of these patterns has been impeded by the fragmentation of documentary sources and the distinctive conditions that obtain in French music printing in the late sixteenth century. These problems have obscured the parallels between the social and musical cultures of the royal court of France and those of better-known north Italian centres.

My purpose here is to trace the careers of Girard de Beaulieu and Violante Doria at the French royal court; abundant but previously unstudied archival material helps to document the new professional circumstances their lives exemplify. The establishment of their role in the creation of the *Balet comique de la royne* (1581) is a central point of my argument. The vocal showpiece they sang on

[6] Studies of female singers include T. Carter, 'Finding a Voice: Vittoria Archilei and the Florentine "New Music"', in L. Hutson (ed.), *Feminism and Renaissance Studies* (Oxford, 1999), pp. 450–67, and L. Stras, 'Recording Tarquinia: Imitation, Parody and Reportage in Ingegneri's "Hor che'l ciel e la terra e'l vento tace"', *Early Music*, 27 (1999), pp. 359–77. Richard Wistreich, 'Giulio Cesare Brancaccio and Solo Bass Singing in Sixteenth-Century Italy' (Ph.D. thesis, Royal Holloway, University of London, 2002), treats the career of the famous Neapolitan basso. The best-known example of a singing couple in Italy is no doubt Giulio Caccini and Lucia di Filippo Gagnolanti; the couple whose careers show the most striking parallels with those of Doria and Beaulieu was formed by Alessandro Striggio and Virginia Vagnoli (see below).

that occasion not only underlines their deployment of the technical skills that would come to characterise the 'new music' of the early Baroque, it is a solo dialogue, a genre usually considered typical of the seventeenth century. Their duo from the *Balet comique* was, in fact, the only solo dialogue to appear in print as such in France before 1611. Yet traces of other similar duo performances survive in contemporary polyphonic prints. When read against the documentary evidence of Beaulieu and Doria's careers and interpreted in the light of the *Balet comique* and of later publications of solo song, late sixteenth-century musical sources suggest that the seventeenth-century solo dialogue had deep roots in the performance culture of the preceding decades. A mirror of changes in the milieu that produced it, the French dialogue of the late Renaissance symbolises the centrality of new concepts of civility to the fabric of the court and the musical practices and institutions it fostered.

BEAULIEU AND DORIA AT COURT, OR, WHO WROTE THE *BALET COMIQUE DE LA ROYNE*?

Beaulieu's name is usually invoked by modern scholars writing on the *Balet comique de la royne*, one of the entertainments performed during the October 1581 wedding celebrations for Henri III's favourite, the duc de Joyeuse, and the queen's sister, Marguerite de Lorraine-Vaudémont.[7] Celebrated in its own time, the *Balet comique* occupies a no less eminent place in modern music-theatrical history. In accounts of French ballet, the *Balet comique* inevitably figures as the most important court spectacle of the late Renaissance; as the first such entertainment to feature a continuous narrative, it is normally characterised as a significant forerunner of French opera, and it has been accorded an influence over Italian dramatic music of the early seventeenth century as well.[8] Yet despite the event's iconic status, the question of who was responsible for the music remains vexed.

[7] B. de Beaujoyeulx, *Le balet comique de la royne, faict aux nopces de Monsieur le Duc de Joyeuse et madamoyselle de Vaudemont* (Paris, 1582; facs. edn. with introduction by M. M. McGowan, Binghamton, 1982). For a modern edition, see *Le balet comique de la royne, 1581*, trans. and ed. C. and L. MacClintock (Rome, 1971). On the wedding festivities, see F. A. Yates, 'Poésie et musique dans les *Magnificences* au mariage du duc de Joyeuse', in *Musique et poésie au XVI*e *siècle* (Paris, 1954), pp. 241–64.

[8] On contemporary reactions to the *Balet comique*, see McGowan's introduction to Beaujoyeulx, *Le balet comique*, pp. 39–42. News of the event was widely disseminated

The violinist Balthazar de Beaujoyeulx described the genesis of the *Balet comique* in his preface to the print that appeared the year after its performance. According to Beaujoyeulx, the queen, Louise de Lorraine-Vaudémont, charged him with devising an entertainment for her contribution to the wedding festivities; his response was an innovative project that would 'make the ballet speak, and the drama resound and sing'.[9] After approving Beaujoyeulx's plans, Louise assigned Nicolas Filleul to write the poetry and the royal painter Jacques Patin to design and execute the scenery for Beaujoyeulx's scenario. For the music, Beaujoyeulx says:

> She commanded likewise the sieur de Beaulieu (who is one of her servants) to make and prepare in his home all that could be said to be perfect in music, based on the ideas that would be given to him by me, serving as subjects for the material. In which [task] he performed so well that he (whom the most perfect musicians say excels in their art) surpassed himself . . .[10]

through ambassadorial reports and even through popular song: the *Sommaire de tous les recueils des plus excellentes chansons* (Paris, 1583), fols. 2ᵛ–5ᵛ, contains a 'Chanson nouvelle du mariage de Monsieur le Duc de Joyeuse . . . sur le chant, Quand ce beau printemps je voy' with a description of the *Balet comique*. Modern discussions of the work are legion. It occupies a central role in histories of court ballet: H. Prunières, *Le ballet de cour en France avant Benserade et Lully* (Paris, 1914; repr. New York, 1970) and M. M. McGowan, *L'art du ballet de cour en France 1581–1643* (Paris, 1963); it is a principal focus of recent studies in dance (e.g. T. M. Greene, 'Labyrinth Dances in the French and English Renaissance', *Renaissance Quarterly*, 54 (2001), pp. 1403–66). Beaujoyeulx's place in the title of J. R. Anthony, *French Baroque Music from Beaujoyeulx to Rameau*, rev. edn. (New York, 1978) indicates his conviction that the *Balet comique* was the herald of a new musical era; he points out (p. 28) that the tradition of regarding it as central to the development of French dramatic music goes back to the mid-eighteenth century at least. Other typical accounts include articles in *The New Grove Dictionary of Opera*, ed. S. Sadie (London, 1992), i, pp. 293–4, s.v. 'ballet de cour' by M. E. C. Bartlet (where the *Balet comique* appears as the most important early example, standing at the head of a tradition that stretches through to the eighteenth-century *opéra-ballet*) and ii, pp. 271–7, s.v. 'France' by D. Charlton with R. Langham-Smith (in which the main body of the article begins with the *Balet comique*, described as 'the most celebrated of [late Renaissance] proto-operatic events'). Prunières and, more recently, Iain Fenlon have posited French court ballet and particularly the *Balet comique* as a model for Italian musical theatre (H. Prunières, *L'opéra italien en France avant Lulli* (Paris, 1913; repr. New York, 1971), pp. xxiv–xxvi); I. Fenlon, 'The Origins of the Seventeenth-Century Staged *Ballo*', in id. and T. Carter (eds.), *Con che soavità: Studies in Italian Opera, Song and Dance, 1580–1740* (Oxford, 1995), pp. 13–40; and I. Fenlon and C. MacClintock, s.v. 'Beaujoyeux [*sic*], Balthasar de', in *The New Grove Dictionary of Music and Musicians*, 2nd edn., ed. S. Sadie (London, 2001; henceforth *New Grove II*). Interest in the *Balet comique* has recently led to a full-length collection of essays on the work: M. T. Dellabora (ed.), *'Une invention moderne': Baldasare da Belgioioso e il 'Balet comique de la Royne'* (Lucca, 1999).

[9] 'Ainsi j'ay animé et fait parler le Balet, et chanter et resonner la Comedie . . .' Beaujoyeulx, *Le balet comique*, 'Au Lecteur' (unfoliated prefatory material).

[10] 'Elle commanda pareillement au sieur de Beaulieu (qui est à elle), qu'il fist et dressast en son logis tout ce qui se pouvoit dire de parfaict en musique, sur les inventions qui

Beaujoyeulx adds that Beaulieu was aided by musicians of the *chambre du roi*, especially a certain 'maistre Salmon'.

Later in the print Beaujoyeulx describes a central moment of the *Balet comique*, the entry of a car representing a giant fountain drawn by three sea horses, carrying the queen and her ladies-in-waiting costumed as water nymphs. Seated at the base of the fountain were two musicians: 'Above and behind the [sea horses'] tails were two other thrones, in one of which was seated the sieur de Beaulieu, playing Glaucus, called by poets the god of the sea; and in the other, the *damoiselle* de Beaulieu his wife, holding a lute, likewise playing Tethys, the goddess of the sea . . .'.[11] In the accompanying engraving, we see the singers at the front of the car; 'la damoyselle de Beaulieu' is indeed playing a lute, while her partner is holding a bass bowed string instrument (Figure 1). The subsequent pages include music for a dialogue for bass and soprano in praise of the queen. Florid and vocally demanding solo interventions by Glaucus and Tethys alternate with a five-part vocal and instrumental refrain performed by royal chamber musicians representing tritons or sea gods.[12]

In nearly all modern histories and music dictionaries, the 'sieur de Beaulieu' of the *Balet comique* is identified as a 'Lambert de Beaulieu', an error apparently first made by François-Joseph Fétis in his *Biographie universelle des musiciens*. Fétis discovered a letter from the emperor Rudolph II, sent some months after Henri III's assassination in 1589, in which Rudolph asked his ambassador in France, Auger Busbecq, to find and hire Lambert de Beaulieu, a bass who sang admirably to his own accompaniment and who had been in Henri's service. Without any other documentary material

luy seroyent par moy communiquees, servants au suject de la matiere. En quoy il s'est si heureusement comporté, que luy (que les plus parfaicts Musiciens disent exceller en cest art) s'est surmonté luy-mesme . . .'. Beaujoyeulx, *Le balet comique*, fol. 3^{r}. Jacqueline Boucher has shown that the 'sieur de la Chesnaye' to whom Beaujoyeulx attributes the poetry was the well-known poet Nicolas Filleul and not an otherwise unknown courtier, as has often been supposed. J. Boucher, *Société et mentalités autour de Henri III* (Ph.D. diss., Université de Lyon II, 1977; Paris, 1981), iii, p. 1053.

[11] 'Au deçà et delà de leurs queues estoyent deux autres chaires, en l'une desquelles s'asseoit le sieur de Beaulieu, representant Glaucus, appelé par les poetes Dieu de la mer: et en l'autre la damoyselle de Beaulieu son espouse, tenant un luth en sa main, et representant aussi Tethys, la deesse de la mer . . .'. Beaujoyeulx, *Le balet comique*, fol. 16^{r}. The title *damoiselle* was used for gentlewomen not of the first rank; the word *dame* was reserved for the Virgin Mary, queens, princesses, and members of the highest nobility. Neither refers to marital status.

[12] Beaujoyeulx, *Le balet comique*, fols. 19^{r}–21^{r}.

Figure 1 'Figure de la Fontaine' (detail) from B. de Beaujoyeulx, *Le balet comique de la royne* (Paris, 1581). Cliché Bibliothèque Nationale de France

to corroborate or contradict this information, Fétis reasonably supposed that the 'Lambert de Beaulieu' the emperor hoped to recruit was the 'Sieur de Beaulieu' cited in the print of the *Balet comique* as responsible for the music.[13]

Fétis's identification has been accepted by generations of scholars, who have continued to ascribe the music of the *Balet comique de la royne* to the 'Lambert' of Rudolph's letter.[14] Yet no 'Lambert de Beaulieu' figures in any extant French royal account from the period 1560–90 or in any other contemporary document that has so far come to light. There are, however, dozens of payments and references in court documents to Girard de Beaulieu. Knowledge of some of these led Frances Yates to revise her own attribution of the *Balet comique* to Lambert, and to argue that Girard was the musician concerned; Jacqueline Boucher's exhaustive research into French court archives led her to a similar conclusion.[15] Music historians have continued to associate the *Balet comique* with 'Lambert', however, usually without noting the existence of Girard or else claiming that he was a different individual. For example, *The New Grove Dictionary of Music and Musicians* supplies separate entries for Girard and Lambert de Beaulieu; that under Girard's name asserts that he was a music teacher and only possibly a composer, not to be identified with Lambert, the creator of the music for the *Balet comique*.[16]

[13] F.-J. Fétis, *Biographie universelle des musiciens*, 2nd edn. (Paris, 1873; repr. Brussels, 1963), i, pp. 283–4, s.v. 'Beaulieu'. The letter appears in Rudolph II, *Divi Rudolphi imperatoris, caesaris augusti epistolae ineditae . . .*, ed. Bernard, count de Pace (Vienna, 1771), p. 210; its text is reproduced in the Appendix. None of the letters in this collection has subsequently been re-edited, and the location of the count de Pace's sources is unknown. No response appears in Busbecq's published correspondence (C. T. Forster and F. H. Blackburne Daniell, *The Life and Letters of Ogier Ghiselin de Busbecq*, 2 vols. (London, 1881)).

[14] These include Dellabora, introduction to *'Une invention moderne'*, pp. 35 and 38; McGowan, introduction to Beaujoyeulx, *Le balet comique*, p. 38; *Le balet comique*, ed. MacClintock and MacClintock, p. 11, as well as the vast majority of music dictionaries and textbooks. The only modern recording of the *Balet comique* (dir. Gabriel Garrido, K617080, rec. 1997) attributes it to Lambert de Beaulieu.

[15] Boucher, *Société et mentalités*, iii, pp. 1057–8. In *The French Academies of the Sixteenth Century* (London, 1947; repr. with foreword by J. B Trapp, 1988), p. 238, Yates followed the usual attribution of the *Balet comique* to 'Lambert'; she revised this in 'Dramatic Religious Processions in Paris in the Late Sixteenth Century', *Annales Musicologiques*, 2 (1954), pp. 251–2. I asserted Girard's authorship and performance of the *Balet comique* in *Courtly Song*, 200–1 and 234, but without presenting the detailed evidence discussed here to support my contention.

[16] *New Grove II* s.v. 'Beaulieu, Girard de' and 'Beaulieu, Lambert de' by F. Dobbins. Dobbins also writes that Marin Mersenne attributed the *Balet comique* to Girard (though Dobbins discounts the attribution). This is not entirely correct: while Mersenne praised Girard

A look at the archival material summarised in the Appendix shows this hypothesis must be mistaken. Girard de Beaulieu was a prominent singer who occupied a central role in the musical establishment of the royal court from at least 1572 until his death in 1590. The court's records confirm that he was a bass; that he was initially attached to the queen's household, and gained a position in the royal *musique de chambre* under Henri III; that he was married to a Genoese singer, Violante (often called Yolande or Yolante) Doria, who was also a member of the queen's entourage; and that they were regularly remunerated as a couple.[17] One account describes him as a singer to the *lire*, a word frequently used in contemporary French to describe the *lirone*, a bass bowed string instrument similar to the one Glaucus plays in Figure 1, widely used in the late sixteenth and early seventeenth centuries to accompany the voice.[18] In the context of the *Balet comique*, the

de Beaulieu's excellent bass singing (see below), he did not explicitly connect him with the performance or composition of the ballet.

[17] Beaulieu is identified as a bass in the records of the Puy d'Evreux for 1581 and on a list of royal household members in 1584. Violante Doria is identified by name as Beaulieu's wife in accounts of 1577 (where she is described as Genoese), 1580, 1582, 1584, 1585, 1586, 1587 and 1588; in other accounts she appears only as 'sa femme'. Unless otherwise noted, locations and summaries for all archival documents cited are listed in the Appendix, where they can be found by consulting the entries under the relevant year.

[18] Although Beaulieu is usually named in court records as a *chantre*, in accounts of 1572 he figures as a 'chantre et joueur d'instrumens', and in 1577 he is named as a 'joueur de lyre devant sa Magesté'; he and his wife together are called 'musiciens et joueurs de luth' on the queen's household accounts in 1584, suggesting that both regularly accompanied their own singing as they did in the *Balet comique*. On the *lirone* see especially *New Grove II* s.v. 'Lirone' by E. Headly; see also I. Woodfield, *The Early History of the Viol* (Cambridge, 1984), pp. 179–80. Rudolph II's letter uses the Latin word *lira* to describe Beaulieu's instrument; Fétis translated this as a lute, but it seems likely that the *lire* (i.e., *lirone*) was what Rudolph intended. In literary works the French word *lire* can be ambiguous because of its employment in classical and metaphorical contexts, but in court archives the usage is clearer; secretaries differentiate the words *lire* and *luth* fairly consistently (as in treasury accounts of 1572, when Joachim Thibault de Courville was paid for the composition of pieces 'qui se reciteront sur la lyre et le luth'; Paris, Bibliothèque Nationale de France (henceforth BNF), Clairambault 233, p. 3598). The word *viole* also figures in such accounts, so that *lire* is probably more often a term for a *lirone* than a bass viol, despite the fairly loose nature of bowed string terminology in this period. Blaise de Vigenère's discussion of the ancient Greek lyre in *Les images ou tableaux de platte-peinture de Philostrate Lemnien Sophiste*, trans. and annotated by Vigenère (Paris, 1578) makes this clear: after remarking that many scholars claim that the ancient lyre and cithara were the same instrument, Vigenère says that others think the ancient lyre was like the modern *lire*, 'la lyre propre, celle dis-je de maintenant, faitte à maniere de violle qui se joue avec l'archet' (the real lyre, I mean the lyre of today, made in the manner of a viol and played with a bow) (fol. 89^{r}). Mersenne's discussion of the construction of the *lire* (*Harmonie universelle, contenant la theorie et la pratique de la musique* (Paris, 1636; facs. edn. with introduction by François Lesure, Paris, 1963), iii, pp. 204–8, simi-

most telling documents are those from the early 1580s, contemporary with the event's production: Girard de Beaulieu appears on both extant lists of royal household members from this period, those of 1580 and 1584 (along with Jacques Salmon, Beaujoyeulx's 'maistre Salmon' of the *chambre du roi*); and receipts for payments to Girard de Beaulieu and Violante Doria together survive from 1580 and 1582.

Although royal documents do often refer to 'Beaulieu' or 'Monsieur de Beaulieu' without including a first name, the consistency of the payments (despite the fragmentary condition of court accounts, there are fairly continuous records from a period of nearly twenty years) and the frequent inclusion of his spouse render improbable the possibility that we are dealing with two different individuals. It is yet more implausible that the 'sieur de Beaulieu' named by Beaujoyeulx could be another court singer with the same skills and identical surname who – despite being responsible for the music of the most famous court spectacle of the decade – left no traces in royal records of the period. The man who oversaw the musical component of the *Balet comique* and sang the part of Glaucus was certainly Girard de Beaulieu. While the description leaves several question marks over his exact role (how did Salmon and other musicians help him? did he devise any or all of the dance music as well as vocal numbers?) we can reasonably assume that he created most of the solo vocal music, and certainly the pieces he himself performed. Girard was also no doubt the singer Rudolph hoped to engage for imperial service, but when the emperor wrote to his ambassador he was far from Paris and probably going on hearsay. He may have been misinformed or simply made an error in the musician's given name, for a search of court records reveals no Lambert de Beaulieu in any branch of royal service at the time of Henri III's death.[19]

larly describes the late Renaissance *lire* as a *lirone* and distinguishes it from the viol (*viole*) to which it is related; Mersenne states that the instrument is commonly used in France 'pour accompagner la voix et les recits'. See Brooks, *Courtly Song*, p. 312n, for other instances of *lire* as a term for a bowed string instrument.

[19] Rudolph's informant may have been his sister Elizabeth of Austria, who had returned to the imperial court in 1575 following the death of her husband Charles IX of France. After a lapse of nearly fifteen years, Elizabeth or Rudolph may have confused Beaulieu with another noted musician, Lambert Du Fay, who was *maître de musique* for the king's brother François d'Anjou in the 1570s and still a member of his household in 1584 (Paris, BNF fr. 20614, fol. 74^{v}). Du Fay may also be the person referred to in Olivier de Magny's

Despite the confusion over his identity, Girard de Beaulieu has attracted some attention from modern scholars; the 'damoyselle de Beaulieu' has received virtually none. Yet the earliest record of a payment to the couple concerns a gift not to Beaulieu but to Violante Doria. Royal treasury accounts for 1572 register a present on 2 January to Doria for her *étrennes*, or New Year's gift. Here she is identified as 'la seignore Violante Doria l'une des damoiselles de la Royne' (the *signora* Violante Doria, one of the queen's ladies), indicating both her Italian origin and her position as a lady-in-waiting to the reigning queen, Elizabeth of Austria. A subsequent entry in the same account records a royal gift of 750 livres to Beaulieu and Doria together. The sum is generous, representing over three times the annual salary of most of the king's chamber musicians in that year.[20] This gift is also highly unusual in the context of royal domestic accounts: Beaulieu and Doria's payment as a couple – which occurs regularly in subsequent records – is unique in the entire *maison du roi* for the reigns of Charles IX and Henri III.

In the inscription of the 1572 gift, as in most later documents, Beaulieu is described as 'chantre et joueur d'instruments' of the king; Doria is not mentioned by name but simply characterised as 'sa femme'. In general, the fashion in which she is described in royal records aligns neatly with the model Billon proposed in the *Fort inexpugnable*, where he posited a situation in which male singers had musical wives under their tutelage and control. In documents where Doria does appear independently, she is almost invariably called a lady-in-waiting rather than a musician. Such gestures in contemporary records pose serious difficulties for understanding the activities of professional women musicians in early modern France.[21] The music provided for her in the *Balet comique* makes it clear that Doria must have been a singer of great skill, but there

Odes (1559) – in which Magny compared a musician named only as 'Lambert' to Arcadelt and Saint-Gelais as a singer to the lute – not 'Lambert de Beaulieu', as has sometimes been suggested (for example, in F. Lesure, *Musicians and Poets of the French Renaissance*, trans. E. Gianturco and H. Rosenwald (New York, 1955), p. 78; the poem is included in Magny, *Les odes amoureuses de 1559*, ed. M. S. Whitney (Geneva, 1964), pp. 10–14).

[20] With few exceptions, chamber musicians received 200 livres per year on the *état de maison* of 1572–4 (Paris, Archives Nationales (henceforth Paris, AN), KK 134, fols. 51^r–52^r; see Brooks, *Courtly Song*, pp. 395–8).

[21] On the difficulty of interpreting extant records, see *ibid.*, pp. 200–2.

is no way of telling how and to what extent her talents were responsible for the considerable rewards the couple received from royal patrons (did she devise her own solo lines for the *Balet comique* duo, for example?). There is only the slimmest archival support for the *Balet comique*'s evidence that she was a musician: in 1584, she and Beaulieu appear together on the queen's chamber budget as 'musiciens et joueurs de luth' and on the royal treasury records as 'chantres ordinaires de la chambre [of Henri III]', the plural nouns confirming that both she and Beaulieu played and sang. Like the payment to Beaulieu and Doria as a couple, however, these two records represent a telling departure from previous practice: Violante Doria was the first woman to be paid explicitly for musical services in any royal account of the sixteenth century, including those of the queens and royal siblings as well as those of the treasury and *maison du roi*. In fact women were rarely paid for anything in the king's household, and even the queen's official entourage, despite the inclusion of ladies-in-waiting, was predominantly male. Doria's presence itself in the records – even when named only as Beaulieu's wife – is a sign of important changes not only in French musical culture but in the structures of the court it inhabited.

Despite Beaulieu's identification as a 'singer and player of [Charles IX]' in the 1572 gift payment, his absence from contemporary lists of the king's household suggests that both singers were primarily attached to the queen. An entry in the 1572 list of royal pensioners supports this impression: an annual pension of 200 livres was awarded to 'Beaulieu et sa femme vallet de chambre de la royne' (Beaulieu, *valet de chambre* of the queen, and his wife). Elizabeth of Austria, who married Charles IX in 1570, had connections with a number of celebrated musicians, including Lassus, Philippe de Monte and Maddalena Casulana, both before and after her marriage.[22] It is unclear whether Doria

[22] When Lassus visited the French court in 1571, he carried letters for Elizabeth from her uncle Albrecht of Bavaria and his heir Wilhelm (see H. Leuchtmann, *Orlando di Lasso* (Wiesbaden, 1976), i, pp. 155–7); Lassus' visit may have been partly due to her encouragement. In French treasury records of 1572, a gift of 500 livres to Casulana, who was visiting from the imperial court in Vienna, was made at Elizabeth's request (Paris, BNF Clairambault 233, p. 3471). Monte became master of the imperial chapel in 1568, two years before Elizabeth left for France; his secular motet *Maeror cuncta tenet* is apparently a lament on her departure (the text refers to the weeping of the Rhine and Ister rivers, and closes with the lines 'Huius maestitiae est et tanti causa doloris, Montibus his abitus Regia Nympha tuis' [The cause of this sadness, and of so much sorrow, is the depar-

and Beaulieu were already part of Elizabeth's household before she left the imperial court, and much remains to be learned about their activities before 1572.[23] But the singers' attachment to the queen's retinue is significant for more than sheer chronology, for it gestures towards the kind of music-making in which they specialised: performances appropriate for the entertainment of the queen's entourage and for occasions when the king and his male retinue visited the chambers of the queen and queen mother, Catherine de Médicis, for conversation and diversion. Such gatherings were the location for courtly behaviour of the type most famously described by Castiglione, whose *Book of the Courtier* enjoyed enormous success in France as elsewhere in Europe.[24] In this context it is worth noting that Castiglione reserved special praise for self-accompanied singing – particularly singing to a bowed string instrument, one of Beaulieu's specialities – as the best kind of music-making for his perfect courtier.[25] Accomplished women singers were also a feature of such gatherings at contemporary Italian courts, most notably in Ferrara, where the French king's cousin, Alfonso d'Este, placed virtuoso female singers in his wife's entourage and organised private musical entertainments in her chambers for honoured visitors.[26] And it is precisely in these

ture of the Royal Nymph from these your mountains], a play on Monte's name). The motet was published in Monte's only chanson collection, *Sonetz de P. de Ronsard* (Paris 1575), with a preface by the royal chamber musician Jacques Antoine de La Chappelle dedicating the volume to Elizabeth's brother-in-law, François d'Anjou.

[23] Neither musician appears on the list of names of those to be assigned to her *maison* on her arrival in France (Paris, BNF Cinq cents de Colbert 7, fols. 81^r–89^r and 391^r–412^v) nor on her *état de maison* for 1570–1 (Paris, BNF Clairambault 356, fols. 7 ff.). The Genoese Doria family was allied to the emperor Maximilian II, however, so a prior connection between Violante and Elizabeth seems possible. Beaulieu was certainly French: he is never described as a foreigner in contemporary notarial records (which because of French property law and the *droit d'aubaine* almost invariably specify the origins of non-French citizens). He and Doria probably married by 1565 at the latest, as they had a daughter of marriageable age in 1580.

[24] For a contemporary account of conversation in the queens' chambers, see P. de Bourdeille, seigneur de Brantôme, *Oeuvres complètes*, ed. L. Lalanne (Paris, 1864–82), viii, pp. 376–7; Brantôme also comments on the excellent music offered to these gatherings by Catherine de Médicis's singers.

[25] J. Haar, 'The Courtier as Musician: Castiglione's View of the Science and Art of Music', in R. W. Hanning and D. Rosand (eds.), *Castiglione: The Ideal and the Real in Renaissance Culture* (New Haven, 1983), pp. 174–5; Brooks, *Courtly Song*, p. 153. On Castiglione as a manual for French courtly behaviour, see P. Burke, *The Fortunes of the Courtier: The European Reception of Castiglione's* Courtier (Cambridge, 1995), pp. 42–5 and 73–5.

[26] Henri III apparently heard one such private concert in Ferrara on his way through Italy to take up the throne of France in 1574; his protegé Anne de Joyeuse was treated to a

contexts that the singing styles that would characterise the 'new music' in Italy were often deployed.

After the death of Charles IX in 1574 and the accession of his brother Henri III, the musicians became members of the household of the new queen, Louise de Lorraine-Vaudémont.[27] Beaulieu may have served the troublesome youngest brother of the Valois clan, François d'Anjou, as well; he appears in the accounts of Anjou's *écurie* in 1575 in a list of musicians to whom table expenses were owed. At that time he had not yet obtained an official position in the *maison du roi*: he does not appear among the chamber musicians in the household list prepared for the new king in 1575.[28] But he had gained a place as one of Henri III's domestic officers by 1577, when receipts from the royal treasury include a record of Beaulieu receiving wages as a 'chantre de la chambre du Roy' at the normal rate of 200 livres per year. Another receipt from the same year records that 'Girard de Beaulieu chantre de la chambre dudit seigneur et Yolande Doria genevoise sa femme, l'une des damoiselles de la royne' (Girard de Beaulieu, chamber singer of [Henri III] and Violante Doria, Genoese, his wife, one of the queen's ladies) received the substantial sum of 2,000 livres as payment of an annual royal pension.

From 1577 extant documents also begin to reflect Beaulieu's close connections with other members of Henri's chamber music group. In July and December 1577 he acted as procurator for two chamber singers, Thesée Du Port and Jehan de Valot, collecting portions of their wages for them. In September 1578, the royal organist Guillaume Costeley, then mainly living in Evreux, took advantage of a stay in Paris to swear out a power of attorney enabling Beaulieu and another keyboard player from the chamber, Nicolas de La Grotte, to receive payments from the royal

performance by Duke Alfonso's famed *concerto* in 1583. See A. Newcomb, 'Courtesans, Muses or Musicians? Professional Women Musicians in Sixteenth-Century Italy', in J. Bowers and J. Tick (eds.), *Women Making Music: The Western Art Tradition, 1150–1950* (Urbana, Ill., 1986), pp. 94–8; and L. Stras, '*Onde havrà 'l mond'esempio et vera historia*: Musical Echoes of Henri III's Progress through Italy', *Acta Musicologica*, 72 (2000), pp. 21–4.

[27] Auger Busbecq wrote to Elizabeth's father Maximilian II on 9 February 1575 that Catherine de Médicis had ordered Elizabeth to send nearly all of her attendants to wait thereafter on Louise, who married the new king on 15 February. See Forster and Daniell, *The Life and Letters of Ogier Ghiselin de Busbecq*, ii, p. 52.

[28] Paris, BNF fr. 7007, fol. 125^{r-v}.

treasury on Costeley's behalf. Links with Costeley probably played a part in a trip to Evreux in November 1581, a month after the *Balet comique*, when Beaulieu and five other royal chamber singers assisted in performances for the Puy d'Evreux, the musical competition in honour of Saint Cecilia that Costeley had helped to found in 1575.[29] The same individuals figured in the creation of Henri III's penitential confraternity of L'Annonciation de Nostre Dame in January 1583. The manuscript listing the names of the founding *confrères* stipulates that the singers were responsible for providing music for the group's devotions and processions.[30] These men, the core of the king's chamber music ensemble, were the only singers retained in royal service in 1584, when Henri III cut large numbers of officers from the royal *état* in an effort to reduce the cost of his entourage.[31] Beaulieu's continuing association with his collaborator on the *Balet comique*, Jacques Salmon, is confirmed by royal treasury accounts of 1586, when a New Year's gift of 200 écus was awarded to the two musicians to share between them.

The royal pension list of 1578 specified that Beaulieu and Doria were to receive 200 livres per annum as a pension from the king and 1,000 livres from the queen, suggesting that even after Beaulieu gained a post in the royal chamber the couple were still considered members of the queen's entourage. This idea is supported not only by Beaujoyeulx's claim in the *Balet comique* that Beaulieu was one of Louise's servants, but also by Louise's *état de maison* from 1584, one of the very few documents from her household to have survived. Here the singers appear together – identified as 'musiciens et joueurs de luth de la Royne' – with joint yearly wages of 400 écus. In addition to wage payments, extant receipts indicate that their annual royal pension in the 1580s amounted to

[29] *Puy de musique érigé à Evreux, en l'honneur de Madame Sainte Cécile, publié d'après un manuscrit du XVIe siècle*, ed. T. Bonnin and A. Chassant (Evreux, 1837), pp. 23–4. The others were François de Lorigny (bass), Jacques Salmon (taille), Claude Baliffre (hautecontre), Jacques Busserat and Mesme Jacquin (both castrati); they were joined by royal cornett player Nicolas Delinet. All were members of the royal chamber in the early 1580s (see the royal *états de maison* for 1580 and 1584, Paris, BNF Dupuy 127, fols. 91^r^–92^r^ and Paris, AN, KK 139, fols. 33^r^–34^r^; transcribed in Brooks, *Courtly Song*, pp. 402–5).

[30] The group, augmented by the *taille* Martin Mingeon and the famous castrato Estienne Le Roy, was listed under the rubric 'Huict Musiciens de la Chambre du Roy'. Paris, BNF fr. 7549, fols. 4^v^ and 21^r^.

[31] Only seven adult singers were retained; of those listed above, Busserat was let go. Paris, BNF Dupuy 489, fol. 13^r^.

666 écus, bringing their yearly income to over 1,000 écus even before any gifts or extra payments were bestowed.[32]

Another gauge of their success is the advantageous marriage they arranged for their daughter. In December 1580, Marguerite de Beaulieu, identified as the daughter of 'noblehomme Girard de Beaulieu vallet de chambre ordinaire du roy et de damoiselle Violante Doria dame de la Royne', contracted to marry Anthoine de Minard, seigneur de Villemain, a nobleman and landowner, son of a financial officer of the *hôtel du roi*. Her dowry of 8,000 écus was well within the range common among the minor nobility at Henri III's court and far above the sums generally available for the daughters of musicians. The document is one of a handful to claim that Beaulieu was himself a minor noble, perhaps another factor in arranging such a match for his daughter. The marriage took place in the spring of 1581, and subsequent documents registered at the Châtelet of Paris along with the marriage contract deal with the payment of the dowry in instalments in 1581 and 1582. Two are notarial acts drawn up in Beaulieu's house, on the rue Champfleury in the parish of Saint-Germain-l'Auxerrois. The rue Champfleury ran at a right angle to the north wall of the main royal residence in Paris, the Louvre, and was parallel to the rue de l'Autruche, site of several large *hôtels* belonging to the wealthiest and most powerful members of Henri III's court. When the court was in Paris, Beaulieu and Doria were thus strategically placed in the centre of its activities.[33]

While Marguerite de Beaulieu married a noble, another daughter, Claude de Beaulieu, followed in her mother's footsteps as a royal musician. The last payment record in which Violante Doria figures is a fragment of the treasury accounts for 1588, which includes a joint payment to Doria and Beaulieu of a portion of their annual pension. There is no further mention of Doria in royal records; she may have died, fallen ill or retired from service at

[32] The écu became the main unit of accountancy after the 1578 monetary reforms, and the livre tournois (formerly the principal unit for expressing sums) became merely an accounting term for a third of an écu. The pension of 666 écus 2/3 was thus equivalent to 2,000 livres before the reform; a receipt from 1577 for that amount suggests that the singers' annual pension had in reality already reached that considerable sum, despite the pension list of 1578 awarding them only 1,200 livres in principle.

[33] On the street and the parish, see J.-P. Babelon, *Nouvelle histoire de Paris: Paris au XVIe siècle* (Paris, 1986), pp. 225–7; a contemporary map showing the rue Champfleury appears on p. 214.

court. In the queen's household list for the following year, her place was taken by her daughter: the joint position formerly occupied by Beaulieu and Doria was now awarded to Beaulieu and 'Claude de Beaulieu sa fille musicienne et jouëuse de lut de la reyne' (his daughter Claude de Beaulieu, musician and lute player to the queen) with the same yearly wage of 400 écus.

On 1 August 1589, in the same year that Claude de Beaulieu was included with her father on the queen's accounts as a lutenist, Henri III was assassinated and France plunged deep into civil unrest. The following May, Emperor Rudolph wrote to Auger Busbecq to request him to offer Beaulieu a post, probably highly attractive, given the appalling situation in France.[34] Busbecq may never have contacted the singer, however, or if he did, it may already have been too late, for Beaulieu himself died later the same month. The parish register of Saint-Nicolas-des-Champs that recorded his funeral on 25 May 1590 identified him as *maître de musique* of the chevalier d'Aumale, a member of the Guise family, and specified that he was then living on the rue Saint-Martin in Paris.[35]

The archival documents that preserve traces of Beaulieu and Doria's careers show how profoundly different their circumstances were from those of Arcadelt, Sandrin or Janequin and other 'renomméz Musiciens de l'Eürope' at whom François de Billon's rhetorical firearms were aimed. Though a few prominent musicians under François I were minor nobles, aristocratic status was the exception rather than the rule, and noble musicians were generally polyphony chapel members before their appointment to positions in the royal chamber.[36] Beaulieu was apparently a gentleman; he never took orders and was married to a woman who was herself probably from a noble family.[37] Though he must have

[34] De Pace includes Rudolph's letter among the dispatches sent on 8 May 1590 (Rudolph II, *Divi Rudolphi . . . epistolae ineditae*, pp. 209–11).

[35] Y. de Brossard, *Musiciens de Paris 1535–1792: actes d'état civil d'après le fichier Laborde de la Bibliothèque Nationale* (Paris 1965), p. 26.

[36] The nobleman Antoine de Longueval, for example, was a chapel member as well as a royal *valet de chambre* under François I; see R. Sherr, 'The Membership of the Chapels of Louis XII and Anne de Bretagne in the Years Preceding their Deaths', *Journal of Musicology*, 6 (1988), pp. 67–8, and Brooks, 'From Minstrel to Courtier'.

[37] My inquiries to the Doria-Pamphilij archive in Rome have so far yielded no information about Violante Doria's genealogy; I would like to thank Cinzia Ammannato for her research on my behalf. The name 'Violante', however, occurs in earlier generations of the branch of the Doria family that included the famous admiral Andrea, making it likely that the singer was related, even if distantly.

sung polyphony, and sometimes religious music (in Henri III's confraternities, and for table blessings and other similar occasions for which the king's chamber group was responsible) he never held a chapel position, and both he and Doria seem to have excelled primarily as self-accompanying solo singers. Both took starring roles in court spectacle as well as performing in more intimate settings.

Beaulieu and Doria's careers had much in common with those of contemporary Italian musicians who have received more consistent attention from historians;[38] the resemblance is hardly surprising, given the close dynastic, political and cultural links between the major European courts of the period. The singers' relationship is in many ways a mirror of the setting in which their careers unfolded: a Franco-Italian couple like Henri II and Catherine de Médicis, Beaulieu and Doria flourished at the courts of Italian-speaking monarchs who were well aware of fashions at the courts of their cousins south of the Alps and determined to match or exceed them in brilliance and sophistication. As in Italy, the importance of courtly *divertissements* and of 'private' settings and mixed-sex sociability (following the model of civility manuals) to the courtly aesthetic created a milieu in need of services that musicians such as Beaulieu and Doria could provide. Their success testifies to the rising value of chamber music; representing in

[38] The most striking parallels concern the lives of their near contemporaries Alessandro Striggio and Virginia Vagnoli. Scion of an aristocratic Mantuan family, Striggio spent most of his career as a courtier-musician in Florence. He was a frequent participant in court *divertissements*, and though principally celebrated as a performer on the lute and *lirone*, he enjoyed close links with the court at Ferrara and composed music reflecting the singing experiments associated with the Ferrarese *concerto* and with early monody. Virginia Vagnoli, who married Striggio in 1571, was a famed singer and lutenist, also of noble origin. Both musicians had connections with the imperial court and were the object of several (unsuccessful) recruitment efforts by the emperor Maximilian II, who in 1566 attempted to secure the services of Vagnoli for the entourage of the empress Mary of Spain. There is even a possibility that Beaulieu or Doria met Striggio in Vienna, Paris or Munich during Striggio's 1567 tour of European capitals. During the trip to Paris, Striggio was lavishly welcomed at the court of Charles IX, who offered handsome enticements to the musician to enter French service. Though Striggio refused the offer and eventually returned to Florence, the incident testifies to the assiduous efforts *c.*1570 to recruit chamber musicians with his skills for the royal court. Further on Striggio and Vagnoli, see *New Grove II* s.v. 'Striggio, Alessandro (i)' by I. Fenlon; D. S. Butchart, 'The Letters of Alessandro Striggio: An Edition with Commentary', *RMA Research Chronicle*, 23 (1990), pp. 1–78; and F. Piperno, 'Diplomacy and Musical Patronage: Virginia, Guidubaldo II, Massimiliano II, "Lo Streggino" and Others', *Early Music History*, 18 (1999), pp. 259–85.

essence a professionalisation of the attainments of the perfect courtier and the *donna di palazzo*, their careers set important precedents for the structure of the royal musical establishment in the following century.[39]

LE PLAISIR DE VOUS ÉCOUTER SEROIT DOUBLE

Documentary sources preserve an array of fascinating material on the careers of these two singers; despite the inevitable gaps, the records permit the trajectory of their professional lives to be traced in more detail than has been possible for any but a handful of sixteenth-century musicians in France. But such documents almost completely fail to convey anything of what Beaulieu and Doria sang for their royal patrons or how they sang it. Contemporary printed musical sources can provide some answers to these questions, but like the archival records that obfuscate attempts to reconstruct Violante Doria's activities, contemporary prints in many cases obscure almost as much as they reveal. In the case of musical sources, however, it is Beaulieu's voice that is most often in need of recovery, for it is the bass singer whose distinctive contributions to contemporary musical style are most completely masked by the conventions of late sixteenth-century print.

Beaulieu and Doria's attachment to the secular realm of the court musical establishment suggests that vernacular chansons were one cornerstone of their repertory. The published music of Beaulieu's comrades in the *chambre du roi* consists almost exclusively of chansons, including some of the earliest examples of the strophic songs later known as *airs de cour*: most notably in the *Musique* of Guillaume Costeley (1570) and in Nicolas de La Grotte's *Chansons de P. de Ronsard* (1569).[40] La Grotte published a second collection of songs in 1583, and a few strophic *airs* by Jacques Salmon were included in the anthology *Vingtquatrieme livre d'airs et chansons* of the same year.[41]

[39] See Brooks, 'From Minstrel to Courtier', and ead., *Courtly Song*, pp. 79–80.

[40] G. Costeley, *Musique de Guillaume Costeley, organiste ordinaire et vallet de chambre, du treschretien et tresinvincible Roy de France* (Paris, 1570); N. de La Grotte, *Chansons de P. de Ronsard, Ph. Desportes et autres* (Paris, 1569). La Grotte's volume was the most successful strophic song print of the period, with four subsequent editions in 1570, 1572, 1575 and 1580.

[41] N. La Grotte, *Premier livre d'airs et chansons à 3. 4. 5. 6. parties* (Paris, 1583); *Vingtquatrieme livre d'airs et chansons à quatre et cinq parties* (Paris, 1583).

The handful of extant pieces attributed to Beaulieu himself are of the same type. They appear in Fabrice Marin Caietain's *Airs* of 1576, which contains four songs credited to 'Beaulieu' and three by another renowned court singer, Joachim Thibault de Courville, amid the pieces attributed to Caietain.[42] Caietain, a Neapolitan composer in the service of the Guises, explained in his preface that since he was liable to make errors in setting French texts, he consulted Beaulieu and Courville in order to represent the stresses of the language accurately in his music. He praises both musicians for their excellence in singing to the *lire* as well as for their composition of *airs*, calling them the Orpheus and Arion of France.[43] A connection with Guise musicians fits with Beaulieu's welcome into the household of the chevalier d'Aumale after Henri III's assassination.[44] And the association with Courville suggests that Beaulieu was involved with one of the more remarkable humanist undertakings of the later sixteenth century, Jean-Antoine de Baïf's Académie de poésie et de musique. Courville was the fellow 'entrepreneur' who founded the Academy in collaboration with Baïf; its Sunday afternoon concerts were the venue for performances of *musique mesurée à l'antique*, settings of Baïf's French poems in

[42] *Helas que me faut il faire*, *Rosette pour un peu d'absence*, *Blessé d'une plaie inhumaine* and *Si tost que vostre oeil m'est blessé* are attributed to 'Beaulieu' in Caietain, *Airs mis en musique à quatre parties* (Paris, 1576); for a modern edition, see *Fabrice Marin Caietain*, ed. J. A. Bernstein (The Sixteenth-Century Chanson, 4; New York, 1995). Two chansons, settings of obscene mock-rustic texts in a imitative polyphonic idiom, are attributed to 'Beaulieu' in the *Quart livre de chansons composées à quatre parties par bons et excelens musiciens* (Paris, 1553); given their early date (twenty years before any documentary evidence of Beaulieu's activities at court) it is unclear whether these are Girard's work or that of another musician (perhaps the Parisian Mathurin de Beaulieu cited in a parish record of 1574; see Brossard, *Musiciens de Paris*, p. 26).

[43] 'Et pour-ce que je suis de nation et langue estrangere je pouvoy manquer a bien approprier les Airs sur les lettres françoises, Mais comme ceux qui veullent profiter aux estudes hantent les lieux ou s'en fait la profession, Moy pareillement me defiant de mes forces, (car je n'ay aucune honte de le declairer,) ay frequenté l'escole de Messieurs de Courville et Beaulieu, l'ung [l']Orphée l'autre l'Arion de France, leur vertu et nostre amitié me permettent de les appeller ainsi, car ilz ne sont seulement excelents aux recits de la Lyre, mais tresdoctes en l'art de Musique, et perfaits en la composition des Airs, que les grecs appellent Melopoee, suivant leurs avertissements et bons avis J'ay corrigé la plus part des fautes que J'avoy peu faire en n'observant les longues et breves de la lettres.' Caietain, *Airs mis en musique à quatre parties*, fols. 1^v–2^r; a facsimile appears in *Fabrice Marin Caietain*, plate 1. Caietain's comments provide further evidence that Beaulieu was a native Frenchman.

[44] Jacques Salmon too enjoyed Guise patronage: in 1577, he appeared on an *état de maison* for Louis de Lorraine, cardinal de Guise, as a chamber musician (Paris, BNF Clairambault 816, fol. $203^{r–v}$).

imitation of classical metres. Caietain's *Airs* contains the earliest printed examples of *musique mesurée*, including the three songs by Courville as well as three others by Caietain himself.[45] Though Beaulieu's own *airs* are all settings of conventional rhymed verse by the court poet Philippe Desportes, the appearance of his music in the collection and the link between his name and Courville's suggest that Beaulieu (and probably Doria as well) was involved in the performance of the new measured music.

All the pieces attributed to Beaulieu and his circle – whether *musique mesurée* or conventional song – were published as vocal polyphony. But the majority are homophonic strophic *airs* suitable for performance by a solo singer, with the remaining parts arranged for lute or another instrument. Many of these pieces, and others like them, were regularly published as songs for voice and lute in the early seventeenth century. They also appear as lute songs in a few sixteenth-century manuscripts and a scattering of print sources. Virtually all the songs in Nicolas de La Grotte's *Chansons*, for example, appeared as arrangements in lute tablature with the superius line in white mensural notation in Adrian Le Roy's *Livre d'airs de cour miz sur le luth* (1571), the first book explicitly to connect this repertory of strophic songs to court usage. Although solo lute performance may have been the primary intention of Le Roy's collection, the inclusion of the texted vocal line and the information supplied in the preface leave little doubt that the pieces could be, and probably usually were, executed as accompanied song.[46] Three manuscript sources copied in the 1590s present similar songs in unambiguous versions for voice and lute.[47] The problem of aligning the tablature and the vocal part without using large amounts of expensive paper discouraged music printers from adopting the lute song format on more than a few occasions before 1600. But despite their usual publication format, it takes

[45] The standard source on the Academy remains Yates, *The French Academies*; on the relationship of Caietain's *Airs* to its activities, see also Bernstein's preface to *Fabrice Marin Caietain*, p. xiv. Beaulieu's association is discussed further in Brooks, *Courtly Song*, p. 240.

[46] On Le Roy's *Livre d'airs de cour*, see Brooks, *Courtly Song*, pp. 13–20. For a detailed examination of the performance issues raised by the book, see J. Le Cocq, 'French Lute Song, 1529–1643' (D.Phil. thesis, Oxford University, 1997), i, pp. 11–20, and id., 'The Status of Le Roy's Publications for Voice and Lute or Guitar', *The Lute*, 35 (1995), pp. 4–27.

[47] Oxford, Bodleian Library, MS Mus. Sch. d.237 (*c.*1597); Valenciennes, Bibliothèque Municipale, MS 429 (copied in stages, 1586–1606) and Aix-en-Provence, Bibliothèque Méjanes, MS 147 (203)-R312 (*c.*1600). See Le Cocq, 'French Lute Song', i, pp. 80–7.

no great leap of imagination to see such *airs* as an important part of the repertory of Beaulieu and Doria, who could perform these graceful strophic pieces to their own accompaniment for the entertainment of the queen's entourage.

Somewhat more difficult to trace are pieces they might have sung together. That they did so on at least one occasion, however, is incontestable: their participation in the *Balet comique*, the only documented instance of their performance of a specific piece of music, was as a couple, and their solo dialogue from the *Balet comique* can provide a springboard for exploring a larger repertory. In the sixteenth and seventeenth centuries, the designation 'dialogue' could be used for pieces in which voices or groups of voices alternate or contrast, or to refer to settings of texts in which two or more characters converse.[48] 'Dialogue' in the latter case is a function of the poetry rather than of compositional or performance style, and Don Harrán has argued that only settings of such texts should be considered as musical dialogues.[49] In what follows, I shall use 'dialogue' to refer to musical settings of dialogue texts, and 'performance in dialogue' to refer to performance practices featuring alternation between solo singers, whether or not the text they sing is strictly speaking a dialogue. French music prints from before 1600 contain a large number of dialogue texts, set in a range of musical styles: as through-composed chansons, as strophic *airs* or as sets of pieces linked in chanson-response pairs or longer cycles. All were published, however, as polyphonic works for four or more voices; the unique exception is the *Balet comique* dialogue performed by Beaulieu and Doria in 1581.

Yet performance in dialogue by self-accompanying solo singers had been a feature of French court life for at least fifteen years before the *Balet comique*. In 1565, when Catherine de Médicis and Charles IX went to Bayonne to meet his sister Élisabeth, queen of Spain, the festivities culminated in a tournament between courtiers costumed as English and Irish knights; as a preliminary, deputies from both sides presented a musical request to the king that the knights be allowed to settle in combat the relative merits

[48] See J. Whenham, *Duet and Dialogue in the Age of Monteverdi* (Ann Arbor, 1982), i, pp. 181–200; and *New Grove II*, s.v. 'Dialogue' by J. Whenham and D. Nutter.

[49] D. Harrán, 'Towards a Definition of the Early Secular Dialogue', *Music & Letters*, 51 (1970), pp. 37–50.

of virtue and love. Two singers to the *lire* – identified as Thibault de Courville and Guillaume Le Boulanger, sieur de Vaumesnil, by the payment records for their costumes – sang alternate stanzas of a strophic poem to their own accompaniment, interspersed with instrumental interludes for violin and lute. Though the music has been lost, the text of the piece is preserved in a description of the event.[50]

Two years later, in January 1567, a similar performance figured in celebrations for the baptism of the son of the secretary of state Nicolas de Neufville, Sieur de Villeroy, and Madeleine de Laubesbine. Pierre de Ronsard's paeon to the ladies attending the banquet, *Autant qu'on voit aux cieux*, was first printed in 1569 with the rubric 'Stanzas quickly made to play on the *lire*, one player answering the other'; the poem consists of quatrains alternately marked 'Player I' and 'Player II'.[51] A musical setting for four voices appeared in the same year in La Grotte's *Chansons*, and it seems likely that this represents an arrangement of the version performed in 1567 by two soloists.[52] Another of Ronsard's occasional poems, *Le soleil et nostre roy*, was sung during carnival celebrations at court in 1571. The earliest version of the text, copied in late 1570 or early 1571 into a manuscript poetry album owned by Villeroy and Laubespine, is labelled 'Comparison of the sun and the king constructed in stanzas to be sung by two *lire* or lute players who will answer one another, who will be seated in a chariot

[50] *Recueil des choses notables qui ont esté faites à Bayonne* . . . (Paris, 1566), ed. in V. E. Graham and W. M. Johnson, *The Royal Tour of France by Charles IX and Catherine de' Medici: Festivals and Entries 1564–66* (Toronto, 1979), pp. 357–62; see also pp. 46–7. The costume payments figure in Paris, AN, KK 130, fols. 78^r–79^v, 81^r–82^v, 89^r–90^v, 222^r–223^v and 226^v–227^r. The violinists were the Burgundian Dominique Davon and the future creator of the *Balet comique*, Balthazar de Beaujoyeulx. On Vaumesnil, see *Oeuvres de Vaumesnil, Edinthon, Perrichon, Raël, Montbuysson, La Grotte, Saman, La Barre*, ed. A. Souris, M. Rollin and J.-M. Vaccaro (Corpus des Luthistes Français; Paris, 1974), pp. xiii–xv.

[51] 'Stances prontement faites pour jouer sur la Lyre, un joueur repondant à l'autre'. The poem first appeared in Ronsard's *Sixiesme livre des poëmes* (1569): see P. de Ronsard, *Oeuvres complètes*, ed. P. Laumonier, revised and completed by I. Silver and R. Lebègue (Paris, 1914–75), xv, pp. 136–41.

[52] La Grotte, *Chansons*, pp. 77–9; the song also appears in Le Roy, *Livre d'airs de cour*, in a print format more closely resembling the circumstances of the first performance. The third edition of La Grotte's collection (1572) includes a setting of another occasional piece by Ronsard, *Tel qu'un petit aigle sort*; in Ronsard's works, the poem – a celebration of the future Henri III's victories over the Huguenots at Jarnac in 1569 – was identified as a 'Chant triomphal pour jouer sur la lyre' (Ronsard, *Oeuvres*, xv, p. 61) though it is unclear if this refers to dialogue or solo performance.

in front of his Majesty'.[53] This poem too was soon published in a homophonic four-voice musical setting, this time by Caietain; his piece appears in his *Airs* of 1576 along with the songs of Beaulieu and Courville. Like *Autant qu'on voit aux cieux*, the music of *Le soleil et nostre roy* was printed as polyphony, so that without the rubrics from poetic prints and manuscripts, it would be difficult to guess that the song was initially conceived for dialogue performance by solo singers. Neither poem is obviously a dialogue text: although each strophe is a self-contained unit, alternate strophes consist of statements (in praise of the ladies, in praise of the king) rather than questions and responses.

We know the names of the performers only for the Bayonne event; for *Autant qu'on voit aux cieux* and *Le soleil et nostre roy*, the word 'joueurs' used to describe the executants could again refer to two men. The masculine plural could also be used for a mixed-sex pair such as Beaulieu and Doria, however, and as we have seen, extant archives suggest that their success at the French court was already considerable by 1572. Another record from the summer of 1574, when Henri III travelled through Italy on his return from Poland to take up the crown of France after the death of Charles IX, confirms that French monarchs had developed a taste for female solo vocal performance – and perhaps duo performances by a mixed pair of solo singers – by the 1570s. The manuscript recording Henri's expenses while in Venice includes a gift of 40 écus to 'the German Martha and her husband, who were twice sent for to sing and play the lute and viol'.[54] The reference is to a

[53] 'Comparaison du soleil et du Roy faicte par stances pour estre recitée par deux joueurs de lire ou de luth qui respondront l'un à l'autre, lesquelz seront assis dedans le chariot devant sa Majesté'. Paris, BNF fr. 1663, fol. 45ʳ. On this manuscript, see J. Lavaud, *Philippe Desportes (1546–1606): un poète de cour au temps des derniers Valois* (Paris, 1936), pp. 46–58, and P. Champion, *Ronsard et Villeroy: les secrétaires d'état et les poètes d'après le manuscrit français 1663 de la Bibliothèque nationale* (Paris, 1925). When the poem was printed in 1571, the rubric was revised to reflect the circumstances of the actual performance by two singers to the *lire* ('Comparaison du Soleil et du Roy faitte par stances, qui fut recitée par deux joueurs de Lyre, lesquels estoient assis dedans un chariot devant sa Majesté'; see Ronsard, *Oeuvres*, xv, pp. 349–54). Villeroy and Laubespine were not only active patrons of court poets, but also maintained a musical establishment including a chapel of professional singers (see Michel Brenet [Marie Bobillier], *Les musiciens de la Sainte-Chapelle du Palais* (Paris, 1910; repr. Geneva, 1973), pp. 124 and 138–9; and E. C. Teviotdale, 'The Invitation to the Puy d'Evreux', *Current Musicology*, 52 (1993), pp. 11–12).

[54] 'la Marthe Thudesque, et a son mary qui ont esté mandez deux foix pour chanter et sonner du luth et de la viole'. Paris, BNF fr. 3321, fol. 20ᵛ. The wording of the payment is ambiguous, but suggests that both musicians sang and played. On musical enter-

young singer from Mechelen known only as 'Martha', who entered the service of the emperor Maximilian II around 1570, and her husband, the imperial chamber musician Mauro Sinibaldi.[55] Martha was among the most celebrated musicians of Maximilian's court, where Henri had stopped for several days after leaving Poland and before setting off for Italy. She and her husband – another musical couple like Striggio and Vagnoli, or Beaulieu and Doria – were probably included in the entourage assembled in Vienna to accompany Henri on his subsequent voyage until his own retinue, left behind during his precipitous nocturnal departure from Poland, was able to join him.[56] Whether or not Martha and Sinibaldi sang together or in dialogue, this gift (a generous sum, and the only payment to a named musician in the manuscript) suggests that Henri, during whose reign Beaulieu and Doria were most successful, was fond of solo singing with lute and viol and particularly prized the female voice.

With these contexts in mind, we can return to the duo from the *Balet comique*. As for the other accompanied solo vocal music for the event, only the melodic lines appear in the print (see Example 1). The text begins with ten quatrains alternating between the characters, with Glaucus' interventions cast in alexandrines and Tethys' responses in heterometric stanzas of eight- and ten-syllable lines. The text is a true dialogue, that is, each of Glaucus' strophes poses a question or makes a statement to which Tethys'

tainments during Henri's stay in Venice, 17–27 July 1574, see D. Nutter, 'A Tragedy for Henry III of France, Venice, 1574', in A. Morrogh, F. S. Gioffredi, P. Morselli and E. Borsook (eds.), *Renaissance Studies in Honor of Craig Hugh Smyth: History, Literature, Music* (Florence, 1985), pp. 591–611.

[55] See R. Lindell, '*Martha gentile che'l cor m'ha morto*: Ein unbekannte Kammermusikerin am Hof Maximilians II', *Musicologica Austriaca*, 7 (1987), pp. 59–68, and id., 'Filippo, Stefano and Martha: New Findings on Chamber Music at the Imperial Court in the Second Half of the Sixteenth Century', in *Atti del XIV Congresso della Società Internazionale di Musicologia: trasmissione et recezione delle forme di cultura musicale*, ed. A. Pompilio, D. Restani, L. Bianconi and F. A. Gallo (Turin, 1990), iii, pp. 869–75.

[56] Henri certainly enjoyed musical entertainments in Vienna. In the dedication to his *Madrigali di Filippo de Monte a cinque voci. Libro quinto* (Venice, 1574), signed from Vienna on 10 October, Philippe de Monte wrote of the pleasure the French king had recently taken in Monte's music (Stras, 'Musical Echoes', p. 9). Henri's own musicians (no doubt including his keyboard player, Nicolas de La Grotte) followed from Poland about a week behind him, performing with great success for Maximilian after Henri had already left for Venice: on 24 July the Ferrarese envoy to the imperial court wrote that they were then in Vienna, and that the emperor had showered them with gifts (E. Durante and A. Martellotti, *Cronistoria del concerto delle dame principalissime di Margherita Gonzaga d'Este* (Florence, 1979), p. 131).

Toutes les stances se chantent soubz ce chant icy,
reste la derniere qui est interlocutoire.

Example 1 [Girard de Beaulieu], *Mais que me sert Tethys ceste escaille* (first strophe only), from Beaujoyeulx, *Le balet comique*, fols. 19r–21r

Example 1 *Continued*

La reprise du dialogue.

Example 1 *Continued*

Example 1 *Continued*

Example 1 *Continued*

strophe supplies an answer or commentary. After each exchange, singers and players representing marine gods take up the final two phrases of Tethys' music in a five-part harmonisation. The superius line of the five-part refrain is largely the same as in Tethys' solo, though it is notated in half the former rhythmic values and employs different ornamentation. The final part of the text, in prose, is described in the print as 'interlocutoire': it features a series of short questions from Glaucus alternating with Tethys' responses. This section is manifestly designed as a vocal showpiece, including elaborate diminutions of a type today more frequently associated with Italian music and court spectacle of the period.

One striking aspect of the entire piece is the behaviour of the solo bass line. Unlike the melodically conceived soprano part – which moves mainly by step and approaches cadential pitches through the leading note or the note above – the bass displays the characteristic motion of bass lines of contemporary polyphony, tracing fourths, fifths and octaves on a regular basis and almost invariably approaching cadence pitches by a leap of a fourth or fifth. For example, the final phrase of the music repeated for each of the rhymed stanzas (bars 28–37) begins by tracing the fourth *b♭–f*, and outlines the fifth *f–c′* and the *g–G* octave before cadencing from *d* to the modal final, *G*; it can easily be harmonised using the chords of one of the most common singing formulae of the period, the *romanesca*. In the interlocutory section, these interval patterns remain prominent, especially at cadence points, despite their clothing in decorative passage work (see bars 47–8, for example).

This is the only dialogue we know to have been composed for and performed by Beaulieu and Doria. It may have been a unique occasion: a one-off performance of 'marriage' in the context of the wedding festivities for Joyeuse and as a celebration of the existing marriage of Louise de Lorraine-Vaudémont and Henri III.[57] It is

[57] The latter badly needed affirmation, in the light of the queen's inability to produce an heir and to counter the persistent accusations of homosexual practice levelled at the king and his *mignons* (including Joyeuse himself) by *ligueurs* and Protestant pamphleteers throughout Henri's reign. See J. Cady, 'The "Masculine Love" of the "Princes of Sodom" "Practising the Art of Ganymede" at Henri III's Court: The Homosexuality of Henri III and his *Mignons* in Pierre de L'Estoile's *Mémoires-Journaux*', in J. Murray and K. Eisenbichler (eds.), *Desire and Discipline: Sex and Sexuality in the Premodern West* (Toronto, 1996), pp. 123–54.

clear that Beaulieu and Doria must often have performed separately, especially once Beaulieu had gained a place in the royal chamber; the court of the late sixteenth century was still largely peripatetic, and the entourages of the queen and king were often physically apart. Beaulieu may also have followed the retinues of François d'Anjou or one of the Guise princes at times when they were travelling separately from the main body of the court. It is hard to believe, however, that during nearly twenty years of court service the *Balet comique* was the only instance in which Beaulieu and Doria sang together. Their regular remuneration as a couple is suggestive but inconclusive (though the record that 'la Marthe' and her husband performed together for Henri III in Venice helps to strengthen the case). More compelling is the evidence that dialogue performance was a familiar mode of execution for self-accompanying singers at the French court from the 1560s at the latest. Furthermore, musical dialogues participated in the discourse of civility at the very heart of contemporary concepts of courtliness. This discourse spawned a whole range of cultural artefacts imitating and perfecting courtly conversational exchange, ranging from the civility manuals themselves to poetry and romance, and must certainly be seen as a strong encouragement to the musical enactment of these ideals.[58]

Dialogue performance by the pair is unlikely to have been a unique event; but the print of the *Balet comique* in which this duo is preserved *is* a unique publication. Unlike the vast majority of French music prints, it was not designed as a blueprint for the production of subsequent performances. It was a luxuriously presented narration of a fabulous occasion, to be savoured as the record of an event of historical significance: the sixteenth-century equivalent of a lavishly illustrated coffee-table book on the coronation of Elizabeth II or the wedding of Charles and Diana.[59] Written-out music is one component that contributes to the effect, a visual representation of sound analogous to the engravings

[58] Brooks, *Courtly Song*, p. 234.

[59] After Elizabeth II's coronation, Novello published a souvenir book uncannily like the account of the *Balet comique*, containing descriptions of the proceedings, texts for all the prayers and orations, and notated music for everything the Westminster Abbey Choir performed: *Coronation of Her Majesty Queen Elizabeth II: The Form and Order of the Service and the Music Sung in the Abbey Church of St. Peter, Westminster, 2 June 1953* (London, 1953).

showing costumes and scenery; Beaujoyeulx did not intend that anyone should mount performances of the music any more than he expected his readers to build their own replicas of the sets. The run-of-the-mill music prints of the period have a radically different function. They do not generally reflect any specific performance of the pieces they contain, but present the material in a standard format that could be adapted to suit the music-buyer's needs. In late sixteenth-century France, this standard format was vocal partbooks. Thus the situation for dialogues is similar to that of solo songs: if any traces of Beaulieu and Doria's other dialogue performances survive, they are camouflaged by the printing convention of four-voice polyphony.

The question is how to work backwards from the polyphonic prints to the solo dialogue performances they obscure. In two cases I shall examine here, early seventeenth-century versions of pieces that were first published many years earlier as polyphony suggest how dialogues were performed by soprano and bass in the late sixteenth century. Both set texts that elaborate variants of the type of mixed-gender exchange that characterised late sixteenth-century courtly love discourse. Both texts, like that of the *Balet comique*, feature a question–answer or statement–response relationship between the interventions; though the evidence of pieces such as *Autant qu'on voit aux cieux* and *Le soleil et nostre roy* shows that strophic songs whose texts were not true dialogues could be performed by soloists in alternation, dialogue texts seem positively to invite such performance by their clear differentiation of personae. To my mind, these pieces can be productively read as metaphors both for the careers of the singers who performed them and the social setting in which they flourished. And the conclusions drawn from the examination of these dialogues have wider implications both for the contemporary performance of solo song and for significant aspects of the period's musical aesthetics.

In strophic dialogues, exchanges between the characters may occur by strophe, or their voices may alternate at shorter intervals within the stanza. (The *Balet comique* dialogue provides a sample of both kinds of alternation, by strophe in the first five exchanges and then within the strophe for the final stanza.) Where subject voices alternate from stanza to stanza, sixteenth-century polyphonic print sources make no musical distinction between them: only a single strophe is underlaid, and subsequent strophes, for either speaker, employ the same music. Polyphonic dialogues in which the voices alternate within strophes often use a similar procedure: the responding speaker employs a recomposed version of the material given by the initiating subject, sometimes involving little more than changes to accommodate the final cadence. A good example is *Que ferez vous, dites madame*, published in Didier Le Blanc's *Airs de plusieurs musiciens, sur les poësies de P. Desportes, et autres des plus excelens poëtes de nostre tems* (Paris, 1579). A modern edition appears in *Monuments de la musique française au temps de la Renaissance*, ed. Henry Expert (Paris, 1925). As its title indicates, this collection contains music by various (unnamed) composers; notably, it features arrangements of the melodies of three of the four pieces attributed to Beaulieu in Caietain's 1576 *Airs*.[60] Like the songs earlier attributed to Beaulieu, *Que ferez vous* is a triple-metre *air*, and like them it sets a text by Philippe Desportes. The poem treats a staple subject of courtly love, constancy in absence, through the questions of the male interlocutor to a woman separated from her lover. The text consists of nine quatrains rhyming *abab*, each quatrain beginning with two lines in a masculine voice and closing with two lines of feminine response. The musical setting follows the verse structure, employing similar rhythms for all four phrases and the same melody (with some reharmonisation in the second appearance) for the *a* rhyme in the first and third lines of each quatrain. The music for the *b* rhyme of the second and fourth lines is also related, but melody and harmony are adjusted to provide a cadence on D at the end of the second line and a closing cadence on the modal final, G, at the end of the fourth (Example 2).

Though it is published as a four-voice vocal arrangement, two solo singers could perform this piece as a dialogue by assuming one of the subject voices and playing the other parts on an instru-

[60] Le Blanc's book contains arrangements of the same melodies used by Beaulieu for *Blessé d'une plaie inhumaine*, *Helas que me faut-il faire* and *Si tost que vostre oeil m'eust blessé*. The melody of the fourth piece attributed to Beaulieu in Caietain's book, *Rosette pour un peu d'absence*, appears in Chardavoine and in Besard (see *Airs de cour pour voix et luth (1603–1643)*, ed. A. Verchaly (Paris, 1961; repr. 1989), p. xxix). It is not clear whether the attributions in Caietain refer to entire pieces, that is, the melody and the accompanying voices, or whether it is simply the arrangements in polyphony that were Beaulieu's work.

Example 2 *Que ferez vous, dites ma Dame*, from Didier Le Blanc, *Airs de plusieurs musicians* (1579)(first strophe only). After *Monuments de la musique française*, ed. Expert, pp. 30–1

ment, just as they would have done for solo *airs*. Modern musicians might assume that in doing so the singers always performed the melody of the sections corresponding to their character, and that the lower parts furnished the material for accompaniment. That this was probably not the case – at least for the duos for soprano and bass that we can imagine Doria and Beaulieu performing – is shown by a later arrangement of *Que ferez vous* published in Gabrielle Bataille's *Airs de differents autheurs mis en tablature de luth . . . troisiesme livre* (Paris, 1611). This was the third in a highly successful series of books of solo songs with lute accompaniment that Pierre Ballard began publishing shortly after 1606, when he formally took over the music-printing business founded by his father Robert and his partner Adrian Le Roy some fifty years earlier. One of Pierre's first ventures was to launch a series of stunningly elegant lute song books employing an ingenious new use of type originally designed for other purposes. The new layout was not only beautiful but practical as well; for the first time, the problems of aligning the vocal lines with the tablature were neatly and economically solved. For the first six books in his series, Ballard collaborated with the royal lute player Gabriel Bataille, who collected and arranged the music. The repertory was chosen from fashionable recent works by court composers, particularly Pierre Guédron, but also contains a large number of older songs, many of them in circulation for more than thirty years but previously published only in polyphonic format.[61]

In Bataille's anthology, *Que ferez vous* appears as a dialogue for bass and soprano with lute accompaniment; the first two poetic lines are notated in bass clef, and lines 3 and 4 supply the woman's response in treble clef (Example 3). Although Bataille notates the piece with the rhythmic flexibility characteristic of later prints of *airs*, his soprano solo is an embellished version of the same melody that appears in Le Blanc's superius for the woman character's lines. The bass solo is not a melody in the modern sense of the

[61] See J. Le Cocq, 'Experimental Notation and Entrepreneurship in the Seventeenth Century: The *air de cour* for Voice and Lute, 1608–1643', *Revue de Musicologie*, 85 (1999), pp. 265–75; G. Durosoir, *L'air de cour en France, 1571–1655* (Liège, 1991), pp. 111–52. Le Cocq considers the books as a bold entrepreneurial step by Ballard and Bataille in appealing to new markets for this type of song. The typography of the collections (which used type originally designed as spinet tablature) will be discussed in Laurent Guillo's forthcoming study of the Ballard firm. I am grateful to M. Guillo for sharing his work prior to publication.

Example 3 *Que ferez vous, dites Madame*, from *Airs de differents autheurs . . . troisiesme livre*, ed. Bataille (1611), fols. 66v–67r (first strophe only)

Example 4 *Que ferez vous*, melody from Le Blanc superimposed on the bass from Bataille. The sections marked with asterisks represent clashes where the melody used by Bataille differs from that of Le Blanc

word, but – like the music for Glaucus in the *Balet comique* – a bass part similar to those found in contemporary polyphony. At first glance this section looks unrelated to Le Blanc's version of the male speaker's lines: it does not follow the melody, nor does it duplicate Le Blanc's bass. But in fact putting Le Blanc's melody together with Bataille's bass produces a reasonably satisfactory contrapuntal match (Example 4). Discrepancies occur only at bars 2–3 and 11 (at corresponding positions in the first and second couplet of the text, marked with asterisks in Example 4) where the melody as Bataille knew it was slightly different from Le Blanc's, generating a different harmonisation.[62] That is, Bataille's song is not based on Le Blanc. Both Bataille and Le Blanc present different harmonisations – with correspondingly different bass parts – of much the same strophic song, which probably circulated primarily in the form of a tune to which different arrangement techniques were applied. One such technique apparently involved the extraction of a bass part for performance by a male singer, allowing the song to be executed as a dialogue for male and female soloists. What seems unusual about this from the modern perspective is that the bass part was clearly considered a self-sufficient solo line without the superius melody, which does not even appear in the lute part of the bass singer's sections in Bataille's arrangement.

Bataille's third book contains one further dialogue for solo singers: *Pastoureau m'ayme tu bien?*, on a pastoral text by Jean Passerat. Born in 1534, Passerat was a poet under the protection of Henri de Mesmes, *maître des requêtes* at the court of Henri III. Virtually none of his vernacular poetry was published before his death in 1602; a posthumous publication contains the first printed version of the dialogue.[63] But the poem had been circulating in manuscript at the French royal court for many decades. It figures in a poetry album compiled *c.*1564–5 for Marie de Montmorency, and it appears in an album copied in the early 1570s for Nicolas de Neufville and Madeleine de Laubesbine (the same manuscript that contains the earliest version of Ronsard's *Le soleil et nostre roy*).[64] Both volumes include numerous poems circulating with musical settings in contemporary prints.[65] Both also contain several dia-

[62] Bataille's soprano part (Example 3, 3rd system, on 'corps') shows that the melody he knew moved to *d″* rather than *c″* at the spot corresponding to the downbeats of bars 3 and 11 in Example 4. The reason for the bass *c* in Example 4, bar 2 is less obvious, but if the melody Bataille knew proceeded *d″–e♭″–d″* at this point (as his superius line suggests) instead of *b♭′–d″–c″*, this harmonisation too would work.

[63] *Recueil des oeuvres poétiques de Jean Passerat lecteur et interprete du Roy* (Paris, 1606); see J. Passerat, *Les poésies françaises,* ed. P. Blanchemain (Paris, 1880; repr. Geneva, 1968), i, pp. 141–3. Here and in the setting in Bataille, the first word is spelled 'Patoureau'; all other sources use the orthography 'Pastoureau', which I adopt here for the sake of consistency.

[64] The poem appears in the Montmorency album, Paris, BNF Rothschild IV.2.3, on fols. 109^{r}–110^{r}; see E. Picot, *Catalogue des livres composant la bibliothèque de feu M. le baron James de Rothschild*, iv (Paris, 1912), pp. 584–91. On the Villeroy manuscript, Paris, BNF fr. 1663, see n. 53 above; the dialogue is on fols. 42^{r}–43^{r}.

[65] Poems known in contemporary musical settings include Passerat's ode in *vers mesuré*, *Ce petit dieu colere archer leger oyseau* (Rothschild IV.2.3, fol. 69^{r-v}, and fr. 1663, fol. 84^{v}, set to

logue poems, including the anonymous *Hola hola Karon*, an exchange between a soul and the guardian of Hell (a poem type frequently set to music), and Baïf's dialogue *O Liz' objet de mon amour fidelle*, a portion of which appears in musical setting as *Lise que j'aime sur tout* in Didier Le Blanc's second book of *airs*.[66] *Pastoureau m'ayme tu bien?* also survives in a contemporary musical setting, in Jean de Castro's *Livre de chansons à cincq parties . . . avec une pastorelle à VII en forme de dialogue* (Antwerp, 1586). Although the preface was signed from Antwerp, the collection appeared only a few years after Castro was forced by the troubles in the Low Countries to seek refuge in France, where he may first have become familiar with Passerat's text.[67]

The structure of the poem is unusual, consisting of five strophes of six-syllable lines, each followed by a refrain of two three-syllable couplets ('Comme quoy? / Comme toy / Ma rebelle / Pastorelle'). The strophes vary in length: the first is a rhyming couplet; strophes 2 and 5 are quatrains composed of two couplets; and strophes 3 and 4 are *huitains* of four couplets (see Table 1). A further complication is that the changes between speakers occur at different places in each strophe. Part of the poem's attraction lies in the lively volley between the characters: the shepherdess's exasperated attempts to dictate the terms of her suitor's love-talk produce rapid shifts in voice, as she proposes responses for him and mimics his unsatisfactory replies. The frequent inclusion of phrases such as 'You should say . . .' and 'Don't say . . .', followed by quotes or parodies, combines with the employment of reflexive

music in Le Blanc's *Airs de plusieurs musiciens*) and Philippe Desportes's *Quand je pense aux plaisirs* (Rothschild IV.2.3, fols. 87ʳ–88ᵛ; set in Caietain's *Airs mis en musique*). Both manuscripts also contain poems for which no musical setting is known but whose construction – strophes plus repeating refrains – betrays a musical intent or origin (for example, *Mettez moy là et en tous lieux*, Rothschild IV.2.3, fol. 116ʳ⁻ᵛ), as well as the texts of occasional pieces identified as having been sung on particular occasions (*Ce chevalier d'invincible puissance*, a poem by Ronsard with the rubric 'Ceci a esté chanté à l'hostel de Lorraine le dimanche gras 1571', fr. 1663, fol. 88ᵛ).

66 *Hola hola Karon* appears in Rothschild IV.2.3, fols. 107ᵛ–108ʳ; on Charon dialogues set to music, see R. Wistreich, 'Seventeenth Century English Charon Dialogues: A Study of Literary Sources and Contexts' (unpublished M.A. diss., University of Birmingham, 1988). Baïf's poem appears in fr. 1663, fols. 8ᵛ–9ʳ; the musical setting is in D. Le Blanc, *Second livre d'airs des plus excelants musiciens de nostre tems* (Paris: Le Roy & Ballard, 1579).

67 In the preface to his *Second livre de chansons, madrigalz et motetz à trois parties* (Paris, 1580), signed from Lyon on 1 January 1580, Castro explains his reasons for coming to France. On Castro's French connections, see Brooks, 'Jean de Castro, the Pense Partbooks and Musical Culture in Sixteenth-Century Lyons', *Early Music History*, 11 (1992), pp. 91–149.

Table 1 *Jean Passerat*, Pastoureau m'ayme tu bien? *as set in Jean de Castro*, Livre de chansons à cincq parties . . . avec une pastorelle à VII en forme de dialogue (*Antwerp: Phalèse and Bellère, 1586*)

Text	Text structure	Translation	Musical structure
Pastoureau m'ayme tu bien?	a	'Shepherd, do you love me well?'	A
Je t'ayme dieu sçet combien.	a	'I love you, God knows how much.'	
Comme quoy?	Refrain	'Like what?'	Refrain
Comme toy		'Like yourself,	
Ma rebelle		my rebellious	
Pastorelle.		shepherdess.'	
Ce propos tant affaité	b	'This precious talk	B
En rien ne m'a contanté,	b	Doesn't please me at all.	
Pastoreau sans mocquerie,	c	Shepherd, without joking,	C
M'ayme tu, dy je te prie	c	do you love me, I pray you tell me,	
Comme quoy?	Refrain	like what?'	Refrain
Comme toy		'Like yourself,	
Ma rebelle		my rebellious	
Pastorelle.		shepherdess.'	
Tu m'eusses respondu mieux	d	'You would have done better to say	B′
Je t'ayme comme mes yeux,	d	"I love you like my eyes".'	
Trop de haine je leur porte	e	'I bear too much hate for them,	D
Car ilz ont ouvert la porte,	e	for they opened the door	
Aux ennuys que je resceu	f	to the cares I gained	E
Deslors que je t'apperceu,	f	as soon as I saw you	
Quand ma liberté fut prise	g	and my liberty was taken away	C′
Des beautez que tant je prise.	g	by those beauties I cherish so much.'	
Comme quoy?	Refrain	'Like what?'	Refrain
Comme toy		'Like yourself,	
Ma rebelle		my rebellious	
Pastorelle.		shepherdess.'	
Pastoureau parle autrement	h	'Shepherd, speak otherwise	B″
Et me dy tout franchement	h	and tell me honestly,	
M'ayme tu comme ta vie?	c′	do you love me like your life?'	F
Non, car elle est asservie	c′	'No, for my life is enslaved	
A cent et cent mil' ennuys	i	by a hundred hundred thousand cares	G
Donc aymer je ne la puis,	i	so that I cannot love it,	
N'estant plus qu'un corps sans ame	j	since I am but a body without soul	C″
Par trop cherir une dame.	j	for having loved a lady too much.'	
Comme quoy?	Refrain	'Like what?'	Refrain
Comme toy		'Like yourself,	
Ma rebelle		my rebellious	
Pastorelle.		shepherdess.'	
Laisse là ce comme toy,	k	'Leave off this "like yourself",	B‴
Dy je t'ayme comme moy,	k	say, "I love you like myself".'	
Je ne m'ayme pas moymesme.	l	'I don't love me myself.'	C‴
Dy moy doncques si tu m'ayme,	l	'Tell me then if you love me	
Comme quoy?	Refrain	like what?'	Refrain
Comme toy		'Like yourself,	
Ma rebelle		my rebellious	
Pastorelle.		shepherdess.'	

constructions (e.g. 'Je ne m'ayme pas moymesme') to produce a pleasing tangle of subject positions and direct and indirect speech in every stanza. An excellent example of courtly pastoral, the poem illustrates the kind of witty erotic repartee in which Castiglione's perfect courtiers were meant to excel.

Castro's setting is for seven voices divided into two groups, a three-voice high ensemble (superius I, contratenor I and tenor I) representing the shepherdess, and a four-voice group (superius II, contratenor II, tenor II and bass) that sings the shepherd's lines. The poem's irregular construction precluded composition as a straightforward strophic song in the style of *Que ferez vous*. But like the music of more conventional strophic *airs*, Castro's piece is almost unrelievedly homophonic, and the lines for each interlocutor are clearly marked off by simultaneous rests and cadences, so that there is no overlap in the exchange between the characters. And although the piece is fully written out in the source, the strophic structure of the text is represented in Castro's setting by the use of repeated material for the four- and eight-line stanzas. The music for the two couplets of the quatrains returns with only minor alterations for the first and last couplets of the *huitains*, so that the beginnings and ends of the four final strophes are marked by the same music (represented by letters B and C in the right column of Table 1). The strophic effect is reinforced by the unvarying refrain at the end of each stanza.

While the vocal groupings remain largely consistent, the tenor I and tenor II parts often contribute to the music for the opposing choir (as in Example 5, bars 27–34, when tenor II sings with the three-voice group). Textural variety also figures in the refrain, consisting of a statement of the first refrain line 'Comme quoy' by the high voices representing the shepherdess, followed by the shepherd's response for the low-voice choir, using the last three lines of refrain text. These three lines are then repeated by the entire seven-voice ensemble, using the same music enriched by the addition of the extra voices (see Example 6a; the gesture is repeated at each of the four subsequent appearances of the refrain, bars 35–47, 77–89, 119–31 and 146–60). Techniques such as these, including the representation of gender by tessitura and the disposition of the vocal groups, had become typical of seven-voice dialogues after Willaert began to employ them in the late 1530s

Example 5 Jean de Castro, *Pastoureau m'ayme tu bien?* from *Livre de chansons à cinq parties* (1586), bars 25–34

Example 6a Castro, *Pastoureau*, bars 1–20

Example 6a *Continued*

Example 6b *Patoureau m'ayme tu bien?* from *Airs de differents autheurs*, ed. Bataille, bars 1–5. After *Airs de cour*, ed. Verchaly

(though the dialogues of Willaert and his followers are rarely as unremittingly homophonic as Castro's piece). David Nutter suggests that Willaert's dialogues were performed in Venetian academies by solo singers with instrumental accompaniment; he proposes that only the highest vocal line of each choir was sung, since generally only these parts carry the complete text.[68] The dialogue arranged by Castro was certainly also performed by solo voices: but in this case, the version of the piece preserved by Bataille shows that one of the vocal soloists could be a bass.

Bataille's 1611 *Pastoureau m'ayme tu bien?* uses a variant of the poem that matches that published in Passerat's 1606 *Recueil des oeuvres poétiques*; Castro's text is closer to the earlier manuscript

[68] See Nutter, 'Dialogue', in *New Grove II*.

versions, particularly that in Paris, BNF fr. 1663.[69] But despite the textual divergence, Bataille's dialogue is an arrangement of the same piece set for seven voices by Castro. As in Bataille's version of *Que ferez vous*, the music is rhythmically notated in a looser declamatory style, in contrast to Castro's strict triple metre. This difference apart, all the shepherdess's lines are lightly ornamented versions of the music of Castro's superius I part, the highest line of the three-voice ensemble representing the woman's voice. And the solo bass part in Bataille largely duplicates the bass line from Castro's second choir. In many sections the duplication is exact, most notably in the opening of the dialogue and in the refrain (see Examples 6a and 6b). In others, some variation and octave transposition occurs (as in Examples 7a and 7b, where a descent from *B*♭ to *F* in Castro is matched by an ascent to *f* in Bataille). In a few sections the bass in Bataille is almost completely different, a concomitant of different harmonisation (Examples 8a and 8b). Even when it deviates from the bass part in Castro, however, Bataille's bass solo retains its character as a line functionally different from the melodically conceived soprano part, echoing the role of the bass in polyphony and duplicating the lowest line of the lute accompaniment throughout. Like the bass solo of the duo from the *Balet comique*, it moves largely in fifths, fourths and octaves, and it invariably doubles the lowest pitch of cadential sonorities rather than approaching the cadence pitch by whole tone.

Pastoureau m'ayme tu bien? resembles the *Balet comique* dialogue not only in the behaviour of the bass line, but in a basic component of its structure: the enhanced repetition of music from the end of each stanza in a ritornello-like fashion (this seems to have been a feature of the lost 1565 dialogue sung at Bayonne by Courville and Vausmesnil as well, though the 'refrain' in that case was instrumental). In the *Balet comique*, this involves the repetition and elaboration of the final two phrases of each of Tethys' strophes by a five-part vocal and instrumental ensemble. In Castro's setting of *Pastoureau m'ayme tu bien?*, the refrain first performed in alternation by the two groups representing the shepherd and shepherdess is

[69] The principal differences are in the final line of the third strophe, which appears as 'De ton oeil qui me maistrise' in Bataille and the Passerat print (instead of 'Des beautez qui me maistrise'), and in the order of the first two lines of the second strophe, which is reversed in Paris, BNF Rothschild IV. 2.3 and in the 1606 print.

Example 7a Castro, *Pastoureau*, bars 69–76

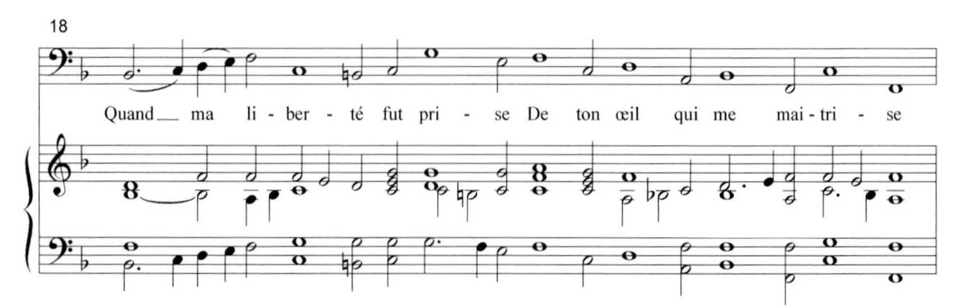

Example 7b *Patoureau*, ed. Bataille, bar 18

amplified by repetition of the shepherd's refrain material by the full seven-voice ensemble (as in Example 6a). In Bataille's version, this full-choir material becomes a solo statement by the soprano shepherdess (as in Example 6b), which could seem odd since the words she is singing properly belong to the shepherd character. This was probably performed, however, with the bass repeating his final refrain phrase from the preceding measure (echoing the bass of the lute accompaniment, which repeats the material exactly) so that each strophe finishes with a simultaneous performance by both singers of 'Comme toy ma rebelle Pastourelle' in place of Castro's full-ensemble repetition.

Support for this idea comes from another pastoral dialogue, *Berger que pensés vous faire?*, published as a piece for bass and soprano with lute accompaniment in Bataille's fourth book of *airs* in 1613, and in a polyphonic version in a 1617 collection of five-voice *airs de cour* by Pierre Guédron.[70] Guédron moved in court circles from 1583 at the latest, first as a member of the chapel of Louis de Lorraine, cardinal de Guise, and then as a royal chamber singer.[71] His Guise and royal connections brought him into personal contact with La Grotte, Costeley, Caietain, Salmon, Beaulieu and Doria, and he was intimately familiar with the style of the late

[70] The voice and lute version appears in *Airs de différents autheurs . . . quatriesme livre* (Paris, 1613); the polyphonic arrangement in Guédron, *Troisieme livre d'airs de cour à quatre et cinq parties* (Paris, 1617). Editions of both appear in *Airs de cour*, ed. Verchaly, pp. xliv–xlv and 56–7.

[71] Guédron attended the Puy d'Evreux in 1583 as a member of Louis de Lorraine's chapel; the records of the Puy state that although his voice was then changing, he sang the *hautecontre* part 'fort bien' (Bonnin and Chassant, *Puy de musique*, pp. 27–8). Further on Guédron see L. de La Laurencie, 'Un musicien dramatique du XVIIe siècle français: Pierre Guédron', *Rivista Musicale Italiana*, 29 (1922), pp. 445–72, and D. L. Royster, 'Pierre Guédron and the *air de cour*, 1600–1620' (Ph.D. diss., Yale University, 1973).

Example 8a Castro, *Pastoureau*, bars 54–68

Example 8a *Continued*

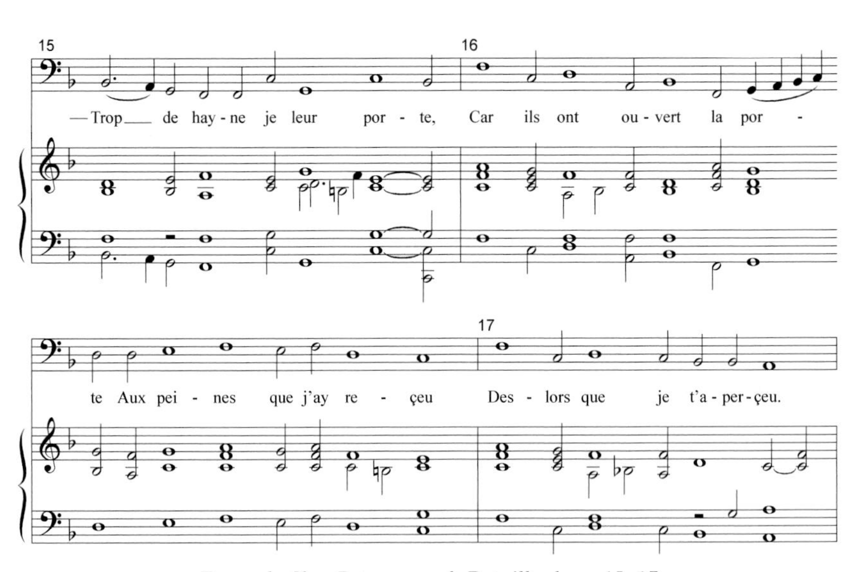

Example 8b *Patoureau*, ed. Bataille, bars 15–17

sixteenth-century *air de cour*. The most important practitioner of the genre during the reign of Henri IV, he was not only the composer of the lion's share of attributed music in Bataille's anthologies but also the dedicatee of the first volume of the series (1608). As in the case of *Berger que pensés vous faire?* his songs regularly circulated in both solo and polyphonic versions.

In this case, however, the piece in the polyphonic collection is not a true arrangement in polyphony, but rather a dialogue for bass and soprano with lute accompaniment (featuring the earliest appearance of a printed continuo part in France) and a short polyphonic statement at the end of each strophe; the three inner parts are *tacet* for all but the final measures. As in the *Balet comique* duo, and as in Castro's setting of *Pastoureau m'ayme tu bien?*, the full group repeats the final phrase of each stanza, here the shepherd's statement 'Philis, vous me baiserez'. The full ensemble's reiteration of the final line of text is represented in Bataille's version of *Berger que pensés vous faire?* by the soprano shepherdess and the bass shepherd joining in together; Bataille and Ballard managed to print the section in this fashion because the piece is short and straightforwardly strophic, meaning that there was room at the end of the stanza to add an extra stave below the lute tablature for the second vocal part (see Figure 2). This printing solution was technically impossible for the lute-and-voice version of *Pastoureau m'ayme tu bien*, because of its length and continuous composition; but it seems likely that in performance the bass would join the soprano for the final refrain lines simply by repeating his previous phrase in tandem with the lute repetition of the same material.[72]

The dialogue for solo singers is often considered a creature of the seventeenth century, a phenomenon made possible by the widespread adoption of continuo accompaniment and the consequent new possibilities for solo vocal writing.[73] The similarities between the *Balet comique* dialogue and the pieces preserved in

[72] Simultaneous singing of a final section after an initial exchange in alternation continued to be a feature of French solo dialogues later in the seventeenth century; see, for example, Etienne Moulinié, *Respects qui me donnez la loy* (1629); Antoine Boësset, *Mourons Tirsis* (1632); François de Chancy, *Faut-il mourir sans espérance* (1635); and François Richard, *Cloris attends un peu* (1637), all transcribed in *Airs de cour*, ed. Verchaly. Simultaneously circulating polyphonic versions existed for both the Richard and Boësset dialogues.

[73] See, for example, Whenham, *Duet and Dialogue*, i, p. 183; Nutter and Whenham, 'Dialogue', *New Grove II*.

Figure 2 Pierre Guédron, *Berger que pensés vous faire?*, from *Airs de differents autheurs . . . quatriesme livre*, ed. G. Bataille (Paris, 1613), fols. 65[v]–66[r]. Reproduced by permission of the British Library

Figure 2 *Continued*

Bataille suggest, however, that the Baroque solo dialogue rested on a performing heritage that extended well back into the previous century. Particularly compelling is the evidence of a body of common structures for dialogues and for a tradition in the way solo parts were created for bass singers. The construction of bass parts was conditioned by the habits of polyphony, but I think it may be a mistake to consider Bataille's dialogues for voice and lute to be necessarily 'based on' pre-existing polyphonic compositions. The bass line of the *Balet comique* duo acts in a similar way, though the piece was manifestly conceived from the beginning as a dialogue for solo singers. So the relationship between Bataille and Castro, for example, may not be quite as straightforward as that of a lute song 'arrangement' of a polyphonic 'original', or vice versa; both may be arrangements or versions that circulated simultaneously. This concept resonates too with what we know about compositional process for this repertory. Guédron, for example, whose technique is probably representative of that of the previous generation of court singer-composers as well, apparently wrote *airs* as pieces for superius and bass, for which the inner parts would be filled in (perhaps not even by the composer himself) loosely for lute or in a more contrapuntal fashion for voices, depending on which was required.[74] Leaving aside the question of print dates – a red herring since the impetus to print dialogues in the way they appear in Bataille did not exist before Pierre Ballard took over his father's firm – it seems plausible that solo dialogue versions of both *Pastoureau m'ayme tu bien?* and *Que ferez vous dites madame* existed in performance, by Girard de Beaulieu, Violante Doria and other court singers, at the same time that polyphonic arrangements of these pieces were appearing in print.[75]

[74] Royster, 'Pierre Guédron and the *air de cour*', pp. 180–2. Royster's conclusions are based on the evidence of letters from Malherbe sent in February–March 1610 about a poem written at Henri IV's command for Charlotte de Condé. The second letter contains a manuscript of Guédron's setting of the text, likewise written at the king's behest, presented as a melody with text and an untexted bass line. The letters are quoted and the musical manuscript transcribed in *Airs de cour*, ed. Verchaly, pp. xxxix–xl. Le Cocq ('French Lute Song', i, pp. 211–13), on the basis of this and other evidence drawn from earlier sources, argues convincingly for the soprano–bass framework as the compositional basis for the entire *air de cour* repertory from the 1590s at the very latest and probably as early as the 1560s.

[75] An Italian coda to this hypothetical scenario is provided by settings of Ottaviano Rinuccini's adaptation of Passerat's dialogue text, 'Bel pastor dal cui bel guardo', set to music as a dialogue for soprano and bass by Marco da Gagliano and for soprano and

Although I have been motivated by a desire to unearth a potential repertory for my protagonists rather than a wish to make recommendations to performers, my reading of Bataille's lute songs and earlier polyphonic prints does have some consequences for modern performance practice. Bataille's dialogues provide models for the interpretation of earlier dialogue settings, published only as polyphony, in which masculine and feminine subject voices alternate between or within strophes of text: male and female soloists can perform the line corresponding to their range – that is, with bass singers extracting bass lines, and sopranos performing melodies – adding appropriate ornamentation, with harmonies supplied by instrumental accompaniment. A significant number of pieces published in French sources in the last third of the sixteenth century lend themselves well to this treatment. Examples include settings of pastoral dialogue texts similar to *Pastoureau m'ayme tu bien?*, such as *Reveillez vous belle Catin*, *Bergere de quelle façon*, *Vous me jurez bergere*, *Mon dieu que pouroy-je faire*, *J'aymeray tousjours ma Philis*, *Berger quelle adventure estrange* and *Dieu te gard Catin*, all of which were published in polyphonic collections of *airs* from the 1580s and 1590s.[76] A number of these have refrains (*Reveillez vous belle Catin* and *Bergere de quelle façon* in fact share the same refrain) and these should probably be performed by both soloists together.

tenor by Claudio Monteverdi. (F. Chiarelli, 'Per un censimento delle rime di Ottavio Rinuccini', *Studi Italiani*, 2 (1990), pp. 133–63, has confirmed the traditional attribution of 'Bel pastor' to Rinuccini set aside in *Claudio Monteverdi, madrigali e canzonette. libro nono*, ed. A. M. Monterosso (Cremona, 1983), p. 45. Verchaly (*Airs de cour*, p. xxviii), unaware of the early manuscript versions of the Passerat poem, followed Théodore Gérold in incorrectly reversing the relationship of the French original and the Italian imitation.) Gagliano's setting appeared in Piero Benedetti's *Musiche* (Florence, 1611); Monteverdi's was published in 1651 in the posthumous ninth book of madrigals. For a comparison of Gagliano, Monteverdi and Bataille/Castro, see S. Leopold, 'Der schöne Hirte und seine Vorfahren', in P. Cahn and A.-K. Heimer (eds.), *De musica et cantu: Studien zur Geschichte der Kirchenmusik und der Oper. Helmut Hucke zum 60. Geburtstag* (Hildesheim, 1993), pp. 471–80. (Leopold lays the poem out correctly on pp. 474–5; the text as printed in Monterosso's edition makes no poetic sense.) Rinuccini visited the French court in 1601, 1602–3 and 1604, well before the appearance of Passerat's text in print (1606) or the publication of the musical setting in Bataille (1611). Although Beaulieu and Doria were long gone by the time Rinuccini came to France, it is tempting to speculate that he first heard Passerat's poem in a dialogue setting performed by other French singers.

[76] The first three were included in Jehan Planson's *Airs mis en musique à quatre parties par Jean Planson Parisien tant de son invention que d'autres Musitiens . . .* (Paris, 1587; subsequent editions appeared in 1588, 1593 and 1595); *J'aymeray tousjours ma Philis* appeared in *Airs de court mis en musique* (Paris, 1595), and *Mon dieu que pouroy-je faire* was added to the augmented edition of that collection that appeared in 1596. *Berger quelle aventure* and *Dieu te garde* figure in *Airs de court mis en musique . . .* (Paris, 1597).

These observations about dialogue singing in the late sixteenth century also prompt reflection on issues of wider significance. If basses regularly sang solo lines similar to those in the *Balet comique* duo when performing dialogues, what did they sing when they performed alone to their own accompaniment? Could it have been ornamented versions of bass parts similar to those in the polyphonic prints of *airs de cour*, with or without the associated melody in the instrumental accompaniment? The evidence of the dialogues suggests that in attempting to answer these questions we might do well to suspend our own notions of what constitutes a satisfactory melodic line, and to re-examine some of our assumptions about musical transmission. Richard Wistreich's work indicates that Italian basses probably regularly created solo performances around bass parts similar to those we see in polyphony.[77] The special formulae for bass singers in ornamentation treatises of the period provide plenty of solutions for filling in the characteristic angularities of bass parts with passagework (and applying their formulae to a typical bass part from an *air de cour* – such as those attributed to Costeley and La Grotte – results in a line closely akin to Beaulieu's in the *Balet comique*).[78] This hypothesis also receives strong support from later French sources; in Mersenne's *Harmonie universelle*, for example, one of the examples of ornamentation supplied for the *air N'esperez plus mes yeux* involves three different solo versions of the bass line of the song.[79] Considering the bass and superius lines of repertories such as the *villanella* and *air de cour* as complementary but detachable entities, liable to be transmitted in musical sources separately as well as together, each susceptible to independent deployment as well as simultaneous execution, also helps to illuminate some of the characteristic

[77] Wistreich, 'Giulio Cesare Brancaccio', pp. 197–220.

[78] An early model for the procedure, which furthermore confirms the hypothesis that lines other than the superius were considered a satisfactory basis for solo performance, appears in Diego Ortiz, *Trattado de glosas sobre clausulas y otros generos de puntos* (Rome, 1553). Ortiz supplies sample solo viol pieces based on the different lines of a madrigal and a chanson; in both cases the first 'recercada' is derived from an ornamented rendition of the bass line of the piece. He also furnishes models for bass viol lines derived from the bass movement of contemporary singing formulae such as the *romanesca*, highlighting the connections between the procedures of improvising bass lines around the bassus of polyphonic pieces and creating new bass lines around the patterns of well-known formulae.

[79] Mersenne, *Harmonie universelle, contenant la theorie et la pratique de la musique*, ii, p. 413.

quirks of the dissemination of Renaissance singing formulae such as the *romanesca* and *ruggiero*. Finally, the refrains that so often punctuate dialogues offer support for a simple mode of reconstructing duos out of the repertory of printed polyphony, through the simultaneous execution of soprano and bass lines and the filling in of inner parts with lute or *lirone*.

My conclusions about the genesis and performance of solo dialogues are more speculative than many of those I can draw from archival documents that testify to Doria and Beaulieu's activities; while musical sources allow me to say something about what they may have performed, most of what what was valued about their singing is necessarily irretrievably lost. Nevertheless, I find it useful to think of Bataille's dialogues as distant echoes of their songs, which can contribute a valuable perspective to our understanding of a lost performing culture. The dialogues can stand as a metaphor for the lives of the singers who performed them and for the changing social setting that supported their careers; but only a reading around and through the musical sources can render the metaphor meaningful. Another kind of testimony to these vanished voices is provided by Marin Mersenne, who in the early seventeenth century wrote nostalgically about the royal musicians who created what he considered a golden age of French singing. Listing the famous performers of the past, Mersenne asserted that 'Girard de Beaulieu, bass of the *chambre du roi*, sang better than any other'.[80] Mersenne included no such glowing tribute to Violante Doria, though her visibility in contemporary records is so much higher than that of any other of her sex that we can picture her as a woman of exceptional gifts. We can imagine, too, that the pleasure that François de Billon prophetically assured his contemporaries would result from duo singing was experienced by those fortunate enough to hear them perform together.

University of Southampton

[80] 'Girard de Beaulieu Basse de la Chambre du Roy, a mieux chanté que nul autre . . .', *ibid.*, i, sig. Av^{v} ('Premiere Preface generale au lecteur').

APPENDIX

Girard de Beaulieu and Violante Doria: Documents

Records from royal accounts are also presented in abbreviated form in the entries s.v. 'Beaulieu' and 'Doria' in Brooks, *Courtly Song*, pp. 423–6 and 463–5; in this Appendix, they are augmented with material from notarial documents and other printed and manuscript sources to present a complete documentary portrait of Beaulieu and Doria's activities.

1572 Royal treasury accounts, record for 2 January: 50 livres paid as *étrennes* to 'la seignore Viollante Doria, l'une des damoiselles de la Royne'. Paris, BNF Clairambault 233, p. 3096.

Royal treasury accounts, record for 29 June: 750 livres paid as a gift 'tant à luy que à sa femme' to 'Girard de Beaulieu chantre et joueur d'instrumens [of Charles IX]' for their upkeep 'à la suitte de sa Ma^{té} ou ilz sont ordinairement'. Paris, BNF Clairambault 233, p. 3356.

List of royal pensions for 1572: 200 livres per annum awarded to 'Beaulieu et sa femme vallet de chambre de la royne.' Paris, BNF fr. 7007, fol. 74^{r}.

1575 Stable accounts, François d'Anjou: 'Beaulieu' is listed among musicians to whom table expenses are owed (to a total of 365 livres). Paris, AN, KK 236, fol. 436^{v}.

1576 Fabrice Marin Caietain, *Airs mis en musique à quatre parties* (Paris: Le Roy & Ballard), including four pieces by 'Beaulieu'.

1577 Receipt, 11 April: 'Girard de Beaulieu chantre de la chambre [of Henri III] et Yoland Doria genevoise sa femme, l'une des damoiselles de la Royne' receive 2,000 livres in payment of a royal pension for the year 1577. Paris, BNF fr. 26728 (Pièces originales 244), dossier 'Beaulieu', pièce 25.

Receipt, Poitiers, 9 July: 'Girard de Beaulieu vallet de chambre du Roy', as procurator for the royal chamber singer Thesée Du Port, confirmed by an act of procuration passed in Rome on 3 December 1575, receives 50 livres on Du Port's behalf in payment of the latter's wages for the January quarter of 1577. Paris, BNF fr. 26160, pièce 549.

Receipt, Paris, 21 December: 'noble homme Girard de Beaulieu chantre de la chambre du Roy' receives 200 livres in payment of his wages for 1577. Paris, BNF fr. 26160, pièce 657.

Receipt, Paris, 21 December: 'noble homme Girard de Beaulieu varlet de chambre du Roy', as procurator for the royal chamber singer Jean de Valot, as confirmed by an act of procuration passed on 12 May 1577, receives 50 livres on Valot's behalf in payment of the latter's wages for the January quarter of 1577. Paris, BNF fr. 26160, pièce 658.

1578 List of royal pensions for 1578: 200 livres per annum awarded to 'Beaulieu vallet de chambre de la Royne joueur de lyre devant sa Magesté et sa femme'; specified as a supplement to the 1,000 livres per annum they were to receive from the queen. Paris, BNF Dupuy 852, fol. 42r.

Notarial act, Paris, *étude* of Jehan Marchant (rue Saint Honoré), 13 September: Guillaume Costeley, 'organiste et vallet de chambre ordinaire du Roy', names 'les sieurs de Beaulieu et La Grotte aussy vallets de chambre ordinaire du roy' as his procurators, authorized to receive from the royal treasurers on Costeley's behalf payment of any royal gifts, pensions or salary. Paris, AN, Minutier Central ET/XC/128.

[1578] List of royal pensions, undated (appears to be a different redaction of the 1578 list, or a draft for 1579): 200 livres per annum awarded to 'Beaulieu et sa femme vallet de chambre de la Royne'; specified as a supplement to the 1,000 livres per annum they were to receive from the queen. Paris, BNF Dupuy 127, fol. 14r.

1580 List of royal household officers (*état de maison*) for Henri III: 'Girard de Beaulieu' is listed in the category 'chantres', with yearly wages of 66 écus 2/3. Paris, BNF Dupuy 127, fol. 92r.

[1580] Fragment of royal treasury accounts: order for payment of 166 écus 2/3 to 'Girard de Beaulieu chantre de la chambre [of Henri III] et Yolant Doria sa femme' for the January quarter's payment of their annual pension. Paris, BNF fr. 26170, fol. 49r.

1581 15 October, performance of the *Balet comique de la royne*.

Entry in the foundation charter of the Puy d'Evreux. The 'sieur de Beaulieu . . . bassecontre' and five other royal musicians assist in performances at the Puy for seven days around the feast of Saint Cecilia, 21 November. Evreux, Archives départementales de l'Eure, Série D^{4}, edited in *Puy de musique érigé à Evreux, en l'honneur de Madame Sainte Cécile, publié d'après un manuscrit du XVIe siècle*, ed. T. Bonnin and A. Chassant (Evreux, 1837), pp. 23–4.

1582 Fragment of royal treasury accounts, expenditures approved by Henri III at Fontainebleau on 6 August: order for payment of 166 écus 2/3 to 'Girard de Beaulieu vallet de chambre et chantre de la chambre [of Henri III] et Yolande Doria sa femme' for the April quarter's payment of their annual pension. Paris, BNF n. a. f. 1441, fol. 12^{v}.

1583 20 January, foundation of the royal penitential confraternity of L'Annonciation de Nostre Dame. 'Monsr de Beaulieu' is listed among the members, bracketed together with seven others under the rubric 'chantres'; 'M. de Beaulieu' and the same others listed as 'Huict Musiciens de la Chambre du Roy' who will be responsible for singing *fauxbourdons* and other music for the group's devotions. Paris, BNF n. a. f. 7549, fols. 4^{v} and 21^{r}.

1584 List of household officers (*état de maison*) for Louise de Lorraine-Vaudémont: 'Monsieur [blank] de Beaulieu et [blank] sa femme musiciens et joueurs de luth de la Royne' are listed in the category 'autres personnes que la royne a voullu estre adjoustées au present estat', with joint yearly wage of 400 écus. Paris, AN, KK 530/ 15, no. 13.

List of household officers (*état de maison*) for Henri III: 'Girard de Beaulieu' is listed in the category 'chantres', with yearly wages of 66 écus 2/3. Paris, AN, KK 139, fol. 33^{r}.

List of household officers to be retained from Henri III's yearly *état* as part of a reorganization of the *maison du roi*: 'Beaulieu bassecontre' listed in the category 'Vois ordinaires' (i.e., in daily service). Paris, BNF Dupuy 489, fol. 13^{r}.

Fragment of royal treasury accounts, expenditures approved by Henri III at Saint-Maur on 15 August: order for payment of 166 écus 2/3 to 'Girard de Beaulieu et Yolande Doria sa femme' for the April quarter's payment of their annual pension. Paris, BNF n. a. f. 1441, fol. 30r.

Fragment of royal treasury accounts, expenditures approved by Henri III on 3 December: order for payment of 166 écus 2/3 to 'Girard de Beaulieu et Yolante Doria sa femme chantres ordinaires de la chambre [of Henri III]' for the previous January quarter's payment of their annual pension. Paris, BNF 26170, fol. 132v.

[1584] Fragment of royal treasury accounts, undated: order for payment of 333 écus 1/3 to 'Girard de Beaulieu chantre [of Henri III] et Yolande Doria sa femme' for a half year's (July–December) payment of their annual pension. Paris, BNF fr. 26170, fol. 135v.

1585 Receipt, 25 September: 'Girard de Beaulieu vallet de chambre ordinaire [of Henri III]' receives 100 écus in payment of a royal gift. Paris, BNF fr. 26728 (Pièces originales 244), dossier 'Beaulieu', pièce 26.

1586 Fragment of royal treasury accounts, expenditures approved by Henri III at Paris, 10 February: order for payment of 200 écus (100 écus each) in *étrennes* to 'Girard de Beaulieu et Jacques Salomon chantres ordinaires de la chambre [of Henri III]'. Paris, BNF n. a. f. 1441, fol. 40r.

Register of the Châtelet de Paris, 2 July. Inscription at the Châtelet of a series of notarial documents dating back to 1580, concerning the marriage and dowry of Marguerite de Beaulieu. The documents include: (1) Marriage contract between Anthoine de Minard, seigneur de Villemain, age 23, son of the late Pierre Minard, seigneur de Villemain et Laquette, conseiller du roi et maître des requêtes ordinaire de l'hôtel du roi, and of the late Claude de Laquette; and Marguerite de Beaulieu, 'fille de noblehomme Girard de Beaulieu vallet de chambre ordinaire du roy et de damoiselle Violante Doria dame de la Royne'. The dowry will be 8,000 écus, the balance of which will be paid in three instalments. The contract dated from 23 December 1580, and was signed at Blois, where the court was then residing, in the *basse court* of the château, where Beaulieu and Doria were lodged. (2) Documents concerning the payment of the balance of the dowry: 2,166 écus 1 tiers on 5 May 1581; 1560 écus 2 tiers on 11 August 1581; 3773 écus on 15 February 1582. The act notarising the last instalment was passed 'en l'hostel dudit Sieur de Beaulieu size à Paris rue Champfleury'. (3) Act testifying that the conditions of the marriage contract have been met in full, passed 2 July 1586 'en la maison dudit Sieur de Beaulieu size à Paris rue Champfleury paroisse Saint Germain l'Auxerrois'. Paris, AN, Y 127, fols. 441^{r}–444^{r}.

List of *placets* (formal requests) presented to Henri III; request presented 10 December 1586, signed by the king 7 March 1587: 'De Beaulieu chantre de la chambre' requests the office of surveyor of the Ile de France, vacant as a result of the death of the incumbent and (he claims) not entailed or promised to anyone else. Marginal note in the hand of Henri III: 'Accordé s'il dict vray'. Paris, BNF fr. 21480, fol. 25^{v}.

1587 List of *placets* presented to Henri III; request presented 7 March 1587, signed by the king 13(?) March: 'Beaulieu' reiterates his request for the office of surveyor of the Ile de France; entry crossed out in the hand of Henri III, suggesting that the request was denied. Paris, BNF fr. 21480, fol. 48^{r}.

Fragment of royal treasury accounts, expenditures approved by Henry III at Paris, 5 April: order for payment of 180 écus (30 écus each) to 'Girard de Beaulieu valet de chambre' and 5 others (two dancers, a barber, a watchmaker and the royal harpist Mathieu Monnier) as wages for the January quarter. Paris, BNF n. a. f. 1441, fol. 65^{r}.

Fragment of royal treasury accounts, expenditures approved by Henry III at Paris, 6 July: order for payment of 180 écus (30 écus each) to 'Girard de Beaulieu vallet de chambre' and the same others as on 5 April as wages for the April quarter. Paris, BNF n. a. f. 1441, fol. 65^{r}.

Fragment of royal treasury accounts, expeditures approved by Henri III at the camp of Pluviers, 9 October: order for payment of 166 écus 2/3 to 'Girard de Beaulieu vallet de chambre [of Henri III] et damoiselle Yolande Doria sa femme' in payment of the January quarter of their annual pension; order for payment of 180 écus (30 écus each) to 'Girard de Beaulieu vallet de chambre' and the same others as on 5 April as wages for the April [*sic*] quarter. Paris, BNF n. a. f. 1441, fols. 179^{v} and 188^{v}–189^{r}.

1588 Fragment of royal treasury accounts, expenditures approved by Henri III at Blois, 2 October: order for payment of 166 écus 2/3 to 'Girard de Beaulieu vallet de chambre ordinaire du roy et Yolande Doria sa femme' in payment of the July quarter of their annual pension; order for payment of 60 écus to 'Girard de Beaulieu vallet de chambre ordinaire [of Henri III]' as wages for April and July quarters. Paris, BNF n. a. f. 1441, fols. 233ᵛ and 245ʳ.

1589 List of household officers (*état de maison*) for Louise de Lorraine-Vaudémont: 'Monsieur [blank] de Beaulieu et Claude de Beaulieu sa fille musicienne et jouëuse de lut de la reyne' are listed in the category 'autres personnes que la reyne a voulu estre adjoustez au present estat', with joint yearly wage of 400 écus. Paris, BNF Clairambault 1216, fol. 68ᵛ.

1590 Letter from Emperor Rudolph II to Auger Busbecq, [8 May]:

Intelleximus, Galliae Regem, qui nuper in vivis esse desiit, habuisse musicum quendam Bassum a voce rara, qui sibi ipse lira succinat, celebrem, cui Lamberto de Beaulieu sit nomen. De eo mandamus tibi, ut diligenter inquiras, &, ubi hominem inveneris, cum eo, ut se nostris musicis aggregari honestis & aequis conditionibus sinat, & aulae nostrae se dedat, agas. Quidquid autem effeceris, ejus nos prima quaque opportunitate certiores facias, & si quid amplius erit, ut hoc tempore non esse non potest, quod in publicis operae pretium. Caeterum tibi benigna nostra gratia semper integra manet.

Rudolph II, *Divi Rudolphi imperatoris, caesaris augusti epistolae ineditae*, ed. Bernard, count de Pace (Vienna, 1771), p. 210.

Parish register of Saint-Nicolas-des-Champs, Paris, 25 May: funeral of Girard de Beaulieu, identified as the *maître de musique* of the chevalier d'Aumale, at the time of his death living in Paris on the rue Saint-Martin. Y. de Brossard, *Musiciens de Paris 1535–1792: Actes d'état civil d'après le fichier Laborde de la Bibliothèque Nationale* (Paris, 1965), p. 26.

Early Music History (2003) Volume 22. © *Cambridge University Press*
DOI:10.1017/S0261127903003024 Printed in the United Kingdom

ARDIS BUTTERFIELD

ENTÉ: A SURVEY AND REASSESSMENT OF THE TERM IN THIRTEENTH- AND FOURTEENTH-CENTURY MUSIC AND POETRY

The medieval term *enté*, meaning 'grafted', has a long and varied history in musicological study. It is usually held to refer to the practice of grafting a refrain (whether text or melody or both) onto a longer work, such as a motet voice. For modern scholars its chief importance lies in its association with the thirteenth-century motet:[1] it has been discussed principally in its role as a classificatory term, where it occurs as a rubric in several medieval manuscript lyric collections, and is also mentioned (in Latin) in a well-known passage from the musical treatise *De musica* (*c.*1300)

An earlier version of this article was read at the Medieval and Renaissance Music Conference, University of Bristol, July 2002. I would like to thank Suzannah Clark, Yolanda Plumley, Bonnie Blackburn and, in particular, Elizabeth Leach for their comments on a subsequent draft. Judith Peraino's interesting article, 'Monophonic Motets: Sampling and Grafting in the Middle Ages', *Musical Quarterly* 85 (2001), pp. 644–80 (published March 2003) unfortunately appeared just after mine had already gone to press. I was glad to see that many of our arguments concur.

Examples 1–4 are taken from Hans Tischler's edition *The Earliest Motets (to circa 1270): A Complete Comparative Edition*, 3 vols. (New Haven and London, 1982) by kind permission of Yale University Press. Example 5 is taken from Gordon A. Anderson's edition *Compositions of the Bamberg Manuscript: Bamberg, Staatsbibliothek, Lit. 115 (olim Ed.IV.6)* (Corpus Mensurabilis Musicae, 75; American Institute of Musicology, 1977), by kind permission of the American Institute of Musicology. Examples 6–7 are taken from Hans Tischler, Susan Stakel, and Joel C. Relihan, *The Montpellier Codex* (Recent Researches in the Music of the Middle Ages and Early Renaissance, 2–7; Madison, Wis., 1978–85), with the kind permission of A-R Editions.

[1] The term is current in the work of F. Gennrich, *Bibliographie der ältesten französischen und lateinischen Motetten* (Summa Musicae Medii Aevi, 2; Darmstadt, 1957); *Repertorium organorum recentioris et motetorum vetustissimi stili*, ed. F. Ludwig (Wissenschaftlicher Abhandlung, 7; Halle, 1910; repr. New York, 1964); *Polyphonies du XIIIe siècle*, ed. Y. Rokseth, 4 vols. (Paris, 1935–9); *Motets of the Manuscript La Clayette: Paris Bibliothèque Nationale, nouv. acq. f. fr.13521*, ed. Gordon A. Anderson (Corpus Mensurabilis Musicae, 68; American Institute of Musicology, 1975); and *Compositions of the Bamberg Manuscript: Bamberg, Staatsbibliothek, Lit. 115 (olim Ed.IV.6)*, ed. Gordon A. Anderson (Corpus Mensurabilis Musicae, 75; American Institute of Musicology, 1977).

by Johannes de Grocheio.[2] After a period of settled usage in the work of such scholars as Friedrich Ludwig, Friedrich Gennrich and Yvonne Rokseth, the term has been freshly examined by Mark Everist, and the settled usage declared incorrect.[3] Everist's stimulating revisionary argument has ensured that we cannot continue to use the term without care. It seems appropriate to consider the implications of his case more fully, and take the opportunity to reassess the term in the light of his arguments. In particular, since he proposes that a *motet enté* is characterized by a specifically musical technique, his work raises the issue of how far in that case we are to understand grafting as a textual procedure. This essay attempts two kinds of assessment: one, a revisiting of the term in relation to the motet; and the other, a wider, historical look at the term in poetic as well as musical contexts.

One source of confusion in modern usage is that it has always been easier to identify a grafting procedure in the texts than it has in the music. For Ludwig and Gennrich, and subsequent editors of motets, a *motet enté* can be readily identified as one that has a text in which a refrain has been split and its two halves used to frame the text.

Hé! amorettes,
Trop mi destraigniez;
C'est morteis pechiez,
Cant lai belle amerousette
Ne mi daigne ameir,
Ne sans li ne puis dureir,
Car mes fins cuers me semont
Ke je die a lai doucette
Saverouzette:
M'ocireiz vos dont?[4]

Hey, darling, you torture me too much; it is mortal sin when the beautiful little darling does not deign to love me, and I cannot endure without her. For my noble heart urges me to say to the charming girl, "are you going to kill me then?"

Yet although this seems straightforward enough, in practice difficulties arise. Refrain texts are often so indistinguishable from any

[2] For the relevant passage, see C. Page, 'Johannes de Grocheio on Secular Music: A Corrected Text and a New Translation', *Plainsong and Medieval Music*, 2 (1993), pp. 17–41.

[3] M. Everist, *French Motets in the Thirteenth Century: Music, Poetry and Genre* (Cambridge, 1994), ch. 4.

[4] *Recueil de motets français des XIIe et XIIIe siècles*, ed. Gaston Raynaud, 2 vols. (Paris, 1881–3), ii, p. 16, no. 47.

routine expression of love or sorrow in a motet text that it is hard to be sure that one is present, unless it happens to have a correspondence in another text.[5] Musically, although the tune of a refrain may stand out from its context when it is cited within the body of a voice-part, when a composer starts a piece with a refrain he tends to use the musical material to shape the rest of the piece. It becomes more difficult in that case to recognize the graft. Ironically, in addition, since the melodies of refrains have received less systematic attention than the texts, musicologists have not explored the cross-referencing among motet melodies fully enough to develop an understanding of grafting that takes proper account of the music. It remains implicit that – in the current state of scholarship – we are more likely to notice a textual than a musical graft. For this reason, the settled sense of a *motet enté* among Gennrich *et al.* is more reliant than one might expect on the structure of the texts. In the following discussion I will therefore begin with an account of the literary meanings of *enté*. The very few medieval usages of the word in relation to musical compositions will be viewed against this background, as well as in relation to each other. Further, later, examples of medieval usage will then be considered. My purpose is to place the term in as wide a frame of reference as possible in the hope of gaining a better understanding of its textual resonances, of its musical resonances, and of the two together. The process may help to illumine some aspects of medieval compositional practices in ways that go beyond the merely literary or the merely musical.

I

The word *enté* functions primarily as a metaphor. Its meaning is drawn from horticulture, where grafting refers to two kinds of process, splitting and joining. It is most commonly used in literary texts quite directly of fruit, flowers and trees. As Baudouin de Condé, for example, a mid-thirteenth-century poet, explains:

[5] This particular refrain (*Rondeaux et refrains du XIIe siècle au début du XIVe*, ed. N. H. J. van den Boogaard (Paris, 1969) (hereafter vdB), refr.793) occurs in three other contexts: two motets and the satiric romance *Renart le Nouvel* by Jacquemart Giélée, ed. H. Roussel (Société des Anciens Textes Français; Paris, 1961).

de bone ente
Vient bons fruits[6]

from a good graft comes good fruit

The idea here seems to be the one still current among gardening cognoscenti – that judicious improvement of the stock yields superior fruit. This literal sense is readily transferred by extension into figurative meanings, such as when the Virgin is described as a grafted flower, or flowering tree. In just the same way, by a natural logic, is the poet's lady:

Dame gente,
Sour toutes autres florie ente
(*Le Roman du castelain de Couci*, 7672–3)[7]

Noble lady, a flowering graft above all others

Sa face n'est pale ne tainte,
ainz est plus clere et rovelente
qe n'est en mai la flor en l'ente,
d'une color et fresche et fine
(*Le roman de la poire*, 1664–7)[8]

Her face was not pale or flushed, but rather brighter and rosier than the flower on a grafted tree in May, of a refined, fresh colour.

From here, one can find many examples of its use in the language of love, the term being applied, as in the following, to the sorrows of the heart:

Car trop griefment en son cuer enté
Le mal d'amours qui est entré
(*Le Roman du castelain de Couci*, 5691)

For the sorrow of love which has entered is too painfully grafted within his heart

Mon cuer fu si en vous enté
Quonques puis ne len pos retraire
(*Voir Dit*, 1976–7)[9]

My heart was so grafted in yours that I could never afterwards draw it out again from there

There seems to be a broader sense here of the actual process of insertion: the graft of love, as it enters within the heart, causes

[6] *C'est li contes dou Mantiel*, in *Dits et contes de Baudouin de Condé et de son fils Jean de Condé*, ed. A. Scheler, 3 vols. (Brussels, 1866–7), i, p. 80, ll. 2–3.

[7] Jakemés, *Le Roman du castelain de Couci*, ed. M. Delbouille (Société des Anciens Textes Français; Paris, 1936).

[8] *Le roman de la poire par Tibaut*, ed. C. Marchello-Nizia (Société des Anciens Textes Français; Paris, 1984).

[9] *Le Livre dou Voir Dit (The Book of the True Poem)*, ed. D. Leech-Wilkinson, trans. R. Barton Palmer (Garland Library of Medieval Literature, 106A; New York and London, 1998).

pain as it takes root. Godefroy's dictionary ascribes separate meanings of 'fixed' or 'brought in'; but these seem to me to be largely unnecessary, since the underlying notion of grafting as a physical process remains strongly present in these figurative contexts.[10]

Various points can be made about these usages. Perhaps the first (most obviously) is that *enté* is not merely a technical term: it has a wide currency. It is important to recognise it as a common metaphor in the language of love, for this means that it is part of the common stock of language that makes up the texts of motets, chansons, narratives and refrains. To describe it as common, however, is not to imply that it is a dead, or redundant, metaphor. This can perhaps best be illustrated by a particular frame of reference that surrounds the grafted tree. The grafted tree has a special resonance in romance: when heroines sit under such a tree, a supernatural or mystical event often occurs. This usage passes over into Anglo-Norman, and occurs in English as 'ympe tree'.[11] Herodis is sitting under an 'ympe tre' in *Sir Orfeo* when she is abducted by the king of the underworld.[12] She passes into a strange half-world of shadows, semi-substantial figures, and scenes of terrifying gloom, where Orfeo, in seeking her, glimpses fellow creatures caught in moments of grotesque physical

[10] Modern glossators categorise the word in various ways: under *ente*, q.v. *enter*; *ante*, q.v. *anter*; *hanter*; *entrer* (Godefroy; *Altfranzösisches Wörterbuch*, ed. Adolf Tobler and Erhard Lommatzsch, 10 vols. (Berlin, 1925–76); A. J. Greimas, *Dictionnaire de l'ancien français*, 2nd edn (Paris, 1968); *Recueil général des jeux-partis français*, ed. A. Långfors, A. Jeanroy and L. Brandin, 2 vols. (Paris, 1926); K. Bartsch, *Chrestomathie de l'ancien français (VIIIe–XVe siècles) accompagné d'une grammaire et d'un glossaire*, 12th edn, rev. L. Weise (New York, 1958).

[11] The *MED* gives 'ympe' as either grafted or orchard tree. Further discussion of the Anglo-Norman and English terms can be found in Constance Bullock-Davies, '"Ympe-tre" and "Nemeton"', *Notes and Queries*, n.s. 9 (1962), pp. 6–9, and Alice E. Lasater, 'Under the Ympe-Tre or: Where the Action is in *Sir Orfeo*', *Southern Quarterly*, 12 (1974), pp. 353–63. Bullock-Davies proposes a transference of meaning from the Celtic 'nemeton' (a sacred clearing in a wood), via Old French 'nante' to Middle English 'nympe' and hence 'ympe'. Lasater traces 'ympe' from Old English 'impian' (Old High German 'impfon') meaning 'graft', and also 'offspring', 'small demon' or 'child'. She suggests a correspondence between the ympe-tre and the grafted apple tree of the Celtic otherworld.

[12] *Sir Orfeo*, ed. Anne Laskaya and Eve Salisbury, *The Middle English Breton Lays* (TEAMS Middle English Texts; Kalamazoo, Mich., 1995), line 70 and note. The heroine falls asleep 'soz une ente' in the Anglo-Norman romance *Tydorel*; 'ympe' also occurs in the Auchinleck manuscript version of *The Seven Sages of Rome* (560–1). Other related romance references include *Sir Gowther* (lines 67–72), which contains an episode where a woman is accosted by a demon while lying under a tree; *Launfal* (lines 223 ff.); *Sir Degaré* (lines 70 ff.); *Guingamor* (lines 422–95); *Graelent* (lines 220–79); *Cleomadés* (lines 5617 ff.); and *Sir Gawain and the Green Knight* (lines 718–25). Chaucer parodies the topos in his *Sir Thopas* (lines 796–806) and the *Wife of Bath's Tale* (lines 878–80).

transition, such as the moment of giving birth, or of being killed, with their limbs in contorted positions.

In such a context, the notion of grafting implicitly has a powerful role in structuring meaning. One further example, from *Le Roman de la poire* by Tibaut, that combines various figurative and literal meanings of grafting, shows how the work is founded on these meanings.

> De Dieu soit beneoite l'ante
> qui ainz pot enfanter tel fruit
> (*Poire*, 469–70)

May the graft be blessed by God that can now give birth to such fruit

Here, the narrator is describing the qualities of the tree after which the roman is named. This tree is a grafted tree, belonging to a well-known medieval species of pear, 'de Saint Riule' or 'Saint Rieul'. Not only was the pear itself prized, it is mentioned several times in fabliaux and romance contexts, for instance as a comparison for the marriage of a peasant and a noblewoman.[13] Such a reference draws attention to the obvious sexual connotations of grafting and reproduction.[14] Likewise inserting itself into the hot nexus of erotic and spiritual meanings attached to fruit trees, the *Roman de la poire* depicts the lady biting into the pear and offering it to her lover. He, explicitly comparing himself to Adam when he took the apple (l. 453), finds that the sweet taste penetrates his heart. The rest of the work springs from this root: structurally it is built around refrains that similarly both cut into and generate its text.[15] This is not the place to give a fuller account of the significance of grafting in medieval romance more generally, but it may be said that both these examples give witness to a larger cultural fascination with the transitional and the hybrid. In specific, descriptive ways and through more subtle, implicit and complex means, the idea of grafting articulates a medieval obsession with the key creative practices of splicing new material into old, or of reworking the fragmentary into new structures.

[13] *Vingt trois manières de vilain*, cited in *Le roman de la poire*, ed. Marchello-Nizia, p. 134, n. to line 406.

[14] Cf. Chaucer's *The Merchant's Tale*.

[15] For further discussion of this work, see Sylvia Huot, *From Song to Book: The Poetics of Writing in Old French Lyric and Lyrical Narrative Poetry* (Ithaca, NY and London, 1987), and Ardis Butterfield, *Poetry and Music in Medieval France from Jean Renart to Guillaume de Machaut* (Cambridge, 2002), pp. 246–52.

II

Having looked briefly at some of these literary contexts, I want now to turn to the more technical uses of *enté*. I will be making reference to examples from the thirteenth and fourteenth centuries. Several of these are notoriously opaque to interpretation. Nonetheless, it may be profitable to view them alongside one another, and then, by considering one or two in more detail, attempt to draw out some comparisons and provisional conclusions.

Looked at as a group, the examples involve a variety of genres: motets, dits, ballades and rondeaux. This in itself is worth stressing: for whatever we conclude about the *motet enté*, for instance, needs to be brought into relation with what we can observe or deduce in other genres. As far as the motet is concerned, two references can be tied to specific surviving repertories: the first is a rubric that occurs in the margin of Paris, Bibliothèque Nationale de France, fr. 845, the second is a (slightly less specific) reference in *Le Jeu du Pelerin* to the *motets entés* of Adam de la Halle.[16] Fr. 845, one of a group of four chansonniers (*KNPX*), begins in the usual way with trouvère chansons collected by author.[17] Towards the end of the manuscript (fol. 184^{r}) is copied a group of fifteen monophonic pieces, labelled in the right-hand margin 'Ci commencent li motet enté'. It is always interesting to find generic descriptions in medieval writing – largely because they are often so tantalisingly difficult to interpret – and this direct attachment of a term to a group of pieces invites analysis.

What then, do we find? Briefly, the collection comprises non-strophic monophonic pieces. The texts are characteristic of motet voices in having short lines and often repeated rhyming sounds; most are fairly short in length. What makes them distinctive as a group is the disposition of refrains: in each a refrain text has been split so that, in the classic grafting procedure, its first line becomes the first line of the motet text, and its second line the last line of the motet:

[16] Adam de la Halle, *Le Jeu de Robin et de Marion, précédé du Jeu du Pèlerin*, ed. K. Varty (London, 1960), p. 66, line 91.

[17] *K* = Paris, Bibliothèque de l'Arsenal, 5198; *N* = Paris, Bibliothèque Nationale de France, fr. 845; *P* = Paris, Bibliothèque Nationale de France, fr. 847; *X* = Paris, Bibliothèque Nationale de France, n. a. fr. 1050 ('Chansonnier Clairambault').

Hé amors, morrai je?
qui l'a deservi?
Li regarz que fis vers li,
qui m'ont mis en tel usage,
tant me plot, quant je la vi;
car je l'aim a heritage
sanz avoir merci.[18]

Hey love, will I die? Who has deserved it? The looks that I cast towards her, which have put me in such a condition – it pleased me so much when I saw her; for I love her for always, *without having mercy.*

This textual pattern also occurs in other motet collections, notably in Oxford Douce 308, in which, as it happens, four of the same pieces are copied.[19]

Musically, as Mark Everist has shown, the works of this group are distinctive in the degree to which they collectively display examples of melodic repetition from line to line. His case is that this form of melodic parallelism is so different from the rest of the motet repertory that we should consider it to be the defining characteristic of this collection. In short, these are to be considered as *motets entés* because of the musical repetitions that they contain, and not for any other reason. He calls on us to 'stop calling pieces *motets entés* that simply divide a refrain into two and place it at the beginning and end of a voice-part'.[20] For Everist, the grafted aspect of

[18] fr. 845, fol. 184c: no. 346 in *The Earliest Motets (to circa 1270): A Complete Comparative Edition*, ed. H. Tischler, 3 vols. (New Haven and London, 1982), ii; also Motet no. 2 in *Recueil de motets français*, ed. Raynaud, ii, p. 62.

[19] Nos. 345, 350, 357 and 359 (*The Earliest Motets*, ed. Tischler) correspond to Oxford, Bodleian Library, Douce 308, nos. 50, 28, 44 and 9 respectively (*Recueil de motets français*, ed. Raynaud, ii, pp. 1–38). The motets occur in the seventh (untitled) section of the manuscript: this contains 101 pieces, of which sixty-three in modern terminology are 'motets' (or 'motets entés' as Ludwig described them, *Repertorium*, I, 1, pp. 207–13) and thirty-eight 'rondeaux'. Everist is reluctant to agree that these fifteen pieces in fr. 845 conform to the usual definition of a *motet enté*, on the grounds that eight of the refrains, identified as such by modern editors, are not attested elsewhere. However, this may be an overscrupulous approach to the definition of refrains if it is being used to argue first that the lack of correspondence proves that they cannot be refrains, and second that this proves that the grafting technique is not present. One of the refrains he cites as unattested, for instance, has a first line that occurs in nine other contexts (see vdB, refrs. 825 and 824). Given the clear pattern of splicing evident in seven of the pieces, and the similarity in form, sentence structure and verbal formulas of the first and last lines of the other pieces, it seems reasonable to assume that that these unattested lines are also functioning as refrains. For an extended discussion of the problem of defining pre-existent material in relation to the peculiar taxonomy of the refrain, see Butterfield, 'Repetition and Variation in the Thirteenth-Century Refrain', *Journal of the Royal Musical Association*, 116 (1991), pp. 1–23.

[20] *French Motets*, p. 89.

these motets is to be identified with the melodic repetition: it is the melodic repetition, and the melodic repetition alone, which makes these *motets entés* as opposed to any other type of motet.

I will shortly consider the nature of these musical repetitions more closely. Everist's broader argument deserves some initial comment. He does an important service to our understanding of these pieces. The notion of a *motet enté* in Ludwig and Gennrich is in danger of degenerating into an unhelpful all-inclusiveness. As a consequence, it is often used to refer to any type of refrain citation. Yet this does not do justice to the instances of quite specific usage in medieval contexts of which this group in fr. 845 is a case in point. Untrammelled by a pre-conceived notion of grafting, Everist is prepared to take a fresh look at these pieces and recognise in them quite different and new features. In addition, he remedies the lack of attention previously paid to musical analysis of *motets entés* by means of an argument that unusually centres on the musical rather than the textual procedures evident within them.[21]

Yet the very originality of this approach has attendant risks. Intent on giving the term a greater specificity, Everist privileges the use of the term *motet enté* in this context above any other. His method is to seek some common feature among these particular pieces and deduce that this explains the term in general. In trying to assess this suggestion, various kinds of evidence might be brought into play. One line of approach (and the main purpose of this essay) is to place this group of pieces – and their marginal designation – alongside other material either also described as 'grafted', or else displaying similar characteristics.

In this case, the difficulties of interpretation are compounded in several directions. These pieces are very unusual in being at once supplied with musical notation, monophonic, non-strophic, and structured as textual grafts. The best textual comparisons, in Douce 308, have no musical notation. The polyphonic motets often do contain individual voice-parts with similarly structured texts, but it is not easy to compare single with multiple texts, and even less clear that a monophonic structure in music has the same principles of construction as polyphony. With all these restrictions,

[21] The parallels in these fr. 845 motets are also noted in *Earliest Motets*, ed. Tischler, ii, pp. 1546–56, who nonetheless draws different conclusions from those of Everist.

it is hard to be confident that a single feature – in this case the musical repetitions – holds the key to a process which, as we have seen, was conceived in much broader cultural terms.

The fr. 845 pieces are indeed full of repeated musical phrases and patterns. I have found only two exceptions.[22] In general, the most common feature is the repetition of the opening lines and the last: there is some variation in this, since sometimes it is only the first (or second) line that is repeated in the last, or else a portion of it. Thus in no. 345, lines 1 and 2 are recapitulated in lines 10 and 11 (see Example 1).[23] In the case of no. 347 (a ten-line piece), it is the last part of line 1 and the whole of line 2 which

Example 1 *Douce dame debonaire*, BN fr. 845, fol. 184r–v,
ed. Tischler, *The Earliest Motets,* ii, no. 345

22 Nos. 346 and 358. This is a more generous estimate than Everist's, who counts more cautiously only ten out of the fifteen as having these internal repetitions (though without specifying which).

23 Also nos. 351, 355, 356. The first and last lines only are repeated in nos. 354, 357 and 359.

are repeated in the last part of line 9 and the whole of line 10 (see Example 2). Some pieces extend the repetition further, such as nos. 348, 350, 353 and especially 355: in these, the musical refrain material is reused throughout the piece.

Example 2 *Tres haute amor jolie*, BN fr. 845, fol. 184v, ed. Tischler, *The Earliest Motets*, ii, no. 347

Two points may be made: first, the process in the texts is not the same as that in the music. Whereas in the motet texts the first and last lines are different (because they form the two halves of a split refrain), in the music they are the same. The composer is tying the piece together musically in a way which is more obvious than it would be from the words alone. At first sight, this is confusing. We appear to have two radically different techniques, one involving splitting textual phrases, the other repeating musical ones. Moreover, the relation between the textual and musical phrases appears to be far from organic. The music is separable from the refrain text, and applied, in some cases, to several other text lines. These pieces seem to uncouple the textual and musical identities of a refrain, and hence weaken the notion of a refrain as a single textual and musical unit.

Yet a closer look at no. 355 reminds us that these procedures are not as unfamiliar as they seem (see Example 3). In this piece, with the exception of two lines in the middle, there are only two main motifs: A and B (with a smaller sub-motif B′). They alternate as follows: ABABBB′CDBB′AB. This pattern is recognisably related to the variable forms of the thirteenth-century *rondets de carole*, dominated as they are in musical terms by the melody of the refrain.[24] In short, this technique of tying a piece together by repeating the refrain melody is central to composers of early rondeaux forms. The refrain melody is repeated through the strophic lines before being reattached to a repeated refrain text.

Example 3 *He Dieus, que ferai*, BN fr. 845, fol. 189, ed. Tischler, *The Earliest Motets*, ii, no. 355

[24] Butterfield, *Poetry and Music*, pp. 46–9, 92–3.

What we see in fr. 845 is an extension of this process. Interestingly, these monophonic *motets entés* use musical means to give even greater structural prominence to the refrain. We can further see this from the way that nearly all of them prepare the ending by splicing onto it a transitional section of the refrain music given at the start.

A provisional conclusion, then, from this consideration of the musical and textual features of the fr. 845 *motets entés* is that the techniques of splitting and repeating are not, after all, distinct, nor are they mutually exclusive. They may be happening separately in the texts and music, but this should not lead us to regard them as isolated activities. In fact, what seems to be happening is that the grafting is taking place from the music to the text, so that the music of one half of the refrain text is being grafted onto the other textual half.

It may be helpful here to bring in some other examples of refrain citation in motets for comparison. One way of making the comparison is to trace some refrain links between the fr. 845 motets and other pieces. This alerts us to some intricate patterns of cross-referencing. For instance, no. 358 (Example 4) is framed by the following refrain:

> *Amoureusement . . .*
> *me tient li maus que j'ai* (vdB, refr. 144)

This also occurs, with the same melody, in the triplum of the well-known motet *Amourousement mi tient li maus que j'ai* (9)/*Hé, amours, mourrai je* (10)/OMNES (M1) (Bamberg, Staatsbibliothek, Lit. 115, no. 43; see Example 5).[25] Its occurrence here shows clearly how a single line in one piece can occur as two fragments in another. Yet, as I have discussed elsewhere,[26] this motet also shows how various and multiple motet refrain usage can be. Splitting and grafting processes occur not only separately in motetus and triplum, but also across the voice-parts. In this case, the refrain '*Hé, amours! mourrai je sans avoir merci?*' is cited twice, once in the motetus (where it is split across the text) and again in the triplum (where it is inserted in the middle). Ingeniously it is combined

[25] This motet also occurs in Montpellier, Bibliothèque de l'École de Médecine, H196, fols. 114v–115v, and Rome, Biblioteca Apostolica Vaticana, Reg. Lat. 1490, fol. 114.

[26] Butterfield, *Poetry and Music*, pp. 228–31.

Example 4 *Amorousement*, BN fr. 845, fol. 189v,
ed. Tischler, *The Earliest Motets*, ii, no. 358

with a further refrain (*Dieus d'amours, vivrai je longuement enssi?*), in a double process of splitting and grafting, whereby the final refrain line of the motetus (*sans avoir merci*) serves as a continuation of both the opening refrain fragment (*Hé, amours, mourrai je*) and also of the second refrain (*Dieus d'amours*) inserted in the same voice-part. *Sans avoir merci* can be grafted in seamlessly (the musical seam is less smooth) to the semantic structure of both refrain lines:

Hé, amours! mourrai je . . .	*sans avoir merci?*
Dieus d'amours, vivrai je longuement enssi . . .	*sans avoir merci?*

To add to the cross-citational texture of the motet, *Dieus d'amours, vivrai je longuement enssi?* from the motetus recurs as the last two lines of the triplum.

Bamberg, no. 43: Triplum	Bamberg, no. 43: Motetus
Amourousement mi tient li maus que j'ai;	*Hé, amours, mourrai je* pour celi
pour ce chanterai:	cui j'ai trestout mon eage
Ay mi!	de cuer et de cors servi?

Example 5 *Amourousement mi tient li maus que j'ai/Hé, amours, mourrai je*/OMNES, ed. Anderson, *Compositions of the Bamberg Manuscript*, motet no. 43

Example 5 *Continued*

Hé, amours! mourrai
je sans avoir merci?
Ay mi! las! ay mi!
je muir pour li,
et nepourquant vuill je chanter
pour moi deduire et pour moi deporter;
las! que porrai je devenir?
nule riens tant ne desir;
or me di,
Dieus d'amours, vivrai
je longuement enssi?

Si fort m'a d'amours la rage saisi
que riens ne feroit pour mi
mes cuers fors penser a li.
Ay mi!
Dieus d'amours, vivrai
je longuement enssi?
Di pour les seins Dieu, languirai
je sans avoir merci?

Triplum: *The pain that I have holds me in love*, therefore I will sing: Alas, *Hey Love, will I die without having mercy? Oh, alas, oh, I am dying for her*, but nevertheless I want to sing to amuse and distract myself; *Alas, what will become of me? there is nothing at all that I desire so much*; I now say to myself, *God of Love, will I live long like this?*

Motetus: *Hey, Love, will I die* for her whom I have served with heart and body all my life? So strongly has the madness of love seized me that my heart would do nothing for me except think of her. Alas! *God of Love, will I live long like this?* Tell me, for God's saints' sake, will I languish *without having mercy?*[27]

All these cases of textual cross-reference and patterns of combination are matched in the music. Example 5 presents an analysis of the motet as including five repeated motifs. The composer sometimes repeats refrain text lines with the same melody, and sometimes attaches the melody to a new line of text. For example, in all the repetitions of *Hé, amours! mourrai je* (1), and *Dieus d'amours* (3) the music and text remain the same. However, the first part of the melody for *Amourousement mi tient* (4) is also given to the first part of *las! que porrai je devenir?* and similarly the music for *Hé,*

[27] This text is based on Anderson's. I have modified it slightly by removing the quotation marks in the triplum. The translation also deliberately avoids quotation marks since to include them would raise issues of interpretation that it would not be possible to discuss adequately here.

amours! mourrai je (1) is given to a non-refrain line 'que riens ne feroit pour mi' in the motetus. There is also a fifth motif that is used to connect three separate non-refrain lines.

This motet is a particularly flamboyant example of refrain citation. Sometimes described as a refrain cento, it may be compared with some eighteen other pieces whose voice-parts draw on several refrains at once.[28] Everist has argued that we should restrict our use of the term refrain cento to a mere three works. But since the term is in any case a modern one, there seems a danger of circularity in the attempt to create a watertight category from it. The term *enté*, by contrast, being medieval, provides no guarantee for a modern reader of clear-cut definition. On the contrary, the very variety of contexts argues for a certain suppleness and flexibility in its meanings. From this point of view, Bamberg no. 43 is interesting, not for how it can be categorised now, but for what light it can shed on the practices of refrain citation visible in fr. 845. Again, we should distinguish between the textual and musical evidence. Textually and musically, it confirms that grafting is an identifiable procedure: we see in it a 'whole' refrain that is split in fr. 845. The textual games that are played in and across the voice-parts present a view of the text as a kaleidoscopic collection of fragments that can be radically rearranged, yet still display a coherent surface. Musically, the play of parts is much more complex than in any of the monophonic pieces in fr. 845, yet it shares with them a re-grafting of music to text that serves to reinforce the melodic patterns of the refrains. Notably, it shares with them the procedure of preparing the ending by grafting onto it a section of the refrain music given at the start.[29]

There are some further questions and points of interest here. Some of these relate to issues of punctuation and layout. I have presented the text as it is edited by Gordon Anderson, where, following conventional practice, italics are used to mark out the refrains. It should be pointed out, first of all, that not all the italicised lines in the triplum are attested elsewhere. In other

[28] Everist, 'The Refrain Cento: Myth or Motet?', *Journal of the Royal Musical Association*, 114 (1989), pp. 164–88; and *French Motets*, pp. 117–19.

[29] For further discussion of this piece, see also Everist, *French Motets*, pp. 117–20 and 167. He comments on the use of divided refrains, but not as a type of grafting, since he has rejected any association of this practice with the term *enté*.

words, there are concordances for *Amourousement mi tient li maus que j'ai*, *Hé, amours! mourrai je sans avoir merci?* and *Dieus d'amours, vivrai je longuement enssi?*, but not for the rest. Strictly speaking, therefore, we have no outside textual corroboration for identifying any other lines as refrains. Here the musical parallels may be brought into consideration. Since, as we have just noted, the music for *Amourousement mi tient* is also assigned to the first part of *las! que porrai je devenir* there might be an argument for identifying the latter as a refrain on the grounds that this 'new' piece of text has been attached to a 'old' refrain melody. If a refrain can be identified by its words, even when those words are attached in different contexts to more than one melody, then logically it can equally be identified by its melody, even when that melody is attached in different contexts to more than one set of words. Yet one other parallel we noted, in which the music for *Hé, amours! mourrai je* in the triplum is given to the line 'que riens ne feroit pour mi' in the motetus, suggests that this logic is unlikely to apply in every case without some qualification. 'Que riens ne feroit pour mi', for instance, unlike many attested refrain texts, is not a completed remark or exclamation.

It is not my purpose to 'solve' the question of how many refrains there are in this motet so much as to comment on the kind of interpretative significance that attaches to musical and verbal repetitions and their interconnections. At what point do we recognise a repetition as a graft, or a graft as manifesting itself as a repetition? We are straying into the shadowy area of musical and verbal identity, and the kinds of patterns of recognition that begin to enable us to construct such identities. The practice of grafting is peculiarly located in this area since it creates pieces that are not just intertextual but which contain a surface recognition of intertextuality. *Amourousement mi tient* shows particularly well how fluid the borderline is between a musical or verbal repetition that cements a listener's prior knowledge of a refrain and one that creates a new aural identity for a piece of text or music (or both).

The potential complexity of this process in the words can be appreciated when one begins to think through the issue of how a modern editor might punctuate these two texts. Do the refrains signify changes within the register and voice of the texts, or are they contained within an all-embracing first-person speaker?[30] Again, we seem to have more than one possibility. In the triplum, two refrains are directly introduced as distinct forms of utterance: 'or me di, *Dieus d'amours, vivrai je longuement enssi?*' and 'pour ce chanterai: Ay mi! *Hé, amours! mourrai je sans avoir merci?*' The third such introduction ('et nepourquant vuill je chanter pour moi deduire et pour moi deporter; *las! que porrai je devenir? nule riens tant ne desir*') is so emphatic that it presumably explains van den Boogaard's decision to identify the latter as a further refrain. However, in the motetus, where there is a split refrain, that sense of difference between one form of utterance and another is smoothed away: '*Hé, amours, mourrai je* pour celi cui j'ai trestout mon eage de cuer et de cors servi?' Here, the listener's prior knowledge of the refrain (if he or she possesses it) is explicitly undermined by the grafting process: the distinct edges of the refrain have been planed down and the join rendered all but invisible. Grafting, in other words, involves the strange practice of both drawing attention to a sense of verbal and musical identity yet at the same time effacing it. For such a process, the term 'intertextuality' itself might seem too inflexible.

I have selected *Amourousement mi tient/Hé, amours mourrai je*/OMNES for discussion because it shares a refrain with one of the fr. 845 *motets entés*. There is a further cross-reference between it and another of these motets, for the second line of the refrain (*me tient li maus que j'ai*) also occurs as the last (grafted) line of no. 348. This detail confirms the relevance of the comparison, in that it shows the same refrain involved compositionally in several grafting manoeuvres. Two more motet clusters, this time not directly associated with any of the fr. 845 motets, help to explore further examples of grafting. The first pair, Tischler nos. 80 and 101, has been chosen because the two-line refrain that finishes the motetus of one (no. 80) is split and framed around the text of the triplum in the other (no. 101) (see Example 6). The text and music of the refrain remain the same in both contexts. An example like this might be thought to represent a classic case of the *motet enté*. Yet even here, there are complications. It immediately becomes

[30] For further discussion of refrains as forms of citation, see Butterfield, *Poetry and Music*, ch. 15, pp. 243–70.

Example 6 (a) *Je m'en vois/Tieus a mout/OMNES*;
(b) *Dieus je n'i os aler/Amors, qui m'aprist/ET SUPER*,
ed. Tischler, Stakel and Relihan, *The Montpellier Codex*, ii, nos. 80 and 101

difficult to compare them with the fr. 845 pieces because of the differences between monophony and polyphony. In what way does a grafting procedure in one voice affect our interpretation of the whole motet? Moreover, both no. 80 and no. 101 have additional refrains incorporated in the middle of the voices. In practice, it is rare to find any two motets that share identical grafting techniques.

The second cluster involves three pieces: nos. 159, 195 and 291 (Tischler). Here again we find a full statement of a refrain in two separate works (nos. 195 and 291) and the same refrain split in two in another (no. 159) (see Example 7). The difference is that no. 159 contains the same split refrain sung simultaneously in both motetus and triplum. Although the texts are the same, the music is thus different: the music for this refrain in the motetus in no. 159 is very close to that in no. 195 (and in no. 291), but there is new music in no. 159 for the same words in the triplum. This kind of graft serves to emphasise the words of the refrain more than its music; at the same time, the melody of the last line of the refrain in the triplum in no. 159 is an exact repeat of the fourth line.

It is clear, even from this brief discussion, that the apparently simple procedure of splitting a refrain in the context of a motet stimulated many structural variations in the texts and the music.

Example 7 (a) *A vos, douce debonaire/OMNES*;
(b) *Bien met Amours son pooir/Dame, alegiés ma grevance/A Paris*;
(c) *Emi, emi, Marotele/Emi, emi, Marotele/PORTARE*,
ed. Tischler, Stakel and Relihan, *The Montpellier Codex*, ii, nos. 195, 291 and 159

Example 7 *Continued*

Without seeking to claim too much from a small a choice of examples, it may be reasonable to conclude that they raise more than one issue. One concerns melodic analysis: repetition, per se, is clearly not confined to the motets in fr. 845. It may be that we need to refine our sense of repetition as a musical procedure before proceeding too far with the work of definition. Another concerns the relation between grafting in music and grafting in poetry. This is a delicate, and fascinating area. As I shall go on to argue, and has already been part of the argument so far, it seems essential to recognise that one cannot be understood in isolation from the other. The sheer weight of textual reference in the word *enté* makes it a necessary, and not merely a relevant context for musical practice.

The direct evidence for medieval usage of the terminology of grafting is indeed largely literary. Before turning to this, however, we should consider that other example of the term in the context of motets: the description in the *Le Jeu du Pelerin* of Adam de la Halle's motets as 'entés'. Rogaus and Warnier are discussing the pilgrim's news that 'maistre Adan' is dead. Questioned sceptically by Warnier, Rogaus talks of Adan in glowing terms as someone who could compose and sing:

> . . . ains savoit canchons faire,
> Partures et motés entés;
> De chi fist-il à grant plentés –
> Et balades, je ne sai quantes. (90–3)

[rather] he knew how to compose songs, jeux-partis and motets entés. He made a great number of those, and I don't know how many ballades.

It is striking to find this rare reference to the term uttered so casually: it straightaway implies that it was a current term, and a common genre. It also appears to group all Adam's motets under this heading. The pieces are not, however, so homogeneous as those in fr. 845. They vary in length, number of voice-parts, and structure. The only common feature among them is the use of refrains: no. 2, *De ma dame vient/Diex, comment porroie/Omnes*, which, like *Amourousement mi tient li maus que j'ai* (Bamberg, no. 43) is based on the tenor *Omnes*, cites four refrains altogether in the two upper parts.[31] Yet grafting practices in certain of Adam's motets are pervasive.[32] Once again it seems we cannot narrow the meaning of *enté* to the particular characteristics of the motets in fr. 845. The term evidently had a wider frame of reference.[33]

There do not appear to be any other uses of 'enté' that are applied directly to pieces that either survive with or were clearly intended to have musical notation.[34] A halfway exception to this is the heading in the index of Paris, Bibliothèque Nationale de France, fr. 146 announcing the works of Jehan de Lescurel:

> Balades rondeaux et diz entez sus refroiz de rondeaux les quielx fist iehannot de lescurel dont les commencemenz sensuivent (fol. B^{va})

ballades, rondeaux and dits grafted on refrains of rondeaux composed by Jehannot de Lescurel, the openings of which now follow

The two *dits entés* of Jehan de Lescurel, explicitly named as such in the manuscript, are strophic 'narratives' in the first person,

[31] Ed. Nigel Wilkins, *The Lyric Works of Adam de la Hale: Chansons, Jeux Partis, Rondeaux, Motets* (Corpus Mensurabilis Musicae, 44; Rome, 1967).

[32] For examples and further discussion, see Butterfield, *Poetry and Music*, pp. 279–83.

[33] Other examples occur in works associated with Arras: for example, see Adam de la Halle, *Dit d'amour*, stanza VII, 76–9, ed. A. Jeanroy, in 'Trois dits d'amour du XIIIe siècle', *Romania*, 22 (1893), pp. 45–70; and Jeu-parti no. XXVI, line 44 (Jehan Bretel a Jehan de Grieviler), in *Recueil général des jeux-partis français*, ed. Långfors, Jeanroy and Brandin.

[34] One further reference can be traced to the Chansonnier de Mesmes, lost in a fire in 1807. According to notes taken by the sixteenth-century scholar Claude Fauchet, one division of the manuscript contained the rubric 'Ci commencent li motet ente' on fol. 247. See Theodore Karp, 'A Lost Medieval Chansonnier', *Musical Quarterly*, 48 (1962), pp. 50–67 and Janet Espiner-Scott, *Documents concernant la vie et les oeuvres de Claude Fauchet* (Paris, 1938), pp. 266–71.

with inset refrains after each nine-line strophe. What marks them out is the inclusion of music for each refrain: this gives them a part-narrative, part-musical character. In their strophic structure, these *dits entés*, 'Gracieuse, faitisse et sage' and 'Gracieus temps est', resemble the strophic *saluts*; to have music written in for the refrains, however, makes them unique among these, and suggests rather a comparison with the *chanson avec des refrains*. Lescurel's pieces, on the face of it, have little in common with motets. It seems, in other words, that in finding a shared terminology, we have not (at least ostensibly) found a shared practice. To accommodate the meaning of *enté* apparent in the motets of fr. 845, we would have to widen the textual sense of grafting from being a process of dividing refrains and enclosing the text within the fragments to one of dividing a text regularly *by* refrains. (In this extended sense, not only the strophic *saluts* but several of the longer *romans* and *dits à refrains*, including the semi-lyric pieces in *Fauvel*, could be held to share an analogous compositional procedure.) Musically, there is no direct comparison since there is no music for the stanzas.

However, if we look more closely at the textual grafting, the process by which the stock is joined to the shoot, then it is possible that some points of comparison can be found between the textual practice in Lescurel and the musical practice in fr. 845. Each refrain (they vary in length from one to four lines) is rhymed in to the previous strophe, so that the final rhyme of the strophe is the same as that of the last line of the refrain. Rhyme in the narratives that cite songs is the most common kind of rapprochement between a song and its narrative context: this begins with some of the songs in Renart's *Rose* and continues in the majority of later thirteenth-century narratives. In general, there is a *vers de transition*: the line immediately before or after the citation bears the same rhyme as the first (or last) line of the song:

> Et pour lui plus reconforter
> Commenche cest ver a chanter
> A clere vois haute et levee:
>
> > Amors, quant m'iert ceste painne achievee
> > Qui si me fait a grant dolour languir?
> > (*Le Roman de la violette*, 2336–40)[35]

[35] Gerbert de Montreuil, *Le Roman de la violette ou de Gerart de Nevers*, ed. D. L. Buffum (Société des Anciens Textes Français; Paris, 1928).

And to comfort himself further he begins to sing this song aloud in a high, clear voice:

Love, when will this torment be finished that causes me to languish like this in such sorrow?

The melodic repetitions in the fr. 845 motets could be viewed in the same light as forms of musical rhyme, or to coin a phrase, *sons de transition*.

III

This final section turns to fourteenth-century examples, none of which refers to pieces with music. A connection is provided by the Lescurel *dits entés*. The rubric contains a possible ambiguity: in 'Balades rondeaux et diz entez', strictly, 'entez' could qualify 'balades' and 'rondeauz' as well as 'diz'.[36] At first sight this seems implausible, since it would imply the awkward construction 'rondeaux entez sus refroiz de rondeaux'.[37] Before dismissing the possibility entirely, it is interesting to compare a less well-known rubric from the *Trésor amoureux*. This late fourteenth-century work (at one stage tentatively ascribed to Froissart) is a large lyric anthology organised into a loose narrative sequence, rather like some of the sequences by Charles d'Orléans. The narrative, in a self-conscious manoeuvre, contains explicit and highly detailed formal instructions from Amours to the poet on how he should compose his book: the number of rhyming couplets it should have, the precise arrangement and number of ballades and rondeaux. He even tells him to incorporate a table of refrains and a first-line index. The whole work begins with the following rubric:

Divisé en .IIIJ. parties de lignes coupletes. Et en chascun nombre des balades sont .XIJ. rondeaulx entez ens es balades qui s'ensuivent, comme divisié est en la fin du premier nombre des coupletes et commence ainsi:

Divided into four parts of rhyming couplets. And in each group (lit. number) of ballades are twelve rondeaux grafted into the ballades that follow, as is stated at the end of the first number of couplets, and the beginning is as follows:

This explanation is echoed in the narrative:

[36] There is enough syntactical flexibility in the passage cited above from the *Jeu du Pelerin* for this ambiguity to be present there as well. However, the likelihood is less strong: 'canchons' occurs on a separate line, and in any case only one of Adam's surviving thirty-six has a refrain. There are, in fact, no surviving 'balades' as such.

[37] As Everist also notes, *French Motets*, p. 81.

> Des rondeaulz y veuil trente six,
> Justement entez et assis,
> Douze en chascun nombre des trois . . .
> Douze balades esliras,
> Où les douze rondeaulz liras
> Quant tu les y aras entez. (749–51; 753–5)[38]

I want thirty-six rondeaux there, properly grafted and well placed, twelve in each group of three . . . You will choose twelve ballades where you will read the twelve rondeaux when you will have grafted them there

A little later, Amours explains how the table and index are to be constructed:

> Les premieres lignes prendras
> De tes balades, et mettras
> Les refrains avec (769–71)

You will take the first lines of your ballades, and will put refrains with them

What happens in practice is that the work is divided into four narrative sections. In between each section occur groups of ballades: the first has forty-four, the second forty, and the third another forty-four. These ballade clusters are in turn divided by sets of rondeaux, in three groups of twelve. Each set of rondeaux is grafted by rhyme onto the ballades. To take an example, Ballade 19 is preceded by an eight-line rondeau. The first line of this rondeau becomes the first line of the ballade, and the second line of the rondeau becomes the last line of the ballade stanza (the refrain).

Not only does the *Trésor* give a remarkably explicit account of the process of grafting, it even sets up a means of summarising the process in tabular form. Thus each group of ballades has its own table set out in the manuscript (Brussels, Bibliothèque Royale Albert Ier MS 11140) listing the opening line and the refrain line of each ballade, which are, of course, where appropriate, equivalent to the two-line refrains of the *rondeaux entés*. In this work we do indeed have 'balades entez sus refroiz de rondeaux', a possible reading of the Lescurel rubric. The *Trésor* attests to a variety of points about grafting. Perhaps the most important is the insistence on the refrain as the key element: it both creates the means by which the grafting can take place, and provides the locus of transition between one genre and another. Strikingly, it not only shares but also fixes as a specific procedure the defining textual

[38] *Le trésor amoureux*, ed. A. Scheler, in *Oeuvres de Froissart: poésies*, 3 vols. (Brussels, 1870–2), iii, pp. 52–305.

characteristic of the *motets entés* of fr. 845. The splicing action once more dominates.

This account of fourteenth-century usage cannot finish without some mention of two more well-known fourteenth-century references to *enté*, in Machaut's *Prologue* and Deschamps' *L'Art de Dictier* respectively. Both are hard to interpret.[39] In the case of Machaut, we should note first that he uses the term twice in the *Voir Dit*: in a chanson baladee and a rondeau respectively:

Des que premiers oy retraire	Since first I heard mentioned,
De vous dous amis debonnaire	My sweet and debonair lover,
La valeur et la grant bonte	Your worthiness and great virtue,
Mon cuer fu si en vous ente	My heart has so grafted itself onto you
Quonques puis ne len pos retraire	That I could never separate it.
(*Voir Dit*, chanson baladee 26, 1973–7)[40]	(trans. Leech-Wilkinson and Palmer, p. 141)
Tres dous amis iay bonne volente	Very sweet darling, I am most willing
De vous donner ioie et pais et mercy	To grant you joy, peace, and mercy,
Et dacroistre vo bien et vo sante	To increase your benefit and well-being,
Tres dous amis iay bonne volente	Very sweet darling, I am most willing.
Car dedens vous ay mon fin cuer ente	For onto yours I've grafted my own heart
Pour ce que voy quil me wet amer ci	Because I see it wishes me to love there.
Tresdous amis iay bonne volente	Very sweet darling, I am most willing
De vous donner ioie et pais et mercy	To grant you joy, peace, and mercy.
(*Voir Dit*, rondel 34, lines 3003–10)[41]	(trans. Leech-Wilkinson and Palmer, p. 199)

[39] G. Reaney, 'The Poetic Form of Machaut's Musical Works: I. The Ballades, Rondeaux and Virelais', *Musica Disciplina*, 13 (1959), pp. 25–41, at pp. 25–6; U. Günther, 'Zitate in franzözischen Liedsätzen der Ars Nova und Ars Subtilior', *Musica Disciplina*, 26 (1972), pp. 53–68; W. Arlt, 'Aspekte der Chronologie und des Stilwandels im französischen Lied des 14. Jahrhunderts', in *Aktuelle Fragen der musikbezogenen Mittelalterforschung: Texte zu einem Basler Kolloquium des Jahres 1975 = Forum musicologicum*, 3 (1982), pp. 193–280. For other references, see Lawrence Earp, *Guillaume de Machaut: A Guide to Research* (New York and London, 1995), p. 204, n. 45. Work on citational practices in Machaut and other fourteenth- and fifteenth-century composers has grown extensively more recently: see, for instance, M. Bent, 'Deception, Exegesis and Sounding Number in Machaut's Motet 15', *Early Music History*, 10 (1991), pp. 15–27 and 'Polyphony of Texts and Music in the Fourteenth-Century Motet: *Tribum que non abhorruit/Quoniam secta latronum/Merito hec patimur* and Its "Quotations"', in Dolores Pesce (ed.), *Hearing the Motet: Essays on the Motet of the Middle Ages and Renaissance* (New York, 1997), pp. 82–103; Yolanda Plumley, 'Citation and Allusion in the Late *Ars nova*: The Case of *Esperance* and the *En attendant* Songs', *Early Music History*, 18 (1999), pp. 287–363; Elizabeth Eva Leach, 'Fortune's Demesne: The Interrelation of Text and Music in Machaut's *Il mest avis* (B22), *De fortune* (B23) and Two Related Anonymous Balades', *Early Music History*, 19 (2000), pp. 47–79; and Jacques Boogaart, 'Encompassing Past and Present: Quotations and their Function in Machaut's Motets', *Early Music History*, 20 (2001), pp. 1–86.

[40] *Le Livre dou Voir Dit,* ed. Leech-Wilkinson and Palmer, p. 140.

[41] *Ibid.*, p. 198.

In both cases, he uses *enté* as a rhyme word: this, with obvious wit, enables the figurative meaning of his grafted heart to be enacted in the grafting pattern of the rhyme.

The context in the *Prologue* is less carefully crafted: he simply uses the term as a form of classification. The God of Love has commanded him to compose the following genres with the aid of Esperance, Dous Penser and Plaisance:

> . . . dis et chansonnettes
> Pleinnes d'onneur et d'amourettes,
> Doubles hoquès et plaisans lais,
> Motès, rondiaus et virelais
> Qu'on claimme chansons baladées,
> Complaintes, balades entées,
> A l'onneur et a la loange
> De toutes dames sans losange
> (*Prologue*, V, 11–18)[42]

dits and little songs full of honour and love, double hoquets and pleasing lais, motets, rondeaux, and virelais that are called chansons balladées, complaintes, ballades entées to the honour and praise of all women without deception

The classification is unexpected because it does not appear elsewhere: are we to assume that he means it in a specific sense, or as a way of referring to his ballades in general? Again it seems likely, as Gilbert Reaney and Ursula Günther have proposed, that he is alluding to aspects of refrain citation, in particular the way in which many of his ballades share refrains and other lines in self-referring sequences, and also with *formes fixes* by other authors, such as Adam de la Halle, Jehan de la Mote and Thomas de Paien. Our discussion of other usages, particularly in the *Trésor*, might suggest that Machaut's sense of ballade structure was rather more dominated by grafting procedures than we commonly assume. In other words, he perhaps conceived the composition of *formes fixes* quite fundamentally as a matter of working with given refrain structures, many of which were borrowed.[43]

[42] Guillaume de Machaut, *Oeuvres*, ed. E. Hoepffner, 3 vols. (Société des Anciens Textes Français; Paris, 1908, 1911, 1921), i, p. 6.

[43] For important detailed explorations of these processes, see Plumley, 'Citation and Allusion'; Leach, 'Fortune's Demesne'; and Boogaart, 'Encompassing Past and Present'. On Machaut's term *ballade entée*, see further Plumley, p. 287 and n. 2. Her fine essay, in exploring grafting processes in Machaut's younger contemporaries, finds the practice 'could take on altogether more subtle form than the classic "cut and paste" style of grafting' (p. 289). See also Boogaart on grafting in Machaut's motets (pp. 2–3 and n. 6 and 63–4 and n. 120). He makes the interesting case that Machaut grafts material from

Although we might expect that Deschamps would use the term similarly to Machaut, especially in a work dedicated to the principles of composing *formes fixes*, the reference does not quite overlap. The general context is indeed ballade composition; however his mention of *enté* occurs as part of a discussion of chansons royales. Their envoys, he says, must be grafted by rhyme onto the chanson:

Et doivent les envois d'icelles chancons qui se commencent par "princes" estre de cinq vers entez par eux aux rimes de la chancon sanz rebrique; c'est assavoir deux vers premiers, et puis un pareil de la rebriche; et les ij autres suyans les premiers, deux concluans en substance l'effect de la dicte chancon et servens a la rebriche. Et l'envoy d'une balade de iij vers ne doit estre que de trois vers aussi, contenans sa matere et servans a la rebriche, comme il sera dit cy apres:[44]

The envoys of these songs, which begin with 'Princes', must be of five lines themselves grafted onto the rhymes of the chanson, not counting the refrain; that is, two first lines and then one line rhyming with the refrain; and then, two more following, these two essentially concluding the effect of this song and serving to introduce the refrain. The envoy of a balade of three lines must also have only three lines, containing its substance and serving to introduce the refrain, as will be said hereafter.

In broad terms, his description is very reminiscent of the instructions in the *Trésor*: there is a similar compositional sense of a procedure of fitting two elements together by rhyme. When we try to interpret this interesting passage in more detail we find that several further issues are raised. First, it must be acknowledged that, in a way that is characteristic of Deschamps throughout this work, his remarks are tantalising rather than wholly enlightening; he often contradicts himself, or is inconsistent, and his examples rarely illustrate his precepts. There is a good instance of the latter here, for having specified that an envoy must have five lines he provides an example of one with four. Moreover, it is not entirely clear whether he is writing about chansons royales or ballades. His

grands chants (and not just lower-register refrains) into his motets. On possible connections between the term *ballade entée*, citational procedures in Machaut's *Louange des Dames*, the *motet enté* and the *Trésor amoureux*, see references in Earp, *Guillaume de Machaut: A Guide*, p. 261. Elizabeth Leach has kindly drawn my attention to two further cross-references (not in Earp): the refrain of Machaut's ballade 'De petit po' (B18) is in Adam de la Halle's motet no. 2 (triplum), and the refrain of Machaut's ballade *Beauté qui* (B4) occurs as the refrain of the fourth ballade of Jean de le Mote, 'Le Regret Guillaume'. As Hoepfner first noted, Machaut drew on the 'Regret Guillaume' in his ballade *On ne porroit* (B3); see Earp, p. 352.

[44] E. Deschamps, *L'Art de Dictier*, ed. and trans. Deborah Sinnreich-Levi (East Lansing, Mich., 1994), pp. 78–9.

discussion of envoy form appears to be based on those of the chansons royales, yet this example is of a ballade stanza. Deschamps composed 136 chansons royales: these have five strophes, an envoy and no refrain, yet his comments here discuss the use of a refrain and his example also possesses one (repeated at the end of the envoy).

Which form he is discussing may perhaps be put to one side for the moment in favour of pondering his term 'rebriche'. I have referred to it as meaning 'refrain', but as Deborah Sinnreich-Levi observes, Deschamps employs both terms in his treatise, once in the same sentence:

> chanson balladees, qui sont ainsi appelles pour ce que le refrain d'une balade sert tousiours, par maniere de rubriche a la fin de chascune couple d'icelle, et de la chanson balladee de trois vers doubles a tousiours, par difference des balades, son refrain et rebriche au commencement[45]

> Chanson baladées are so called because the refrain of a balade always functions, in the accepted manner, at the end of each strophe, whereas the chanson baladée of three paired sections always has its refrain and musical refrain at the beginning

Sinnreich-Levi makes the interesting suggestion that one term might be referring to musical repetition, the other to textual repetition[46] and translates the above passage accordingly. Another layer of meaning must also derive from 'rubric' (the spellings *rebrique*, *rebriche* and *rubriche* are all found in *L'Art de Dictier*). Since it seems hard to see a consistent distinction of meaning in Deschamps' usage, it may be preferable to interpret his sense fairly inclusively. The connections between musical and verbal repetition, and their marking on the page are, after all, of key importance.

To return to the ambiguities of form: a song's form is something that can be apprehended in a number of ways. It is perceived as a particular set and type of repetitions (a ballade has one kind, a *chanson baladée* has another) that are at once heard aurally, as words and notes, and registered on the page. Deschamps, writing in the second half of the fourteenth century, is giving us a double view of music and poetry as form, and music and poetry as writing. His own treatise holds a position somewhere between the abstract and the material, the prescribed and the practised, the heard, the

[45] *Ibid.*, pp. 62–3.
[46] *Ibid.*, p. 113, note to 62.

seen and the read. The very fluidity of relation between his own writing in the treatise and the examples he provides is revealing of the status of song in the period. When he writes that 'le refrain d'une balade sert tousiours, par maniere de rubriche' he seems to be referring to the function of a refrain as both a sign of form and a means of translating that form into writing. Refrains, in thirteenth- and fourteenth-century manuscripts, are highlighted visually in a wide range of ways, by illumination, an enlarged initial, musical stave or full notation, and on occasion, by being written in red.[47] Deschamps' terminology appears to draw on an understanding of the refrain as an element whose visual prominence on a page comes to seem part of its formal meaning. In seeing a refrain as a 'rubriche', Deschamps is like the author of the *Trésor*. The *Trésor* and *L'Art de Dictier* are comparable in the way that they each bring the art of commentary into the art of composition.

Once we acknowledge the wider implications of Deschamps' use of 'rebriche', it may be possible to come a little closer to understanding his (somewhat obscure) comments on grafting. Two points are worth emphasising: he plainly sees grafting as partly being a matter of rhyme ('cinq vers entez par eux aux rimes de la chancon'). In addition, he twice uses the phrase 'servens a la rebriche'. This is not easy to translate. But it gives prominence once more to the refrain. A possible interpretation is that he sees the grafting process as a way of preparing the link between strophe and refrain: the grafted lines help to summarise or conclude the 'substance' of the song and bring it back to its formal focus or refrain.

IV

This discussion of literary usages of *enté* has found that they share a common attention to the fundamental structuring potential of a refrain, and also to the use of rhyme as a means of linking disparate elements within formal structures. In my last example, I return to a musical reference from the turn of the century. This is Grocheio on the *cantilena*:

[47] Butterfield, *Poetry and Music*, ch. 10, pp. 171–90.

Est etiam alius modus cantilenarum, quem *cantum insertum* vel *cantilenam entatam* vocant, qui ad modum cantilenarum incipit et earum fine clauditur vel finitur.

There is also another kind of *cantilena* which they [i.e. the Parisians] call 'ornamented song' or 'grafted song'. It begins in the manner of *cantilene* and ends or comes to a close in their fashion.[48]

I quote here Christopher Page's edition and translation of these lines: he restores the reading 'entatam' from the manuscripts, which Rohloff had emended to 'entratam', seeing in this reading a likely reference to the French verb *enter*. This is an important and highly plausible affirmation of one of the manuscript readings; what is perhaps not quite so clear is the reason for translating 'insertus' as 'ornamented'. This seems an over-elaborate rendition of a term whose plain sense would fit just as well, if not rather better, with the idea of grafting. In trying to follow Grocheio's meaning here, one is taken back to a very similar definition earlier in the treatise:

Cantilena vero quaelibet rotunda vel rotundellus a pluribus dicitur eo quod ad modum circuli in se ipsam reflectitur et incipit et terminatur in eodem. Nos autem solum illam rotundam vel rotundellum dicimus cuius partes non habent diversum cantum a cantu responsorii vel refractus.

There are indeed many who call any cantilena a 'rotunda' or 'rotundellus' because it turns back on itself in the manner of a circle, beginning and ending in the same way [i.e. with a refrain]. However, I only call the kind of song a 'rotunda' or 'rotundellus' whose parts have the same music as the music of the response or refrain. (pp. 24–6)

I confess I find it hard to unravel these two definitions, not, I am sure, because Grocheio is unclear or confused, but simply because the assumptions on which he was relying for comprehension are not easy for us at this distance to reconstruct. There seems to be material here for more than one kind of interpretation. What I take him to be saying is that the *cantilena*, in general, is the kind of song that begins and ends with a refrain. Although this tempts some people to call them all rondeaux, he prefers to reserve that term for those types of song where the music of the refrain is repeated in the rest of the song. We then come to the *cantus insertus* or *cantilena entata*. He is quite clear that this is another type of song. Yet this type begins and ends like the 'normal' *cantilena*. The only clue Grocheio gives us as to why it is different occurs in the words *insertus* and *entatus*. Implicitly, he also seems to me to be

[48] Page, 'Johannes de Grocheio', p. 27 and n. 41.

saying that it is not a rondeau either. From his earlier definition, this must be because 'its parts' do not 'have the same music as the music of the response or refrain'. It follows that if the *cantilena entata* is using the refrain, it must be doing so in a way that distinguishes it from rondeaux. This brings us back inexorably to the grafting, which implies not a circular form of citing refrains, but (from ordinary French usage) splicing. It is hard not to conclude from all this that musical repetition, as an exclusive procedure, does not figure highly in Grocheio's definition of grafting.[49] Indeed, one possibility is that Grocheio's use of *insertus* or *entatus* refers to the texts rather than the music. We saw earlier the intimations of such a distinction in Deschamps in his use of terms which appear to refer to the text of a refrain separately from its music.

This effort to bring together a variety of medieval references to grafting seeks to show that the concept is likely to be broader rather than narrower than we thought. It encompasses both musical and poetic techniques. The very preponderance of literary references may seem disappointing from a musical point of view; at the same time, it provides a cumulative sense of the frequency with which medieval writers associated grafting with a spliced text. It reminds us, in addition, not to attach too much explanatory weight to any one reference, since the overall conceptual framework is perhaps surprisingly inclusive.

Several conclusions can be drawn. The fr. 845 motets are indeed characterised by an unusual degree of musical repetition; they also have the trademark splicing of refrain texts. Much as we may want to emphasise the musical repetitions, we cannot ignore the textual grafts. Most explicitly of all in the *Trésor amoureux*, but throughout a wide range of sources from the mid-thirteenth to the late fourteenth century, the term *enté* has a deep yet also precise metaphorical meaning of splicing and joining. The depth and range of its linguistic field is enough to mean that it is a term we cannot afford to understand in a limiting way. In addition, a variety

[49] At the same time, Grocheio's implied recognition of the association of *cantilena entata* with the *rondellus* could be said to confirm the point that certain types of grafting practice, in musical terms, are not so far from the melodic repetitions characteristic of rondeau forms (see above, p. 78).

of authors, composers and theorists use the term technically as well as more commonly. Their way of using a term technically, as we have seen, is not necessarily the same as ours; rather than reject it on these grounds, however, these very differences in methodology might encourage us not only to re-examine our own use of technical terminology, but more fundamentally, our ways of making and identifying categories. This is perhaps especially true of the fourteenth-century authors, at whose historical moment the making visible of categorical thinking is an imperative creative activity.

The fr. 845 motets are also a telling case in point since it seems possible to learn from them that musical repetition and textual splicing are not mutually exclusive techniques. They show that grafting is a musical process, and a textual process, but that it may also involve grafting music onto text and text onto music. Once we consider grafting in polyphonic motets the complexities of the activity increase even further, rather like 3-D chess, to include the grafting of music, text, or both, not just within a single voice, but from one voice to another. The *enté* process shows that there is a connection between two things that we often think of as separate – textual citation and musical repetition. It is important, moreover, to note that the word 'refrain' has always ambiguated – often problematically for musicologists and literary historians alike – between these two practices (which one might equally call textual repetition and musical citation).

If the examples in this essay have in part confirmed the importance of repetition to grafting procedures, then they have also underlined its ambivalence as an analytic tool. Observing patterns of repetition in motet voices is partly to observe how structures of recognition are built up freshly within a piece as well as on the audience's prior knowledge of a text or melody (or of a texted melody). Grafting depends on the prior existence of stock and shoot: yet once the join has been crafted, it may not always be visible. Medieval composers and writers take pains with the transitions between old and new: again, we can observe the making of these transitions within melodies and texts, in *sons de transitions* as well as *vers de transitions*. In both musical and verbal terms, rhyme is crucial: the use of verbal rhyme makes a refrain integral to a poetic structure; similarly the use of musical rhyme helps to integrate a split refrain musically since the second half of the refrain is preceded by a melodically 'open' phrase which it closes. These various means of removing the autonomy of the old material while also respecting it appear to be at the heart of grafting.

For fourteenth-century authors and composers, grafting is further associated with writing. The linking power of refrains, their usefulness as a means of connecting different genres, authors and individual pieces, is seen by the author of the *Trésor* to be a means of writing, displaying and ordering a work on the page. Deschamps' intriguing use of the term 'rebriche' in the context of a treatise on composition further implies that refrains, the fundamental material of grafting, are contributing to a process in which songs and their verbal subtleties are expected to have a presence on the page as well as in the ear.

It is tempting to shy away from the metaphorical aspects of *enté* because they do not seem to give us access to precise enough analytic categories. But the sheer pervasiveness of the term amongst writers, composers and scribes requires us to take it seriously in all its variety of implication. Peter Burke, in his account of cultural history, has written of metaphor as a means of understanding the 'collective imagination'. He finds himself 'driven to metaphor in the attempt to conceptualise conceptual change'.[50] Following through the metaphorical richness of *enté* brings us closer to the breaks and joins of medieval compositional practices, to the means by which the hybrid creation is nurtured into new life.

University College, London

[50] P. Burke, *Varieties of Cultural History* (Cambridge, 1997), p. 179.

Early Music History (2003) Volume 22. © *Cambridge University Press*
DOI:10.1017/S0261127903003036 Printed in the United Kingdom

YOLANDA PLUMLEY

AN 'EPISODE IN THE SOUTH'? ARS SUBTILIOR AND THE PATRONAGE OF FRENCH PRINCES

Scholars have long been aware of the intriguing fact that the late fourteenth- and early fifteenth-century French song repertory survives almost exclusively in non-French sources. Most of the principal collections of chansons copied between *c.*1380 and 1420 – that is, in the period corresponding roughly to the reign of Charles VI, sources like *PR*, *Pit*, *ModA* and *FP* – derive from Italy;[1] further witness to the circulation of this repertory south of the Alps is found in additional, fragmentary sources, such as *Lu*, *SL* and *GR*. In comparison, the number of French songs preserved in manuscripts of northern provenance is remarkably slight. Moreover,

Research for this essay was assisted by a grant from the Arts Faculty, University College Cork. I thank Anne Stone and Bonnie Blackburn for their comments. The excerpt from Machaut's Ballade 33 in Example 1 is taken from Leo Schrade's edition in Polyphonic Music of the Fourteenth Century, iii, and is used by kind permission of Oiseau-Lyre. Examples 2 and 3 are taken from Willi Apel's editions in *French Secular Compositions of the Fourteenth Century* (CMM 53, i–ii) and are reproduced by permission of the American Institute of Musicology.

Abbreviations used in this article are as follows:

BNF	Paris, Bibliothèque Nationale de France
FP	Florence, Biblioteca Nazionale, Panciatichi 26
GR	Grottaferrata, Biblioteca dell'Abbazia, E.b.XVI
Iv	Ivrea, Biblioteca capitolare, MS 115
Lei	Leiden, Bibliotheek der Rijksuniversiteit, MS BPL 2720
Lu	Lucca, Archivio di Stato, MS 184
ModA	Modena, Biblioteca Estense, α.M.5.24
Ox	Oxford, Bodleian Library, Canon. misc. 213
Penn	Philadelphia, University of Pennsylvania Libraries, Fr. 15
Pit	Paris, Bibliothèque Nationale de France, f. it. 568
PR	Paris, Bibliothèque Nationale de France, nouv. acq. fr. 6771
SL	Florence, Archivio di San Lorenzo, MS 2211
Tu	Turin, Biblioteca Nazionale, J.II.9
Trém	Paris, Bibliothèque Nationale de France, nouv. acq. fr. 23190
Ut	Utrecht, Universiteitsbibliotheek, 6 E 37

1 The obvious exceptions here would be the late Machaut manuscripts and *Trém* (which was copied at least in part in 1376).

those works that do survive in such sources (and these are mostly Flemish fragments) are generally simple works in classic Ars nova style; hardly any songs from the repertory we associate with Ars subtilior feature in these collections at all.[2]

This situation may not surprise us, however, because the traditional and still prevailing view is that Ars subtilior was a product of the south. This hypothesis dates back to the earliest assessments of this repertory in modern scholarship, and it is reflected in particular in discussions concerning the Chantilly codex, perhaps the most significant repository for French Ars subtilior songs.[3] Scholars have generally been united in believing this manuscript to have originated in the south, a consensus reached on palaeographical grounds – the scribe was clearly not French and seemingly a southerner – but one strongly influenced also by the number of textual references to southern patrons. Archival studies have helped to strengthen this hypothesis by highlighting the musical importance of key southern courts – notably papal Avignon but also the secular courts of Aragon, Foix, Navarre – and by uncovering biographical details linking specific composers to one or other of these centres.[4] However, opinion as to where precisely the Chantilly codex originated has varied over the years: Navarre, Foix, Avignon, Aragon and most recently Milan have in turn all

[2] Isolated exceptions include three songs from the Chantilly codex that survive also in Flemish fragments: Suzoy's ballade *Prophilias* and the anonymous *Adieu vous di*, transmitted in *Ut* (along with a couple of other anonymous songs in this style), and Egidius's *Roses et lis* (contratenor only) in *Lei*. In a round table discussion on the meaning of Ars subtilior at the conference The Chantilly Codex Reconsidered (Nouveaux regards sur le Codex Chantilly), Tours, September 2001, there was general consensus that Ars subtilior should be understood not as a style period but rather as a style repertory. Opinions differed, however, as to precisely which elements define the style. My own definition in this essay is a broad one, embracing not only complex notational and rhythmic features (notably, proportional rhythms and novel note symbols) but also other stylistic features present in works written between *c*.1380 and *c*.1410, including extensive syncopation and sequence, large-scale formats and formal interrelationships, and experimentation with pitch organisation.

[3] For a discussion of these early reports on the manuscript, see Y. Plumley and A. Stone, *The Manuscript Chantilly, Musée Condé 564: Facsimile and Introduction* (forthcoming), and E. R. Upton, 'The Chantilly Codex (F-CH 564): The Manuscript, its Music, its Scholarly Reception' (Ph.D. diss., University of North Carolina at Chapel Hill, 2001), pp. 7–39.

[4] See notably, R. Hoppin and S. Clercx, 'Notes biographiques sur quelques musicians français du XIVe siècle', in *Les Colloques de Wegimont, II: L'Ars Nova* (Paris, 1959), pp. 63–92; U. Günther, 'Zur Biographie einiger Komponisten der Ars subtilior', *Archiv für Musikwissenschaft*, 21 (1964), pp. 172–99; A. Tomasello, *Music and Ritual at Papal Avignon* (Ann Arbor, 1983); H. Anglès, *História de la música medieval en Navarra* (Pamplona, 1970); M. C. Gómez-Muntané, *La música en la casa real Catalano-Aragonesa 1336–1442*, i (Barcelona,

been proposed as the likely centre where the musical repertory was not only copied but where much of it had its genesis.[5]

In many ways, the characterisation of Ars subtilior as an 'episode in the south' has helped make sense of the overall development of musical style in the period.[6] Indeed, this repertory fits uncomfortably into what we generally construe as the broad trends of stylistic development in the age, apparently bequeathing little to the subsequent generation, which, rather, seems to have taken its cue from the 'classic' Ars nova style of Machaut and his contemporaries. Reinhard Strohm recently offered an elegant explanation for this state of affairs. He proposed that during the Schism the simpler Ars nova style continued to be cultivated in Paris and northern France. Here it fused with a 'lateral' tradition that remained quite distinct from the 'central' Ars subtilior, which, he suggested, became increasingly isolated in the south.[7]

1979); G. Reaney, 'The Manuscript Chantilly, Musée Condé 1047', *Musica Disciplina*, 8 (1954), pp. 59–113.

[5] See Plumley and Stone, *The Manuscript Chantilly*, for relevant bibliography and a summary of the various viewpoints.

[6] In his review of Willi Apel's 1950 edition of late fourteenth-century songs and in response to Apel's location of the 'manneristic' style in the years *c.*1370–90, Otto Gombosi said the following: 'it seems to me that the manneristic style is limited in space just as much as in time. It is an episode in the South with occasional radiation in the North. Yet the North had a continuous and changing tradition of its own that leads from Machaut and his circle directly to the Parisian masters of the early fifteenth century. Netherlandish elements get gradually mixed into it.' See '[Review of] *French Secular Music of the Late Fourteenth Century* ed. by Willi Apel (Cambridge, Mass., 1950)', *Musical Quarterly*, 36 (1950), pp. 603–10, at p. 607. Apel later revised his ideas concerning when the various stylistic changes occurred in 'The Development of French Secular Music during the Fourteenth Century', *Musica Disciplina*, 27 (1973), pp. 41–59. He located a post-Machaut style (defined by works that are more advanced than Machaut but less than Ars subtilior) in *c.*1350–70. The 'manneristic' (Ars subtilior) style he now redated *c.*1360, suggesting that it emerged in Avignon (this early date was on the basis of the presence of Matheus de Sancto Johanne's *Inclite flos* in *Iv*, which was then believed to date to *c.*1360). The 'modern' style he saw as starting *c.*1380. He conceded that these styles probably overlapped but confirmed Gombosi's association of Ars subtilior with the south: 'the style of Machaut may have been cultivated by some conservative composers after 1380 or later. The influence of the post-Machaut style may have continued into the modern style . . . so that the manneristic style would appear as a lateral development confined to the southern part of France . . .' (*ibid.*, p. 51).

[7] In Strohm's view, the transmission of these two style repertories to Italy reflects their geographical polarisation: the simpler repertory crossed the Alps via Burgundian Flanders, while its Ars subtilior counterpart was disseminated through, and in large part generated by, the Francophile court of Giangaleazzo Visconti of Milan. See R. Strohm, *The Rise of European Music* (Cambridge, 1993), chapters 1–2, and esp. pp. 62–4, and his essay, 'The Ars Nova Fragments of Ghent', *Tijdschrift van de Vereniging voor Nederlandse Muziekgeschiedenis*, 34 (1984), pp. 109–31.

In this essay, I shall reassess the evidence for the geographical currency of Ars subtilior songs and present new findings that I believe undermine the notion that there was a 'north–south' divide in the cultivation of musical styles in the late fourteenth century. Closer scrutiny of the Chantilly song repertory permits us to relate a significant number of works to the patronage of the French fleur-de-lis princes, Louis d'Anjou and Jean de Berry, who now emerge as leading patrons of music in this period. These princes' role in the governing of the realm caused them to spend much of their time in Paris, but various political situations contributed to their frequent and often long-term implantation in the Languedoc and in Avignon. Surviving biographical information attests to similar mobility on the part of certain musicians, casting further doubt on the plausibility that separate musical traditions prevailed in north and south. But it is evidence from the surviving songs themselves that perhaps bears most vivid witness to my case: musical and textual interrelationships linking specific works indicate quite clearly that Ars subtilior songs and those of the 'northern' post-Machaut tradition were cultivated and enjoyed within the same cultural milieux.

ORDERS OF EVIDENCE: ARS SUBTILIOR AND THE SOUTH

Three main categories of evidence have been used to support the case for a southern provenance for the Chantilly songs and to link them to specific centres: first, references in the texts to specific patrons; second, biographical information concerning specific musicians; and, third, circumstantial evidence regarding the cultivation of music at specific courts.

The privileging of one or the other of these orders of evidence has resulted in a bewildering range of opinions concerning the provenance of both repertory and manuscript. Paulin Paris, one of the first to appraise the Chantilly codex in the 1860s, believed it came from Foix on account of the number of textual references to Count Gaston 'Febus' III, a view shared by certain later scholars, including Gilbert Reaney and Gordon Greene.[8] Others, like Nino Pirrotta, Willi Apel and Craig Wright, thought, on the basis

[8] For bibliography and a summary of these various viewpoints, see Plumley and Stone, *The Manuscript Chantilly*.

of biographical and circumstantial evidence in particular, that Avignon was a more likely candidate. Drawing on elements from all three orders of evidence, Terence Scully subsequently argued for an Aragonese provenance, while most recently Strohm has proposed the court of Giangaleazzo Visconti (r. 1378–1402) in Milan-Pavia.

The courts of Foix, Aragon and Milan

Explicit textual references to certain patrons or courts may seem to provide one of the most suggestive links between a composer and a patron. Such references, however, are comparatively rare in the fourteenth-century chanson repertory, and where they do occur they are often obscure: though doubtless the identity of the intended recipient would have been obvious to the original audience, we are left to unravel whatever clues we can find and to argue for the most plausible interpretation.

As intimated above, many have been struck by a seemingly significant number of textual allusions to the house of Foix and this has led some scholars to place the manuscript there. Two songs, *Se July Cesar* by Trebor and *Se Galaas* by Cuvelier, indeed make specific reference to Gaston 'Febus' (d. 1391), and a third, *Se Alixandre*, also by Trebor, to his heir, Mathieu de Castelbon (d. 1398). The identification of these patrons is clear because the various texts refer to them either by name or by describing their motto, heraldic devices or territories. These cases have encouraged vaguer allusions to the classical god Phoebus in other songs from the manuscript, notably *Phiton, phiton* by Magister Franciscus and the anonymous ballade *Le mont Aon*, similarly to be connected with the house of Foix. While our knowledge of topical events together with some slim evidence for Gaston's musical tastes renders these interpretations plausible, the question arises how much we can or should extrapolate from allegorical references of this kind.[9] Even where we are dealing with an explicit allusion to a historical figure, should we necessarily conclude that the work in question was written from a position within that court?

The songs by Cuvelier and Trebor mentioned above are cases

[9] I discuss these works and their connection to Gaston Febus below.

in point. Cuvelier composed another song (also preserved uniquely in the Chantilly codex) that points resolutely to the north. This is *En la saison*, which praises the Breton noble Olivier du Guesclin, kinsman of the famous Bertran, Constable of France. Given the theme of this work, it seems highly plausible that our composer is the Jean le Cuvelier (or Cavelier), courtier of Charles VI, who wrote a chronicle of Betran's life in the 1380s and who is probably identical with the poet Jacquemart le Cuvelier who served Charles V in the 1370s.[10]

Trebor seemingly has more solid southern credentials. In addition to the two songs for Foix, he wrote another, *En seumeillant*, that refers to the campaign to conquer Sardinia planned by the Aragonese during the reign of Johan I (1387–95).[11] Trebor's *Quant joyne cuer* has also been linked to southern courts, notably Navarre or Aragon, because of its reference to an unnamed patron's red and gold heraldry.[12] The composer's presence in either Foix or Aragon would conveniently account for all these allusions, since the courts were closely linked. Aragon in particular is known to have been an active musical centre: Johan I, a keen music-lover and himself a composer, expended considerable energy in trying to lure the best musicians of the day to his court, and many of those he employed were French.[13] Indeed, musicologists have noted

[10] For what is known about the chronicler, see 'Cuvelier', *Dictionnaire des lettres françaises: le moyen âge* (rev. edn, Paris, 1992), p. 363. It is generally assumed that the two songs attributed in the Chantilly codex to J. O. or J. Cun. are by Cuvelier; for a discussion of this and arguments for Cuvelier's authorship of *En la saison*, see Y. Plumley, 'Cuvelier', in *Die Musik in Geschichte und Gegenwart* (*MGG*²), *Personenteil*, v (Kassel, 2001), pp. 191–2, and Plumley and Stone, *The Manuscript Chantilly*.

[11] Léopold Delisle, in the report dated 6 July 1868 that he prepared for Henri, duc d'Aumale, following the latter's acquisition of the manuscript in 1861, was the first to connect this work with this event, which he dated to 1389. A. Pagès explains the references in the ballade to a prophecy made in 1288 that a hundred years later the Aragonese would vanquish the Moors; though the song could mark this anniversary, Pagès points out that it could have been written any time during Johan I's reign (1387–96) since the campaign in Sardinia was prepared but never carried out; see *La poésie française en Catalogne du XIII*^e^ *siècle à la fin du XV*^e^ (Toulouse and Paris, 1936), pp. 61–2. If so, in line with my suggestions below concerning Trebor's connection with the Duke of Berry, the ballade could have been prompted by a rumour circulating in the French court in 1393 that the campaign was imminent (*ibid.*, p. 62 n. 2).

[12] See W. Apel, *French Secular Compositions of the Fourteenth Century* (Corpus Mensurabilis Musicae, 53; Rome, 1972), i, p. xliii, and Reaney, 'The Manuscript Chantilly', p. 78 n. 69; Reaney suggested that while Gaston Febus also wore red and gold, he was not a king so could be discounted.

[13] See esp. Gómez-Muntané, *La música en la casa real Catalano-Aragonesa*.

with interest the presence in the Aragonese records of certain names reminiscent of Chantilly composers, notably Jaquet de Noyon and Gacien Reyneau.[14] Maria Carmen Gómez sought to identify Trebor with a singer named Trebol who served briefly in the chapel of Johan's brother and successor, Martin I, in 1408–9;[15] she suggested that the name was an anagram and that this singer was identical with the Jean Robert who served in the chapel of Charles III of Navarre some years earlier, and also with Borlet, another composer represented in Chantilly 564. This hypothesis in turn encouraged her to link not only *Quant joyne cuer* to Aragonese patronage but also *Passerose de beauté*: the latter, which refers to a wedding but in highly allegorical terms, she proposed was written in connection with the wedding of Johan to Yolande de Bar rather than with that of Jean, duc de Berry as earlier proposed by Gilbert Reaney.[16]

Attractive though it is, Gómez's hypothesis concerning the identity of this composer relies on our accepting the various transmutations of his name – Trebor, Trebol, Borlet, Robert – and also that the two musicians from Aragon and Navarre were one and the same. In fact, even if we accept that Trebor's real name was Trebol or Robert, there are candidates active elsewhere with whom we might choose to identify him.[17] Despite this, the circumstantial evidence concerning musical life in the Aragonese court together with the reference to Aragon in *En seumeillant* has proved irresistible: Gómez's biographical reconstruction has thus far

[14] Some attempts have been made to identify three minstrels, Jacomi lo Begue, Jacomi Capeta and Johani Sent Luch, with composer Jacob de Senleches, but Gómez-Muntané has contested these identifications; see *ibid.*, pp. 40–1.

[15] M. C. Gómez-Muntané, 'La musique à la maison royale de Navarre à la fin du Moyen-Age et le chantre Johan Robert', *Musica Disciplina*, 41 (1987), pp. 109–51.

[16] *Ibid.*, pp. 145–6, and Reaney, 'The Manuscript Chantilly', pp. 76–7.

[17] This includes two further musicians called Robert who served in the Aragonese chapel. Robertus Creque served in the chapel of Johan I in 1394 and in 1406 was in the papal chapel in Avignon; see Tomasello, *Music and Ritual at Papal Avignon*, p. 263 and Gómez-Muntané, *La música de la casa real*, p. 91. Robertus Nyot served as chaplain in Aragon in 1379–80 and 1382–3 but went on to serve in the chapel of Benedict XIII alongside Haucourt, Hasprois and Watignies (Watignies also served in Aragon in the late 1370s); *ibid.*, p. 93 and Tomasello, *Music and Ritual at Papal Avignon*, p. 263. Another candidate might be the Jean Robert who was master of the boys at Reims cathedral. It may be that Trebor was not an anagram after all: there are musicians with similar names, such as the minstrel Triboul, who served Charles VI of France in 1387, and Tibaut Tribolet, who worked at the court of Navarre in 1390; see Y. Plumley, 'Trebor', *The New Grove Dictionary of Music and Musicians*, 2nd edn (London, 2001), xxv, pp. 709–10.

passed unchallenged, and some have even renamed Trebor 'Jean Robert'.[18]

The case of Trebor is an interesting one because it illustrates our desire to align biographical information, however tenuous or scant, with apparent textual clues, and to use circumstantial evidence for the patronage of music at specific centres to corroborate our interpretations. The traditional view that the Chantilly manuscript and much of its repertory originated in the south arguably has led to a certain circularity of thinking, whereby texts of ambiguous content have been interpreted – and biographies constructed – according to, and in order further to corroborate, this 'fact'.

This is particularly well illustrated by Terence Scully's study of the Chantilly manuscript.[19] Building on the work of Gómez, Günther and others, Scully connected a large proportion of the works with the Aragonese royal family on the basis of their textual content. This in turn was fuelled by his conviction that the manuscript itself was copied at the court of Barcelona; he presented a linguistic study of the texts that he believed definitively confirmed the Catalan nationality of the scribe. Recent reappraisal of the linguistic profile of the texts, however, suggests otherwise;[20] there is no longer any compelling reason to link the manuscript and its repertory to Aragon.

The general conviction concerning the 'southerness' of the Ars subtilior song repertory has also stimulated a recent proposal that much of it – and indeed the Chantilly manuscript – may have derived from the court of Giangaleazzo Visconti in Milan-Pavia. The Francophile tastes of this court have been the subject of considerable interest in recent years, and a certain number of musical works have been plausibly connected with that cultural

[18] Notably Strohm, *Rise of European Music*, p. 55, and two recordings by the Ferrara Ensemble, *Balades a iii chans* (Arcana, 1995, CD A 32) and *Fleur de Vertus* (Arcana, 1997, CD A 40) refer to the composer as Johan Robert.

[19] T. Scully, 'French Songs in Aragon: The Place of Origin of the Chansonnier Chantilly, Musée Condé 564', in K. Busby and E. Kooper (eds.), *Courtly Literature: Culture and Context. Selected Papers from the 5th Triennial Congress of the International Courtly Literature Society, Dalfsen, The Netherlands, 1986* (Amsterdam and Philadelphia, 1990), pp. 509–21.

[20] See Plumley and Stone, *The Manuscript Chantilly.*

centre.[21] Much has been made of the presence of Visconti mottos in two French songs from this period, Ciconia's *Aler m'en veut* and Philipoctus de Caserta's *En atendant souffrir*. The citation of the latter and two further songs by Philipoctus in Ciconia's *Sus une fontayne* led to the irresistible hypothesis that the two composers met under the patronage of Giangaleazzo Visconti.[22] Reinhard Strohm postulated that Philipoctus may never even have left Italy: for him, the court of Giangaleazzo Visconti emerged not only as a centre for the dissemination of Ars subtilior into Italy but as the focal point for its composition, and, more recently, the most likely place of origin of the Chantilly manuscript.[23] However, while we can be confident that French songs were heard at Giangaleazzo's court – there survives a collection of French lyrics written there for which musical settings apparently existed, and at least two French minstrels served this patron[24] – the evidence for linking the Chantilly collection to Milan remains highly circumstantial.

Papal Avignon: the junction of north and south

In my opinion, the evidence cited by scholars to situate specific Chantilly songs in Foix, Aragon or Milan is too slight for us to draw any definitive conclusions about the provenance of the Chantilly song repertory as a whole.[25] As we have seen, very little

[21] See J. Nádas and A. Ziino, *The Lucca Codex: Il Codice Mancini. An Introductory Study and Facsimile Edition* (Ars Nova, 1; Lucca, 1990), pp. 38–46. *ModA*, which shares a significant number of concordances with Chantilly, is thought by some to have links with the Visconti; see, however, the most recent study of this source in Anne Stone's introduction to the facsimile edition (Lucca, forthcoming).

[22] Strohm, *The Rise of European Music*, p. 60.

[23] *Ibid.*, p. 59, and 'Filipotto de Caserta, ovvero i francesi in Lombardia', in F. Della Seta and F. Piperno (eds.), *Festschrift for Nino Pirrotta on his 80th Birthday* (Florence, 1980), pp. 65–74. Strohm argued a connection with the Chantilly manuscript and the Visconti court in a paper presented at the conference The Chantilly Codex Reconsidered.

[24] The manuscript is London, British Library, Add. 15224. Two of the song texts are known from *ModA* in song settings by Johannes de Janua and Matteo da Perugia. The two French minstrels who worked there are Jaquet de Noyon, who may be the composer of a song in Chantilly and who served in Aragon, Milan and for the Duke of Anjou (see below), and Everli, who served Johan of Aragon and Louis duc d'Orléans.

[25] Certainly, the hypothesis has also been influenced by the apparent southern origin of the scribe. However, pinpointing the scribe as Italian rather than Catalan, as now seems most likely, does not necessarily help us determine the place of origin of the repertory: songs – like musicians and, for that matter, scribes – travelled. The manuscript might have been copied close to papal circles, possibly at the councils of Pisa or Constance. Florence also seems a distinct possibility in view of what we know about the early ownership of the manuscript, the close relationship with *FP* and the evidence that exists for the circulation of French songs there.

if any biographical information has come to light that allows us to connect specific composers to those centres. Such details are, indeed, generally hard to come by; however, if we are to privilege this kind of evidence as a significant indicator of the currency of a style or repertory, then we surely need to concede that at present the most tangible evidence we possess points to Avignon.

Three composers of the Ars subtilior generation represented in the Chantilly codex and elsewhere can be connected to the papal chapel at Avignon in the 1380s and 1390s. Matheus de Sancto Johanne (d. before 1391) is documented as a singer in the papal chapel between 1382 and 1386, while Jean Haucourt (Johannes Altacuria) and Jean Symonis dit Hasprois (Haspre) served there between 1393 and 1403/4. The specificity of Matheus's and Hasprois's names renders plausible the identifications of these musicians with the Chantilly composers; in the case of the former a connection with the pope is corroborated by the text of his ballade *Inclite flos* (see below). The appearance of Haucourt's name alongside that of Hasprois in the Avignon records and his beneficial profile, together with the placement of his isorhythmic rondeau beside a similar work by Matheus in the Chantilly codex, help confirm the composer's identity with the Avignon singer.[26]

Between them, these three composers wrote eight of the ninety-nine songs of the Chantilly collection. Matheus de Sancto Johanne is represented there by five songs (which gives him one of the highest profiles in the collection) while Haucourt is attributed one song and Hasprois two. Several other Chantilly composers have also been linked with papal Avignon, though here the evidence is more ambiguous. Appearing alongside Haucourt and Hasprois in a list of papal singers from 1393 is the name Franciscus, and some have speculated that this was the Magister Franciscus who composed the song *Phiton, phiton*.[27] Equally ambiguous is the identification of

[26] As I have suggested elsewhere, Matheus's isorhythmic rondeau seems to allude to another song by Haucourt; see 'Intertextuality in the Late Fourteenth-Century Chanson', *Music & Letters*, 84 (2003), pp. 355–77. Both men originated in Laon and shared the location of certain of their benefices.

[27] For details about the lists of singers in the chapel of Clement VII and Benedict XIII, see Tomasello, *Music and Ritual at Papal Avignon*, pp. 64–72. The papal singer Franciscus has been identified with Burgundian singer Jean François, who is believed to be the author of several compositions found in certain fifteenth-century sources; see C. Wright, *Music at the Court of Burgundy 1364–1419: A Documentary History* (Brooklyn, NY, 1979), p. 63. On the compositions attributed to François, see Tomasello, *Music and Ritual at*

composers Guido and Jean Vaillant with members of the pope's chapel active slightly earlier, respectively Guido de Lange and Johannes Valentis.[28] One Chantilly composer, however, who surely spent time in Avignon is Jacob de Senleches. The text of his ballade *Fuions de ci* suggests that he had been working for Queen Eleanor of Castile, sister of Johan I of Aragon, until her death in September 1382. A record of the court of Navarre dated April 1383 indicates that by then Senleches had become harpist to Cardinal Pedro de Luna, the future pope Benedict XIII.[29]

The number of songs in the Chantilly manuscript by composers whom we may thus link with papal Avignon – Matheus de Sancto Johanne, Jean Haucourt, Jean Symonis de Hasprois, and Jacob de Senleches – totals twelve. If we add to these the other songs that refer explicitly to pope Clement VII (1378–94) in their texts – Egidius's *Courtois et sages* and Philipoctus' *Par les bons gedeons* – and other works by these composers in the Chantilly collection, the sum reaches eighteen. This figure represents nearly a fifth of the total songs in the codex.

On the face of it, then, and on the basis of the kind of textual and biographical evidence that musicologists have tended to privilege, Avignon emerges as a more credible converging point – if not the place of origin – for a significant portion of the Chantilly song repertory than any one of the southern secular courts discussed above.

Circumstantial evidence is, of course, not lacking, for it is safe to say that Avignon enjoyed at this time a reputation for music-making that was second to none. Here congregated the best sacred and secular musicians of the day, and it is here that secular princes, as well as prelates, came to recruit their musical personnel. These secular potentates included not only southern rulers like Johan of Aragon but also figures that we associate with the north, notably the French fleur-de-lis princes, Philippe de Bourgogne and his

Papal Avignon, p. 226; Wright, *Music at the Court of Burgundy*, p. 64; and V. Newes and Y. Plumley, 'Franciscus, Magister', *MGG*², *Personenteil*, vi, pp. 1581–3.

[28] For the composer Guido we lack a surname to confirm this identification; on Guido de Lange, see Tomasello, *Music and Ritual at Papal Avignon*, p. 227. The name Jean Vaillant is rather common and the date of the relevant Avignon singer on the early side (on Vaillant and alternative candidates, see below).

[29] Anglès, *História de la música medieval en Navarra*, p. 225.

brother Jean de Berry. The latter hired several musicians directly connected with the papal chapel, including colleagues of Haucourt and Hasprois, and certain of these recruits divided their time between the papal chapel and one or both of these princely courts.

In the remainder of this essay, I shall explore some evidence for musical patronage of Ars subtilior songs by the French princes, and specifically by Louis d'Anjou and Jean de Berry in the 1380s and 1390s. What I shall propose is that the cultural orbit of these French princes was far from being detached from activities in the south and in no way represented a distinct and more old-fashioned musical context. Indeed, I suspect that it was the intersection between this princely milieu and the papal court of Avignon and the fluidity of movement of musicians between the two cultural orbits that gave rise to a significant number of the songs by the Ars subtilior generation that survive in the Chantilly codex.[30]

THE MUSICAL PATRONAGE OF THE FRENCH PRINCES

The French royal court had, of course, enjoyed a strong tradition of musical patronage during the reigns of Jean II (1350–64) and Charles V (1364–80). The great composer Guillaume de Machaut had close contacts with the French court for most of his career, and he penned various works for members of the royal family. Jean de Berry later owned one of the complete works manuscripts, and it was for this same prince that Machaut wrote *La fonteinne amoureuse* c.1360; it has recently been suggested that Jean de Berry may also have commissioned *La prise d'Alixandrie*.[31] Clearly, there was a keen appreciation of music and poetry of the highest order within this royal and princely milieu, and though patchy, the surviving records suggest that in the last two decades of the four-

[30] The extent to which the courts on the peripheries of French culture, notably those of Giangaleazzo Visconti and Johan I, drew musicians from the French courts has also perhaps not been emphasised enough. French musicians seem to have circulated between the various courts; these included chapel singers, like Robertus Nyot, Colinet le Forestier and Johannes de Watignies (Colinet served in the Burgundian chapel and that of Gaston Febus), as well as minstrels like Everli and Jaquet de Noyon. On French musicians in Aragon, see Gómez-Muntané, *La música en la casa real*, and G. Mele, 'I cantatori della cappella di Giovanni I, il cacciatore', *Anuario Musical*, 41 (1986), pp. 63–104. The exchange could go both ways; see below, n. 79.

[31] F. Autrand, *Jean de Berry: l'art et le pouvoir* (Paris, 2000), pp. 60–1.

teenth century, sacred and secular musicians continued to thrive in this cultural orbit.

From 1380 onwards, following the death of Charles V, the late king's younger brothers, the Dukes of Anjou, Berry and Burgundy, dominated the political scene. The political ambitions of the fleur-de-lis princes translated into the cultural domain: their ever-growing desire to demonstrate their power and prestige was strongly reflected in their patronage of the arts, including music, and the splendour of their courts soon matched even that of the monarch. The recruitment of musical personnel by these personages was informed by the same discernment that led to their employment of the foremost and most advanced exponents of visual and plastic arts, such as architecture, manuscript illumination, poetry, jewellery and metalwork.[32]

Archival evidence attests to the employment of secular minstrels by the king and French royal princes throughout this period, and this was matched by the patronage of musicians to provide for musical performance of the liturgy. The role of Philippe de Bourgogne as music patron from the 1380s onwards has been extensively explored, and several composers of the pre-Dufay generation, including Fontaine, Grenon, Tapissier and possibly Cordier, have been shown to have been employed at his court or that of his son, Jean-Sans-Peur.[33] The surviving works of these composers are in the 'modern' style, which has thus come to be closely associated with Franco-Burgundian circles. Recent research has shown that following the death of Philippe le Hardi several of these Burgundian composers and their musician colleagues went on to serve in Jean de Berry's Sainte-Chapelle. The presence there of composers like Guillaume Le Grant, Cesaris, Grenon, Paullet and Fontaine has tended to reinforce existing impressions that the French princely courts were dominated by music of a simpler and essentially northern tradition. This may have been the case in the early years of the fifteenth century, but what kind of music did these princes cultivate in the last decades of the fourteenth?

The evidence of *Trém*, which is known to have belonged to

[32] See the various comments by Guillebert de Metz in his *Description de la Ville de Paris* written in the early fifteenth century, edited in A. Le Roux de Lincy and L. M. Tisserand, *Paris et ses historiens au XIVe et XVe siècles* (Paris, 1867).

[33] Wright, *Music at the Court of Burgundy*.

Philippe le Hardi, suggests that songs and motets in the Ars nova tradition continued to be cultivated at the French courts in the late fourteenth century.[34] However, though scarce, traces of Ars subtilior composers in the service of the French princes are not entirely lacking. By the 1370s, both Louis d'Anjou and Jean de Berry had their own household chapels,[35] and, as we shall see, at least two (and possibly three) composers from the Chantilly codex can be placed in their employment. Moreover, I believe that further works from this collection can be connected with these patrons by their musical and textual content. The evidence presented below concerning the patronage of these two princes suggests that the milieu of cultivation of Ars nova, Ars subtilior and modern styles was not, therefore, necessarily distinct. Indeed, the differences in style between the repertories might therefore be better accounted for by chronology – or by a composer's choice of stylistic register – rather than by disparate geographical currencies.

Louis, duc d'Anjou

After the death of Charles V in 1380, Louis, duc d'Anjou, the eldest of the three surviving brothers, was appointed regent for the period of Charles VI's minority. Louis's political standing is reflected in many aspects of his cultural patronage. We know that he collected many books and, in particular, that he built up an extraordinary collection of jewellery and other fine metalwork.[36] Relatively little is known about Anjou's patronage of secular and sacred musicians, other than isolated traces in the records, but we do know that by 1357 he already had a household chapel at his ducal palace at Le

[34] For an inventory and reappraisal of the dating of the contents of this source, see M. Bent, 'A Note on the Dating of the Trémoïlle Manuscript', in B. Gillingham and P. Merkley (eds.), *Beyond the Moon: Festschrift Luther Dittmer* (Musicological Studies, 53; Ottawa, 1990), pp. 217–42.

[35] Wright, *Music at the Court of Burgundy*, p. 55, where mention is made that Louis d'Anjou supported six singers including a 'chapellain et teneur' called Pierre le Bretois (BNF f. fr. 11863, fol. 27), and that in 1372 Jean de Berry maintained six chaplains, one clerk and two choirboys at a cost of over 2,000 francs per annum.

[36] An inventory of Louis d'Anjou's jewellery still exists in the Bibliothèque Nationale: for details, see H. Moranvillé, *Inventaire de l'orfèvrerie et des joyaux de Louis I, duc d'Anjou* (Paris, 1906). Christian de Mérindol believes the inventory was copied in 1382 by Louis himself, immediately prior to his departure to Italy; see *Le Roi René et la seconde maison d'Anjou: emblematique, art, histoire* (Paris, 1987), p. 33. On the jewellery of the French princes in this period, see R. Lightbown, *Mediaeval Jewellery* (London, 1992).

Mans.[37] By the late 1370s, Louis's chapel was sizeable, comprising a master chaplain, along with nine other chaplains and four clerks.[38] The prince's premature death in 1384 probably deprived French music of one of its leading patrons in this period. The monk of Saint-Denis attested to the prince's piety and stated that of all the princes, Louis maintained the largest number of musicians to sing the offices and that he rewarded these servants with great liberality.[39] One or other of these musicians may have been responsible for an anonymous ballade from *PR*, *Los, pris, honeur*, that bears the acrostic 'Loys de France et de Valois' and describes Louis d'Anjou's escutcheon.[40]

Matheus de Sancto Johanne

Interestingly, one of the few of Anjou's ecclesiastical musicians to be named in the historical record is Matheus de Sancto Johanne. As we have seen, Matheus is one of the Chantilly composers who served in the papal chapel at Avignon, from 1382 to 1386. A papal supplication dated 1378 reveals that prior to this he had been a clerk in the household chapel of Louis d'Anjou.[41] Recent research has shed further light on Matheus's earlier career: in 1366 he belonged to the household of Enguerrand de Coucy, who, like the Dukes of Anjou, Berry and Burgundy, was a hostage in England following the Treaty of Brétigny in 1360.[42] That Matheus was present at least for a time in England is suggested by the mention of

[37] In September 1357 Louis assigned the personnel 'lieu et habitations honnettes en son manoir et cite du Mans'. See Mérindol, *Le Roi René*, p. 44.

[38] BNF f. fr. 27509 (P.O. 1025) 'dossier de Douxmesnil' (23456), no. 4. These payments were made while Anjou was in the south (at Toulouse, Avignon, Montélimar).

[39] 'circa cultum divinum eciam jugiter insistebat et devote, assidueque Deo psallencium clericorum numero ultra omnes regni principes delectabatur, quos omnes vestibus et stipendiis annuis remunerabat habunde'; *Chronique du religieux de Saint-Denis contenant le règne de Charles VI de 1380 à 1422*, ed. and trans. M. L. Bellaguet, repr. with introduction by B. Guenée (Paris, 1994), i, pp. 328–9.

[40] *Los, pris, honeur* is in the Machaut style and is stylistically similar to a fellow work in *PR*, *Bonté de corps*, that features an acrostic and describes the heraldry of Bertrand du Guesclin, Anjou's companion-in-arms, who died in 1380. It is puzzling that the acrostic in *Los, pris* does not list Anjou among Louis's possessions, since he acquired it in 1350, though the refrain describes the heraldry of Anjou and the missing third stanza might have contained such a reference.

[41] K. Hanquet, *Documents relatifs au Grand Schisme*, i: *Suppliques de Clement VII (1378–9)* (Analecta Vaticano-Belgica, 8; Rome, 1924), p. 109, no. 347.

[42] G. Di Bacco and J. Nádas, 'The Papal Chapels and Italian Sources of Polyphony during the Great Schism', in R. Sherr (ed.), *Papal Music and Musicians in Late Medieval and Renaissance Rome* (Oxford, 1998), p. 47 n. 7.

the name 'Mathieu de Seintjon' in a letter of safe-conduct to France dated 1368 written on behalf of Coucy's mother-in-law, Queen Philippa.[43] Matheus's contact with Louis d'Anjou during or before this sojourn in England presumably facilitated his later entry into the prince's household chapel.

Matheus was not the only musician to join Louis d'Anjou's service after spending time in England during the captivity of the French hostages in the 1360s. A minstrel named Jean de Pountoyse who had previously been in England is identified as one of the duke's musicians in 1374.[44] Isolated records indicate that several such minstrels were employed at the Angevin court during this period. In 1370, there is mention of payment to a minstrel called Regnaudin de Compiègne,[45] a musician who apparently went on to serve Jean de Berry and to visit the Aragonese court in 1383.[46] Also in Louis' service, in 1368, was Conrat l'Alement,[47] while in 1380 there is mention of a *menestrel de bouche* named Nycholas le Viellare.[48]

Jaquet de Noyon

The presence of secular minstrels in the prince's pay is hardly surprising, since the extant records indicate that most princes, along with the king and other nobles, had at least a few such musicians in their service.[49] Of rather greater significance for us

[43] A. Wathey, 'The Peace of 1360–1369 and Anglo-French Musical Relations', *Early Music History*, 9 (1989), pp. 144–50. The two rotuli that connect Matheus with Enguerrand dated 1366 were probably written during one of Enguerrand's periodic visits to his domains in northern France. Matheus's documented presence in England makes it all the more likely that he was the self-professed Frenchman who wrote a motet *Are post libamina*, which is ascribed to 'Mayshuet' and survives in the Old Hall manuscript.

[44] BNF, collection Clairambault 215, no. 83. The record of payment was made the same day as that to Jaquet de Noyon, mentioned below. On Pountoyse in England, see Wathey, 'The Peace of 1360–1369', pp. 134, 148.

[45] BNF f. fr. 11863, fol. 26^r.

[46] The Aragonese records mention payment to three minstrels of Jean de Berry in 1383, Raynaldinus de Compenya, Peraylardus and Bauderius; see Gómez-Muntané, *La música en la casa real*, p. 72.

[47] This may be one and the same as Conrrad, a German minstrel of the count of Foix, who visited the court of Navarre in 1361; see Anglès, *História de la música medieval en Navarra*, p. 362.

[48] M. Douet-d'Arcq, *Choix des pièces inedites relatifs au règne de Charles VI* (Paris, 1863), i, pp. 185–6.

[49] For a list of Anjou's minstrels, see B. Prost, *Inventaires mobiliers et extraits des comptes des ducs de Bourgogne de la maison de Valois* (Paris, 1902), i, pp. 240–1. For minstrels serving other French nobles, see also the documents presented in Appendix B of Wright, *Music at the Court of Burgundy*, pp. 179–211 and in Gómez-Muntané, *La música en la casa real*, pp. 68–73.

is the presence in Louis's employ of the minstrel Jaquet de Noyon. A record of payment made in Nîmes (Languedoc) and dated 28 October 1374 identifies Jaquet de Noyon as a string-player of Louis d'Anjou; the document instructed that he was to be rewarded for entertaining the duke and paid 60 gold francs to buy a harp and to travel to the minstrel schools.[50]

It seems plausible that this minstrel was the composer of the song *Puisque je sui fumeux* from Chantilly 564, which, as mentioned earlier, is jointly attributed to the papal singer Jean Simon de Hasprois.[51] Though we cannot be certain, it is entirely possible that Jaquet's time at the court of Anjou overlapped with that of Matheus de Sancto Johanne. Moreover, another connection with composers represented in the Chantilly collection occurs in a payment record of the court of Navarre that indicates that he visited there on the same day in 1383 as fellow harpist Jacob de Senleches. In any case, it is clear that the Jaquet de Noyon named in the Angevin record in 1374 is the same as the string-player and harpist of that name who served Johan of Aragon between 1377 and 1379 and again in 1393, and Giangaleazzo Visconti in the 1380s.[52] The story of this musician's itinerant career provides a fascinating case study of the fluidity of movement between northern and southern courts, and so it seems appropriate to explore it here in some detail.

How precisely Jaquet's transfer from the Angevin to the Aragonese court came about is unknown, but it seems that he was not alone in making such a career move. Two other minstrels documented in Louis's service between 1368 and 1370, Thomassin de Chaumont and Thibaut de Varennes, had transferred to the household of Johan of Aragon some time earlier; in 1371, these two musicians formed part of the first four-minstrel consort (*cobla*)

[50] BNF, collection Clairambault 131, no. 134.

[51] An inscription following the text residuum attributes the text to Hasprois and – implicitly – the music to Noyon; for the arguments for this interpretation, see Plumley and Stone, *The Manuscript Chantilly 564*.

[52] Jaquet de Noyon is mentioned in a document of payment from the court of Aragon dated December 1377 that pays him for three months' service. In March 1378 he formed part of an ensemble of musicians that travelled to the minstrel schools in Bruges; in July 1379, he again attended the minstrel schools. After working for Giangaleazzo in the 1380s, Jaquet returned once more to serve Juan of Aragon in 1393. See Gómez-Muntané, *La música en la casa real*, pp. 55, 141 and 145–6.

established by Johan in February of that year.[53] Such musical exchanges between the two courts at this time were facilitated by Louis's appointment as lieutenant of Languedoc in 1364 and the proximity of his residences in Toulouse, Montpellier and Carcassonne to that of Johan of Aragon in Perpignan. Close ties already existed between the two courts.[54] In 1352, Louis had been officially betrothed to one of the daughters of Pedro IV, but the planned marriage was interrupted by the events following the battle of Poitiers (1356) and by his subsequent marriage to Marie de Blois. Relations between Aragon and Anjou remained unsoured, however, and between 1365 and 1370 there was a regular exchange of ambassadors between the court of Barcelona and Anjou's southern court. From 1370, however, Louis's territorial ambitions in Roussillon brought him into conflict with his southern neighbour, and for most of that decade relations were extremely bitter.[55] Matters only improved in 1379 when Clement VII promised Anjou the kingdom of Adria in Italy, drawing the prince's attentions elsewhere. Marriage negotiations then resumed, this time between Louis's eldest son and Johan's daughter.

The transfer of the Angevin musicians to the court of Aragon in the 1370s may have been continuing a tradition of musical exchanges that perhaps began when Louis first settled in the Languedoc in the mid-1360s. By the time Jaquet moved south in the late 1370s, however, relations between the two courts were bad. That Jaquet left Anjou's service without the prince's blessing

[53] Thomassin de Chaumont and Thibaut de Varennes (Vaurenes) are referred to in an Angevin court record dated 1368 (BNF, collection Clairambault 215, no. 8); Thibaut is referred to again in 1370 (BNF, f. fr. 11863, fol. 26ʳ). It seems that they had passed into the service of the infante Johan of Gerona by 1371 (Gómez-Muntané, *La música en la casa real*, p. 33). Thomassin is described in a letter from Johan dating from later that year as 'feel ministrer nostre Thomas de Jaumont' (*ibid.*, p. 132); he is mentioned twice as 'Thomasi' in letters dated 1372 (*ibid.*, p. 133). Thibaut went on to work for Johan's brother Martin (the future king Martin I), for whom he was still working in 1382.

[54] The following account concerning Aragonese and Angevin relations is based on that given in E. Labande, *La politique mediterranéenne de Louis Iᵉʳ d'Anjou et le rôle qu'y joua la Sardaigne* (Cagliari, 1957), pp. 4–20.

[55] Anjou supported the deposed Jacques III of Majorca against Aragon. After Jacques's invasion of Roussillon, lands lying on Aragon's border, and his subsequent death in 1375, Louis d'Anjou bought the rights from Jacques's successor and swore to invade Roussillon within two years. He was distracted from this mission, however, by political events elsewhere but relations with Aragon had by now grown bitter. In 1376, the case between Anjou and Aragon was brought before the Pope and over the next few years mediations continued but the situation remained tense as Anjou continued his intrigues.

is implied by a letter from Johan to the Viscount of Canet, a coastal town west of Perpignan, dated March 1378, just a few months after Jaquet's move to Aragon. In the letter, Johan explained that Jaquet de Noyon was setting off for the minstrel schools and desired to travel by sea from Canet-de-Mar to Aigues-Mortes to avoid taking the usual land route via Beziers, where he knew the duc d'Anjou and his men to be.[56]

We can only speculate as to when and where Jaquet participated in the composition of the Chantilly song *Puisque je sui fumeux*. The ballade text, apparently by Hasprois, features eleven-line stanzas, suggesting a date of *c.*1390.[57] The text attests to Hasprois's familiarity with the poetic scene in the royal milieu in and around Paris, for it echoes a series of poems by Deschamps written between 1368 and the late 1380s, probably in connection with a society for comic verse (*puy des sots*) based in Vertus.[58] Jaquet might

[56] The letter is transcribed by M. C. Gómez-Muntané in 'Quelques remarques autour du virelai "Tel me voit et me regarde" de Senleches, un exemple de l'avant-garde musicale au temps du Gaston Fébus (1343–91)', in J.-P. Darrigand (ed.), *L'amour courtois des troubadours à Fébus. Actes des recontres-communications de image/imatge à Orthez* (Orthez, 1995), pp. 146–7. The enmity between Aragon and Anjou at this time affected certain other decisions taken by Johan concerning his musical personnel. In August 1379, Johan contracted his representative in the curia, the Viscount of Roda, to obtain six good singers from Avignon for his chapel; see Gómez-Muntané, *La música en la casa real*, p. 198. He instructed that some were to be unmarried and able to play instruments, and that they were to bring with them all the chants of the Mass and a book containing motets and chansons; but Johan was at particular pains to specify that *none* of them should have served the Duke of Anjou. See Gianpaolo Mele's correction to Gómez-Muntané's reading of Johan's request for notated music, which clarifies that he asked for two separate collections, one containing liturgical music and the other secular songs, in 'Una precisazione su un documento di Giovanni duca di Gerona e primogenito d'Aragon riguardante la sua cappella musicale', *Anuario Musical*, 38 (1983), pp. 255–60. In November 1379, Johan also wrote to Cardinal Pedro de Luna requesting him to free one of his singers to join his court (Gómez-Muntané, *La música en la casa real*, p. 200); this may have been Johannes Rogier de Wattignies, who was in Pedro de Luna's service in 1378 and is later documented in Aragon; see Wright, *Music at the Court of Burgundy*, p. 62. Wattignies later served in the chapel of Benedict XIII (Pedro de Luna), alongside Hasprois and Haucourt, and was resident at Laon cathedral alongside Haucourt in the first decade of the fifteenth century; see Plumley, 'From Court to Cathedral: Musicians *c*1400 and the Politics of Princely Power', forthcoming.

[57] As Gilles Dulong points out, this is a rare form for the ballade; there is only one other example in the Chantilly codex (*Toute clerte m'est obscure*). Further examples can be seen among the works of Deschamps and Charles d'Orléans and in the *Livre des Cents Ballades*. See Dulong, 'La ballade polyphonique à la fin du Moyen-Âge. De l'union entre musique naturelle et musique artificielle' (thèse de musicologie, Université de Tours François-Rabelais, Conservatoire National Supérieur de Musique et de Danse de Paris, 2000), pp. 170–2.

[58] See I. S. Laurie, 'Eustache Deschamps: 1340?–1404', in D. M. Sinnreich-Levi (ed.), *Eustache Deschamps, French Courtier-Poet: His Work and his World* (New York, 1998), pp. 4–5. Vertus, near Reims, was Deschamps's county of origin and it was also closely linked with the house of Orléans, since it belonged to Duchess Valentina's father, Giangaleazzo Visconti.

have encountered the text when he stopped off in Avignon on his trips northward to the minstrel schools, or at one of the princely courts in Paris, where the musicians of both Johan of Aragon and Giangaleazzo Visconti were frequent visitors. Jaquet's whereabouts after 1393 remain unknown; he may have returned to Visconti service or to French princely circles.[59] Whether or not our song – or at least its text – originated in Paris is unknown, but the presence of its lyric in two poetry anthologies indicates its continued circulation in the orbit of the royal courts in Paris well into the 1420s.[60]

Other Chantilly songs linked to Louis d'Anjou

Several other composers in Chantilly 564, in addition to Matheus de Sancto Johanne and Jaquet de Noyon, may be linked to the musical patronage of Louis d'Anjou. As I have discussed elsewhere, the three *En attendant* songs by Philipoctus de Caserta, Jacob de Senleches and Galiot cite the well-known rondeau *Esperance*, which itself seems to have Valois connections.[61] I believe the *En attendant* songs date from the time of Louis d'Anjou's coronation as king of Naples and Sicily in March 1382, following the prince's entry into Avignon and his reception by the Pope a month earlier.

Philipoctus' *Par le grant sens d'Adriane* refers to the imprisonment of Jeanne of Naples by Charles of Durazzo and names Louis as her rescuer,[62] allowing the song to be dated to around February 1382, when Charles VI pledged support for Louis d'Anjou's Italian

[59] It even seems conceivable that Jaquet returned to the service of Louis d'Anjou after leaving that of Johan of Aragon in 1379; in July of that year, the latter wrote to a merchant of Montpellier, a city belonging to Anjou, to request news of Jaquet and his colleagues.

[60] See M. Connolly and Y. Plumley, 'Crossing the Channel: French Lyrics in England in the Early Fifteenth Century', in P. Ainsworth and G. Croenen (eds.), *Patrons, Authors and Workshops: Books and Book Production in Paris circa 1400* (Leuven, in press).

[61] Louis of Bourbon adopted the motto 'Esperance' in 1366 following his return to France after his sojourn as hostage in England. Evidence from the 1380s reveals that this device and another Bourbon device, the flying stag, was also used by Charles VI (on the latter device see n. 65); see Y. Plumley, 'Citation and Allusion in the Late Ars Nova: The Case of *Esperance* and the *En attendant* Songs', *Early Music History*, 18 (1999), pp. 287–363. On the Valois use, see also A. Hedeman, *Of Counselors and Kings: Three Versions of Pierre Salmon's* Dialogues (Urbana-Champaign, 2001), p. 92. The rondeau *Esperance* also alludes to the text of Machaut's ballade *En amer a douce vie*.

[62] See N. Wilkins, 'Some Notes on Philipoctus de Caserta (*c*1360?–*c*1435) with the Ballade Texts and an Edition of the Regule Contrapuncti', *Nottingham Medieval Studies*, 8 (1964), pp. 82–99.

campaign. Philipoctus' ballades *En atendant souffrir* and *Par les bon gedeons* and Matheus de Sancto Johanne's *Inclite flos* probably date from a similar time since they evoke the alliance formed between Louis d'Anjou, Bernabò Visconti, Amadeus of Savoy and Clement VII in that same month.[63] Philipoctus' presence in this Angevin–Avignon milieu is further suggested by a citation of text from his ballade *En remirant* in Matheus's ballade *Sans vous ne puis*;[64] perhaps he came over in the service of one of the Neapolitans who frequented the Angevin court at this time.

I propose that the complex of songs that can be linked to the *En attendant* series suggests that at least a portion of the songs from the Chantilly codex were written at a similar time by a network of composers frequenting the same cultural and political milieu. This group included Philipoctus de Caserta, Jacob de Senleches, and Matheus de Sancto Johanne, all of whom, as we have seen, have a connection with Avignon. Galiot, about whom nothing is known, also participated in this series, as apparently did the elusive J. O. or J. Cun, who modelled the text of *Se Genevre* on that of the anonymous ballade *Se Lancelot*, a song clearly familiar to French royal patrons.[65] One might also add to this circle of composers Haucourt, Jaquet de Noyon and Hasprois. As we have seen, from 1382 Matheus de Sancto Johanne moved to the papal chapel, where he probably overlapped with Haucourt and Hasprois.[66] This contact would explain the pairing of two 'isorhythmic' rondeaux by Matheus and Haucourt in the Chantilly codex,

[63] It was in February 1382 that King Charles VI sent assurances of support for Louis's mission to release Jeanne of Naples, who had been imprisoned by a rival claimant to the throne, Charles of Durazzo. In a paper read at the conference on fourteenth- and fifteenth-century music, Novacella, 2000, John Nádas and Giuliano Di Bacco presented new findings that indicate that Matheus transferred to the papal court at the time of Louis d'Anjou's departure for Italy.

[64] See Plumley, 'Ciconia's *Sus une fontayne* and the Legacy of Philipoctus de Caserta', in Philippe Vendrix (ed.), *Ciconia, musicien de la transition* (Paris, in press), and the discussion below. In a paper presented at the conference The Chantilly Codex Reconsidered, Giuliano Di Bacco traced a Philippus Andree to Avignon in this period; the *Tractatus de diversis figuris* (*Tractatus figurarum*) is variously attributed to Philippus Andree and to Philipoctus de Caserta.

[65] *Se Lancelot* is listed in the index of *Trém*, a source believed to have originated close to the royal court; as in the case of *Esperance*, the text may also relate to one of the heraldic devices used by Charles VI and Louis of Bourbon; see Plumley, 'Citation and Allusion', pp. 344–5.

[66] Ursula Günther suggests that Hasprois and Haucourt were in Avignon by 1391 at the latest. See 'Zur Biographie', pp. 186–7.

and an apparent intertextual relationship between that of Matheus and another rondeau by Haucourt that survives in *Ox*.[67] Finally, the collaboration between Jaquet de Noyon and Hasprois (both colleagues of Matheus at one time or another) strengthens the impression that a significant number of songs from Chantilly 564 derived from a relatively circumscribed set of composers.

Louis d'Anjou's presence in the south – and, in particular, the constant exchanges that took place between his headquarters at the royal chateau of Beaucaire and the papal court following Clement's election in 1378 and especially after Louis's appointment as heir to Provence and Naples two years later – seems to provide a context for some of this musical activity and exchange.[68] What is apparent in any case is that the *En attendant* complex was intended for the same cultural circles that cultivated and appreciated songs of the 'simpler' Ars nova tradition: *Esperance* and *Se Lancelot*, with their royal connections, were clearly well known both to the Ars subtilior composers responsible for the series and, we must presume, to its intended audience.

Jean, duc de Berry

After Louis d'Anjou's premature death in 1384, his younger brothers Jean de Berry and Philippe de Bourgogne emerged as the dominant figures in the French political scene. Philippe de Bourgogne's importance as a musical patron in the last two decades of the fourteenth century has long been recognised.[69] Several composers associated with the 'modern' style of the pre-Dufay generation – including Fontaine, Tapissier, Carmen and possibly Cordier – were in Philippe's service in the last years of the fourteenth century. The notion that music at the Burgundian court essentially reflected the northern tradition has seemed corroborated by the absence of any Ars subtilior composers in the records. However, it remains possible that the composer Magister Franciscus from the Chantilly codex was the Burgundian singer Jean François; moreover, it should not be overlooked that this and several other singers in the Burgundian chapel moved in the same circles as the

[67] See Plumley, 'Intertextuality in the Late Fourteenth-Century Chanson'.

[68] On the constant communication between the Angevin and papal courts, see A. Coville, *La vie intellectuelle dans les domains d'Anjou-Provence de 1380 à 1435* (Paris, 1941), pp. 7, 20.

[69] Notably, Wright, *Music at the Court of Burgundy*.

composers Haucourt and Hasprois, with whom their career paths frequently crossed.[70]

Jean de Berry's stature as a music patron has only very recently begun to emerge. Two recent studies have revealed that the prince, who previously was noted for his patronage of the visual and decorative arts, employed some of the leading musician-composers of the early fifteenth century at his Sainte-Chapelle in Bourges. This included several musicians known to us from songs preserved in *Ox*, notably Jean Cesaris, Guillaume le Grant, Nicolas Grenon and Paullet.[71] Writing after Jean de Berry's death in 1416, the chronicler of Saint-Denis commented how the prince's piety prompted him to maintain a great number of chaplains to sing God's praises and the Mass day and night; he noted too how the prince took care to compliment these servants when the service was longer or more elaborate than usual.[72] Jean de Berry's obvious concern to employ the best musicians of the day in the last years of his life renders it surprising that so little evidence has come to light to link him with the song repertory of the 1380s and 1390s, the period of his political ascendancy.

The duke of Berry's newly acquired status in the 1380s was reflected in the intensification of a programme of building that he had begun in the 1370s. The prince employed some of the leading sculptors, painters and other artisans of the day to embellish his various hotels and chateaux in and around Paris and in his territories, edifices that quickly became renowned for their splendour. Musical patronage represented another means by which such a powerful political figure could enhance his political prestige. Such motivation surely underlay Philippe de Bourgogne's decision to establish a full household chapel following his inheritance of

[70] On this, see in particular Plumley, 'From Court to Cathedral'.

[71] See P. Higgins, 'Music and Musicians at the Sainte-Chapelle of the Bourges Palace, 1415–1515', in *Atti del XIV Congresso della Società Internazionale di Musicologia*, iii (Turin, 1990), pp. 689–701; and F. Pilleboue, 'La Sainte-Chapelle de Bourges: maîtrise et musiciens (XVe–XVIe siècles)' (unpublished doctoral diss., École Nationale des Chartres, 1990); I am very grateful to Mlle Pilleboue for making her dissertation and her research notes available to me.

[72] 'Circa Dei servicium devote semper intentus, magnum capellanorum numerum in domo sua habebat, qui diurno, nocturno quoque tempore, sibi laudes divinas et missarum sollempnia altissonis vocibus decantabant; quos et tociens collaudabat quociens illa honestius et prolixius solito peragebant.' *Chronique du religieux de Saint-Denis*, vi, pp. 32–3.

Flanders in 1384.[73] In this act, Philippe was years behind his elder brothers: as we have noted, Louis d'Anjou had established his own household chapel by the 1360s, while Jean de Berry had formed a household chapel of six chaplains, one clerk and two choirboys by 1372.[74]

From the beginning, Jean de Berry's chapel formed an integral part of his court. When the prince set off on his regular journeys to his various estates or to the south, the personnel of his chapel travelled with him. Thus in 1385, when the Duke of Berry, then in his second lieutenancy of Languedoc, spent three months in Toulouse, the members of the chapel numbered among the 150 courtiers in his retinue.[75] Within each of the prince's main residences the chapel enjoyed a privileged physical position within the courtly space. In the 1380s, a new chapel was built for the chateau at Mehun-sur-Yèvre (Berry) and an even grander Sainte-Chapelle was provided for Berry's palace at Riom (Auvergne). In the 1390s, as Berry reached the pinnacle of his political power, his political ambitions were mirrored in his plans for a second Sainte-Chapelle, this time for his new palace at Bourges; this was to be modelled on the chapel of the royal palace in Paris. The grandiose design is explained by its intended purpose: it was to serve as the duke's funerary monument.[76]

It was to this splendid establishment that were attracted some of the leading young musicians of the early fifteenth century mentioned above and known to us from works in *Ox*. But Berry's Parisian residence, the Hôtel de Nesle, which he acquired in 1381, also possessed a fine chapel, and it was here that his daily spiritual needs were nurtured when in the capital, which, especially from 1392, became his principal residence. By the 1390s, the size of the duke of Berry's court had grown to some 250 members, a physical manifestation of the prince's powerful political position as leading

[73] Philippe recruited musicians, mainly from Avignon, to join a number of singers he had inherited from the chapel of his late father-in-law, Louis de Mâle. On Philippe's chapel, see Wright, *Music at the Court of Burgundy*, ch. 4, pp. 55–83.

[74] See above, n. 35.

[75] BNF, f. fr. 10369, cited in F. Lehoux, *Jean de Berri* (Paris, 1966–8), ii, pp. 161–2; see also Autrand, *Jean de Berry*, p. 303.

[76] The design was influenced by Philippe de Bourgogne's funerary chapel at Champnol, which was consecrated in 1388; see M. Meiss, *French Painting at the Time of Jean de Berry: The Late Fourteenth Century and the Patronage of the Duke* (London and New York, 1967), i, p. 38.

peer of the realm.[77] His household chapel reflected this expansion; by this date it comprised ten chaplains, six clerks, a *chasublier*, six *sommeliers* and a *varlet de chapelle*. Among these was Jean Charité, the composer of a 'modern-style' rondeau preserved in *Ox*, who appears to have grown up at Berry's court, and several musicians shared with the Burgundian court.[78]

All this confirms that Jean de Berry was a significant patron of musicians in the 1380s and 1390s. We have plentiful indication too that he employed minstrels also in these years but linking known composers from the period to the prince has proved more difficult.[79] Only two composers associated with the Ars subtilior generation, Jean Vaillant and Solage, have thus far been connected with this prince; interestingly, both are represented principally in the Chantilly codex.

Jean Vaillant has been identified with a *clerc des offices de l'ostel* in the duke's retinue in 1377 and with a *secretarius ac custos sigilli* named in 1387,[80] but this is difficult to confirm since the name is not uncommon. Indeed, there was a singer in the chapel of Innocent VI in 1356 named Johanni Valhant as well as a poet from the Poitou called Jean Vaillant who composed an *abregé du roman de Brut* for Louis de Bourbon in 1391, both of whom have been suggested as possible candidates.[81] Finally, there was also a singer in the chapel of Queen Isabeau in 1401 named Jehannin Vaillant.[82] It seems very probable that the Chantilly composer had Parisian connections. The anonymous poetry treatise known to us as *Les règles de la seconde rhétorique* mentions a poet-composer of the post-Machaut generation called Jean Vaillant who ran a music school in the capital. That this was our composer seems corroborated by a Hebrew text that apparently presents a late transmission of

[77] Autrand, *Jean de Berry*, p. 313.

[78] A full list of the personnel in 1398 can be seen in Paris, Archives Nationales, KK 254, fol. 41; see Plumley, 'From Court to Cathedral'.

[79] On minstrels in his employ, see U. Günther, 'Die Musiker des Herzogs von Berry', *Musica Disciplina*, 17 (1963), pp. 80–1. Among other records documenting his employment of minstrels are some from the court of Aragon dated 1380 and 1383; see Gómez-Muntané, *La música en la casa real*, pp. 71–2. In 1376, Johan asked to borrow two of Berry's harpists (*ibid.*, p. 181, doc. 165); in 1392, it was Johan who loaned some minstrels to Berry (*ibid.*, pp. 188–9, doc. 194).

[80] See Günther, 'Die Musiker des Herzogs von Berry', pp. 82–3.

[81] *Ibid.*, p. 84.

[82] Wright, *Music at the Court of Burgundy*, p. 82 n. 211.

Vaillant's teaching.[83] This text indicates that the master referred in his teachings to the Ars subtilior ballade by Galiot, *Le sault perilleux*, which survives uniquely in Chantilly 564. Despite the simpler style of most of Vaillant's songs, it thus seems that he was contemporary and familiar with the Ars subtilior repertory. His rhythmically sophisticated ballade in the Chantilly codex, *Pour ce que ne sai gaires*, seems to confirm his pedagogic activities. A further connection with the capital appears in a note after the residuum of his rondeau *Dame doucement / Doulz amis* in Chantilly, which reads 'compilatum fuit parisius anno domini MCCC sexagesimo nono'. The identification of the composer with the servant of the duke of Berry is thus not implausible, especially given that from the 1390s the prince made Paris his principal residence.[84]

The only explicit reference to the Duke of Berry in the Chantilly repertory occurs in Solage's ballade *S'aincy estoit*, which names 'bon Jhean, duc gentilz de Berry' and celebrates him as 'la flour du monde'. This connection with Solage is surely significant, for he is the best-represented composer in the manuscript.[85] Unfortunately, no tangible information concerning this musician has come to light. We should not assume that Solage was a nickname, since references to people called Jean Soulas or Soulages pepper the archives; indeed, there was a canon and *bourgeois* of Reims cathedral in 1388 called Jean Soulas, who may be identical with the *bourgeois* of that name who swore an oath of allegiance to Jean-Sans-Peur in Paris in 1418.[86] The name Solage may, therefore, be

[83] The most recent discussion of this text and its content is in A. Stone, 'The Ars Subtilior in Paris', *Musica e storia*, 10 (2002), pp. 373–404. I am grateful to the author for sharing this with me prior to its publication.

[84] On Berry's presence in the capital, especially from 1392, see Autrand, *Jean de Berry*, p. 307; this contradicts Strohm's suggestion that the prince spent most of his later years in Bourges; see *The Rise of European Music*, p. 63.

[85] Only *Pluseurs gens voy* and *Le mont Aon* (assuming the latter is by Solage) appear in another source, that is, in the last fascicle of *FP*, which is of course closely related to Chantilly 564.

[86] In *Calextone qui fut*, the poet-composer appears to name himself in the text ('soulage'). One of the attributions to Solage in the Chantilly codex contains the initial J wrapped into the name in a not dissimilar fashion to that found in the presentation of the name J. Senleches. The name Jean Soulas is not uncommon even in the present day. On the canon at Reims of this name (Johannes Solacii) see *Fasti Ecclesiae Gallicanae*: *répertoire prosopographique des évêques, dignitaries et chanoines de France de 1200 à 1500*, ed. P. Deportes (Turnhout, 1998), iii, p. 414, and for the bourgeois in Paris in 1418 'maistre Jehan Soulas', see Le Roux de Lincy and Tisserand, *Paris et ses historiens*, p. 385. The name Soulages also existed; Guillaume de Soulages, count of Canillac, represented Bernard d'Armagnac when the latter married Berry's daughter Bonne in 1392 (Autrand, *Jean de Berry*, p. 290).

a surname, and it is perhaps significant that there exist two villages called Soulages in the Auvergne, in what were then the territories of Jean de Berry, one near Riom (the duke of Berry's capital in the region), and the other some kilometres west; there is also a hamlet near Bourges called Solas.

Solage's ballades *Calextone* and *Corps femenin* feature acrostics that spell 'Cathelline' and there has been speculation that these works were dedicated to Catherine of France, who married Jean de Berry's second son (Jean) in 1386.[87] Catherine was a very popular name at the time so this identification is difficult to confirm. An alternative candidate might be the granddaughter of Philippe de Bourgogne, born in 1393, or the daughter of the Duke of Lancaster, whom Jean de Berry was apparently considering marrying in 1388, before he settled for Jeanne de Boulogne (see below).[88]

Two further songs by Solage strengthen our suspicion that the composer was active within the cultural orbit of the French princely courts. His rondeau *Fumeux fume*, like Hasprois–Noyon's *Puisque je sui fumeux*, is a fanciful essay that echoes Deschamps's 'Fumeur' poems. As previously noted, Deschamps was closely connected with Louis d'Orléans, the brother of Charles VI and nephew of Jean de Berry. Another connection with Louis d'Orléans is hinted at in Solage's virelai *Joieux de cuer*, which evokes the motto 'a bon droit' used by Louis's wife, Valentina Visconti.[89]

I believe the connection between Jean de Berry and the Chantilly collection goes beyond the association with the composer

[87] See Günther, 'Die Musiker des Herzogs von Berry', p. 87. Gilbert Reaney connected these two ballades with the Duke of Berry's second marriage in 1389, but this was as a result of a muddle on his part; see Upton, 'The Chantilly Codex', pp. 279–81.

[88] Froissart suggested that Berry was contemplating the match. Despite some anomalies in his account (and the fact that by September 1388 Catherine had married the Infante of Castile), it is possible the project existed; see the discussion in F. Lehoux, *Jean de Berri*, ii, p. 231. The identification of the acrostics with Catherine of Lancaster was first proposed by Léopold Delisle in his 1868 report on the Chantilly manuscript and also suggested by J. Guiffrey in his *Inventaires de Jean duc de Berri* (Paris, 1894), ii, p. 52 n. 1. It is worth noting that the name is given in its northern French or Flemish form, 'Cathelline', and, moreover, that Catherine of Alexandria was one of favourite saints of the Valois, and especially of Jean de Berry.

[89] See Plumley, 'Crossing Borderlines: Points of Contact between the Late Fourteenth-Century French Lyric and Chanson Repertories' (forthcoming in *Acta Musicologica*). Deschamps's Ballade DCCLXXI, which celebrates this lady, identifies her by using this same motto: see *Œuvres complètes d'Eustache Deschamps*, ed. A. Queux de Saint-Hillaire and G. Raynaud (Paris, 1878–1903), iv, pp. 269–70.

Solage. In the remainder of this essay, I shall demonstrate how, though there are no further explicit references to the prince in the form of citation of mottos or heraldic devices, some more subtle clues exist that enable us to connect a series of works from the Chantilly codex with this patron.

Songs for the marriage of Jean de Berry and Jeanne de Boulogne in 1389

Years ago, Gilbert Reaney suggested that both Trebor's *Passerose* and Egidius's *Roses et lis* were composed for the union of Jean de Berry and Jeanne de Boulogne in 1389.[90] Both songs, which Reaney noted share the line 'En Engaddy la precieuse vigne', speak of a wedding but in highly allegorical terms. Some thirty years later in her article about the composer Trebor, Maria Carmen Gómez contested Reaney's suggestion and proposed that the songs were composed in connection with the marriage of Johan of Aragon and Yolande de Bar, which took place in 1380.[91] Gómez drew attention to the presence of shared musical as well as textual material in the two songs. However, she dated the songs to ten years apart: *Roses et lis*, she suggested, was written in Avignon in 1380 as the bride passed on her way to the wedding,[92] while *Passerose* she related to the tenth anniversary of the union. According to this interpretation, Trebor's song is modelled on that of Egidius. My own findings permit us to refine our understanding of these two songs and to corroborate the validity of Reaney's hypothesis: I believe the songs by Trebor and Egidius were written at a similar time and that they formed part of a complex of citation songs prompted by the marriage of Jean de Berry and Jeanne de Boulogne in the spring of 1389.

As I have reported elsewhere, *Passerose de beauté* indicates that Trebor was very well acquainted with the mainstream Ars nova song repertory.[93] The textual incipit of the song is identical with that of an anonymous song transmitted in *PR* and *Pit*, and also echoes another one, *Passerose flours excellente*, which is preserved uniquely in *Pit*. A line in the third stanza, 'Soit tart, tempre, vespre,

[90] Gilbert Reaney, 'The Manuscript Chantilly', pp. 76–7.

[91] Gómez-Muntané, 'La musique à la maison royale de Navarre', pp. 145–6.

[92] As mentioned above, another song by this composer, *Courtois et sages*, is in praise of Clement VII.

[93] 'Intertextuality in the Fourteenth-Century Chanson'.

main, heure tarde', alludes to the song *Soit tart, tempre, main ou soir*.[94] Furthermore, the refrain of Trebor's *Passerose* is identical with that of the ballade *Dedens mon cuer* by Grimace, a composer represented in the Chantilly codex by a number of other works.

The reference to Grimace's song is significant, for the textual theme of *Dedens mon cuer* echoes another Machaut-style ballade that I suspect was also in the mind of the composers of *Passerose* and *Roses et lis*. As can be seen in Figure 1, *Dedens mon cuer* elaborates the same subject as the anonymous song *En mon cuer est un blanc cine pourtrait* – describing how the portrait of a beautiful lady is etched on the narrator's heart – and shares vocabulary with the anonymous lyric (indicated in Figure 1 in boldface).

I now believe that the shared textual and musical material that links *Passerose* and *Roses et lis* did not originate in Egidius's *Roses et lis*, as has usually been assumed, but was probably culled from another source or sources.[95] I suspect the source for the musical borrowings was *En mon cuer est un blanc cine pourtrait*.

En mon cuer is significant for the present discussion concerning the musical patronage of Jean de Berry, for its text makes an explicit reference to one of the prince's favourite heraldic devices, the wounded swan or 'blanc cine navré', a point that seems hitherto to have been overlooked.[96] Jean de Berry adopted this device *c.*1370 and he used it extensively until the end of his life. It appears for the first time, along with his other favourite symbol of the bear,

[94] *Soit tart, tempre* was the subject of several other citations; see L. Welker, '*Soit tart tempre* und seine Familie', in *Musik als Text. Bericht über den Internationalen Kongress der Gesellschaft für Musikforschung Freiburg im Breisgau 1993* (Kassel, 1998), pp. 322–34, and Y. Plumley, 'Playing the Citation Game in the Late Fourteenth-Century Chanson', *Early Music*, 31 (2003), pp. 20–39.

[95] In my article 'Intertextuality in the Fourteenth-Century Chanson', I too assumed that Trebor was citing from Egidius. On closer inspection, however, the shared text and music stand out in *Roses et lis*: the text presents a different orthography for its end-rhyme (*-igne*) from that used elsewhere in the song (*-eigne*), and the music also sounds like a change of gear.

[96] The scribe in *FP* wrote 'eme' instead of 'cine'; this may reflect a misreading of his exemplar (which, if in Gothic script, may easily have provoked such an error), or a copying error caused as he inadvertently replicated the corresponding syllable of line 3 that underlies the same music. Both F. Alberto Gallo in his facsimile edition of *FP* and Willi Apel in his musical edition (CMM 53/ii) interpreted the word as 'e[s]me', though this makes little sense in this context (the masculine noun *esme* signifies thought, opinion, calculation or intention). In Gordon Greene's edition of the song in *French Secular Music* (Polyphonic Music of the Fourteenth Century, 20; Monaco, 1982), Terence Scully provides the more plausible reading 'cine' but neither he nor Greene noted the heraldic implications.

Anon.	*Grimace*
En mon cuer est un blanc cine **pourtrait**	Ded**ens mon cuer** est **pourtrait'** un' ymage
Qu'Amour y a navre si doucement	Qu'il n'est nulz hom qui peust ymaginer
D'un dart d'amours que ma dame y a trait.	La grant beaute de son tresdoulz vysage
En la playe est un rubins d'orient;	**Qu'Amours** y a voulu configurer.
Un signes est que j'aim parfaitement	Le dieu d'amours y fu au deviser,
La douce flour por qui telx maulz j'endure	Qui nuit et jour songneusement la garde;
Quant je la voy en sa propre figure.	Resjouis est quiconques la regarde.
	Si ne me quier partir de son servage
	Tant com vivray, mais ades, sans fausser,
	La vueil servir de tout le mien courage,
	De trestout ce que je porray finer;
	Pour ce, li ay donne mon cuer en garde.
	Resjois est [quiconques la regarde].
	Si la doy bien servir et faire homage,
	Quant nature si la daigna fourmer
	Dedens mon cuer, qui demeure en hostage
	A tous jours mais, tout sien sans decevrer;
	Car il n'est nulz qui penser adeviner
	Que qui la voit que pres lui son cuer n'arde.
	Resjois est [quiconques la regarde].

Figure 1 Textual parallels between Grimace's *Dedens mon cuer* and *En mon cuer*

on his Great Seal, which dates from 1375 or earlier.[97] The swan device featured on many of Jean's possessions, where it was used to identify the owner: books commissioned by the prince featured the device in their illuminations and on their covers, and even his clothes were embroidered with swans. The device rapidly became a symbol of Berry's princely power: it featured in a collection of tapestries he owned known as the *Chambre des cygnes*; one year the

[97] Meiss dates the Great Seal to 1370 or earlier; see *French Painting*, i, p. 95, and ii, fig. 474. Brigitte Bedos-Rezak dates another seal of the Duke of Berry that carries both the bear and swan devices to *c.*1372; see 'Idéologie royale, ambitions princières et rivalités politiques d'après le temoignage des sceaux (France, 1380–1461)', in *Form and Order in Medieval France: Studies in Social and Quantitative Sigillography* (Variorum Collected Studies Series, CS424; Aldershot and Brookfield, 1993), fig. 4, p. 498, and the discussion on p. 485 n. 8. Jean-Bernard de Vaivre dates the seal to the mid-1370s; see 'Le Grand Sceau de Jean, duc de Berry', *Gazette des Beaux-Arts*, 98 (issue 1354) (1982), pp. 141–4 (a photograph taken from a wax impression found in the Bastard d'Estang collection in the Cabinet des Médailles of the BNF can be seen on p. 143). The significance of the duke's two devices has been the subject of some discussion. René d'Anjou's explanation that Jean adopted the bear and the swan to symbolise the name of an English lady named 'Oursine' is probably fanciful; it has been noted that St Ursin was the patron saint of Bourges, and that in any case the combination of bear and swan echoes older symbolism; see Meiss, *French Painting*, i, pp. 95–6.

prince purchased fifty such birds for his menagerie.[98] The surviving inventories of Jean de Berry's possessions indicate furthermore that he gave and received gifts bearing this device, and it is interesting to note that these included two salt cellars bestowed on him as New Year's gifts by members of his chapel, Ascelin Royne and Guillaume Ruilly, in 1404 and 1407, respectively.[99]

The text of *En mon cuer* is suggestive of some such tangible artefact, especially because of its description of the 'rubins d'orient' lying in the wound caused by Love's arrow. The duke of Berry's passion for gemstones was legendary even in his own time, and the ruby, the most highly regarded and expensive gem in this period, was his particular favourite.[100] The oriental (*balas*) ruby was the most esteemed type, and Berry owned several that were so precious and rare that they were given names. Among the many items listed in the inventories that bore the swan device are several that were embellished with rubies in the manner described in *En mon cuer*.[101] These include a magnificent gilt crystal salt cellar in the form of a vessel, set with six rubies and seventeen large pearls; on its lid was a wounded swan in white enamel set with a *balas* ruby in the wound, holding a roll bearing the duke's motto *Le temps venra* ('The time will come').[102] Amongst the prince's reli-

98 Representations of the wounded swan in the borders of Berry's illuminated manuscripts can be seen in the Brussels Hours and the Grandes Heures (see *ibid.*, ii, figs. 178–98 and 219–32 respectively. An early example from before *c.*1385 can be seen in the Heures de Milan (*ibid.*, fig. 491); in the margin is a portrait of Jean de Berry, who is identified by his escutcheon, above which is a wounded swan. On the use of the swan device on Berry's clothing, see *ibid.*, figs. 487 and 500. On the *Chambre des cygnes*, see *ibid.*, i, p. 59 and Guiffrey, *Inventaires*, ii, p. 211, nos. 27–43. On the purchase of live swans, see Meiss, *French Painting*, i, p. 32.

99 See Guiffrey, *Inventaires*, ii, p. 180, items 680–1.

100 See *Chronique du religieux de Saint-Denis*, vi, pp. 32–3, which comments on the prince's regular importation of gems, including rubies, from the Orient. See also Lightbown, *Mediaeval Jewellery*, p. 37, and for some further contemporary accounts of Berry's obsession with gems, see also Meiss, *French Painting*, i, p. 70.

101 Some of his rubies he had sculpted to form the shape of a bear, fly, heart, rose or vase; see Lightbown, *Mediaeval Jewellery*, pp. 14–16. The prince closely directed the design of his own jewels: he had one valuable ruby set with five diamonds to compose a brooch that cost him 90,000 livres tournois; *ibid.*, p. 70. A gold bear enamelled white given by Berry to Jean V, Duke of Brittany was decorated in this way, as was a similar brooch mentioned in a Burgundian in ventory of 1430, which was probably given as a gift by Berry; see *ibid.*, p. 167. In 1411, Berry had a collar with bear pendants, each of which was set with diamonds (*ibid.*, p. 288).

102 'item, une salliere de crystal, garnie d'or, en façon d'une navete et entour VI petites tournelles, garnie de VI balaiz et XVII perles grossettes et sur le couvercle une cigne esmaillee du blanc, navré d'un balay, tenant un roolleau ou a escript "Le temps venra" qui seoit sur un ours d'or.' Guiffrey, *Inventaires*, ii, p. 179, item A679.

gious artefacts (listed in the inventories under *Bulletes, petis reliquieres et paternosters*) we find reference to an item that bore a gem carved in the shape of a man and above it 'un petit cigne, esmaillie de blanc qui a un petit ruby en la poictrine'.[103]

Whether the text of *En mon cuer* was celebrating the gift or commission of a specific precious object cannot be confirmed, though the existence of such an artefact seems likely since the poet compares the wounded swan with seeing the lady 'en sa propre figure'.[104] Precisely when and for which occasion the song was written is difficult to ascertain. However, as we have seen, the presence of the swan device provides a *terminus post quem* of *c.*1370. The musical content of the song corroborates that it could not have been written much before, for the ballade is modelled stylistically on Machaut's ballades *Plourez, dames* (Ballade 32), *Nes qu'on porroit* (Ballade 33) and *Se pour ce muir* (Ballade 36), which date from the early 1360s.[105] Like Machaut's Ballade 36, *En mon cuer* is notated in the B♭ tonal type, a comparatively rare choice in the context of the fourteenth-century song repertory as a whole but a rather more common one among Machaut's songs.[106] It also uses the same major prolation that characterises these Machaut ballades, but the most striking evocation of these older works lies in the use of the highly distinctive descending motif that pervades them.[107] The very opening of *En mon cuer*

[103] *Ibid.*, i, p. 65, item 179.

[104] The linking of literary works to the production of precious artefacts may be seen in the case of Jean de la Mote's *Li Parfait de paon*, which Richard Rouse and Mary Rouse propose was composed in connection with the fabrication of a jewelled peacock by the king's goldsmith Simon de Lille in 1340 for Philippe VI; see 'The Goldsmith and the Peacocks: Jean de la Mote in the Household of Simon de Lille, 1340', *Viator*, 28 (1997), pp. 281–303. The reference in *En mon cuer* to the ruby as the sign of the narrator's perfect love for the lady ('Un signes est que j'aim parfaitement / La douce flour . . .') reflects conventional symbolism of the gem representing truth; see Meiss, *French Painting*, i, pp. 69–70. Two lyrics by Machaut also refer to the ruby: the virelai with musical setting *Foy porter* and the rondeau from the *Loange des dames* (*Lo* 82), whose refrain is 'Blanche com lis, plus que rose vermeille / Resplendissant com rubiz d'Oriant'.

[105] D. Leech-Wilkinson and R. Barton Palmer date these works to between the winter of 1361–2 and the spring of 1364; see *Guillaume de Machaut*: *Le Livre dou Voir-dit (The Book of the True Poem)* (New York and London, 1998), p. xliv.

[106] The B♭ tonal type occurs in less than 6 per cent of fourteenth-century songs overall, but it is considerably more prominent among Machaut's works. See Y. Plumley, *The Grammar of Fourteenth-Century Melody: Pitch Organization and Compositional Process in the Chansons of Guillaume de Machaut and the Ars Subtilior* (New York and London, 1996), pp. 15–16.

[107] This descending motif also appears in other songs by Machaut, but it seems that the composer was reworking this musical idea particularly intensively during the *Voir-dit* period.

Example 1 The incipits of Machaut's Ballade 33 and *En mon cuer*

echoes most closely the beginning of Ballade 33, as can be seen by comparing Example 1a and b.

En mon cuer survives uniquely in a southern source, the Florentine manuscript *FP*. However, its position in that manuscript attests to its northern provenance, for the work appears to have formed part of a small collection of French songs that reached one of the scribes as a set. These songs were used mainly as page fillers, though in the case of *En mon cuer*, a spare folio at the end of the fascicle enabled the scribe to devote a whole page to it.[108] This set of French songs includes several by Machaut and other well-circulated works, such as the anonymous rondeaux *Je languis* and *Quiconques veut* and Pierre de Molins's *De ce que fol pense*.[109] The

[108] The songs in question are those copied by hand E, according to John Nádas's identification of hands in 'The Structure of MS Pantiatichi 26 and the Transmission of Trecento Polyphony', *Journal of the American Musicological Society*, 34 (1981), pp. 393–427.

[109] *De ce que fol pense* also is transmitted in Chantilly, but unlike those songs common to *FP* and Chantilly (that is, those copied into *FP* by hand E), it seems to have followed a distinct line of transmission. On the relationship between these two sources, see Plumley and Stone, *The Manuscript Chantilly*.

general quality of the textual readings suggests that the songs were transmitted in an exemplar of French origin.[110] Like its companions, *En mon cuer* doubtless enjoyed a wider circulation in its day than is now implied by its unique survival in this source; it too surely originated in French princely circles and continued to have currency in that milieu.

The relationship between *En mon cuer*, Trebor's *Passerose de beauté* and Egidius's *Roses et lis* is essentially a musical one, though there are also some textual echoes (compare Figures 1 and 2). The first stanza of *Passerose* refers to a 'cygne' and, as in Egidius's setting, the 'flour' forms the principal subject of the poet's discourse; the loss of the second and third stanzas of *En mon cuer* of course may obscure the existence of more extensive textual interrelationships.

The musical relationship between *En mon cuer* and *Passerose de beauté* and *Roses et lis* is rather more striking. The distinctive phrase that accompanies the setting of 'En Engaddy la precieuse vigne' in Egidius's *Roses et lis* is taken, I believe, from the *ouvert* ending of *En mon cuer* (that is, at the first ending of the *prima pars*); see Example 2, motif (*x*).

While Egidius restricted his borrowing to this one instance, Trebor exploits the anonymous song much more extensively. Scholars have noted the extent to which he reworks his motivic material throughout *Passerose*, but they have not been aware of the inspiration behind this song; comparison with *En mon cuer* suggests that Trebor modelled his song closely on the older work (see Examples 3a and 3b, where common motivic material is labelled).[111]

Passerose shares with the older song its B♭ tonal type, but especially striking is the systematic way in which it culls musical

[110] In a paper presented at the conference The Chantilly Codex Reconsidered, Thomas Brothers suggested that the presentation of certain accidentals (what he termed 'French'-style flats) in these works confirmed that the scribe had direct access to French exemplars.

[111] Both Gómez-Muntané ('La musique à la maison royale de Navarre') and Gilles Dulong ('La ballade polyphonique à la fin du Moyen-Âge') have commented on the reuse of material in *Passerose de beauté*. Dulong notes the recurrence of material first heard at the opening (which he assumes is a citation from *Roses et lis*) in the refrain, and comments that by doing this *Passerose* adopts 'une forme circulaire plus marquée que d'autres texts . . . tout se passe comme si le premier vers sonnait comme un refrain, comme s'il pouvait se confondre avec le refrain' (pp. 254–5). He suggests that the principle of basing the refrain on material from the opening of the ballade as seen in *Passerose* is also found in *En l'amoureux vergier*, a song I link to this complex below; *ibid.*, pp. 255–6.

Trebor

Passe**rose** de beauté, la noble **flour**,
Margarite plus blanche que nul cygne,
Dont Jupiter l'espousa par sa **valor**
Ens Engaddy, la precieuse vigne:
Car du printemps a tous monsstre la douçour
Pour esbahir cuer qui vray amour garde,
Resjouis est quicunqes la regarde.

En son cler vis sont trestuy li gay sejour,
Plaisance, **odour**, honnesté ytres benygne,
Car nature en la produyre mist vigour;
Quant la fourma, y tint sa droyte ligne,
Son dir', compas, mesure et playsant labour,
En son faystis corps droyt com lance e darde:
Resjouis est quicunqes la regarde.

Humble mayngtieng, son doulz renon son atour,
Son noble pris, sa redoubtee **ensigne**
Ne porroit nulz racomter, ne la auctour
Fleytrir ne puet par froidure que vigne.
Tous biens en ly sont composés sanz descours.
Soyt tant tempre, vespre, main heure tarde,
Resjouis est quicunqes la regarde.

Egidius

Roses et lis ay veu en une **flour**
Qui moult flurist et veut fructifier,
Fruis composés de flourie **valour**
Qui les mourans feront vivifier,
Se le soloil l'acompaigne
En Engaddy la precieuse vingne,
Dont la flour fait les mors ressusciter.
Si lo la flour plus que ne puis dicter.

Moult est noble et souverayne **oudour**;
Tost espandra quant le grant jardinier
L'uis ouvrera qui l'enclost en destour
[Et] ses buissons fera rarifier.
Que l'umbre plus ne l'atiengne
Qui le bon fruit empiesche qu'ore viegne
Tel com souloit la flour jadis porter.
Si lo la flour [plus que ne puis dicter].

Le tamps est pres que l'esté oit retour.
L'iver s'en va qui seult mortifier
Lez flours au frive; aspirent par honnour
Et pour neistre veulent redifier
Et [moult] hault lever **l'ensengne**
Qui du ciel vient, a ce qu'a tous souviegne
Que sur tout ce est de magnifier.
Si lo la flour plus que ne puis diter.

Figure 2 The texts of *Passerose de beauté* and *Roses et lis*

Example 2 *Ouvert* ending of *En mon cuer* and related material in *Roses et lis*

material from its model. Trebor introduces a variant of the *ouvert* phrase of *En mon cuer* (motif *x*) in bar 3 (labelled (*x*)), following this immediately with a reference to bars 6–11 in *En mon cuer* (a^1), which itself develops motivic material from the Machaut ballades (motif *a*), first presented in the preceding phrase (bars 2–5). Trebor mirrors the tonal events of bars 14–19 of *En mon cuer*, featuring the same descent to the fifth below the final in the cantus (motif *b*), followed by a brief allusion to motif *x*. Towards the end of the *prima pars* Trebor introduces material from the pre-refrain phrase of *En mon cuer*, alluding to the cadence on D (motif *d*, which

Example 3a *En mon cuer*

Example 3a *Continued*

Example 3b Trebor's *Passerose de beauté*: interrelationships with *En ma cuer*

Example 3b *Continued*

Example 3b *Continued*

is the 'Phrygian' inflection of e♭–d in the cantus) and outlining the cantus descent to unison G (motif *c*). In the *secunda pars*, Trebor reintroduces motif *b*, now in exact form, followed again by a brief reference to motif *x*. In the refrain section, he presents in direct succession the main motivic material culled from his model: he alludes to motif *d*, then reintroduces motif *b*, followed once more by motif *x*, and finally rounds off the song with a recurrence of motif a^1, which likewise appears in the refrain of *En mon cuer*.

What light does the intertextual relationship that links *En mon cuer*, *Roses et lis* and *Passerose* shed on our understanding of the texts of *Passerose* and *Roses et lis*? Both songs allude to a marital union (see above, Figure 2).[112] This is more explicitly expressed in *Passerose*, which extols the perfection of the flower 'Dont Jupiter l'espousa par sa valor / Ens Engaddy, la precieuse vigne'. The 'flour' in this case, which is characterised as both a beautiful hollyhock (*passerose*) and a daisy (*marguerite*) whiter than any swan, seems to refer to the bride. In Egidius's text, the union is alluded to in less direct terms and does not yet appear to have taken place: the text speaks of a flower (*flour*) that is like both a rose and a lily (*lis*) and that is now in full bloom and desiring to bear fruit. In this case, the flower may represent the bridegroom; in stanza 2 there is a suggestion that fruit previously created by the flower had been blighted by the cold, which could be a reference to lost children ('Que l'umbre plus ne l'atiengne / Qui le bon fruit empiesche qu'ore viegne / Tel com souloit la flour jadis porter'). The flower metaphor is often used to symbolise a man, a notable example being Solage's *S'aincy estoit*, where it represents Jean de Berry. I believe Egidius's 'flour' also alludes to this prince, and that, like Trebor's *Passerose*, *Roses et lis* refers to Berry's second marriage that was under negotiation in 1388–9. By 1388, Berry had lost at least four children, including Charles, his eldest son and heir,[113] and the death that year of his first wife had temporarily suspended his potential for producing further 'fruit'.

[112] Elizabeth Randell Upton argues that they were not conceived as dedicatory works in connection with a real wedding; she implies that the two works may not have been linked, the common text merely representing parallel references to the Bible (she overlooks the musical connection); see 'The Chantilly Codex (*F*-CH 564)', pp. 283–92.

[113] On Berry's children from his first marriage, see Autrand, *Jean de Berry*, pp. 256–7. His concern that no male heir would survive him was manifest by 1386; that year he made arrangements that in the event of his death without a male heir, his lands were to revert to the crown in exchange of payments to his daughters; see *ibid.*, p. 297.

The textual parallels between *Passerose* and *Roses et lis* are all too evident, in terms of theme and vocabulary (exact parallels are indicated in bold, similarities in italic font). The flower is the main subject of both, forming the first end-rhyme, which in both cases is paired with 'valour'; as already noted, the first stanzas also share the text line 'En Engaddy, la precieuse vigne'. In the second stanzas, the virtues of the flower are described, and both texts allude to the receding winter and the return of spring, and how this will ensure the flower's survival.[114] Finally, the two poems remind the reader/listener of the nobility of the flower's 'ensigne'. Egidius speaks of the standard's heavenly origins; this is surely a reference to the sacred lineage of the Valois and the celestial origins of their fleur-de-lis emblem.[115] The refrains conclude with a slightly different emphasis: Trebor declares that all who behold the flower are rendered joyful, while Egidius exclaims that he cannot praise the flower highly enough.

The two texts were clearly written as a pair, though it is possible that Trebor's *Passerose* post-dated Egidius's *Roses et lis* slightly, since its text implies that the union had now taken place. However, the musical style of the two songs suggests that the works were roughly contemporaneous.

The historical context

How does all this fit into what we know about the circumstances of Berry's marriage to Jeanne de Boulogne? The main political strategy underpinning this alliance was the French crown's desire to improve relations with the Count of Foix, Gaston Febus. Relations with Febus had been difficult since the 1350s when the French crown appointed his enemy Jean II, Count of Armagnac, lieutenant of Languedoc, a position Gaston coveted.[116] Febus had

[114] In addition to their reference to the 'vineyards of Engaddi', both texts draw on other images from the Song of Songs, especially from ch. 2: Ego *flos* campi et *lilium* convallium (v. 1); *fructus* eius dulcis gutturi meo (v. 3); iam enim *hiems transiit* (v. 11); *flores* apparuerunt in terra nostra (v. 12); vineae *florentes* dederunt *odorem* suum (v. 13); et inclinentur *umbrae*.

[115] See W. H. Hinkle, *The Fleurs de Lis of the Kings of France, 1285–1428* (Carbondale and Edwardsville, Ill., 1991), and C. Beaune, *The Birth of an Ideology: Myths and Symbols of Nation in Late-Medieval France* (Berkeley and Los Angeles, 1991).

[116] The county of Armagnac formed part of the lands ceded to Edward III in Aquitaine, so the count was to become a vassal of the English after the treaty of Brétigny. The marriages of both Jean de Berry and his brother Louis d'Anjou (the latter to Marie, daughter of Charles de Blois, royal candidate to the duchy of Brittany) were both planned

not been appeased when, in 1358, Jean de Berry replaced Armagnac in this role; after the strategic marriage of Jean de Berry to Jeanne, daughter of the Count of Armagnac, Febus resorted to arms and began a campaign to extend his own influence in the south. Though peace was signed between Berry, Armagnac and Foix in 1360, two years later fighting resumed. By this time Jean de Berry was in England, as one of the royal hostages; in 1364 Charles V hesitated whether to appoint Febus as lieutenant in Languedoc, but decided in favour of his brother Louis d'Anjou, who, as we have seen, retained the post until 1379. When in 1380 the lieutenancy was again invested in Jean de Berry, Gaston Febus led an army to Toulouse, the capital of the region, and took the city. Despite making peace with Berry in 1381, the Count of Foix remained a thorn in the side of the French, and in particular that of Jean de Berry, over the coming years.

When Berry's first wife Jeanne d'Armagnac died in 1388 an opportunity presented itself for the French crown to resolve the problems with Gaston Febus once and for all, while simultaneously strengthening Berry's personal position. Jeanne de Boulogne was the daughter of Jean, Count of Boulogne and Auvergne and cousin of Clement VII, and Aliénor de Comminges, cousin of Gaston Febus. When Jeanne's parents separated, her mother entrusted her to Febus' care. Despite the great age difference between Jean de Berry and Jeanne de Boulogne, the match had much to commend it. The Royal Council was keen to pull Febus into the French camp and to establish peace in the Languedoc. With Louis d'Anjou dead, Clement VII wanted Jean de Berry's support for the Avignon cause. Finally, Berry himself coveted the lands in the Auvergne that belonged to Jeanne's father; legal proceedings over the prince's acquisition of Jean de Boulogne's territories were already under way at this time.[117] Jeanne's parents consented to the marriage on 24 July 1388, and three days later the intended sale of the county of Auvergne was agreed before the Parlement.[118] The dukes of Berry and Burgundy began negotiations with the

with the hope of consolidating the French position in the south and west. For this, and the events and diplomacy relating to Jean de Berry's marriage to Jeanne de Boulogne summarised here, See Autrand, *Jean de Berry*, pp. 247–68.

[117] Lehoux, *Jean de Berri*, ii, pp. 232–3.

[118] *Ibid.*, pp. 232–3 n. 1.

Count of Foix in Toulouse; they proffered an official pardon to Gaston for his actions in Languedoc and made arrangements for him to bring the bride to Avignon.

When Febus and his charge failed to appear, Charles VI and his royal council sent an embassy comprising some of the highest-ranking members of the government to meet with Febus in Toulouse. The embassy took a hard line with the recalcitrant count, reminding him of his past infidelities and false promises, and ruled that Berry was to be given the lands in Auvergne whether or not the marriage went ahead. In exchange for the bride, Charles VI agreed to forgive Gaston and to pay him the exorbitant sum of 30,000 francs. Clearly, the match was highly desired. The negotiations were settled at Orthez on 9 March 1389, and led to two acts: the first a formal alliance between Gaston Febus and the dukes of Berry and Burgundy, and the agreement by Gaston that he would hand over Jeanne in Carcassonne before 25 April; the second the marriage of Jean de Berry and Jeanne d'Armagnac.

These events provide a very plausible context for the two songs discussed above. As we have seen, in *Roses et lis* the union is anticipated and the text mentions that the sun is to accompany the flower 'En Engaddy, la precieuse vigne' and that the sun alone can ensure the flower's potential to fruit. It seems plausible that this is a reference to Gaston Febus, whose device was a gold sun and whose sobriquet alluded to the sun god Phoebus,[119] and to the doubt that existed as to whether he would hand over the bride. If this interpretation is correct then the text of *Roses et lis* was probably written in Avignon or Toulouse during or immediately prior to the negotiations between Febus and the French embassy in March 1389. The reference to the 'grant jardinier' who will give the flower freedom to reproduce may be an allusion to Charles VI and his payment to Febus for the bride. In the *Songe du vieil pelerin* (written between 1385 and 1389), Philippe de Mézières represents the king as both the great keeper of the large park (i.e. France) and as the gardener of a large garden filled with white gilded flowers (i.e. fleurs de lis).[120] 'Engaddy', which is defined as the place of the union in both this song and in *Passerose*, may represent

[119] He acquired the sobriquet on account of his blond hair; see *ibid.*, p. 156.
[120] See S. Hindman, *Christine de Pizan's 'Epistre Othéa': Painting and Patronage at the Court of Charles VI* (Toronto, 1986), p. 146.

Carcassonne or Morlaas, the town in Gaston's territory of Béarn where the marriage by proxy ultimately took place on 25 April 1389.

In fact, the 'sun' did not attend this ceremony, and neither did the bridegroom (Berry was represented by the Bishop of Autun). Following this ceremony, Jeanne proceeded with her cortege to Avignon, where Clement VII received her and hosted a grand dinner in her honour. She then made her way to Riom, where, in the early hours of June 6, the marriage was celebrated in the old chapel of Jean de Berry's palace. The festivities lasted four days and were attended by the royal embassy and various nobles and prelates from near and far. Either of these festive occasions provides a plausible context for the composition of Trebor's *Passerose*, in which the marriage apparently has already occurred.

Five dedicatory songs

The 1389 marriage also prompted the poet-chronicler Jean Froissart to write a work: his pastourelle *Assés près dou castiel dou Dable* sets the wedding into a pastoral context, casting the bride and groom as 'le pastourel de Berri / Et la pastoure de Boulongne'.[121] I suspect that this occasion was also the catalyst for a number of other works in Chantilly. As already intimated at the beginning of this essay, it seems highly likely that Cuvelier and Trebor were active in similar circles, for both penned a ballade in praise of Gaston Febus. These two works must date from before the summer of 1391, when Gaston died, but in the light of the evidence explored above, there is no reason to suppose they were written from a position of service within the court of Foix. On the contrary, I would suggest that they derived from musicians working in the Valois camp and that they too were composed in connection with 1389 wedding as part of the political strategy to cement good relations with Gaston.

Trebor's *Se July Cesar* and Cuvelier's *Se Galaas* appear to have been conceived as a pair (see Figure 3). Both are seven-line ballades with ababbcc rhyme schemes and they share one of their rhymes (*-us*). They feature certain general parallels in the text

[121] See the edition by A. Scheler, *Jean Froissart: Poésies lyriques* (Paris, 1872), pastourelle no. 14.

Trebor	*Trebor*	*Cuvelier*
Quant joyne cuer en may est amoureux,	Se July Cesar, Rolant et roy Artus	Se Galaas et le puissant Artus,
Et Jupiter, au palais de Gemynis,	Furent pour conqueste renoumez ou monde,	Samson le fort, Tristain, Ogier n'Amon,
Fet son sejour gay, playsant, deliteux,	Et Yvain, Lancelot, Tristain ne Porus	De ***hardement*** et prouesse cremus,
Au roy puissant viennent de lointain paiz	Eurent pour ardesse los, ***pris*** et faconde,	**Prisie**, doubt furent et de grant non,
Maint chevalier et dames de mout haut ***pris***	Au jor d'ui luist et en armez tous ceuronde	Dont doit on bien le **noble** et haut baron
A sa ***noblee***, dont grant est la ***renon***,	Cyl qui por ***renon*** et ***noble*** sorte	Doubter, **prisier**, portans en sa devise:
Qui ***porte*** d'or et de gueules gonfanon.	"Febus avant" en s'enseigne ***porte***.	Febus avant! Par prouesse conquise!
Son droit atour, ***son maintieng gracieux***	Prouesse, vigour le tienent au dessus;	Car en luy [sont], ce designe Febus,
De la Table Ronde est, a mon avis,	Son avis est moult grant com du roy Esmonde.	Force, pooir et dominacion,
Son ***ardement*** grant, fourt et **courageux**.	Ses anemis greve, dont moult en a mis jus;	Et par avant de chescun est tenus
En dons est larges a tous, grans et petis,	Sa forche bien pert en terre et mer parfonde.	Prous et hardis, **couratgeus** com lion.
Tant que le monde en est touz esbahis	***Ses maintiens sont toudis de la Table Ronde***,	Nuls cuer contre luy ne leve **penon**,
De la noble qu'il a soubz son **penon**,	Leess', deduit, soulas le conforte:	Car en armes **porte** qui bien l'avise:
Qui **porte** [d'or et de gueules gonfanon].	"Febus avant" [en s'enseigne porte].	Febus avant! [par prouesse conquise!]
C'est bien rayson que chans meloudieux	A ly comparer en fais je n'en truis nuls;	De haulte honour et de nobles vertus,
Qui la se tienent et touz autres delis	Deshonnor heit, de vice est quites et monde.	De sens, avis, de **largaiche** et raison
D'armonnie qui tant sont precieux,	En fait de guerre ne vint jamais desporvus;	Est aournes, de che ne doubte nus.
Et bons sonneurs tant plaisants et sobtills	D'autres vertus est il sans per ne seconde.	La fame en queurt **en mainte region**.
A servir tel seigneur soyent ententis;	N'afiert que nuls ne termene ou responde;	Par les lettres rouges sara le non
Pour ly se nomment **en mainte region**	Noblesse de ly chescun reporte:	De luy disant, a tous vous en avise:
Qui porte [d'or et de gueules gonfanon].	"Febus avant" en s'enseigne porte.	Febus [avant! par prouesse conquise!]

Figure 3 Interrelationships between *Quant joyne cuer*, *Se July Cesar* and *Se Galaas*

content (highlighted by dotted underlining) – both begin with a comparison of legendary heroes (both mention Arthur and Tristan) and praise Gaston's prowess, boldness, worth, nobility (stanza 1), both comment that his enemies are powerless against him (stanza 2) and mention his *vertus* (stanza 3). More striking (highlighted by the full underlining) are the shared rhyme words – *Artus* (line 1) and *nuls* (line 15/17) – and the citation of Gaston's motto in an identical position at the beginning the refrain. In musical terms, the songs exhibit a similar rhetorical approach to the setting of Gaston's motto, articulating it by cadences onto unstable *ouvert* sonorities (second or third degree of the tonal type).

My suspicion that these two works were written in connection with the marriage of 1389 is strengthened by Trebor's *Quant joyne cuer*. This is another dedicatory chanson, one that praises a nobleman whose heraldic colours are red and gold. As mentioned earlier, these colours have generally been understood to identify the dedicatee as the king of Aragon or Navarre. However, these interpretations have overlooked an important element in the text that clarifies the identity of the dedicatee. In fact, the text does more than simply cite the dedicatee's heraldic colours: it describes his arms, praising 'he who wears gold and a red *gonfanon*'. The *gonfanon* or *gonfalon* was a three-lobed military ensign that was attached to a lance. Early on, it was an ecclesiastical emblem in France, but in the 1090s it was bestowed by the Pope on the princes of the house of Boulogne, Godefroy de Bouillon and his brothers Eustache III, Count of Boulogne, and Baudouin, who are believed to have carried the ensign on their crusade to capture Jerusalem.[122] The counts of Boulogne were also the counts of Auvergne; Guy II d'Auvergne (1165–1224) and his successors used the red gonfalon on a gold background and this remains the emblem of the Auvergne to the present day.

In the period that concerns us here, the count of Auvergne was

[122] A manuscript of the Chroniques de Charles V (BNF fr. 2813) copied between 1375 and 1379 contains an illumination (fol. 473^{v}) depicting the extravagant *entremet* staged during the visit of Charles IV to the French royal court in 1378. This dramatic entertainment presented an enactment of the First Crusade, using among its props a full-size ship that bore the standard of Godefroy de Bouillon (red gonfalon on gold). A reproduction of this illumination can be seen in L. Hibberd Loomis, 'Secular Dramatics in the Royal Palace, Paris, 1378, 1389, and Chaucer's "Tregetoures"', *Speculum*, 33 (1958), pp. 242–55, at p. 243.

Jeanne de Boulogne's father; as shown in an illumination on the marriage contract of Jeanne and Jean de Berry, Jeanne's arms comprised the red gonfalon on gold and the arms of her new husband.[123] As we have seen, Berry's decision to marry Jeanne was in large part motivated by his desire to acquire the county of Auvergne to add to the ducal territory he had received in 1360. The Jupiter of *Quant joyne cuer* 'qui porte d'or et de gueules gonfanon' thus may represent Jean de Berry. The song is set in the month of May: by this time, the marriage by procuration had just taken place in Morlaas (25 April) and Berry was awaiting the arrival of his bride and the French embassy at Riom, his Auvergne capital. Berry, alias Jupiter, the 'puissant roy' of the gods, was thus turning his thoughts to love; the county of Auvergne was in the bag and it simply remained for it to be bestowed on him officially, as the main part of Jeanne's dowry, at the formal ceremony that took place on 6 June.[124]

This new interpretation of *Quant joyne cuer* is strengthened by a comparison of its text with those of Trebor's *Se July Cesar* and Cuvelier's *Se Galaas* (see Figure 3). Though we can concede that dedicatory songs may be somewhat formulaic,[125] the parallels between *Quant joyne cuer* and the two Febus songs is striking. Once again, the form is identical; moreover, not only are there common vocabulary but often this is located in a very similar position within the relevant poems (the parallels between *Quant joyne cuer* and *Se Galaas* are shown by boldface type, and with *Se July Cesar* by bold italic text). There are no obvious musical citations to link the songs, but there are nevertheless similar elements that may be

[123] A reproduction showing the couple and their respective arms can be seen in Meiss, *French Painting*, ii, fig. 476.

[124] F. Lehoux, *Jean de Berri*, ii, pp. 243–5.

[125] For instance, the word 'renon' (renown) appears in five songs by Trebor, all of which are dedicatory works, and otherwise only in *Lorques Artus* from the Chantilly collection. (Elsewhere, I have located the word only in two lyrics by Machaut, including his musical Ballade 34, *Quant Theseus / Ne quier veoir*, and in three lyrics from the *Tresor amoureux* and one song from *Ox*). Trebor's *En seumeillant* and *Se Alixandre*, for Johan I of Aragon and Mathieu de Foix respectively, share several elements with one another (the comment that many people from afar support the dedicatee, and the use of *vaillant* and *ardis*) and with *Se Galaas*, *Quant joyne* and *Se July Cesar*. Like *Se July Cesar*, *Se Alixandre* compares its dedicatee to heroes of romance and the nine worthies; it shares vocabulary with *Se Galaas* and *Quant joyne cuer* (*renon*, *ensenge*, *terre et mer*, *courageus*). *En seumeillant* shares with *Se Galaas* the comment that the dedicatee is as brave as a lion, as well as the reference to his largesse, which also appears in *Quant joyne cuer*.

Solage

S'aincy estoit que ne feust la noblesce
Du bon Jhean, duc gentilz de Berry,
France perdroit son **pris** et la **prouesce**,
Et le monde seroit amenry.
Quar de certain sa valour
S'estent per tout et luist com le cler [jour];
En tous fais son **noble cuer** habunde,
Quar c'est celi qui est la flour du **monde**.

Nature l'a per sa grant soubtilesce
De ses ***dons*** richement enchievy.
Vaillant et ***preux***, en bien met son adresce
Et noble ator si est prouchan de li,
Dont il n'a per ne greignour,
Ains surmonte tout home par doucor.
Ce sont graces que Dieux en son cuer fonde,
Quar c'est [celi qui est la flour de monde].

Considerer doit chescun la sagesce
De ce seignour ***courageux et hardi***,
Quar c'est un cler mirouer ou jounesce
De chevaliers doit mettre son ottri,
Son volour et son amour,
Quar il sont mis en tres souvrain **honour**
Par sa **vertu**, qui est si tres **parfonde**,
Quar [c'est celi qui est la flour du monde].

Trebor

Quant joyne cuer en may est amoureux,
Et Jupiter, au palais de Gemynis,
Fet son sejour gay, playsant, deliteux,
Au roy puissant viennent de lointain paiz
Maint chevalier et dames de mout haut pris
A sa noblee, dont grant est la renon,
Qui porte d'or et de gueules gonfanon.

Son droit atour, son maintieng gracieux
De la Table Ronde est, a mon avis,
Son ardement grant, fourt et courageux.
En dons est larges a tous, grans et petis,
Tant que le monde en est touz esbahis
De la noble qu'il a soubz son penon,
Qui porte [d'or et de gueules gonfanon].

C'est bien rayson que chans meloudieux
Qui la se tienent et touz autres delis
D'armonnie qui tant sont precieux,
Et bons sonneurs tant plaisants et sobtills
A servir tel seigneur soyent ententis;
Pour ly se nomment en mainte region
Qui porte [d'or et de gueules gonfanon].

Figure 4 Interrelationships between *S'ainsy estoit*, *Quant joyne cuer*, *Se July Cesar* and *Se Galaas*

Trebor

Se July Cesar, Rolant et roy Artus
Furent pour conqueste renoumez ou **monde**,
Et Yvain, Lancelot, Tristain ne Porus
Eurent pour ardesse los, **pris** et faconde,
Au jor d'ui luist et en armez tous ceuronde
Cyl qui por renon et **noble** sorte
"Febus avant" en s'enseigne porte.

Prouesse, vigour le tienent an dessus;
Son avis est moult grant com du roy Esmonde.
Ses anemis greve, dont moult en a mis jus;
Sa forche bien pert en terre et mer **parfonde**.
Ses maintiens sont toudis de la Table Ronde,
Leess', deduit, soulas le conforte:
"Febus avant" [en s'enseigne porte].

A ly comparer en fais je n'en truis nuls;
Deshonnor heit, de vice est quites et monde.
En fait de guerre ne vint jamais desporvus;
D'autres **vertus** est il sans per ne seconde.
N'afiert que nuls ne termene ou responde;
Noblesse de ly chescun reporte:
"Febus avant" en s'enseigne porte.

Cuvelier

Se Galaas et le puissant Artus,
Samson le fort, Tristain, Ogier n'Amon,
De hardement et **prouesse** cremus,
Prisie, doubt furent et de grant non,
Dont doit on bien le **noble** et haut baron
Doubter, prisier, portans en sa devise:
Febus avant! Par prouesse conquise!

Car en luy [sont], ce designe Febus,
Force, pooir et dominacion,
Et par avant de chescun est tenus
Prous et ***hardis, couratgeus*** con lion.
Nuls **cuer** contre luy ne lieve penon,
Car en armes porte qui bien l'avise:
Febus avant! [par prouesse conquise!]

De haulte **honour** et de nobles **vertus**,
De sens, avis, de ***largaiche*** et raison
Est aournes, de che ne doubte nus.
La fame en queurt en mainte region.
Par les lettres rouges sara le non
De luy disant, a tous vous en avise:
Febus [avant! par prouesse conquise!]

Figure 4 *Continued*

more than mere coincidence. *Quant joyne* and *Se Galaas* share a similar sequential passage characterized by a hocket-like exchange between the voice parts (bars 18–21 (= 58–61 of the end) in the former; bars 12–16 in the latter). The half-close on low F♯ at the end of this phrase in *Quant joyne* is echoed in *Se July Cesar* in bars 32–4 and 69–70.[126]

It is tempting to imagine that Solage's *S'aincy estoit*, a song dedicated to Jean de Berry, also belongs with this group. The text form here is different, but there are certain other parallels (see Figure 4, where exact parallels with *Se Galaas* and *Se July Cesar* are shown by boldface, and less exact ones with boldface italics, and connections with *Quant joyne cuer* by underlining). First, the rhymes *monde* and *parfonde* are shared with *Se July Cesar*.[127] Second, references to the dedicatee's nobility (stanza 1), prowess (stanzas 1–2) and virtue (stanza 3) are located in similar positions to those of *Se July Cesar* and *Se Galaas*; all four texts allude to the esteem in which he is held (*pris*, *prisie*). Third, the reference to the nobleman's courage and boldness is shared with *Se Galaas*; the description of his *adresce / Et noble atour* echoes similar praise in *Quant joyne cuer* (second stanzas), while the reference to his largesse parallels similar comments in *Quant joyne cuer* and *Se Galaas*.[128]

[126] See Apel's edition in CMM 53/1, nos. 111 (*Quante joyne cuer*) and 113 (*Se July Cesar*).

[127] These shared rhymes are not enough to establish a direct connection between *S'aincy estoit* and *Se July Cesar*, since they also occur in a range of other lyrics from this period, including *Phiton, phiton* by Franciscus and Meruco's *De home vray* (which features the rhymes *habonde*, *monde*, *parfonde* and *redonde*) from the Chantilly codex. In a paper presented at the conference The Chantilly Codex Reconsidered, Elizabeth Leach argued that Trebor's *Se July Cesar* was modelled on Machaut's *Quant Theseus* (Ballade 34) on the basis of the shared rhymes *monde*, *parfonde* and *ceuronde* and the expression *et terre et mer parfonde*. Though this seems possible, given that Machaut is so often the subject of citation and allusion in the late fourteenth-century repertory, this evidence alone does not seem compelling enough to establish a deliberate relationship here: Trebor also uses *terre et mer* in *En seumeillant*, while the rhymes *parfonde*, *monde* and *suronde* also occur in *Se tu monde estre veuls en ce monde* and *Venez veoir qu'a fait Pymalion*, both in *Penn* (both lyrics are among those with the mysterious attribution to 'Ch'). One of the lyrics from the *Tresor Amoureux*, *Les preux de la Table Reonde*, has in common with the Trebor the rhymes *Table Ronde*, *redonde*, *monde*.

[128] It is worth noting too that the text of *S'aincy estoit* features the image of the sun to praise Jean de Berry, and that this same image appears in *Roses et lis*, where I have suggested it refers to Gaston. *S'aincy estoit* seems to relate intertextually to a lyric from Machaut's *Loange des dames*, *Tout ensement com le monde enlumine*. The two poems share the same form (incidentally, that of *Roses et lis*), that is eight-line stanzas (using decasyllabic lines except for line 5, which has seven syllables) and rhyme scheme (ababccdd), but also rhyme words (*habunde / monde* in stanza 1), and the sun image that represents the qualities of the lady love and the Duke of Berry in the Machaut and the Solage texts respectively.

[Solage]	*Trebor*
Le mont Aon de Thrace, doulz **pais**	Quant joyne cuer en may est amoureux,
Ou resonnent les ***doucours d'armonie***.	Et *Jupiter*, au palais de Gemynis,
A en sa court nuef **dames de haut pris**	*Fet son* **sejour** gay, playsant, deliteux,
Qui de beaute tienent la seygnorie.	Au roy puissant viennent de lointain **paiz**
La tient Phebus son **sejo[u]r**,	Maint chevalier et **dames de** mout **haut pris**
Quar d'elles vient sens, bien et toute honour;	A sa noblee, dont grant est la renon,
Dont cuer d'amant se doit esjoir,	Qui porte d'or et de gueules gonfanon.
Se leur amor il povoit acquerir.	
Les poetes qui furent tant **soubtiz**	***Son droit atour***, son maintieng gracieux
Firent leurs [labours?] et tout' leur estudie	De la Table Ronde est, a mon **avis**,
A bien savoir les amourex **delis**	Son ardement grant, fourt et courageux.
De Libefrois, la fontayne jolie	En dons est larges a tous, grans et petis,
Ou ces dames nuit et jour	Tant que le monde en est touz esbahis
Font [maintes?] chapeaux ***de noble atour***,	De la noble qu'il a soubz son penon,
Desquels avoir n'i poura nulz fayllir,	Qui porte [d'or et de gueules gonfanon].
Se leur amor [il povoit acquerir].	
La gist mes cuers, qui est tres **entendis**	C'est bien rayson que chans ***meloudieux***
Au doulz acors de la grant ***melodie***;	Qui la se tienent et touz autres **delis**
Voir **tant plaisants**, certes qu'il m'est **avis**	***D'armonnie*** qui tant sont precieux,
Riens ne me soit de ma grief maladie;	Et bons sonneurs **tant plaisants** et **sobtills**
Et si scay bien qu'a mon tour	A servir tel seigneur soyent **ententis**;
Trouveray foy, pais, loyaute, amour	Pour ly se nomment en mainte region
En cil qui scet toutes dames servir.	Qui porte [d'or et de gueules gonfanon].
Se leur amor [il povoit acquerir].	

Figure 5 Interrelationships between *Le mont Aon* and *Quant joyne cuer*

Yet more striking is the relationship between *Quant joyne cuer* and another song apparently for Febus, *Le mont Aon*, which I suggest can be attributed to Solage on stylistic grounds.[129] Comparison of the texts presented in Figure 5 reveals striking thematic and structural parallels. Though *Le mont Aon* features eight-line stanzas and *Quant joyne cuer* seven-line ones, the two lyrics share a surprising number of end-rhymes: *pais*, *pris*, *avis*, *delis*, *soubtiz* (*sobtills*), *ententis*.[130] Indeed, further textual echoes link the two

[129] Parallels with other works by Solage can be seen in both text and music. *Le mont Aon* features idiosyncratic tonal shifts and sequences that recall those of Solage's *Fumeux fume* and *Calextone qui fut*. The text uses the same end-rhyme pair *servir / acquerir* in an identical position as *Corps femenin* (last two lines of stanza 3); I have located only one other instance of these end-rhymes within the repertory, in *Bien dire, sagement parler* (also in Chantilly 564), but there the rhymes are split between different stanzas. Like *Corps femenin* too, *Le mont Aon* features the expression *cuer d'amant*, which I have located in only two other works, Cordier's *Se cuer d'amant* and the anonymous ballade *Se Lancelot*.

[130] My database of over 1,200 lyrics from the period revealed only these two examples of the use of *soubtiz* (or variant spellings) as an end-rhyme.

poems, as indicated by boldface (exact parallels) or italics (less exact parallels) in Figure 5.[131] The reference to *armonnie* is unusual in lyrics of this period: I have found only four other instances, and, interestingly, three are lyrics that praise musicians (Vitry or Machaut) and, like *Le mont Aon*, set the scene in Parnassus, home of the nine Muses.[132]

The reference to the Muses in *Le mont Aon* is significant. In Book V of Ovid's *Metamorphoses*, we learn that the nine Muses, the goddesses who live by fount Helicon, were challenged to a song competition by the nine Pierides and won hands down.[133] The song competition is, I believe, the subtext underlying and linking *Le mont Aon* and *Quant joyne cuer*. In the former, the Muses inspire and reward poets with garlands; the narrator is hopeful that he too, despite his *grief maladie*, will find *foy, pais, loyaute, amour* from the man who serves all ladies so well – presumably Gaston Phebus? It is here in Parnassus, where one hears sweet *armonie* and *grant melodie*, that *Phebus tient son sejour*. In *Quant joyne cuer*, Jupiter *fet son sejour* in the palace of Gemini (i.e. in the month of May); but it is in the retinue of this king of the gods that there resound *delis d'armonnie* and *chans meloudieux*.[134] The two poet-composers compete with one another in their attempts to illustrate the musicality of the environment they describe. At the same time it is as if they are comparing the musicality of the two patrons; *Quant joyne cuer* is most specific in attributing musical prowess to the court of its dedicatee, whom the most gifted performers (*bons sonneurs tant plaisants et sobtills*) are eager to serve.[135]

Musically, the songs are interrelated by the hocket-like sequen-

[131] Though seemingly banal, the expression *tant plaisants* I have found only in these two works.

[132] These works are Jean de la Mote's *O Victriens, mondains dieu d'armonie* and Jean Campion's *Sur Parnase a le Mote Cyrre et Nise*, both found in *Penn*, and directed to Philippe de Vitry; Deschamps's *O flour des flours de toute melodie*, which honours Guillaume de Machaut and was set to music by Andrieu in a song that survives uniquely in Chantilly 564 (all three of these poems also refer to the fountain Helicon). Two other instances of *armonnie* in Chantilly 564 are Senleches's *La harpe de melodie* and Suzoy's *Pictagoras*, both on the subject of music and musicians.

[133] See Book V of Ovid, *Metamorphoses*, trans. Frank Justus Miller, 2 vols. (London and New York, 1916), III–IV, ll. 251–678.

[134] I previously suggested that the reference to Jupiter might refer to the planet rather than the god (see 'Trebor' in *New Grove*, xxv, pp. 709–10). The relationship between the works discussed here would seem to confirm the latter interpretation.

[135] The comment concerning the duke's largesse reflects his liberality, which appears sometimes to have attracted criticism; see *Chronique du religieux de Saint-Denis*, vi, pp. 32–3.

tial exchange in the phrases leading to the sectional cadences, which, in both cases, set the textual references to music (as noted above, similar passages also feature in *Se Galaas*). More striking still is that the two songs share their unusually low tessitura and the rare grave register G cantus final, which also features in Egidius's *Roses et lis*.[136]

If, as I have proposed, *Quant joyne cuer* was written in May just before Berry's official acquisition of the county of Auvergne, *Le mont Aon* may date from earlier since Febus did not attend the wedding. Perhaps it was written in March 1389 when the negotiations at Orthez brought Gaston together with the dukes of Berry and Burgundy and the ambassadors of Charles VI. If so, then this song presumably served as the model for *Quant joyne cuer*.

Another song by Solage in the Chantilly codex that I strongly suspect to be tied in with the Berry–Boulogne marriage is *En l'amoureux vergier*. This work develops the *rose* / *vergier* theme of *Passerose* and *Roses et lis*, and also raises the theme of marriage with its mention of the *nueces de Mercure*. But closer inspection of its text reveals some more specific parallels (see Figure 6). The 'a' rhyme (*our*) matches that of both *Passerose* and *Roses et lis*. Indeed, the first end-word, *flour*, is identical, and while this may seem banal, I have found this word to occur in this position in only one other song in the fourteenth-century lyric and song repertory.[137] *En l'amoureux vergier* also shares with the other two song-texts the rhyme *valour* and, with *Passerose*, the rhymes *atour* and *tour* (bold font indicates direct parallels between the three texts, bold italics less exact ones; connections between the Solage and Egidius texts are indicated by underlining). Most striking of all, however, is the parallel with

[136] As I have suggested elsewhere, low G is an unusual cantus final in the polyphonic song repertory, occurring in approximately 6 per cent of the total fourteenth-century chanson repertory (statistics based on the contents of the series Polyphonic Music of the Fourteenth Century (PMFC) 18–22) plus Machaut's songs; see *The Grammar of Fourteenth-Century Melody*, pp. 15–16). Interestingly, half the total cases occur in the Chantilly codex. Of these works, three are connected with the marriage complex discussed here, that is, *Le mont Aon*, *Quant joyne cuer* and *Roses et lis*. The others may also derive from the same musical circles: they are *Onques Jacob* by Vaillant, *Adieu vous di* (which I suspect on stylistic grounds to be by Solage), Trebor's *En seumeillant* and Galiot's *Le sault perilleux*. Given the connections between these works and their composers, could it be that we are witnessing here a repertory composed with a particular performing ensemble in mind?

[137] This is in a ballade from the Cyprus manuscript (*Tu*, fol. 115); as discussed by Elizabeth Leach in a paper given at the conference on fourteenth- and fifteenth-century music, Novacella, 2000, this song was clearly inspired by Machaut's *De toutes flours*. The latter doubtless also influenced Solage's *En l'amoureux vergier*.

Trebor

Passerose de beauté, la noble **flour**,
Margarite plus blanche que nul cygne,
Dont Jupiter l'espousa par sa **valor**
Ens Engaddy, la precieuse vigne:
Car du printemps a tous monsstre la douçour
Pour esbahir cuer qui vray amour garde,
Resjouis est quicunqes la regarde.

En son cler vis **sont** tres***tuy* li gay sejour**,
Plaisance, odour, honnesté ytres benygne,
Car nature en la produyre mist vigour;
Quant la fourma, y tint *sa* ***droyte ligne***,
Son dir', compas, mesure et playsant labour,
En son faystis corps droyt com lance e darde:
Resjouis est quicunqes la regarde.

Humble mayngtieng, son doulz renon son **atour**,
Son noble pris, sa redoubtee ensigne
Ne porroit nulz racomter, ne la *auc**tour***
Fleytrir ne puet par froidure que vigne.
Tous biens en ly sont composés sanz descours.
Soyt tant tempre, vespre, main heure tarde,
Resjouis est quicunqes la regarde.

Solage

En l'amoureux vergier ***vis*** **une flour**
Espaunie par le cours de nature,
Droite eslevee, de vermeille colour,
Belle et plaisant et de gente fayture.
A ceste flour me mis en aventure
De l'aprouchier et son ***oudour*** sentir
Mais quant je fus dedens ce noble ***clos***,
Amors me fist si doucement ravir
Tant que mon cuer la prent tout son repos.

En ce vergier **sont *tuit* li gay sejour**
Qu'onques Amours douna a creature.
La me dreschay remirant la **valour**
De celle flour qu'en ly maynt par droiture.
Et apres luy m'assis sus la verdure
Afin qu'Amours de li me fiest jouir.
Avar! n'est rien vivant, bien dire l'os,
Que j'aime tant, ne riens plus ne desir
Tant [que mon cuer la prent tout son repos].

Et s'au jor d'uy trestout li comte **a tour**
De Europe ou d'Almene tres pure,
Ou des belles que maynt amourex ***tour***
Finent si bieng es nuepces de Mercure
Revenoient pour mi mettre en leur cure,
Tout me seroyt nient contre le pleisir
Que j'ay de li ou tout bien sont reclos,
Quar c'est la flour qu'omis ***ne puet flaitrir***
Tant [que mon cuer la prent tout son repos].

Egidius

Roses et lis ay ***veu*** en **une flour**
Qui moult flurist et veut fructifier,
Fruis composés de flourie **valour**
Qui les mourans feront vivifier,
Se le soloil l'acompaigne
En Engaddy la precieuse vingne,
Dont la flour fait les mors ressusciter.
Si lo la flour plus que ne puis dicter.

Moult est noble et souverayne ***oudour***;
Tost espandra quant le grant jardinier
L'uis ouvrera qui ***l'enclost*** en destour
[Et] ses buissons fera rarifier.
Que l'umbre plus ne l'atiengne
Qui le bon fruit empiesche qu'ore viegne
Tel com souloit la flour jadis porter.
Si lo la flour [plus que ne puis dicter].

Le tamps est pres que l'esté oit re***tour***.
L'iver s'en va qui seult mortifier
Lez flours au frive; aspirent par honnour
Et pour neistre veulent redifier
Et [moult] hault lever l'ensengne
Qui du ciel vient, a ce qu'a tous souviegne
Que sur tout ce est de magnifier.
Si lo la flour plus que ne puis diter.

Figure 6 Interrelationships between *Passerose*, *En l'amoureux vergier* and *Roses et lis*

Passerose that occurs in the first line of the second stanza; the only other instance of 'gay sejour' (but not, incidentally, in this position) I have found in the lyric or song repertory is in Solage's *Tres gentil cuer*. Despite the simpler Machaut-like style of *En l'amoureux vergier*, these parallels strongly suggest that Solage's song was written for the same occasion as *Passerose* and *Roses et lis*.[138]

That the interrelations linking *En l'amoureux vergier* with *Passerose* and *Roses et lis* are more than just coincidence is further suggested by the proximity of the three songs in the Chantilly manuscript. *En l'amoureux vergier* appears on the recto directly preceding the two successive rectos that present *Passerose* and *Roses et lis*:

fol. 20	*En l'amoureux vergier*	Solage
fol. 20v	*Phiton, phiton*	Magister Franciscus
fol. 21	*Passerose de beauté*	Trebor
fol. 21v	*En seumeillant*	Trebor
fol. 22	*Roses et lis*	Magister Egidius
fol. 22v	*Le mont Aon*	[Solage]

A similar pattern where related works appear on successive rectos is found elsewhere in the manuscript.[139] It may be no accident, then, that on the verso following that of *Roses et lis*, we find *Le mont Aon*; nor may it simply be chance that *Le mont Aon* and *Roses et lis* are two of three successive works in the manuscript (the third being Trebor's *En seumeillant*) in the unusual low tessitura with the grave register G cantus final mentioned above. Finally, slotted between *En l'amoureux vergier* and *Passerose*, we find *Phiton, phiton* by Magister Franciscus. Like *En mon cuer*, this ballade is modelled on a work by Machaut, *Phyton le mervilleus serpent* (Ballade 38), and it has generally been assumed to date from the 1370s on account of its simple style. The text criticises Phebus' enemy; this has been understood to refer to Gaston's rival Jean II, count of Armagnac.[140] This work circulated with a number of Machaut-style songs, including two others that appear close by in the Chantilly manuscript: one is *De Narcissus*, also by Franciscus, which can be dated to before

[138] A similar Machaut-style motif is found in both this song (bb. 13–14, 35–6) and in Cuvelier's *Se Galaas* (bb. 41–2).

[139] For instance, the songs by Trebor copied onto fol. 42 and fol. 43 are separated by a song on fol. 42v by Taillandier. Upton's suggestion that the bifolio containing *Passerose* and *Roses et lis* is not in its original order can now be discounted; see 'The Chantilly Codex', pp. 281–2, and Plumley and Stone, *The Manuscript Chantilly*.

[140] Reaney, 'Franciscus' in *MGG* iv (first edn.), pp. 634–6, and Reaney, 'The Manuscript Chantilly', p. 84.

1376 because of its presence in the early part of *Trém*; the other is Grimace's *Se Zephirus / Se Jupiter*, which also refers to 'Phebus'. The precise date of *Phiton, phiton* is open to question but it is worth noting that the refrain of this ballade ends in an identical fashion to *S'aincy estoit*, with the text 'la flour du monde', a phrase I have not encountered elsewhere in the contemporary song or lyric repertory.[141] Was this song also written in 1389, or was it an earlier work that was in Solage's mind when he wrote *S'aincy estoit*?

CONCLUSIONS

The prevailing impression of Ars subtilior as a localised and essentially southern phenomenon needs revision, for it now seems that this style repertory enjoyed a wider currency than previously assumed. The case study presented here centring on *Roses et lis* and *Passerose* confirms that works we have tended to associate with the 'southern' Ars subtilior style were not only appreciated by French royal patrons but were apparently composed for them. Far from representing musical backwaters in the last two decades of the fourteenth century, the French royal and princely courts were centres of musical activity very much at the cutting edge of what has been seen as the 'central' avant-garde tradition. Indeed, a broader consideration of the Chantilly song repertory as a whole supports this point, for many works can be linked to the French princely courts or to activity in or around Paris. The Appendix lists some of the main composers represented in the source for whom there exist clues to connect them with particular patrons.[142] The results reveal that a surprisingly large number of works from the 1380s and 1390s can be linked to the Valois, and in particular to Louis I d'Anjou and Jean de Berry.

[141] The only other instance I have come across is in Christine de Pizan's *Le Livre du chemin du Longue Etude* (see the edition by R. Püschel, repr. Geneva, 1974, l. 3208). Here the phrase is applied to an unnamed French prince, possibly Charles VI, to whom Sandra Hindman has suggested the book was dedicated; see *Christine de Pizan's 'Epistre Othéa'*, pp. 170–80. In the Franciscus, 'la flour du monde' has generally been understood to refer to Gaston Phebus, but one might speculate that it could refer, as in *S'aincy estoit*, to the Duke of Berry. As noted above, Febus was very bitter about the influence that he believed Jean of Armagnac exerted over Jean de Berry; the refrain 'Tu que contens gaster la flour du monde' might thus be understood as a complaint that Armagnac was 'spoiling' Berry (rather than 'tormenting' Gaston).

[142] This table takes into account intertextual connections of the kind explored in this study, in addition to the kind of textual or biographical clues usually considered.

It would, of course, be simplifying matters to conclude that the Chantilly song repertory in its entirety originated within the court of one or the other of these French princes; the collection clearly comprises works of disparate origins and, to some extent, of varying vintages.[143] Having said this, many of the songs that can be placed in the 1380s and 1390s appear to have derived from a network of composers working in close proximity or whose paths at least had occasion to cross. It seems plausible that those composers I have related to the wedding of Jean de Berry and Jeanne de Boulogne – Solage, Trebor, Egidius – were moving in the same musical circles as others familiar to us from the Chantilly collection. As we have seen, composers like Philipoctus de Caserta and Matheus de Sancto Johanne were working within the French princely orbit and also had connections with Avignon. Indeed, I suspect that two intertextually related songs by these two may have been stimulated by the same models that served in the composition of *Passerose* and *Roses et lis*, that is Grimace's *Dedens mon cuer* and the anonymous *En mon cuer*.[144] Participation in citation games of this kind may also suggest links between other Chantilly composers: a textual allusion to the anonymous song *Soit tart, tempre* very similar to that found in Trebor's *Passerose* can be observed in *Se Genevre* by J. O.,[145] while musical allusion to that model is present at the opening of Matheus's *Science n'a nul annemi*.[146]

To allocate all this musical activity to any one court is probably unreasonably reductive; indeed, it may prove more fruitful to think in terms of larger, shared cultural and political milieux than strictly in terms of geography per se. The evidence presented here suggests that many of the late fourteenth-century songs in the Chantilly codex derived from political contexts that brought together secular rulers of north and south and papal Avignon. The mobility of musicians (Jaquet de Noyon provides a good example)

[143] This is suggested by the presence of the Machaut songs and certain older, well-circulated songs, but also those later works (like Senleches's *Fuions de ci*) that point explicitly to an origin elsewhere.

[144] The two works in question are Philipoctus' *En remirant vo douce pourtraiture* and Matheus de Sancto Johanne's *Sans vous ne puis*, which as mentioned above share a line of text. The former is on the theme of gazing at the lady's portrait; like *Dedens mon cuer* and *En mon cuer* it immediately evokes the God of Love and the wound he inflicts on the lover's heart. On the *En remirant* complex, see Plumley, 'Ciconia's *Sus une fontayne*'.

[145] See Plumley, 'Intertextuality in the Fourteenth-Century Chanson'.

[146] See Plumley, 'Playing the Citation Game'.

and their patrons – notably, the long-term implantation in the south of 'northern' patrons like Louis d'Anjou and Jean de Berry – should lead us to question the relevance of polarising style repertories on the grounds of geography. Indeed, the intertextual song complexes that I have associated with one or other of the French princes – the *En attendant* and the *Roses et lis / Passerose* complexes – demonstrate that Ars subtilior and simpler Ars nova-style songs were cultivated in the same milieux.

Finally, prevailing assumptions concerning chronology in the song repertory on the basis of style may also need refining. As we have seen, despite its Machaut-like style, Solage's *En l'amoureux vergier* was probably prompted by the same occasion as the Ars subtilior-style songs examined here by Trebor, Egidius and Cuvelier and his own *Le mont Aon* and *S'aincy estoit*. The case for distinct geographical currency for Ars subtilior and the so-called 'modern' style may also deserve reconsideration. Haucourt and Hasprois are attributed songs in both styles in the Chantilly and Oxford manuscripts respectively, and it seems they moved in similar musical circles to composers of the 'modern' style usually associated with the north, like Cesaris, Paullet, Charité and Grenon.[147] Once again, intertextual relations between works may reflect personal contact or at least activity in similar milieux. *Science n'a nul annemi* by fellow papal singer Matheus de Sancto Johanne (d. before 1391), for instance, demonstrates remarkable parallels with *J'aim. Qui?* by Paullet.[148] Both Matheus and Paullet were active in French princely circles, though Paullet's presence in Jean de Berry's employ has not been documented before 1405. Neither has that of Jean Cesaris, who entered the Bourges Sainte-Chapelle in 1407; however, this composer's familiarity with those musical circles that were apparently responsible for much of the Chantilly song repertory is suggested by the presence of his ballade *Li dieus d'amour* in that collection. Not only does this song's *grande ballade* style suggest that Cesaris was well versed in Ars subtilior

[147] Haucourt was resident in the northern French cathedral at Laon from *c.*1398 to after 1417, and his colleagues there included Grenon, Charité and other musicians working at the court of Berry as well as ex-colleagues from the papal chapel. His familiarity with princely circles surely explains his admittance to the *Cour amoureuse* in *c.*1416. On Haucourt, see Plumley, 'From Court to Cathedral' and ead., 'Musicians at Laon Cathedral in the Early Fifteenth Century', *Urban History*, 29 (2002), pp. 19–34.

[148] See Plumley, 'Playing the Citation Game'.

practices, but certain musical and textual elements imply his familiarity with specific works: a musical sequence in the refrain has more than just a passing resemblance to the oft-cited opening of Philipoctus' *En atendant souffrir*, while its text refrain appears in a similar form in *Lorques Artus* by J. O., another song from the *En attendant* complex.[149] Could it be that Cesaris, Paullet and other composers represented in the Oxford manuscript were active in musical circles close to Jean de Berry in the 1390s or even earlier?[150] This might go some way to accounting for the significant number of Ars subtilior style ballades in those early layers of *Ox* that have been connected with the patronage of this prince.

University College Cork

[149] Since the shared text line ('Si en fera tres grant correccion' in the Cesaris, which appears as 'S'en fera l'on tres grant correccion' in the J. O. song) represents the refrain in *Li dieus d'Amours* and the fourth line of stanza 3 of *Lorques Artus*, it seems more likely that J. O. is doing the citing rather than the reverse; we cannot preclude, however, that both songs derived the line from a third source, though I have not located it elsewhere in the song or lyric repertory.

[150] The possibility that Cesaris had connections with the court of Jean de Berry in the 1390s is suggested by the presence of his name in a supplication by the Archbishop of Bourges dated 1394, a document that seems to have been overlooked. See Plumley, 'Cesaris', *MGG*[2] iv, pp. 606–9.

APPENDIX

Song Composers from the Chantilly Codex: Links to Specific Courts

Composer	*French courts*	*Avignon*	*Foix*	*Aragon*	*Milan*	*Other*	*Origin*
F. **Andrieu**	[Deschamps text]						
Philipoctus de **Caserta**	*En atendant souffir* (Anjou, 1382?) →	←			*En atendant souffir* (Bernabò Visconti, before 1385)		Naples
	←	*Par les bons* (Clement VII, 1378–94)					
	Par le grant senz (Anjou, 1382?)						
		Philippus Andree? (1380)					
Jean **Cesaris**	Ste-Chapelle, Berry [1407–9] ←					Archbishop of Bourges, 1394	Thérouanne
	Li dieus d'amours [link with J. O. and *En attendant* complex]					1400s Paris [Martin le Franc]	
						Angers cathedral 1417	
Baude **Cordier**	Baude Fresnel? Burgundy, 1390s						Rheims

Composer	*French courts*	*Avignon*	*Foix*	*Aragon*	*Milan*	*Other*	*Origin*
Jo. **Cuvelier**						*En la saison* (Olivier du Guesclin)	
			Se Galaas [Gaston Febus, 1389]				Tournai?
	Jaquemart le Cuvelier, *faiseur* of Charles V →	→	→	→	→	→ Jean le Cavelier? [Chronicle of Bertrand du Guesclin, Paris]	
Egidius	*Roses et lis* [Berry, 1389]	*Courtois et sages* (Clement VII, 1378–94)					
Mag. **Franciscus**	←	←	*Phiton, phiton* ('Phebus': Armagnac/Berry?)				
Galiot	*Le sault perilleux* *En attendant d'amer* → (Anjou, 1382?)	→				*Le sault* used by Vaillant in Paris	
Guido [de Lange?]		?clerk in Pope's private chapel 1363				priest Montfort-sur-Risle 1363–92, canon and resident in Rouen; canon of Bayeux (1388); prebend in Londinieres 1388–92	Normandy? (d. 1392)

Composer	*French courts*	*Avignon*	*Foix*	*Aragon*	*Milan*	*Other*	*Origin*
Jean Simon dit **Hasprois**	*Puisque je sui fumeux* [Ja. de Noyon] [Deschamps] *Ma douce amour* (early layer *Ox*)	Benedict XIII (1393–1404)		[Ja. de Noyon]	[Ja. de Noyon]	Benefices northern France, Cambrai	Haspre, diocese of Cambrai
Jean **Haucourt** (Jo. de Alte Curie)	Cour d'amour *c.*1416 *Se j'estoye* *Je demande* (early layer *Ox*)	Benedict XIII (1393–1403)				Benefices Paris (*c.*1400), resident in Laon (*c.*1401–after 1417)	Diocese of Noyon (nr St-Quentin?)
J.O. / J. Cun	*Se Genevre* [*En attendant*] ⟶ *Lorques Arthus* ? [link with Cesaris]						
Matheus de **Sancto Johanne**	Louis d'Anjou (1378) (Anjou, 1382 ?) ⟵	Clement VII (1382–6) *Inclite flos*				Enguerrand de Coucy (1366) Queen Philippa (1368)	Diocese of Noyon (d. by 1391)

Composer	*French courts*	*Avignon*	*Foix*	*Aragon*	*Milan*	*Other*	*Origin*
Jaquet de **Noyon**	Louis d'Anjou (1374)			Johan of Aragon (1377–9; 93)	Giangaleazzo (?138?–91)		Noyon
	Puisque je sui → [Deschamps]	[Hasprois] →	→	→	→	circulating in Paris, *c.*1420	
Gacien **Reyneau**				Martin I? (1399–1429?)			Tours?
Jacob **Senleches**		Pedro de Luna (1383–?) →	→	→		Castile (?–1382) Navarre (1383)	nr Calais?
J. **Solage**	*S'aincy estoit* [Berry, 1389?]					Johannes Solacci? (Jean Soulas) canon at Rheims 1382–88; bourgeois in Paris 1418?	Auvergne or Berry?
	← *En l'amoureux vergier* [Berry, 1389]	←	Le mont Aon ('Phebus', 1389?)				
	Calextone (Catherine of France? pre-1388)						
	Corps femenin (Catherine of France? pre-1388)						
	Fumeux fume [Deschamps]						
	Joieux de cuer (motto Valentina Visconti?) →	→	→	→	*Joieux de cuer* (Visconti motto?)		

Composer	*French courts*	*Avignon*	*Foix*	*Aragon*	*Milan*	*Other*	*Origin*
Trebor	Jean Robert? [Charles VI]			Trebol?, (Martin I, 1408–9)		Johan Robert? (Charles III Navarre, 1398)	
		←	*Se July Cesar* (Gaston Febus, 1389)				
	[Deschamps]	←	←	*En seumeillant* (Johan I, 1387–96)		Jean Robert? (Reims?)	
	Passerose [Berry, 1389]		*Se Alixandre* (Mathieu of Foix, *c*.1393–5)				
	Quant joyne cuer [Berry, 1389]						
Jean **Vaillant**	Secretary of Jean de Berry? [1377–]	Jean Valentis? (papal chapel, 1352–61)				Music school in Paris	
	Jehannin Vaillant? (chapel of Queen Isabeau, 1401)						

Early Music History (2003) Volume 22. © *Cambridge University Press*
DOI:10.1017/S0261127903003048 Printed in the United Kingdom

EDWARD H. ROESNER

LABOURING IN THE MIDST OF WOLVES: READING A GROUP OF *FAUVEL* MOTETS

Il finera car touz iourz vivre
Ne pourra pas.
(He will meet his end, for he cannot live for ever)

The ensemble of texts brought together in the celebrated MS 146 of the fonds français in the Bibliothèque nationale de France, Paris, makes up a complex and many-sided essay on government and kingship, one directed to the French monarch Philip V (1317–22) at or near the beginning of his reign.[1] Its various elements reflect on the problem-laden final years of the rule of his father, Philip IV 'le Bel' (1285–1314), and the troubled succession

[1] Facs. in *Le Roman de Fauvel in the Edition of Mesire Chaillou de Pesstain: A Reproduction in Facsimile of the Complete Manuscript, Paris, Bibliothèque nationale, fonds français 146*, ed. E. H. Roesner, Introduction by F. Avril, N. F. Regalado, and E. H. Roesner (New York, 1990). For a detailed description of the manuscript and its copying history see J. C. Morin, 'The Genesis of Manuscript Paris, Bibliothèque nationale, fonds français 146, with Particular Emphasis on the *Roman de Fauvel*' (Ph.D. diss., New York University, 1992). The most comprehensive examination of the manuscript in all its aspects is *Fauvel Studies: Allegory, Chronicle, Music, and Image in Paris, Bibliothèque nationale de France, MS français 146*, ed. M. Bent and A. Wathey (Oxford, 1998). The present study was completed before I had access to the important monograph by E. Dillon, *Medieval Music-Making and the* Roman de Fauvel (New Perspectives in Music History and Criticism; Cambridge, 2002), or to ead., 'Music "bien escriptez et bien notez" in Paris, Bibliothèque nationale, fonds français 146' (D.Phil. diss., University of Oxford, 1998), on which the book is based. I have tried nonetheless to include citations to her book in the notes when her discussion is complementary to my own. It was already in press when Dillon's article appeared, 'The Art of Interpolation in the *Roman de Fauvel*', *Journal of Musicology*, 19 (2002), pp. 223–63. Work on this essay was begun in conjunction with a seminar on *Fauvel* taught jointly with Nancy Freeman Regalado and Elizabeth A. R. Brown at New York University in 2001. My thinking owes much to the seminar; the contributions of individual faculty (Professor Regalado above all) and students can scarcely be adequately acknowledged here. I am also particularly indebted to M. Cecilia Gaposchkin, who shared her work on the canonisation of Louis IX with me prior to its publication. Thanks also to Margaret Bent, Barbara Haggh, and Bonnie J. Blackburn, who read this paper in various stages of its development and made numerous valuable suggestions, and to Leofranc Holford-Strevens, who improved my readings of several Latin texts.

that followed in 1315 and 1316. Each fascicle of the manuscript, the so-called *Roman de Fauvel*, the *dits* of Geffroi de Paris, the collection of songs and *dits* ascribed to Jehannot de Lescurel, and the anonymous verse chronicle of the years 1300–16, interacts with the others in myriad ways and on many levels to yield a collective commentary on the state of the monarchy and the realm, and an *admonitio* on wise rule.[2]

At the heart of the collection is a greatly expanded and lavishly illustrated version of the two *Livres de Fauvel*, as they are called in MS fr. 146, an account of the horse Fauvel, a creature whose very name embodies the vices and whose principal traits are hypocrisy and greed. *Fauvel* presents a moral exemplum that draws many of its object lessons from the scandals and disasters of recent history. As originally conceived, the anonymous first book is an estates satire that dates itself 1310, at the zenith of the reign of Philippe le Bel. Book 2, ascribed to the royal notary Gervès du Bus, recounts the 'ystoire' (La. v. 1231) of Fauvel; it is pointedly dated 6 December 1314, one week after the death of Philippe le Bel and

[2] The original text of *Fauvel* and the long addition at the end of Book 2 in MS fr. 146 are edited in *Le Roman de Fauvel par Gervais du Bus, publié d'après tous les manuscrits connus*, ed. A. Långfors (Société des anciens textes français; Paris, 1914–19) (the original text cited here as La. v. 1, etc.; the added text cited as La. add. v. 1, etc.). Most of the remaining *Fauvel* text in MS fr. 146 is edited in E. Dahnk, *L'hérésie de Fauvel* (Leipziger romanistische Studien, II/4; Leipzig, 1935) (text cited here as Da. v. 1, etc.; texts of musical works as p.mus. 1, etc.; refrains as ref. 1, etc.; and 'rubrics' as + 1, etc.). The polyphony is edited in *Le Roman de Fauvel*, ed. L. Schrade, Introduction by E. H. Roesner (Les Remparts, 1984), repr. from id., *The* Roman de Fauvel, *the Works of Philippe de Vitry, French Cycles of the* Ordinarium missae, with separate commentary vol. (Polyphonic Music of the Fourteenth Century, 1; Les Remparts, 1956). The monophony is edited in *The Monophonic Songs in the Roman de Fauvel*, ed. S. N. Rosenberg and H. Tischler (Lincoln, Nebr., 1991); A. Butterfield, 'The Refrain and the Transformation of Genre in the *Roman de Fauvel*', in *Fauvel Studies*, pp. 105–59; and S. Rankin, 'The "*Alleluyes, antenes, respons, ygnes et verssez*" in BN fr. 146: A Catalogue raisonné', in *Fauvel Studies*, 421–66. Cf. Le premier et le secont livre de fauvel *in the Version Preserved in B.N. f. fr. 146*, ed. P. Helmer (Musicological Studies, 70/1; Ottawa, 1997) (complete transcription of the texts and music in the MS fr. 146 *Fauvel*). The other material in MS fr. 146 is edited in *Six Historical Poems of Geffroi de Paris, Written in 1314–1318, Published in their Entirety for the First Time from MS. fr. 146 of the Bibliothèque nationale, Paris*, ed. and trans. W. H. Storer and C. A. Rochedieu (North Carolina Studies in the Romance Languages and Literatures, 16; Chapel Hill, 1950); L. A. Holford-Strevens, 'The Latin *Dits* of Geffroy de Paris: An *Editio princeps*', in *Fauvel Studies*, pp. 247–75; *The Works of Jehan de Lescurel: Edited from the Manuscript Paris, B.N. f.fr. 146*, ed. N. Wilkins (Corpus Mensurabilis Musicae, 30; American Institute of Musicology, 1966); and *La Chronique métrique attribuée à Geffroy de Paris. Texte publié avec introduction et glossaire*, ed. A. Diverrès (Publications de la Faculté des Lettres de l'Université de Strasbourg, 129; Paris, 1956). All quotations from *Fauvel* follow the readings in MS fr. 146, even when they are given with Långfors's v. numbers.

at the moment when the downfall of the man who most probably was the immediate model for Fauvel, the king's widely hated financial officer, the chamberlain Enguerran de Marigny, was imminent.[3] It is not clear whether the two books were written together or separately, or by one or different authors.[4] The expanded copy in MS fr. 146 is the earliest one known. In all likelihood it was prepared in the royal chancery not more than two or three years after the completion of the original *roman*, by notaries who were colleagues of Gervès du Bus, perhaps with the involvement of the original author.[5] Apart from *Fauvel*, none of the texts in MS fr. 146 is known from other sources. The expanded version of *Fauvel* is also unique to this manuscript; the new text included in it and much of the music that accompanies it appear to have been composed specifically for this *branche*, or 'edition' of the *roman* and its presentation in MS fr. 146.[6]

[3] The standard monograph on this figure remains J. Favier, *Un conseiller de Philippe le Bel: Enguerran de Marigny* (Mémoires et Documents publiés par la Société de l'École des Chartes, 16; Paris, 1963). See also J. R. Strayer, *The Reign of Philip the Fair* (Princeton, 1980).

[4] *Fauvel* survives in whole or in part in fifteen manuscripts; see the list in Dillon, *Medieval Music-Making*, pp. 283–4. The fact that Book 1 circulated independently while Book 2 evidently did not suggests that the second book was an addition to an already existing text. It may be that the dates given the two books in the text of the *roman* should not be taken at face value. They may have been included not to date the author's work but for a literary reason, to situate the text at particular times in the reign of Philip IV. I am grateful to Elizabeth A. R. Brown for this suggestion. Equally questionable is the ascription to Gervès du Bus, who had been Marigny's chaplain and the recipient of numerous favours from him. Gervès is thus an unlikely candidate for the authorship of this particular text. The ascription may have been introduced in order to provide ironic and somewhat mischievous 'insider' credibility to the account of Marigny/Fauvel's career in Book 2. See E. A. R. Brown, 'Répresentations de la royauté dans les *Livres de Fauvel*', in *Répresentation, pouvoir et royauté à la fin du moyen âge: actes du colloque organisé par l'Université du Maine les 25 et 26 mars 1994*, ed. J. Blanchard (Paris, 1995), pp. 215–35, at p. 217. On Gervès and the men around him who may have been responsible for MS fr. 146, see A. Wathey, 'Gervès du Bus, the *Roman de Fauvel*, and the Politics of the Later Capetian Court', in *Fauvel Studies*, pp. 599–613; and E. Lalou, 'La Chancellerie royale à la fin du règne de Philippe IV le Bel', in *Fauvel Studies*, pp. 307–19. These questions are part of a larger group of uncertainties surrounding the names and dates in MS fr. 146, whether they can be accepted on their face or are there as parts of the 'text' pure and simple.

[5] The new *branche* of *Fauvel* is ascribed to 'Mesire Chaillou de Pesstain' (Da. + 6, on fol. 23^{v}, immediately following Da. vv. 41–8 identifying Gervès as the man who 'trouve' the 'livret'. Lalou, 'Chancellerie', proposes an identification of this enigmatic figure. For a study of the production of MS fr. 146 in the context of the Paris book trade, see R. H. Rouse and M. A. Rouse, *Manuscripts and their Makers: Commercial Book Producers in Paris, 1200–1500*, 2 vols. (London, 2000), esp. ch. 8.

[6] This point, now considered virtually axiomatic, was first made in the introduction to the 1990 facsimile edition of MS fr. 146. Part of the added material was drawn from a work ascribed to a chancery colleague of Gervès, Jehan Maillart, the *Roman du Comte d'Anjou*,

As presented in MS fr. 146, the two books of *Fauvel* retain their status as separate texts; but at the same time they are fused into something more nearly resembling a single entity, and their temporal locus is subtly shifted. The date of 1310 at the end of Book 1 serves to set the scene for a substantial block of added material, a passage beginning 'Regnaut li lyons debonaires' (Da. vv. 15–36, p.mus. 32 and 33) about the late Philippe le Bel (the 'lion'), his forebears Philip III and the sainted Louis IX, and his immediate successors, his eldest son Louis X (1315–16), Louis's posthumous son Jean I (born 13 or 14 November 1316, died a few days later), and Louis's brother Philip of Poitiers, Philip V. To close this sequence of added text and music, Philip V himself receives a motet introduced by the line 'Pour phelippes qui regne ores' (Da. v. 35; p.mus. 33). In effect, this added material moves the narrative forward, away from the 'courteous lion' through the unsettled period leading up to the coronation of Philip V on 7 January 1317. Book 2 omits the date of 1314 that appears at the end of the *roman* in its original form, strengthening the impression that in this presentation the Fauvel story is to be understood as unfolding not only during but also, and perhaps especially, after the time of Philippe le Bel. (The end of Book 2 in MS fr. 146 returns the narrative to Philippe le Bel, however: the *roman* effectively ends on fol. 44^{v} with the motet *In nova fert*, p.mus. 129, which speaks in the present tense of the 'blind lion' and the 'fox' [Marigny] who dominates him. This is part of a systematic reversal of narrative flow noticed by Margaret Bent.[7]) And in MS fr. 146 the attribution to Gervès du Bus is moved from the end of Book 2 to the very centre of the *roman* as a whole, to fol. 23^{v}, in

itself only recently completed – or, at least, carrying the date 1316. See Jehan Maillart, *Le Roman du Comte d'Anjou*, ed. M. Roques (Les Classiques Français du Moyen Âge, 67; Paris, 1931). In its content the *Comte d'Anjou* is closely related to MS fr. 146, and can be seen not only as a source of borrowed material but also as something of a companion text. See esp. N. Black, 'The Politics of Romance in Jean Maillart's *Roman du Comte d'Anjou*', *French Studies*, 51 (1997), pp. 129–37; and ead., *Medieval Narratives of Accused Queens* (Gainesville, forthcoming 2003). For a partial listing of text borrowed from Maillart's *roman*, see M. Roques, 'L'Interpolation de *Fauvel* et le *Comte d'Anjou*', *Romania*, 55 (1929), pp. 548–51; this should be supplemented by N. F. Regalado, 'The *Chronique métrique* and the Moral Design of BN fr. 146: Feasts of Good and Evil', in *Fauvel Studies*, pp. 488 n. 78 and 491 n. 84.

[7] Bent, 'Fauvel and Marigny: Which Came First?' in *Fauvel Studies*, pp. 35–52. We shall return to this motet in Part V, below.

medias res, half-way down the centre column. In effect, the putative author is relocated to the heart of 'his' work, evoking the impression of a single intelligence guiding it all, as though he were at the hub of a wheel, and ready, like Fortune, to turn it without warning.[8]

Although he is seen to drive his work from the centre of the MS fr. 146 *Fauvel*, this 'author' – whoever he may have been in fact – draws the reader's attention to his presence again and again over the course of the *roman*. He is visible in numerous illustrations, and his voice is heard not only in the added text but also in several

[8] *Fauvel* extends from fol. 1ʳ to fol. 45ʳ. However, there is an added bifolium, 28 bis–ter, following fol. 28, introduced late in the copying of the *roman*; with this in place, fol. 23ᵛ is in the exact middle of the fascicle. One of the implications of this is that the presence of the added bifolium was anticipated before the copying of the page some five folios earlier was completed. Although the author ascription does interrupt the narrative flow, its placement in MS fr. 146 is not inappropriate from a thematic standpoint. (See also the discussion of this page in Dillon, 'Art of Interpolation'.) Immediately before the reference to 'G clerc le Roy francois de Rues' (*sic*; Da. v. 41) come *roman* lines (La. vv. 2877–86) in which Fortune affirms that one cannot love both God and the World, and that he who eschews earthly riches will find greater rewards in Heaven; these are given scriptural *auctoritas* in two *versez* that quote the words of Christ, *Nemo potest duobus dominis servire* (p.mus. 53; text from Matt. 6: 24) and *Beati pauperes spiritu quoniam ipsorum est regnum celorum* (p.mus. 54; text from Matt. 5: 3). The ironic juxtaposition of this material with the reference to the notary Gervès, Marigny's protegé, is surely deliberate. A comparable use of symmetry is observable on another structurally significant page, fol. 30ᵛ, the point at which the career of Fauvel is situated in France, Paris, and the royal palace. The centre column begins with six lines from the original state of the *roman* (La. vv. 3195–200); it continues with a monophonic *verse* in praise of Paris as royal capital (p.mus. 73), a miniature depicting the Palais, and a plainchant responsory adapted from the liturgy of the Sainte-Chapelle (p.mus. 74); the column is filled in with six more lines of text, the beginning of the long final expansion (La. add. vv. 1–6). In text, music and illustration, Paris, the Palais and the royal chapel are at the exact centre of the page. The symmetry on fol. 23ᵛ situates the author; that on fol. 30ᵛ is used to locate his moral exemplum.

Our association of the 'author' in MS fr. 146 with Fortune and her wheel would appear to be obvious given the presence of the goddess throughout the *roman* from fol. 1ʳ on. But the placement of the author at the crux of the text might also suggest the use of another symbol as a structuring device, the labyrinth, with its connotations of the evil beast or demon, the warrior or Christ, his Cross, his Advent, his triumph over Death, the perfect city (Troy hence Paris, for example), reversal and palindrome, fallen pride (Icarus), and so on – all topoi that will be encountered over the course of this study. (See the discussion of the labyrinth in C. Wright, *The Maze and the Warrior: Symbols in Architecture, Theology, and Music* (Cambridge, Mass., 2001). I thank Barbara Haggh for suggesting to me the potential significance of this symbol for my reading of *Fauvel*.) To consider the labyrinth as an element of design and content in the 'text' compiled in MS fr. 146 would take the discussion in a somewhat different direction from the path followed here, requiring a study of its own. In the meantime, I note that the number symbolism most directly associable with the labyrinth does not seem to be represented in the musical works considered in this study.

of the interpolated musical works, his moral message delivered in a distinctive tone.[9] Thus, having described how Fauvel and his offspring have trampled 'le jardin de douce France', he remarks, 'Et pour ce que ie m'en courrouce / Ce met ci motet qui qu'en grouce' ('and because I am angry, I am putting this motet here, whoever may grouse about it'), introducing the motet *Quoniam secta latronum/Tribum que non abhorruit/Merito hec patimur* (La. add. v. 1577, Da. vv. 1066–7, p.mus. 120). Through his reactions to the evil epitomised by Fauvel, the 'author' of the assemblage that is MS fr. 146 shapes and focuses (and in some respects, perhaps, subtly modifies) the thrust of the original *roman*. He does this not only through the choice of material added to the original, but also through the ways in which the literary, musical and illustrative elements brought together in the *roman* interact on the page. This can be observed at the very beginning of *Fauvel*, on the first numbered page of the manuscript, fol. 1^r. How the content of *Fauvel* is coloured by the music and other added material, and by the design of the page, and how that content is related to the underlying theme of kingship, is the subject of this study. In Part I we shall look briefly at the text on fol. 1^r, in Parts II–IV at each of the three musical works on the page in turn; in Part V we will consider some appearances of this 'author's' voice in the motets added towards the close of the *roman*, and draw some additional conclusions in Part VI.

I

Folio 1^r of MS fr. 146 brings diverse elements together on an elegantly designed page (see Figure 1). The scribe has surrounded the opening lines of the *roman* with musical and illustrative material that elucidates and comments on the text, the music flanking the *roman* text on both sides, *Favellandi vicium* in column a, *Mundus a mundicia* and *Quare fremuerunt* in column c, and the pictures capping and closing the *Fauvel* text in column b. The whole

[9] On the presence of the author see K. Brownlee, 'Authorial Self-Representation and Literary Models in the *Roman de Fauvel*', in *Fauvel Studies*, pp. 73–103; J.-C. Mühlethaler, *Fauvel au pouvoir: lire la satire médiévale* (Nouvelle Bibliothèque du Moyen Âge, 26; Paris, 1994), deuxième partie; and Dillon, *Medieval Music-Making*, ch. 3 and *passim*. The authorial role of the compiler and scribe is a central topic in Dillon's book.

Figure 1 Paris, BNF f. fr. 146, fol. 1r (*Livres de Fauvel*)
Cliché Bibliothèque nationale de France, Paris

is nicely framed by the elaborate decorative border.[10] The overall impression is one of balance and self-containment. How much *roman* text would appear on the page was itself carefully calculated: Book 1 is an estates satire, an account of how the various classes of society come to curry Fauvel; the opening page is designed as an introduction to the satire, setting the stage for it, so that the first line on the following page, fol. 1^{v}, could begin the satire proper with the figures to whom the *admonitio* as a whole is most immediately directed: 'Rois dus et contes verriez / Pour torcher fauvel allez' ('Kings, dukes and counts can be observed gathering together to curry Fauvel', La. vv. 35–6, lines carrying forward one of the principal themes of fol. 1^{r}; see Part IV, below). The text on fol. 1^{r} reads as follows:[11]

	De fauvel que tant voi torcher	Because of Fauvel, whom I see so often curried
	Doucement sanz lui escorcher	Gently, without being flayed,
	Sui entrez en merencolie	I have entered a melancholy state,
	Pour ce quest beste si polie	Because he is so well groomed.
5	Souvent levoient enpainture	Some often see him in paintings
	Tex qui ne sevent se figure	Who do not know if he represents
	Moquerie sens ou folie	Ridicule, reason, or folly;
	Et pour ce sanz amphibolie	And this is why, without ambiguity,
	Clerement dirai de tel beste	I will say right out loud of such a beast
10	Ce quil men puet cheoir en teste	Whatever may come to my mind about him.
	Fauvel ne gist mes en lestable	Fauvel no longer lies in the stable,
	IL a meson plus honorable.	HE has a more honourable house,
	Haute mengoere demande	He requests a high manger,
	Rastelier bel et assez viande	A fine hayrack, and enough food.

[10] The only other decorative border of comparable size is found on fol. 63^{r}, the start of the *Chronique métrique*. This suggests that the compilers had in mind a two-part work, one an allegorical fable, the other a historical narrative. The parallels and interplay between the two have often been noted in recent scholarship; see, for example, below, n. 14.

[11] I am grateful to Nancy Freeman Regalado for her assistance with this text. The transcription follows the reading, orthography and word division of MS fr. 146, except that (1) seeming copying errors are corrected (and noted); and (2) abbreviations are expanded and distinctions are made between *u* and *v*. Variant readings (other than differences in orthography) are noted. Flourished and decorated majuscule letters are enclosed in boxes, and other unusually prominent letters are underscored. For the most part, the same principles obtain in the editions of the Latin motet texts in Parts II–IV, below. In the music examples I have read the notation in the light of the group of treatises associated with the name of Philippe de Vitry, and above all those collected in *Philippi de Vitriaco ars nova*, ed. G. Reaney, A. Gilles and J. Maillard (Corpus Scriptorum de Musica, 8; American Institute of Musicology, 1964) and related texts, rather than in accordance with the doctrine in the *Pomerium* of Marchetto of Padua, followed in the Schrade edition.

15	Il sest herbergiez en la sale	He has lodged himself in the hall,
	Pour miex demonstrer sa regale	The better to display his royal prerogatives,
	Et non pourquant par sa science	And nevertheless in his wisdom
	Es Chambres a grant reverence	In the Chambers in great honour
	Et es gardes robes souvent	And in the privy chambers
20	Fait toust assembler son Couvent	He soon assembles his Faithful,
	Qui si soingneusement le frote	Who rub him so carefully.
	Quen lui ne puet remanoir crote	No muck can remain on him.
	Fortune contraire araison	Fortune, contrary to reason,
	La fait seigneur de sa meson	Has made him lord of her house.
25	En lui essaucer met grant peine	She labours to raise him on high,
	Car en palais Roial le maine	For in the Royal palace she leads him.
	De lui fere honorer ne cesse	She does not cease to make him honoured.
	Entour fauvel a si grant presse	Around Fauvel there is such a crowd
	De gens de toutes nacions	Of folk from every nation
30	Et de toutes condicions	And from every rank
	Que cest une trop grant merveille	That it is a very great wonder:
	Nia nul qui ne sa pareille	There is no one there who does not make ready
	De torcher fauvel doucement	To curry Fauvel gently.
	Trop ia grant assemblement	There is a great gathering there.

Notes on the text: 5 MS *pointure* (sting, wound, sharp pain); *peinture* also implies misleading speech, false appearance | 6 MS *sa* also in 4 other MSS | 11 *en estable* in all but 3 MSS | 13–14 all other MSS: *Avoir veult haute menjoere Et rastelier de grant afere* | 15 MS *hebergiez* | 16 *sa* in 3 MSS; Långfors prefers *son* | 17 *ne* in all other MSS | 18 *Chambres*: personal or workrooms, private domains, assemblies or administrative bodies, or, by inference in association with l. 19, places where one relieves oneself | 19 *gardesrobes*: wardrobes? antechambers? bedrooms? the room where one keeps his commode? | 20 all other MSS: *Fet il assembler son couvent* | 24 *La* (*L'a*) in 4 MSS; Långfors prefers *Le* | 26 MS *ou*; *en* in 2 MSS; Långfors prefers *el* | 30 *condicions*: classes, stations, walks of life | 32 Långfors, following the other MSS, gives *s'appareille* |

The horse Fauvel, seeking more fodder than was to be had in the stable, has inexplicably been made lord of the house by Fortune. There he holds court, surrounded and curried – flattered – by the throng that flocks to him, sending the author into a fit of melancholy and prompting him to expose the beast to those who might not understand the danger he represents. The passage is self-contained from a textual standpoint, beginning and ending with the theme of the universal currying of Fauvel. The narrative portion is set off from the author's opening apology by a large capital F, one of many 'F words' that are strategically placed in the manuscript. (Note in this regard the first words on the page in column a, 'Favellandi vicium et fex avaricie', and the last words on the page in column c, 'inferunt fauvel et fasuli'.[12] These words at the corners and the pictures of Fauvel at the top and bottom of the middle column create a thematic frame for the page that is complemented by the decorative frame that wraps around most of the writing block.) This F and the emphasised 'IL' (also referring to Fauvel) immediately below it appear next to 'O quale contagium' (p.mus. 1, v. 9; 'Oh, such infection!') in the adjoining column to the left.

The orthography of the scribe identifies the speaker, the author, as Parisian, and the script suggests the royal chancery on the Île de la Cité as the place from which his words issue.[13] The capitalisation of certain words – 'palais Roial', 'Chambres', 'Couvent' – contributes further to the sense of topicality, implying specific places and institutions: this is not just any royal palace, but *the* royal palace; it is *the* 'chambres' and *the* 'couvent'. The setting will be further particularised later in the manuscript, when Fauvel is shown seated on the throne of Dagobert (fol. 11r), and when it is made clear that his palace, called 'Desespoir' in the narrative as expanded in MS fr. 146 (La. add. vv. 117–22), is in fact the royal Palais de la Cité, transformed into a coherent administrative and residential complex by Philippe le Bel and Enguerran de Marigny, and formally inaugurated during the Pentecost festivities of 1313 (fols. 30v–31r).[14] By association, 'regale', 'meson', 'sale' and 'gardes robes' also acquire specific connotations: Fauvel has taken over the palace

[12] These are the last words of the motetus; they are immediately followed on the page by the designation '[T]enor', but of course this is only a label, not text to be read, sung, or heard. The fact that this label, unlike the two other tenor designations on the page, did not receive a decorated capital letter raises the suspicion that it may have been added late in the copying process, after the decorator had done his work. If that is the case, it would be a clear sign of the prominence of the concluding motetus text in the mind of the scribe. The missing initial is but one of the anomalies evident in the copying of the tenor part of *Quare fremuerunt*; see Morin, 'Genesis', 70 n. 34, and Dillon, *Medieval Music-Making*, p. 154.

[13] Thanks to Nancy Regalado, Elizabeth A. R. Brown, and Véronique Sigu for their many observations regarding the nuances in this text.

[14] M. T. Davis, 'Desespoir, Esperance, and Douce France: The New Palace, Paris, and the Royal State', in *Fauvel Studies*, pp. 187–213. Regarding the treatment of the 1313 Pentecost festivities in the *Chronique métrique*, see two studies by E. A. R. Brown and N. F. Regalado, '*La grant feste*: Philip the Fair's Celebration of the Knighting of His Sons in Paris at Pentecost of 1313', in B. A. Hanawalt and K. L. Ryerson (eds.), *City and Spectacle in Medieval Europe* (Medieval Studies at Minnesota, 6; Minneapolis, 1994), pp. 56–86; and '*Universitas et communitas*: The Parade of the Parisians at the Pentecost Feast of 1313', in K. Ashley and W. Hüsken (eds.), *Moving Subjects: Processional Performance in the Middle Ages and the Renaissance* (Amsterdam, 2001), pp. 117–54.

and the government of the King of France, emblematic of the French nation itself, and usurped the royal prerogatives, the readings in the manuscript making it clear that this is a fait accompli, not something that is in the course of happening (see La. v. 24).

Much of this is depicted and reinforced in the two miniatures that frame the text. At the top of the page is shown Fauvel, first tethered at his manger in the stable in the lower left compartment; then led upstairs by the blindfolded Fortune, with someone, probably a page, in attendance at his rear; then at his higher and better provided manger in the great hall, above, where Fortune is engaged in tethering him, and where the beast, now significantly bigger, can indulge his insatiable greed. It is noteworthy that it is Fortune herself who tethers Fauvel, and that she appears to fasten him to the same railing or banister to which he had been hitched in the stable below; it is Fortune who controls his destiny.[15] The architectural border around three sides of the miniature, showing a decorated roof with three small towers, two of them framing a gable, is suggestive of the exterior of Fauvel's palace.[16]

[15] I am grateful to Kathryn Smith for drawing my attention to the tether. See also Dillon, *Medieval Music-Making*, pp. 115–17. The railing to which the tether is attached does not recur again in MS fr. 146, suggesting that it is there only as a hitching rod. The position of the rope on Fauvel's neck and its fastening to the overhead beam are reminiscent of a gallows. On fol. 30ʳ, Fortune condemns Fauvel and his descendants to a terrible fate (La. vv. 3145–52). The beast responds with the motet *Heu Fortuna subdola/Aman novi probatur/Heu me tristis est anima mea* (p.mus. 71, introduced by Da. vv. 1032–9), the lament of the ambitious man betrayed by Fortune. It is interesting that this exemplum of fallen pride dies by hanging on the gallows of Paris at Montfaucon; the cord around Fauvel's neck in the first picture of the beast to meet the eye in the manuscript may, like much else on fol. 1ʳ, as we shall see, look forward to that end. For the most recent study of *Heu Fortuna subdola*, see A. Puca, 'Composing Chant: Tenors and Compositional Practice in the Latin Motets of the Manuscript F-Pn fr. 146', *Yearbook of the Alamire Foundation*, 4 (2002), pp. 297–312. On the crucial role played by the figure of Fortune in delivering the *roman*'s moral message and directing it towards the theme of kingship, see N. F. Regalado, 'Fortune's Two Crowns: Images of Kingship in the Paris, BnF Ms. fr. 146 *Roman de Fauvel*', forthcoming in the festschrift for Lucy Freeman Sandler. Also regarding Fortune see T. Hunt, 'The Christianization of Fortune', *Nottingham French Studies*, 38 (1999), pp. 95–113.

[16] Cf. the picture of the Palais on fol. 30ᵛ, col. b. See also the framing on the picture of Fauvel on his throne, fol. 11ʳ, and the author picture in the adjacent column, and cf. the more 'ecclesiastical' frames on fols. 8ᵛ (depicting the clergy and the Church) and 13ʳ, top (Envy), and the frame surrounding Fortune's palace on fol. 19ʳ. Cf. the 'ecclesiastical' frame in the miniature from Paris, Bibliothèque nationale de France (henceforth BNF), f. fr. 9123 (*Estoire*), fol. 4ʳ, reproduced in A. Stones, 'The Stylistic Context of the Roman de Fauvel, with a Note on *Fauvain*', in *Fauvel Studies*, p. 534; also the frames and the urban profiles depicted in several miniatures in the contemporaneous *Vie de Saint Denis* manuscripts, Paris, BNF f. fr. 2090–92, and f. lat. 13896; and the depictions of the Sainte-Chapelle in the somewhat earlier St Louis Psalter, Paris, BNF f. lat. 10525.

At the bottom of the page Fauvel is seen surrounded by his 'Couvent', the 'grant assemblement' or 'presse de gens de toutes nacions et . . . condicions' – two tonsured clerics, four monks, a cardinal, a pope, a nobleman, and a king with crown. Significantly, the king is placed at the centre of the group.[17] Here and in all the pictures that follow over the course of the *roman*, Fauvel is depicted without his tether: although we are to understand that this cord is always there, in the world of men he appears to reign unfettered. (His unbridled state is affirmed in the *roman*, La. vv. 294–5.) Thus through the use of primarily visual devices – illustration, orthography, page design – a rather general text about the triumph of hypocrisy and greed has been made topical, and pointed in a specific direction. The music on the page lends a further dimension to this text.

II

The *roman* text on fol. 1r suggests that Fauvel's usurpation is all-encompassing, incomprehensible, 'une trop grant marveille', and distressing; but it is the musical works glossing the text that bring the malign impact of Fauvel into clear relief. All three works are classified as 'Motez a tenures sanz trebles' in the index that precedes the *roman* (fol. B).[18] Although they are said to be 'a tenures', the tenor parts themselves are each wholly newly composed, designed to fit an already existing upper voice or at least composed simultaneously with it, as an accompaniment rather than as the sort of foundation usually employed in a motet.[19] All

See also the detailed examination of this question in Dillon, *Medieval Music-Making*, pp. 113–17.

17 See the description of these figures in Mühlethaler, *Fauvel au pouvoir*, pp. 414–15.

18 The index was made before the collection achieved its final form. It was entered by the scribe who copied the Lescurel songs, who Morin believes may have been the man who exercised 'editorial oversight' in the production of MS fr. 146; see Morin, 'Genesis', 69–81. The index effectively turns a *roman* with insertions into something approaching a conventional music manuscript, its contents arranged as though in fascicles, according to genre and the number of voices. More importantly, however, the index bears witness to the centrality of the music in the expanded *Fauvel*: music is not merely a literary embellishment, as it is in other romances with added lyrics; it is central to the compiler's purpose, to delivering his moral message, as central as the *roman* text itself. See also Dillon, *Medieval Music-Making*, pp. 164–9.

19 See most recently A. V. Clark, '*Concordare cum materia*: The Tenor in the Fourteenth-Century Motet' (Ph.D. diss., Princeton University, 1996).

three are unique but based on music or text from the preceding century – each using the material it borrows in a different way, however. All conclude with music and text that is entirely 'new', not based on the model (or, at least, not on the same model as the earlier part of the motet). In each the final thought is set off by a somewhat prominent initial letter. Each motet delivers a different aspect of the *roman* message, but, as we shall see, all three are based on a single premise. All were composed – or, better, arranged – specifically for use in *Fauvel*. They are not the only two-voice motets in the manuscript that were created without using pre-existing melodic material in their tenor voices, but they are the only such pieces that are based on polyphonic models. Thus they form something of a special group within the larger *Fauvel* collection of music.[20]

Column a of fol. 1^{r} is occupied by *Favellandi vicium*/Tenor (p.mus. 1, Schrade no. 1):[21]

	F avellandi vicium	The vice of fauvelling
	et fex avaricie	and the muck of avarice
	optinent nunc solium	are now occupying the throne
	summumque locum curie	and the highest position in the court.
5	munus dat propicium	A gift makes the judge
	iudicem et pium	favourable and gentle.
	lex subit exilium	Law passes into exile,
	et prostat iudicium.	and the judgement of law is up for sale.
	O quale contagium	O what an infection,
10	quante pestilencie	how great the boils
	lateri potencie	that daily plague
	herentes cotidie	the flanks of the mighty!
	voces adullatorie	Flattering voices
	scandunt ad dominium.	ascend to power.
15	fraus imperat iusticie.	Fraudulent justice rules.
	Deus misericordie	Merciful God,
	adhibe hic consilium.	apply here counsel!

Notes on the text: 1 *fex*: sing. of *faeces*, hence the excrement that is the product of Fauvel's greedy eating, the dung that his curriers pick from his coat (Leofranc Holford-Strevens informs me that *fex* does not have the rude connotations of the modern 'shit') / 8 MS *prestat*, emended for sense but preferred by Spanke / 9 *contagium*: also, negative influence, touch, temptation / 14 MS *dominum*, emended in accordance with the rhyme /

[20] Cf. the discussions of these motets in Morin, 'Genesis', ch. 6; and L. Welker, 'Polyphonic Reworkings of Notre-Dame Conductus in BN fr. 146: *Mundus a mundicia* and *Quare fremuerunt*', in *Fauvel Studies*, pp. 615–36.

[21] On Dahnk's reading of the text, see P. A. Becker, *Fauvel und Fauvelliana* (Berichte über die Verhandlungen der Sächsischen Akademie der Wissenschaften zu Leipzig, philologisch-historische Klasse, 38/2; Leipzig, 1936), p. 23; and H. Spanke, 'Zu den musikalischen Einlagen im Fauvelroman', *Neuphilologische Mitteilungen*, 37 (1936), p. 204.

Fauvel himself is alluded to only once in the motet, in what is the very first word on the page. *Favellandi vicium* describes two plagues holding sway over the throne and the highest position in the court, 'fauvelling' and greed, leading to the corruption of justice. The former is characterised as a 'vice', the latter as a 'fouling' or 'besmirching', as 'dirt'. 'Fauvelling', 'playing the Fauvel game', must entail flattery, hypocrisy, deceit, falsehood, treachery – the evils stressed throughout the motet poem: bribery, the subversion of justice, deceit prevailing over forthrightness. Flattery and greed are also the vices singled out in the adjacent *roman* text (Fauvel's eager curriers, his greed for more fodder) and the ones stressed in the description of the beast that follows further on in the *roman* (the derivation of his name from 'faus vel', 'veil of deceit', the significance of his colour, fauve, etc.; see La. vv. 171–260). Indeed, 'Flaterie' and 'Avarice', the two vices of the motet, are the sources of the first two letters of Fauvel's name.[22] This is a condition prevailing here and now, as the first and last sentences make a point of affirming through their use of 'nunc' and 'hic'.[23] The opening statement is given the status of a motto through its musical treatment: it is set off in both voices by a stroke connoting a general pause, like a *finis punctorum*. This is the only point in the motet where the two voices do not overlap to produce a continuous web of sound (see Example 1).

This opening statement sets the tone not only for this motet, but indeed for the first book of *Fauvel* as a whole, where the vices that seem to be stressed above all are hypocrisy and greed. The ranking of vices shifts in the second book, recounting the courtship and marriage of Fauvel. After an inserted musical work comments on the 'nacio nephandi generis', the vices as a group, the piece

[22] Throughout the Middle Ages Pride and Avarice were given pride of place among the vices by different authors; see L. K. Little, 'Pride Goes before Avarice: Social Change and the Vices in Latin Christendom', *American Historical Review*, 76 (1971), 16–49. Superbia and Hypocrisis are seen as related vices in some schemes, e.g., that of Robert Grosseteste, 'Primo videndum est quid est peccatum', where they stand opposed to the virtue of Humilitatio (this following Aristotle, who held that each virtue was matched by two vices); see S. Wenzl, 'The Seven Deadly Sins: Problems of Research', *Speculum*, 43 (1968), 11–12. On the central role of Hypocrisy in political and eschatological writing in the thirteenth and early fourteenth centuries see R. K. Emmerson and R. B. Herzman, 'The Apocalyptic Age of Hypocrisy: Faus Semblant and Amant in the *Roman de la Rose*', *Speculum*, 62 (1987), 612–34.

[23] See Mühlethaler, *Fauvel au pouvoir*, pp. 199–201 on the 'timeliness' of the version of *Fauvel* in MS fr. 146.

Example 1 *Favellandi vicium* (excerpt)

immediately following singles out Carnalitas and Luxuria for special treatment.[24] These are also the vices emphasised in the descriptions of the wedding feast and tournament included in Book 2 of the MS fr. 146 *Fauvel*: of the thirty-three vices listed among the wedding guests (La. add. vv. 55–75), the first three are Charnalite, Fornicacion, and Advoutire; the large tournament pictures on fols. 39v–40v show first Charnalite and Concupiscence vs.Virginite, then Fornicacion vs. Chastete, and then Orgueil vs. Patience and Gloutonnerie vs. Abstinence.[25]

Implicit in this motet text is a theme that recurs throughout the *roman*, both in its original form and markedly so in the expanded version in MS fr. 146, the idea of *mundus inversus*, that the normal order has been negated or reversed, with evil dominating good, lawlessness justice, and hypocrisy honesty. The subversion of justice and the rule of law is the dominant theme of the motet. Just rule is one of the central tenets of good kingship in

24 P.mus. 35, *O Nacio nephandi generis/Condicio nature defuit/Mane prima sabbati*; p.mus. 36, *Carnalitas Luxuria in favelli palacio presunt*.

25 See also N. F. Regalado, 'Allegories of Power: The Tournament of Vices and Virtues in the *Roman de Fauvel* (BN MS fr. 146)', *Gesta*, 32 (1993), pp. 135–46.

late Capetian France.[26] The coronation *ordo* that was probably used at the crowning of Philippe le Bel in 1285 and that is certainly representative of the customs prevailing at the time of the compilation of MS fr. 146, includes a commitment (*promissio*) by the new king, responding to a clerical admonition to respect and defend the privileges of the Church and the law, that 'debitam legem atque iusticiam servabo' ('I will serve under the law and in accordance with justice').[27] This motet tells us that the promise has been abrogated – or, more likely, never made, that Fauvel does not sit legitimately on the throne. Kingship has been taken over by unworthy and probably unsanctioned, unsanctified elements. We know from the surroundings of the motet on fol. 1r that it is the legitimacy of the Throne of France that has been compromised.

The plea to God to summon his 'consilium' that closes the motet is, like much else in *Fauvel*, double-edged: it can be read as a petition for aid, counsel; it can also be read as a plea for help from an assembly of councillors. (To a medieval reader it might also have evoked an association with the *consiliarius* of the celebrated messianic prophecy in Isai. 9: 6, a connection that will find support in the discussion of *Quare fremuerunt* in Part IV, below. Be that as it may, this *consilium* stands in pointed contrast to the other counsel mentioned in the poem, the dung-smeared individual in verse 2 who occupies the 'highest position in the court' – the monarch's principal counsellor. It can also be understood as the antithesis of the 'couvent' that Fauvel has gathered around himself, according to the *roman* text.) This plea is set off from the foregoing complaint and given visual emphasis by an unusually large initial. But it stands apart musically as well. There is a significant change in the style of the musical setting towards the close of this final phrase with the introduction of text-bearing semibreves, the only ones in the piece; this speeding up of declamation is followed by

[26] See the discussion of the primacy of justice in Capetian royal thinking in M. C. Gaposchkin, '*Ludovicus decus regnantium*: The Liturgical Office for Saint Louis and the Ideological Program of Philip the Fair', pt. 6 (forthcoming).

[27] *Ordines coronationis Franciae: Texts and Ordines for the Coronation of Frankish and French Kings and Queens in the Middle Ages*, ed. R. A. Jackson, 2 vols. (Middle Ages Series; Philadelphia, 1994–2000), ii, p. 383. See also M. C. Gaposchkin, 'The Sanctification and Memorialization of Louis IX of France, 1297–ca. 1350' (Ph.D. diss., University of California, Berkeley, 2001), p. 248.

Example 2 *Favellandi vicium* (conclusion)

a written out 'cadential retard' in both voices that slows the pace to movement in perfect longs, thereby imparting a sense of closure (see Example 2).

The musical disjunction of the final phrase operates on a less obvious level as well: the preceding part of the motet uses music drawn from an already existing motet (we shall consider the implications of this presently), but the concluding plea is set to new music. The plea can thus be seen not only as a focusing of the thrust of the work, but also as something of an extension to it. Since the text is apparently newly composed throughout, and consequently could have been as long or short as the poet/composer wished, it is noteworthy that he did not craft his poem so that the entire text would fit within the limits dictated by his model. It seems likely therefore that he wanted 'new' music for this 'new' appeal to God. But the composer may have had other motives for extending the work beyond the length of his model: he may have wanted to reach a particular length. If the general pause is not assigned a specific duration, the work is seventy perfections long; if the pause is read as the theoretical equivalent of a long, as in Example 1, the length is seventy-one perfections. The implications of this will become clear in Parts IV–VI, below.

Joseph Morin has shown that *Favellandi vicium* is based on the triplum line of a three-voice motet composed in the earlier thirteenth century and surviving with the texts *De gravi seminio/In corde* in Ma and W_2 (in the former source without the tenor, in the latter without the triplum, however), and with the texts *Cum li plus desesperes/Bien me doi/In corde* in W_2, again, and Mo.[28] The triplum melody is taken over more or less in toto as the motetus line of *Favellandi vicium*; the only variations between the two that are significant for our purpose have already been mentioned, the general pause and the extension at 'Deus misericordie'. A new tenor is composed around this motetus.

Neither Morin nor anyone else has explained why the *Fauvel* composer chose this particular motet as his source for *Favellandi vicium*. It is doubtful that he selected it because of the thrust of its French motet texts: the French texts are love lyrics of a sort found in numerous motets of the period, the complaints of a despairing lover impelled to sing.[29] It is possible, however, to make a case for at least an oblique relationship between the thirteenth-century Latin version and *Favellandi vicium*. That text celebrates the Franciscan Order, which is said to fill the world with the zeal of its love (for Christ). Given the 'royal' thrust of *Favellandi vicium*, this Franciscan locus may not be without resonance for the new motet, since there were intimate ties between the *fratres minores* and the French Throne, cultivated from early on in the reign of

[28] Morin, 'Genesis', pp. 325–44. Ma: Madrid, Biblioteca nacional, MS 20486, fols. 2ᵛ–3ʳ (a late addition to the manuscript); W_2: Wolfenbüttel, Herzog August Bibliothek, cod. Guelf. 1099 Helmstad., fols. 157ᵛ–58ʳ and 202ᵛ–203ᵛ; Mo: Montpellier, Bibliothèque interuniversitaire, Section de Médecine, MS H 196, fols. 185ᵛ–187ᵛ (in fasc. 5). Ed., among other places, in *Polyphonies du XIIIᵉ siècle: le manuscrit H 196 de la Faculté de Médecine de Montpellier*, ed. Y. Rokseth, 4 vols. (Paris, 1935–9), no. 136; *The Earliest Motets (to circa 1270): A Complete Comparative Edition*, ed. H. Tischler, 3 vols. (New Haven, 1982), no. 93; and *El códice de Madrid: polifonías del siglo XIII*, ed. J. C. Asensio Palacios (Patrimonio Musical Español; Madrid, 1997), no. 3. Cf. Welker, 'Polyphonic Reworkings of Notre-Dame Conductus', pp. 631–4 on the model and on what the original note values may have been.

[29] However, the opening lines of the motetus (not the triplum used by the *Fauvel* arranger), 'Cum li plus desesperes / qui soit chant' ('As the most despairing person there is, I sing'), are suggestive of the mood underlying *Favellandi vicium* and of what we will see is one of its primary themes, speaking out or preaching. The same rhetorical topos, speaking what is thought and felt, is central to the *complainte* that once formed part of the MS fr. 146 *Fauvel* and that now serves as something of a prelude to it on fol. A (see the introduction to the 1990 facsimile, pp. 6 and 28); it is edited and translated in Morin, 'Genesis', pp. 411–19. It must be kept in mind, too, that vernacular love poetry could serve political ends, the poet/lover acting as a political spokesman; see J.-C. Mühlethaler, 'Le poète et le prophète: littérature et politique au XVᵉ siècle', *Le Moyen Français*, 13 (1983), pp. 37–57. Thus the French version of this motet may have more affinity with *Favellandi vicium* than meets the eye. I am grateful to Nancy Regalado for drawing my attention to all this. The French and Latin texts are translated in *The Latin Compositions in Fascicules VII and VIII of the Notre Dame Manuscript Wolfenbüttel Helmstadt* [sic] *1099 (1206)*, i: *Critical Commentary, Translation of the Texts, and Historical Observations*, ed. G. A. Anderson (Musicological Studies, 24/1; Brooklyn, [1968]), pp. 174–7.

Louis IX (1226–70), and peaking in the work of the Order to further the cause of Louis's canonisation (realised in 1297). Indeed, Louis, the model of a latter-day monarch ruling under God – and by extension the King of France, whoever he might have been – was identified in late Capetian royal ideology with Francis himself, and seen to exemplify that saint's virtues and the ideals of the Order (poverty, humility, mystical identification with Jesus as an *alter Christus* living in 'imitatio Christi').[30] These are the qualities stressed in the Latin version of the thirteenth-century model: 'Iam paupertas innolevit, fastum devotio sprevit cordis de sacrario, malum lex dei delevit' ('Poverty has now become ingrained, devotion has dispersed pride from the sacristy of the heart, and the law of God has blotted out evil'). One might draw an ironic comparison between the renunciation of wealth (along with other ties to the material life) pursued by the friars and the 'fex avaricie' of *Favellandi vicium*.

Also linking the Franciscan motet to *Favellandi vicium* is another well-known aspect of the Franciscan persona – preaching. The text of the sixth Matins responsory in *Franciscus vir catholicus*, the proper Office of St Francis, affords an indication of the centrality of preaching in the life of the Order: 'Audit in evangelio quae suis Christus loquitur ad praedicandum missis: hoc inquit est quod cupio . . .' ('He [Francis] hears in the Gospel that Christ says to his disciples to go out and preach: "This", he says, "is what I desire"').[31] As we shall presently see, the theme of preaching, proclaiming the truth, obtains in one of the principal subtexts of *Favellandi vicium*. In this regard, the allusion in the responsory to Luke 10: 1, the account of Christ sending his disciples forth to preach his coming, is noteworthy. The Lucan text is laden with agrarian language, language echoed in *De gravi seminio* (e.g., the opening: 'De gravi seminio quod pater colonis sevit, morti dato

[30] On the relations between the Franciscans and the Throne in late Capetian France see, most recently, Gaposchkin, 'Sanctification and Memorialization', pt. 4.

[31] *Franciscus vir catholicus* was composed in Paris *c.*1232 by Julian of Speyer. For the most recent edns. of the text see *Fontes franciscani*, ed. E. Menestrò and S. Brufani (Assisi, 1996), pp. 1105–21; and the edn., trans., and commentary in *Francis of Assisi: Early Documents*, ed. R. J. Armstrong, J. A. W. Hellmann and W. J. Short, 3 vols. (New York, 1999–2000), i, pp. 311–63. See also the discussion of this passage in relation to the liturgy for St Louis in Gaposchkin, 'Sanctification and Memorialization', pp. 413–14; and ead., 'Typology and Fulfillment in the Franciscan Liturgical Office for Louis IX' (forthcoming).

filio, bone messis seges crevit' – 'From the fertile stock that the Father sowed among his labourers, the gift of the Son to death, waxed the fruit of the bountiful harvest').[32] We shall return to this Gospel text in our discussion of *Quare fremuerunt* in Part IV, below, and also in Parts V–VI. But whatever elements of Franciscan ideology lie behind the choice of model for *Favellandi vicium*, fully to understand the reasons for the choice of model and to grasp more deeply the content of *Favellandi vicium* in its *Fauvel* context, we must look not only at the upper-voice texts of that model but also at its tenor.

The tenor of *De gravi seminio* is a fragment of plainchant drawn from the gradual *Os iusti meditabitur, Lex dei eius*, sung in the Mass for Doctors of the Church, and hence available for use in a number of different feasts in the Sanctorale. In most motets the tenor controls every aspect of the composition, its length and overall rhythmic idiom, its tonality and the melodic profiles of its upper voices, and, often, its message.[33] In this case it is not the liturgical occasion, the tenor melody itself, or the text of the tenor, 'in corde' ('in his heart'), by itself that is significant, but rather the full text of the gradual from which it was drawn and the scriptural context from which it was taken in the first instance. The gradual text reads: 'Os iusti meditabitur sapientiam, et lingua eius loquetur iudicium. Lex Dei eius *in corde* ipsius, et non supplantabuntur gressus eius.' This is drawn verbatim from Psalm 36: 30–1: 'The mouth of the just shall meditate wisdom: and his tongue shall speak judgement. The law of his God is *in his heart*, and his steps shall not be supplanted.'[34] (The psalm text is echoed

[32] Asensio Palacios, in *El códice de Madrid*, proposes emending the opening words from 'De gravi seminio', found in both manuscripts, to 'De grani seminio'. This would make the agricultural imagery even more direct.

[33] See esp. Clark, '*Concordare cum materia*'; and ead., 'New Tenor Sources for Fourteenth-Century Motets', *Plainsong and Medieval Music*, 8 (1999), pp. 107–31.

[34] The tenor is M 68 in the motet numbering system of Friedrich Ludwig. Unlike most tenors, which generated numbers of different works, the motets under discussion are the only ones known to have been composed on this chant. Throughout this article, texts quoted from Scripture follow the Vulgate; for the psalms I use the readings in *Biblia sacra iuxta vulgatam Clementinam nova editio*, ed. A. Colunga and L. Turrado, 4th edn. (Biblioteca de autores Cristianos; Madrid, 1965) rather than those of the *Biblia sacra iuxta Latinam vulgatam versionem*: *Liber psalmorum ex recensio Sancti Hieronymi* (Rome, 1953), which antedate what a late medieval reader might have seen. Translations of biblical texts follow the NRSV except for the psalms, which follow Douay–Rheims–Challoner; but I have not hesitated to modify these English renderings when it seemed appropriate.

in the final line of the Latin version of the motet source, *De gravi seminio*: 'malum lex dei delevit' – 'the law of God has blotted out evil'.) The resonance of these lines with the text of *Favellandi vicium* is striking: the plea in the motet for counsel and the opening words of the gradual, that the just shall meditate wisdom and proclaim judgement; the bitter complaint about the destruction of law and justice through bribery, flattery and deceit, and the affirmation that the law of God is in the heart of the just man proclaiming judgement, and that God's law cannot be set aside by something else.

Thus the snippet of text in the tenor of the motet model stands for, calls into play, a larger scriptural passage. It is not only verses 30 and 31 of Psalm 36 that are relevant to *Favellandi vicium*, but in fact the whole of the psalm. Psalm 36 is framed as a comparison of the righteous and the wicked, promising blessings to one and the destruction of the other. It is that destruction for which the final lines of *Favellandi vicium* implicitly ask. Thus, verses 1–2: 'Be not emulous of evildoers [*malignantibus*]; nor envy them that work iniquity [*facientes iniquitatem*]. For they shall shortly wither away as grass, and as the green herbs shall quickly fall.' Introduced at the outset of the psalm is the theme of the reversal of fortune that will befall the evildoer, a motif that plays a dominant role throughout *Fauvel.* Verses 6–7 introduce the theme of justice that will course through the rest of the psalm: 'And he will bring forth thy justice [*iustitiam*] as the light, and thy judgement [*iudicium*] as the noonday. Be subject to the Lord and pray to him. Emulate not the man who prospereth in his way; the man who doth unjust things.' The verses used in the gradual are followed by lines that resonate with the theme of corrupt justice in *Favellandi vicium.* Verse 32: 'The wicked [*peccator*] watcheth the just man [*iustum*], and seeketh to put him to death. But the Lord will not leave him in his hand; nor condemn [*damnabit*] him when he shall be judged [*iudicabitur*].' And later, concerning evildoers who have achieved great power, verses 35–6: 'I have seen the wicked highly exalted [*impium superexaltatum*], and lifted up like the cedars of Libanus. And I passed by, and lo, he was not: and I sought him and his place was not found.' Again, the reversal of fortune.

Thus it was the scriptural context of the tenor in the model of *Favellandi vicium* that rendered its triplum appropriate, even desirable for reworking and reuse in *Fauvel*. The snippet of plainchant in that discarded tenor harks back to the gradual chant from which it was taken and in turn to the psalm from which the gradual drew its text. That is, the thirteenth-century tenor partook of the quality, the message of the parent chant and of its scriptural environment.[35] The tenor was not only the premise underlying the work as a whole, governing its design and content; its influence went further. It imparted a kind of genetic blueprint to the different parameters of the composition, both musical and textual, infusing them with the meaning, the genetic code, so to speak, perhaps of the liturgical situation in which the chant was employed, and certainly of the scriptural text from which it was drawn. That blueprint remained in the other voices as a kind of stem memory, even if the tenor were no longer present. The poet/composer of the *Fauvel* motet was sensitive to all this; for him that genetic marker was evident enough in the triplum of his thirteenth-century model to prompt him to choose that voice for reworking as the opening element in the *Fauvel* collection, thereby imparting that genetic code not only to the reworked piece but also to the collection as a whole.

A reader familiar with the compilation of MS fr. 146 (that is, a reader on the 'inside') would probably have understood the scriptural subtext of *Favellandi vicium* and the dialectic with the motetus text in which it engaged. He may also have been aware of its Franciscan background, and its connotations for the meaning of the *Fauvel* motet. Whether the poet/composer or the compiler of the manuscript expected his readers to recognise this lineage is irrelevant, however: the genetic marker was there whether it was perceived or not; the composer and compiler used it deliberately, if well nigh subliminally, to set the moral tone of their edition of *Fauvel*. The voice of the author rings with scriptural *auctoritas*: implicit in the words he utters in the motet is the affirmation that, with God's law in his heart, he will pronounce judgement on Fauvel, and that the just will prevail over the beast. The evildoer Fauvel 'shall shortly wither away as grass, and as the

[35] Although the Ma version of the motet omits the tenor entirely, the other three states include not only its melody but also its text. It is a measure of the learning of the *Fauvel* composer that he would have been familiar with the source of the tenor melody and its scriptural background.

green herbs shall quickly fall'. The justice that is at the heart of proper kingship will return, and worthy rule will be restored to France.

III

The themes of corruption, filth and the natural order turned upside down that dominate *Favellandi vicium* are also taken up in the two motets that fill the right-hand column on fol. 1r of MS fr. 146, *Mundus a mundicia*/Tenor and *Quare fremuerunt*/Tenor. The setting of *Mundus a mundicia* (p.mus. 2, Schrade no. 2) is based on a thirteenth-century conductus that survives in five manuscripts and that has a strong attribution to Philip the Chancellor.[36] In its *Fauvel* presentation, three lines of text are appended to Philip's stanza:

	Mundus a mundicia	'World' [*mundus*], derived from
	Dictus per contraria	'cleanliness' [*mundicia*] by way of antiphrasis,
	sordet inmundicia	is sullied by the filth of
	criminum	sins.
5	crescit in malicia	It waxes in wickedness,
	culpa nescit terminum	moral turpitude knows no limit.
	Nam sedutrix hominum	For the seductress of mankind,
	favelli nequicia.	the unworthiness that is Fauvel,
	non habet hic dominum	has no master here [in the world].

Notes on the text: 2 *per contraria* cf. La. vv. 1184–5: *Meine tout per antifrasin, C'est a dire par le contraire*; also p.mus. 29, triplum, v. 2: *car tout ce fait par contraire /*

The strident moral tone of this text betrays its early thirteenth-century origins. Filth is linked rhetorically with the idea of the world turned upside down, 'per contraria'. By association, this filth is the *fex* of *Favellandi vicium* across the page and the stable dung that Fauvel has brought with him into the royal palace in the adjoining miniature, and that his curriers try to pick clean from his coat, soiling themselves by doing so. However, this motet

[36] F: Florence, Biblioteca Medicea Laurenziana, MS plut. 29.1, fol. 240v (*a 3*, one strophe only); London, British Library (henceforth BL), Egerton MS 274, fol. 41r (*a 2*, seven strophes, entitled 'de prelatis', among the works ascribed to Philip the Chancellor); Paris, BNF f. lat. 8433, fol. 46r (*a 1*, ascribed to Philip, called a 'prose'); Paris, BNF f. lat. 8237, fol. 13v (text only); Praha, Státní knihovna, Archiv Pražského hradu Kap N 8 (p48), fol. 38r (text only, ascribed to Philip). In its three-voice transmission the conductus is edited in *Three-Part Conductus in the Central Sources*, ed. G. A. Anderson (Notre-Dame and Related Conductus, Opera omnia, 2, Collected Works, X/2; Henryville, Pa., 1986), pp. 31–2.

discloses an aspect of this filth that is different from what we have encountered thus far. The nouns 'crimen' and 'culpa' imply immorality, fornication, and the Original Sin.[37] The text added by the *Fauvel* poet is sensitive to these sexual undertones when in verse 7 it refers to Fauvel as a seducing woman,[38] a traitor or deceiver of mankind, hence an agent of the Devil, that is, most likely, Eve. Tertullian offers an early example of the tone used in much medieval writing on Eve when he says to women bearing her curse, 'You are the Devil's gateway; you are the unsealer of that tree; you are the first deserter of the divine law; you are she who persuaded [Adam], whom the Devil was not strong enough to attack. You destroyed so easily God's image, man. Because of your reward, that is, death, even the Son of God had to die' ('Tu es diaboli janua, tu es arboris illius resignatrix, tu es divinae legis prima desertrix, tu es quae eum persuasisti , quem diabolus aggredi non valuit. Tu imaginem Dei, hominem, tam facile elisisti: propter tuum meritum, id est mortem, etiam Filius Dei mori habuit').[39] Paralleling this line of thought a millennium later, the early twelfth-century Canterbury monk Eadmer, in his important treatise on the Conception of the Virgin, addresses Eve: 'imbued with seed from the manifold traces of perverse desires, you seduced [Adam] into consenting with you by enticing eloquence, presaging in this work of yours that the judgement of the man of God would be true, namely that women make even the wise apostasise' ('e vestigio multiplici perversarum cupiditatum semine imbuta, illecebrosa facundia illum ad tibi consentiendum illexisti, praesignans in hoc opere tuo veram fore futuram sententiam viri Dei, mulieres scilicet apostatare facere etiam sapientes').[40] Citing

[37] See the citations in A. Blaise, *Dictionnaire latin-français des auteurs chrétiens*, rev. H. Chirat (Turnhout, 1993).

[38] The protagonist of Raoul le Petit's *Roman de Fauvain* is a female Fauvel figure. The work is preserved in Paris, BNF MS fr. 571, a manuscript that, although a decade younger than MS fr. 146 and prepared elsewhere, is similar to it, indeed related to it in several respects. See the facsimile of *Fauvain* in *L'Histoire de Fauvain: reproduction phototypique de 40 dessins du manuscrit français 571 de la Bibliothèque nationale (XIVe siècle), précédée d'une introduction et du texte critique des légends de Raoul le Petit*, ed. A. Långfors (Paris, 1914). For the most recent study, see J. H. M. Taylor, '*Le Roman de Fauvain*: Manuscript, Text, Image', in *Fauvel Studies*, pp. 569–89.

[39] Tertullian, *De cultu feminarum lib. II*, in J.-P. Migne (ed.), Patrologia cursus completus series Latina [henceforth PL], 221 vols. (Paris, 1844–64), 1, col. 1305a–b.

[40] *Tractatus de conceptione B. Mariae Virginis*, in PL 159, col. 312d; I am indebted to D. Elliott, *Fallen Bodies: Pollution, Sexuality, and Demonology in the Middle Ages* (The Middle Ages Series; Philadelphia, 1999), for this discussion of Eadmer's work.

Isaiah 64: 6, Eadmer goes on to observe that because of Eve's sin, mankind's relation to God is like sullied menstrual rags ('sicut pannus menstruatae').[41] Thus dirt, seduction and the Original Sin are linked.

Eve is described in much Christian writing as not only gullible but also inconstant, vain, greedy and proud – traits reminiscent of Fauvel. As the Serpent's agent, she herself becomes as the Serpent. Eadmer suggests, following Genesis 3: 5, that she wanted to be as God ('Forte magis putavit Eva se Deum illico fore'),[42] and thus she is comparable to Lucifer. The figure she was most often compared to, contrasted with, in medieval literature is the Virgin.[43] The *seductrix* of *Mundus a mundicia* reigns as an all-powerful harlot queen; as the Queen of 'Mundus' she is, 'per contraria', as it were, the antithesis of the Queen of Heaven. Similarly, Tertullian's *diaboli ianua* contrasts with the *porta celi* of antiphon and motet; she who listened to the Serpent with she who listened to Gabriel; she whose disobedience resulted in death and she whose obedience resulted in eternal life, and Eadmer's source of filth with, paraphrasing Zechariah 13: 1, his 'clear Fountain of David' who washes away the menstrual flow ('fons David patens, in ablutionem menstruatae flue ad nos').[44] 'Eva' is reversed [!] in the 'Ave' with which Gabriel greets Mary at the Annunciation; thus, in the sequence *Missus Gabriel de celis*, 'et ex Eva formans Ave, Evae verso nomine' ('and from "Eve" forms "hail" by turning the name "Eve" around').[45] There is, then, a Marian ele-

[41] Eadmer, *Tractatus de conceptione*, col. 314a.

[42] *Ibid.*, col. 312c.

[43] Thus, in the sequence *Virgini Marie laudes*, 'Eva tristis abstulit, sed Maria contulit natum qui redemit peccatores' ('sad Eve destroyed, but Mary created a son who redeems sinners'). Facs. after London, BL Add. MS 710 in *Le tropaire-prosaire de Dublin*, ed. R.-J. Hesbert (Monumenta Musicae Sacrae, 4; Rouen, 1970), pl. 169; text in *Analecta hymnica medii aevi*, ed. G. M. Dreves *et al.*, 55 vols. (Leipzig, 1886–1922), liv, no. 18. On Eve and Mary see E. Guldan, *Eva und Maria: Eine Antithese als Bildmotiv* (Graz, 1966); A. M. Dubarle, 'Les fondements bibliques du titre marial de Nouvelle Ève', in *Mélanges Jules Lebreton*, 1/*Recherches de science religieuse*, 39 (1951), pp. 49–64; M. Leisch-Kiesel, *Eva als Andere: Eine exemplarische Untersuchung zu Frühchristentum und Mittelalter* (Cologne, 1992); M. Warner, *Alone of All Her Sex: The Myth and the Cult of the Virgin Mary* (New York, 1976), ch. 4; J. A. Phillips, *Eve, the History of an Idea* (San Francisco, 1984), chs. 4 and 5; J. Pelikan, *Mary through the Centuries: Her Place in History* (New Haven, 1996), ch. 3; and, for the scriptural and Patristic background, *Genesis 1–3 in the History of Exegesis: Intrigue in the Garden*, ed. G. A. Robbins (Studies in Women and Religion, 27; Lewiston, NY, 1988).

[44] Eadmer, *Tractatus de conceptione*, col. 314b.

[45] Facs. after Bari, Archivio della Basilica di S. Nicola, MS 1, in *Le prosaire de la Sainte-Chapelle*, ed. R.-J. Hesbert (Monumenta Musicae Sacrae, 1; Macon, 1952), pl. 117; text in *Analecta hymnica*, liv, no. 102. Cf. the antiphon *Ave maris stella*, 'Sumens illud Ave . . .,

ment in *Mundus a mundicia*, introduced subtly and 'per contraria'. We shall return to this in Part IV.

The unbridled sway of this Fauvel/seductress parallels the complaint at the opening of *Favellandi vicium*. Fauvel spreads his (her) filth over the world; wickedness is everywhere. It is the three added lines, verses 7–9, with their allusion to the seductress, that attribute the state of affairs to Fauvel specifically. The last line uses the word 'hic', just as *Favellandi vicium* does in the same location, making clear the immediacy of Fauvel's malign influence. This is not an abstract condition; it is something that is happening now.

Although in its original state Philip's conductus has nine stanzas, each sung to the music of the first, the *Fauvel* poet/composer has used only the first. As Elizabeth A. R. Brown has noted, however, the remaining eight stanzas are also appropriate to the Fauvel theme.[46] In fact, the omitted stanzas carry forward not only the thought of *Mundus a mundicia*, but also that of *Favellandi vicium*, across the page. It is likely that the informed reader of MS fr. 146 would have had access to the original poem, as the person who adapted it for *Fauvel* almost certainly did; if so, it is not inconceivable that he would have realised this 'motet' as a strophic song, with the three Fauvel/Eve lines added to the end of the stanza serving as a refrain, resulting in an unusual hybrid of conductus and motet.[47] At the very least, the informed reader would probably have recalled the entirety of the Chancellor's poem when he encountered its first stanza in MS fr. 146, and had it in mind when he considered the message on fol. 1^{r}.

The motetus voice is essentially the tenor line of the original conductus. Against it a new tenor was composed, flowing homorhythmically with it as an accompaniment.[48] To this polyphonic

mutans Hevae nomen'; 'receiving that 'Ave' . . ., changing Eve's name'; *Antiphonale monasticum pro diurnis horis*, ed. by the Monks of Solesmes (Paris, 1934), p. 705.

[46] Brown, '*Rex ioans, ionnes, iolie*: Louis X, Philip V, and the *Livres de Fauvel*', in *Fauvel Studies*, p. 68. If, as seems likely, the motet was fashioned specifically for MS fr. 146, the creators of the volume probably had the original conductus at hand, and thus would have been familiar with its remaining strophes. It is possible that some other pieces transmitted in MS fr. 146 with fewer than a full complement of stanzas could have been expanded in a similar fashion; one such is *O labilis sortis humane status* (p.mus. 34), based on another conductus by Philip the Chancellor.

[47] See the discussion of genre in Welker, 'Polyphonic Reworkings', *passim*.

[48] Welker, *ibid.*, pp. 618–23, prefers to regard it as a conductus, its designation in the

complex the composer/adapter added music in the same style to accommodate the three additional verses. The new music is twelve perfect longs in length, thirty-six breves. This added music results in a work in which the new material is divided from the old – the state of affairs and the blaming of Fauvel for it – at the Golden Section.[49] The use of the Golden Section as a structuring principle elsewhere in the *Fauvel* repertory raises the likelihood that this was deliberately intended by the composer.[50] We shall return to the planned use of number in this work in Part VI of this study.

IV

Quare fremuerunt/Tenor (p.mus. 3, Schrade no. 3) follows *Mundus a mundicia* in column c of fol. 1r without a break, apart from a decorated initial letter,[51] filling in the remainder of the page.[52]

Quare fremuerunt	Why have they been raging,
gentes et poppuli	the nations and the peoples?
quia non viderunt	Because never have eyes
monstra tot oculi.	beheld so many portents,

manuscript, layout on the page, and single-voice texting notwithstanding. Cf. Morin, 'Genesis', pp. 347–9. The choice of the tenor line for reuse in the new setting is not surprising, since this was always the structural voice in the conductus.

49 Strictly speaking, the Golden Section divides *Mundus a mundicia* into 21:13:8, and our disposition is not quite that. But if we see the division as falling at the start of the following word, on the crucial 'Nam', that puts it at the beginning of the Fauvel extension. It would seem reasonable to admit liberties such as this when considering the presence of the Golden Section in poetry set to mensural polyphony; cf. M. Bent, 'Polyphony of Texts and Music in the Fourteenth-Century Motet: *Tribum que non abhoruit/Quoniam secta latronum/Merito hec patimur* and its "Quotations"', in D. Pesce (ed.), *Hearing the Motet: Essays on the Motet of the Middle Ages and Renaissance* (New York, 1997), p. 102, n. 13. There are twenty-two longs up to this point, ending with '[nescit termi]-num'. The final sonority here is the same as that at the close of the piece as a whole.

50 See Bent, 'Polyphony of Texts and Music', p. 102. For another example, see p.mus. 12: *Qui secuntur castra/Detractor est nequissima vulpis/Verbum iniquum et dolosum abhominabitur dominum* (Schrade no. 9), in which the significant allusion to 'Pinquegnie O vice domine' falls at the Golden Section. On this reference see A. Wathey, 'The Marriage of Edward III and the Transmission of French Motets to England', *Journal of the American Musicological Society*, 45 (1992), pp. 19–21; and id., 'Gervès du Bus', pp. 601–2. The considered use of the Golden Section in medieval polyphony is not universally acknowledged; cf. R. Tatlow, 'Golden Number [Golden Section]', in *New Grove II*.

51 The initial is smaller than the one introducing *Mundus a mundicia*; if it is more elaborate than those used to indicate the tenor voice, that may be at least partly owing to its placement in the margin, affording the flourisher more room to work.

52 Cf. the edition in H. Tischler, 'The Two-Part Motets of the *Roman de Fauvel*: A Document of Transition', *Music Review*, 42 (1981), p. 7.

5	neque audierunt	nor over the course of generations
	in orbe seculi	have old men and little ones
	senes et parvuli.	heard of [so many] conflicts
	prelia que gerunt	that kings and princes wage
	et que sibi querunt	and that they
10	reges et reguli	seek for themselves.
	Hec inquam inferunt	Fauvel and his corrupt little helpers,
	fauvel et fasuli.	I do say, are causing these things.

Notes to the text: 12 *fasuli*: Dahnk suggests *falvuli* in accordance with the 'Fauveaus nouveaus' mentioned later in the *roman* (La. add. v. 1557), but that substitutes a modern concoction for the one offered by the scribe. It may have been derived from ML *vassalus* (retainer) or an OF counterpart, as a diminutive with a Fauvel inflection intended to go with 'gentes et populi', etc. (hence, Fauvel's little henchmen); or from *fas* (right, that which is lawful, divine law, command – hence, a meagre or skimpy moral and legal code). Both connotations may be intended.

Like *Mundus a mundicia*, *Quare fremuerunt* is based on a thirteenth-century conductus, this time on one known only from F.[53] The setting takes over the lone strophe preserved in F without variation, then adds two new lines at the end to relate its message directly to Fauvel (vv. 1–10, 11–12). It differs from *Mundus a mundicia* (and from *Favellandi vicium*, for that matter) in that nothing of the music of its model is used in the *Fauvel* version – or, if it is there, it is so altered that it is scarcely recognisable.[54] Also distinctive – indeed, unique within the corpus of *Fauvel* polyphony – is the musical idiom chosen by the composer, one that combines the homorhythm and contrary motion that dominate *Mundus a mundicia* with the florid decoration of the melodic line found in many of the monophonic vernacular songs in the manuscript, both in the *Fauvel* collection and among the Lescurel songs. Also striking is the overall musical design of the motet: an opening section, written out twice, but with *ouvert* and *clos* endings, setting verses 1–4 and 5–8, and a contrasting section setting for the last four lines, each of the three resulting sections identical in length.[55] If

[53] F, fols. 244^{v}–245^{r}. Edited in *Three-Part Conductus in the Central Sources*, ed. Anderson, pp. 48–9 and xxvii.

[54] Cf. the discussion in Morin, 'Genesis', pp. 349–55 and Welker, 'Polyphonic Reworkings', pp. 622–30. Welker sees the music as having been derived from the bottom voice of the F conductus, which he finds reworked in both voices of the *Fauvel* motet.

[55] If this scheme is reminiscent of the vernacular ballade, it can also be seen, if ordinarily in not quite so balanced a form, in the conductus repertory; see, for example, the monophonic *Beata viscera* attributed to Perotinus by Anonymous IV (edited, among other places, in *1pt Conductus – Transmitted in Fascicule X of the Florence Manuscript*, ed. G. A. Anderson (Notre-Dame and Related Conductus, Opera omnia, 6, Collected Works, X/6;

Mundus a mundicia looks like a hybrid, *Quare fremuerunt* has even more of that aspect.

To come fully to terms with this seemingly modest motet, we must approach *Quare fremuerunt* from (at least) two distinct but complementary directions. One is textual, broadly conceived: we shall examine the work in the light of the sources drawn upon for both its text and its music. The other is structural: we shall consider the design of the motet, evident in text and music alike, as an essential part of its content, and see how it shapes the message of the work. We shall look first at the content of the motet poem, then at the structure of the work, and finally at one aspect of its musical text. To do this, we shall examine three sources drawn upon by the composer in turn.

'adversus Dominum, et adversus Christum eius'

Read without reference to anything else, the message of *Quare fremuerunt* would seem to be straightforward: the *gentes* and *populi* have been fulminating, raging, because of the state of affairs in the land. The world is seeing ominous signs in unparalleled numbers, conflicts without precedent, and rulers who act only out of self-interest, not in that of their subjects and the state. (These same themes are addressed by several of the *dits* of Geffroi de Paris that follow *Fauvel* in MS fr. 146, including *De la comete et de leclipse et de la lune et du soulail*, *Des alliez en latin*, *Des alliez en francois*, *Auisemenz pour le Roy Loys*, and *De Roy phellippe qui ore Regne.*) The poem describing all this may be as much as a century old at the time of its adaptation for *Fauvel*; the crisis is brought into the present, the 1310s, by the added lines: it is happening now because of Fauvel and his band ('inferunt', in verse 11, reinforces the sense of currency that dominates the original poem). These remarks on the corruption and lack of leadership displayed by the 'reges et reguli' complement nicely the text of *Favellandi vicium*, with its references to hypocrisy and greed on and surrounding the Throne

Henryville, Pa., 1981), p. 25). For a somewhat parallel situation to *Quare fremuerunt* cf. the ballade-like *Fauvel* song *Falvelle qui iam moreris*, MS fr. 146, fol. 29^{v}, an adaptation of a conductus text ascribed to Philip the Chancellor (*Homo qui iam moreris*, in F, fol. 428^{v}, among other places); p.mus. 69, edited in *Monophonic Songs*, ed. Rosenberg and Tischler, no. 52. The *Fauvel* indexer was initially uncertain whether to call *Falvelle qui iam moreris* a 'prose' or a 'balade'.

and corrupt judges. Read in the context of the *roman* narrative in column b, these figures must be understood as constituting the leadership of early fourteenth-century France; the 'gentes et poppuli' are the other estates and the populace of the realm who are harmed by their behaviour. The ironic counterpointing in the last line of 'fauvel et fasuli' with both the 'reges et reguli' and the 'gentes et poppuli' underscores syntactically Fauvel's role in the trouble, as does the musical setting of the added lines, which, unlike the treatment of the parallel added passage in *Mundus a mundicia*, flows seamlessly from what had gone before.

The choice of *Quare fremuerunt* to round out the musical package on fol. 1r was undoubtedly sparked by the reference to the 'si grant presse de gens de toutes nacions et de toutes condicions' in the adjacent *roman* text (La. vv. 28–30). Its selection was doubly apt because the 'reges et reguli' of the motet anticipate the reference to kings and nobility that launches the estates satire on the following page. However, if the 'gentes et poppuli' indeed constitute part of Fauvel's 'grant presse', there is likely to be more to them than what we have just suggested: they cannot merely be the people of France oppressed by Fauvel, for they too are part of Fauvel's entourage, just as they too are linked syntactically to the corrupt 'reges et reguli'.

Now the text of *Quare fremuerunt* has a rich tradition behind it, which must be taken into account when reading this motet. Like *Favellandi vicium* it is dependent on a scriptural source, another psalm, in this case Psalm 2. This is most evident at the beginning of the poem, which paraphrases the opening line of the psalm, but in fact verses 1–3 of Psalm 2 would seem directly or indirectly to inform much of the motet text:

1 Quare fremuerunt gentes, et populi meditati sunt inania?	Why have the Gentiles raged, and the people devised vain things?
2 Astiterunt reges terrae, et principes convenerunt in unum adversus Dominum, et adversus Christum eius.	The kings of the earth stood up, and the princes met together, against the Lord, and against his Christ. [Saying]:
3 Disrumpamus vincula eorum, et proiiciamus a nobis iugum ipsorum.	Let us break their bonds asunder, and let us cast away their yoke from us.

To probe the relationship between the psalm and the motet, it will be helpful to consider Psalm 2 in the light of the extensive medieval exegetical tradition that grew up around it. We shall concentrate in particular on the commentary of Thomas Aquinas, which offers a fair example of what a sensitive reader at the time of *Fauvel* would have been likely to find in the psalm, complementing this with exegesis by earlier writers, from St Augustine to Peter Lombard, as appropriate.[56]

In Psalm 2, the *gentes* and *populi* rage and plot against the authority of the true king, the Messiah or 'Christ', the one anointed by God. They are supported in their schemes by the *reges terrae* and *principes*, by those in positions of authority. Aquinas interprets all these figures Christologically, as the people implicated in the persecution of Christ.[57] Thus the *gentes* (the 'nations', or 'Gentiles') are to be understood as the Roman soldiers who came for Christ and who carried out his execution; the *populi* are the Jews who erroneously believed they had killed him;[58] the *reges* are Herod of

[56] *Postilla super Psalmos*, in, among other edns, *Sancti Thomae Aquinatis doctoris angelici Ordinis Praedicatorum opera omnia ad fidem optimarum editionem*, xiv: *Expositio in aliquot libros Veteris Testamenti et in Psalmos I* (Parma, 1863), pp. 152–5; French trans. and commentary in Thomas d'Aquin, *Commentaire sur les Psaumes*, trans. J.-É. Stroobant de Saint Éloy; preface by M. D. Jordan (Paris, 1996); English trans. (with Latin text) by S. Loughlin in 'The Aquinas Translation Project', coordinated by S. Loughlin, on line at http://faculty.niagara.edu/loughlin/Psalms/Psalm_2.html. Quotations from Aquinas are after the Parma edition and Loughlin's translation. Cf. the useful compendium of patristic opinion collected by Peter Lombard in his influential *Magna glosatum*, publ. as *Commentarius in psalmos Davidicos*, in PL 191, cols. 69–77. Testifying to its importance in the thirteenth and fourteenth centuries, the Lombard's *Glosa* seems to have been the primary source for the illustrative cycles and accompanying moralising verses in the psalms portions of the *bibles moralisées*; see T. Alfillé, 'The Psalms in the Thirteenth-Century Bible moralisée: A Study in Text and Image', 2 vols. (Ph.D. diss., Courtauld Institute of Art, University of London, 1992), ch. 3. It is not our intent here to examine the various medieval interpretations of Psalm 2 comprehensively or in any depth. Useful as such an undertaking would be, it would require a book-length study of its own and a much broader purview than the narrow focus of this essay either permits or requires.

[57] Aquinas remarks at the outset of his commentary that the psalm concerns 'the tribulations of Christ', and that 'this [psalm] . . . treats of [David's] kingdom in the figure of the kingdom of Christ. For by David, Christ is suitably signified' ('in hoc procedit ad materiam propriam, scilicet tribulationes suas signantes tribulationes Christi. . . . et de regno eius in figura regni Christi agit. Per David enim Christus convenienter significatur . . .'; *Postilla*, 152). Cf. Peter Lombard, *Commentarius in psalmos Davidicos*, cols. 69c–70b.

[58] Aquinas also remarks that 'a people [*populus*] is a multitude of men associated by legal consent. And thus the Jews are called a people, because they are with and under the law of God. The rest are called gentiles, because they are not under the law of God' ('Populus est multitudo hominum juris consensu sociata. Et ideo Judaei dicuntur populus, quia cum lege et sub lege Dei sunt. Alii dicuntur gentes, quia non sunt sub lege Dei'; *Postilla*, 152). This is admirably clear, but it is apparent from the contexts in which *gentes*, *populi* and *nationes* are used that these words can be multivalent in their connotations, and that their meanings sometimes cross each other. This can be seen, for exam-

Ascalon and Herod Antipas, the former responsible for the Slaughter of the Innocents in an attempt to kill the infant Jesus, the latter responsible for the execution of Christ's herald John the Baptist; and the *principes* are represented by Pilate, who condemned Jesus, and the chief priests of the Temple.[59] That it is these figures who are the speakers quoted in v. 3 was recognised by commentators as early as Jerome and Augustine.[60]

The reading of the opening of Psalm 2 offered by Aquinas was the standard one throughout the Middle Ages. It is reflected in the iconography used to illustrate this psalm, for example in the moralised Bible probably made in 1234 for Louis IX and his wife Marguerite de Provence, Paris, BNF lat. 11560, fol. 2r (Figure 2).[61] Medallion (g) shows the plotters gathered in conspiracy; medallion (h) depicts Christ on the Cross, with the soldier offering him vinegar to drink. The moralising text to the left of the medallions, drawn from the *Magna glosatum* of Peter Lombard, explains the opening lines of the psalm in terms that anticipate Aquinas:

Psalmus id est tractatus iste attribuitur David id est Christo qui agit de se rege et increpat hic Propheta deinde reges et principes id est Herodem et Pylatus et gentes id est milites Romanorum et populos id est Iudeos Christi crucifixores, qui meditati sunt inania id est Christum detinere conati sunt in morte, et hoc frustra quia non impleverunt ut Christe extingueretur.

This psalm, that is, text, is attributed to David, that is, to Christ, who stands as king through him; and this Prophet then rebukes the kings and princes, that is, Herod and Pilate, and the Gentiles, that is, the Roman soldiers and the people, that is, the Jews, the crucifiers of Christ, who considered a vain thing, that is,

ple, in Gen. 10: 1–32, the account of the descendants of Noah: the offspring of Iapheth are described 'in nationibus suis' (v. 5), those of Cham and Sem 'in gentibus suis' (vv. 20, 31), and the whole list is summed up thus: 'Hae familiae Noe iuxta populos et nationes suas. Ab his divisae sunt gentes in terra post diluvium' (v. 32). This blurring of distinctions will be evident in several of the texts presented in this study.

59 Aquinas, *Postilla*, 153. Cf. Augustine, *Enarrationes, 4:* 'Dicitur hoc enim, de persecutoribus Domini'; and Cassiodorus, *Expositio psalmorum I–LXX*, ed. I. Adriaen (Corpus Christianorum Series Latina (henceforth CCSL), 97; Turnhout, 1958), who remarks, p. 40, that vv. 1–3 concern the Jews 'propter passionem Christi', and who offers, pp. 41–2, more or less the same Christological identification of the four groups of rebels as Aquinas.

60 Jerome, *Commentarioli in psalmos*, ed. G. Morin (CCSL 72; Turnhout, 1959), p. 181; Augustine, *Enarrationes in psalmos I–L*, ed. E. Dekkers and J. Fraipont (CCSL 38; Turnhout, 1956), p. 4.

61 On this manuscript see most recently J. Lowden, *The Making of the* Bibles moralisées, 2 vols. (University Park, Pa., 2000), i, ch. 5. Cf. the medallions in the closely related late thirteenth-century Bible, London, BL Add. MS 18719, *ibid.*, i, fig. 89. On the illuminations for Psalm 2 in thirteenth-century Parisian psalters see Alfillé, 'The Psalms in the Thirteenth-Century Bible moralisée', i, pp. 97–8.

Figure 2 Paris, BNF f. lat. 11560, fol. 2r (*Bible moralisée*)
Cliché Bibliothèque nationale de France, Paris

they attempted to drag him to death, but this was thwarted because they were unable to destroy Christ.[62]

Our previous reading of the motet suggested that the *gentes* and *populi* of the poem are in uproar in reaction to the abuses of their *reges* and *reguli*, who have been corrupted by Fauvel. But when the motet is considered against the backdrop of the psalm, it admits a more nuanced reading, one implying not only that the popular rage is on account of Fauvel, but also that it has something of the quality of the foment in the scriptural source. The medieval poet has taken over the verb 'fremo' ('to rage'), using it to characterise the actions not only of the *gentes*, as in the psalm, but also those of the *populi*, suppressing the phrase 'meditati sunt inania', with its implications of deliberation and taking counsel. Aquinas comments that the raging *gentes* of the psalm evince 'minus . . . de ratione' ('a deficiency of the rational powers'), and glosses the verb thus, '*fremuerunt*, quod est bestiarum' ('*fremuerunt*, like the raging of a beast').[63] Whatever the original poet's reasons for the contraction of the psalm verse in the thirteenth-century conductus text, the association with bestiality, and consequently with Fauvel, would not have escaped the man who made the *Fauvel* adaptation. He would also have understood another textual detail that supports a more subtle reading of the motet: the meaning of 'quare' in Christian exegesis. Peter Lombard, following a long patristic tradition, states that the question is to be understood rhetorically, in the sense of 'what use is it that . . .?', rather than literally, in the sense of 'why?'[64] And Aquinas notes, 'he [the speaker] does not ask, but rebukes' ('Non interrogat sed increpat').[65]

[62] Cf. Peter Lombard, *Commentarium in psalmos Davidicos*, cols. 69c–70b: 'iste, id est tractatus iste, qui dicitur psalmus, quia monet ad bene operandum, attribuitur David, id est Christo, qui agit hic de se rege. . . . Primo increpat persequentes et minatur, et loquitur Christus, vel Propheta. . . . VERS. 1. *Quare fremuerunt gentes, et populi meditati sunt inania? Gentes*, id est Romani milites, crucifixores; *fremuerunt*, ut ferae sine ratione: fremere enim ferarum est; *et populi*, scilicet Judaei; . . . *meditati sunt inania*, id est Christum detinere in morte. . . . ; et hoc, *quare?* id est qua utilitate sua? Quasi dicat, frustra, quia non impleverunt, ut Christus exstingueretur. VERS. 2. *Astiterunt reges terrae, et principes convenerunt in unum adversus Dominum et adversus Christum ejus*. *Astiterunt reges*, quasi dicat, non solum populi et gentes, id est minores, contra Christum surrexerunt, sed etiam majores, quia astiterunt, quasi cum mora, mora enim notatur in hoc; *reges terrae*, id est Herodes; *et principes*, id est Pilatus . . .' (the PL text slightly adjusted here for the sake of clarity).

[63] *Postilla*, p. 152.

[64] Peter Lombard, *Commentarius in psalmos Davidicos*, col. 69d: '*quare?* id est, qua utilitate sua? Quasi dicat, frustra, quia non impleverunt, ut Christus exstingueretur'. Cf. Cassiodorus, *Expositio psalmorum*, p. 41.

[65] *Postilla*, p. 152.

Thus the *gentes* and *populi* of MS fr. 146 might be understood to be raging in the manner of beasts, to have become as beasts owing to what Fauvel and his *fasuli* have brought about.[66] They have become as Fauvel; as we intimated, above, they are *fasuli*. In like fashion, the *reges* and *reguli* have taken Fauvel as their leader, and, like the rulers in the psalm, have rejected their true king, the one anointed of God, in favour of Fauvel.[67] Aquinas comments that when the rulers of Psalm 2 seek to rid themselves of the 'yoke' (*iugum*), they are trying to cast off the fetters (*vincula*) of 'royal power' (*regis dominium*).[68] In the spiritual sense, 'in Christo', that 'yoke' is to be understood as 'lex charitatis' ('the law of charity'), and the 'bonds' as 'virtutes, spes, fides, charitas' ('the virtues, faith, hope, charity').[69] Thus, the kings and princes of the psalm have rejected the virtues; their fellows in *Quare fremuerunt*, again, like the *gentes* and *populi* they govern, are Fauvel's *fasuli*, driven by the vices he epitomises rather than guided by Christian virtue. This is confirmed by the next lines of the *roman*, at the top of fol. 1^v, text remarkably reminiscent of Psalm 2: 2, 'Kings, dukes and counts can be observed gathering together to curry Fauvel' (see Part I, above). The other texts on fol. 1^r of MS fr. 146 have already made it clear that the beast, not the anointed king, Christ, presides over the world of *Quare fremuerunt*, the court, and the Throne. *Quare fremuerunt* imparts to this situation a scriptural foundation.

In an elegant touch of irony, the laws of God that the princes

66 The twelfth-century *Glosa ordinaria*, commenting on Lev. 18: 24 ('Defile not yourselves with any of these things with which all the nations [*gentes*] have been defiled, which I will cast out before you') and its surrounding text, defines 'gentes' as 'demons: who on account of their multitude are called all the nations. Who rejoice in every sin: but especially in fornication and idolatry . . .'; cit. after Elliott, *Fallen Bodies*, pp. 126 and 239, n. 2. In Leviticus, these sins are same-sex intercourse and bestiality. This reading of 'gentes' is in harmony with the definition given by Aquinas (see above, n. 58), and it also fits with the thrust of Psalm 2 (the *gentes* do not follow the Levitical laws of God, and seek to overthrow his authority) and with the distinctly demonic character of Fauvel that will be suggested in the discussion to follow.

67 Aquinas: 'Or [*gentes* can be understood] literally: In David's kingdom there were subjugated gentiles and faithful Jews, and both struggled against him' ('Vel ad literam. In regno David erant gentes subjugatae, et Judaei fideles; et utrique moliebantur contra eum'; *Postilla*, p. 152).

68 Aquinas: '"yoke" signifies "royal power". . . . In a kingdom, "bonds" are those things by which the royal power is made firm, such as soldiers, forts, and arms. Therefore, it is appropriate [for rebels] first to destroy these things and then to remove the yoke' ('regis dominium dicitur jugum. . . . Vincula autem sunt in regno illa quibus firmatur potestas regia in regno, sicut milites, castra, et arma. Primo ergo oportet ista dissolvere, et tunc removere jugum'; *Postilla*, p. 153). Cf. Peter Lombard, *Commentarius in psalmos Davidicos*, cols. 70c–71a.

69 *Postilla*, p. 153.

of Psalm 2 conspire to set aside are the very laws and justice that *Favellandi vicium* declares have been corrupted. As in the other texts on the page, the natural order has been upended. The princes who take counsel together against the Lord and his king can be seen as the antithesis of the *consilium* prayed for in the final line of *Favellandi vicium*. Reading that *consilium* Christologically (as evocative of Isaiah's *consiliarius*) like the Christus of *Quare fremuerunt* makes the contrast all the more telling. Even more striking is the parallel that can be drawn between the *populi* that schemed in vain ('meditati sunt inania') in the psalmic background to *Quare fremuerunt* and the *iustus* who will meditate wisdom ('meditabitur sapientiam') in the psalmic subtext to *Favellandi vicium*. The two motets reinforce each other subliminally across the page. The net result is a subtle but powerful statement that the corruption described in *Favellandi vicium* will not stand; the laws of God and the rule of His anointed king cannot be set aside, and the transgressors who plot in vain to do that will be judged and punished.

Although the poet of *Quare fremuerunt* drew specifically on the first three verses of Psalm 2, he doubtless had the complete psalm in mind, the incipit evoking the whole to inform his text on a broader level, just as the content of *Favellandi vicium* is moulded by the entirety of Psalm 36.[70] This will be clear from a brief look at the remainder of the psalm and its exegesis by Aquinas. Much of it is concerned with the entitlement of God's Anointed. Psalm 2: 6 introduces this Christus, who declares, 'But I am appointed king by him over Sion, his holy mountain, preaching his commandment' ('Ego autem constitutus sum rex ab eo super Sion, montem sanctum eius, praedicans praeceptum eius').[71] Aquinas affirms what any medieval reader would have understood, that Sion is Jerusalem, that the king is God's appointed ruler over the people

[70] This would have been true of both the writer of the original conductus text and the poet/composer of the *Fauvel* arrangement.

[71] Thus in the Vulgate, and thus understood by the Latin exegetical tradition; see, for example, Peter Lombard, *Commentarius in psalmos Davidicos*, col. 71d. In the Hebrew, as in modern translations based on it, it is God himself who speaks here: 'I have set my king on Sion.' Cf. the textual commentary in Peter Lombard, *Commentarius*, cols. 74d–76b. Psalm 2 would seem to have originated as a coronation prayer; the 'voice' speaking throughout, whether quoting others or uttering his own words, is likely to be that of either the monarch himself or one of his vassals; see S. R. A. Starbuck, *Court Oracles in the Psalms: The So-Called Royal Psalms in their Ancient Near Eastern Context* (Society of Biblical Literature Dissertation Series, 172; Atlanta, 1999), pp. 161–8. See also P. Auffret, *The Literary Structure of Psalm 2* (Journal for the Study of the Old Testament, Supplement Series, 3; Sheffield, 1977).

of Israel, and that 'his commandment' is the Gospel.[72] In verses 7–9 the king reports the words of God that confirm his authority: 'The Lord hath said to me: Thou art my son, this day have I begotten thee. Ask of me, and I will give thee the Gentiles [this is also Aquinas's understanding of the meaning of *gentes* here] for thy inheritance, and the utmost parts of the earth for thy possession. Thou shalt rule them with a rod of iron, and shalt break them in pieces like a potter's vessel' ('Dominus dixit ad me: Filius meus es tu; ego hodie genui te. Postula a me, et dabo tibi gentes haereditatem tuam, et possessionem tuam terminios terrae. Reges eos in virga ferrea, et tamquam vas figuli confinges eos'). Aquinas's comments on the 'rod of iron' begin with a 'historical' reading:

But because the citizens [*cives*] were ruled one way, and the conquered enemy [*hostes*; Aquinas otherwise calls them *gentes*] in another (citizens were ruled by the guidance of mercy, the enemy by the guidance of harsh justice), thus [the psalmist] says, 'with a rod of iron'. But it is better that this be referred to the spiritual dominion of Christ, for it is necessary that he who rules have a rod. 'The rod of governance, the rod of your kingdom.' It is for this kings are necessary, so that they have the rod of discipline by which they punish transgressors. And because Christ was appointed king by God to rule the people [*populus*], he says: 'You shall rule them with a rod of iron.' He adds 'iron' to designate the inflexible discipline of justice [*iustitiae*]. For the rod by which the Jews were ruled was not made from iron, because they frequently shook themselves free by worshipping idols. But this is an iron rule [*virga*] whereby he governs the Gentiles [*gentes*], because they will no longer withdraw from the dominion of Christ, when the plenitude of the people [*gentium*] shall have entered in.

Sed quia aliter reguntur cives, nam cives reguntur regimine misericordiae, aliter hostes subjugati, scilicet regimine severae justitiae; ideo dicit: *In virga ferrea*. Sed melius est ut referatur ad dominium spirituale Christi: necesse est enim quod qui regit habeat virgam: Ps. 44: 'Virga directionis, virga regni tui.' Ad hoc enim necessarii sunt reges, ut virgam habeant disciplinae qua puniant delinquentes. Et quia Christus constitutus est rex a Deo ad populum regendum, ideo dicit: *Reges eos in virga ferrea*. Et addit, *Ferrea*, ad designandum inflexibilem justitiae disciplinam. Virga namque qua regebantur Judaei, non fuit ferrea, quia frequenter excusserunt se adorando idola. Sed haec est virga ferrea qua regit gentes, quia non recedent amplius a dominio Christi, quando plenitudo gentium intraverit.[73]

Aquinas also interprets the *virga* allegorically, as 'good people' ('bonos scilicet') and the pieces of the shattered wheel as, among other things, 'evil people which were finally destroyed' ('malos qui finaliter conterendi sunt').[74] We shall return to this *virga* presently.

[72] *Postilla*, p. 153. Aquinas adds, 'so that I might rule the people according to God's law' ('sed ut regam populum secundum legem Dei'). Cf. Peter Lombard, *Commentarius*, col. 72a.

[73] *Postilla*, p. 154.

[74] *Ibid.*, pp. 154–5. Cf. Peter Lombard, *Commentarius*, col. 73b–c.

The psalm then admonishes the rebellious *reges terrae* and *principes*, the anointed one still speaking: 'And now, O ye kings, understand: receive instruction, you that judge the earth. Serve ye the Lord with fear: and rejoice unto him with trembling. Embrace discipline, lest at any time the Lord be angry, and you perish from the just way' (vv. 10–12: 'Et nunc, reges, intelligite; erudimini, qui iudicatis terram. Servite Domino in timore, et exsultate ei cum tremore. Apprehendite disciplinam, nequando irascatur Dominus, et pereatis de via iusta').[75] Commenting on this passage, Aquinas is careful to distinguish between the *reges*, to whom is committed the *universalis gubernatio*, 'government overall', and the *iudices*, to whom *speciale iudicium*, 'particular judgement', is entrusted. The former are exhorted to understand ('ad intelligendum'), this supported with a quotation of Proverbs 1: 5, 'he that understandeth, shall possess governments'. Aquinas cites Augustine to the effect that 'the king serves God, in so far as he is a man, by living justly in himself, but in so far as he is a king, by enacting laws against those which are contrary to the justice of God'.[76] The 'judges' (we presume that these include Pilate, mentioned earlier in the commentary as representative of the *principes*), whom Aquinas calls 'teachable' ('tales dicuntur bene docibiles'), are exhorted to 'receive instruction, namely so that they may acquire the form of judgement from others' ('ad erudiendum, ut scilicet ab aliis formam judicii accipiant').[77] (For authority Aquinas quotes Wisdom 6: 2: 'hear, therefore, ye kings, and understand; learn, ye who are judges of the ends of the earth'.) The discipline that the rulers are exhorted to embrace consists of '[God's] commandments and good practices, or adversities, as if an assistance and protection' ('praecepta et bonos mores, vel adversa quasi praesidium et munimentum'). By 'perish from the just way', Aquinas understands '[the path] of justice and the goods of society, which is exceedingly painful to them who have tasted of the sweetness of justice' ('scilicet justitiae et societatis bonorum, quod est valde

[75] Readers as early as Jerome and Augustine understood that this passage is addressed to the *reges terrae* and *principes* of v. 2; see Jerome, *Commentarioli in psalmos*, p. 181, and Augustine, *Epistola CLXXXV (De correctione Donatistarum liber)*, PL 33, cols. 801–2. On the identify of the speaker cf. Peter Lombard, *Commentarius*, cols. 73c–74a.

[76] *Postilla*, p. 155: 'Et notandum secundum Augustinum: quod rex servit Deo inquantum homo, in se juste vivendo, sed inquantum rex, leges ferendo contra ea quae sunt contra Dei justitiam.' His source is Augustine, *Epistola CLXXXV*, col. 801.

[77] *Postilla*, p. 155.

poenosum his qui dulcedinem justitiae gustaverunt'; this echoes Augustine and Peter Lombard, the latter remarking of the *via iusta*, '*Ne pereatis de via iusta*, id est Christo sublati, vel de operatione bona' – '*Lest you perish from the just way*, that is, removed from Christ, or from the good work').[78]

The psalm concludes with a benediction introduced by the theme of anger: 'When his wrath shall be kindled in a short time, blessed are all they that trust in him' (v. 13: 'Cum exarserit in brevi ira eius, beati omnes qui confidunt in eo').[79] Some measure of that wrath is described earlier in the psalm, in verses 4–5, when the Lord derides his rebellious subjects and their rulers, throwing them into confusion, and is, according to Aquinas, sitting 'in judgement' ('in judicio') and 'setting them [the rebels] on his left' ('statuens eos a sinistris'), casting them 'into eternal punishment' – into damnation ('in corde et in anima in aeterna poena').[80]

Many, if not all, of these associations would have occurred to a reader of *Quare fremuerunt*.[81] The anointed king ruling in justice in accordance with the law of God, the rulers who reject the authority of God and his Christ who are admonished in the strongest terms to bow before the authority of the Anointed One – these stand in vivid and stark counterpoint with the dreadful state of affairs conjured up in the motet launched by the psalm's opening lines. In large measure they are also the themes of *Favellandi vicium*. The psalmic background to *Quare fremuerunt* is much more concerned with empowered kingship, however, than is the scriptural foundation of *Favellandi vicium*, the so-called royal Psalm 2 forcefully bringing the motet into line with the central theme of

[78] *Ibid.*, p. 155; Augustine, *Enarrationes in psalmos I–L*, p. 4; Peter Lombard, *Commentarius in psalmos Davidicos*, col. 74c.

[79] The adjective 'iusta' in v. 12, present in both the Roman psalter and the Vulgate, is absent from Jerome's translation from the Hebrew; see *Sancti Hieronymi psalterium iuxta Hebraeos*, ed. H. de Sainte-Marie (Collectanea Biblica Latina, 12; Rome, 1954). Aquinas comments on this: 'Jerome's version has "perish from the way", and "just" is not there. . . . But if "he perishes from the way", he is irretrievable (Job 4). And because he understands nothing, he will perish for ever' ('Litera Hieronymi habet, *Pereatis de via*; non est ibi *justa*. . . . Sed si *perit de via* irreparabilis est', Job 4. Et quia nullus intellegit, in aeternum peribunt'); *Postilla*, p. 155. Cf., however, Jerome, *Commentarioli in psalmos*, p. 182 ('via recta').

[80] *Postilla*, p. 153.

[81] It is conceivable that the *Fauvel* arrangement of *Quare fremuerunt* is modelled not only on the content of Psalm 2 but also on its structure. The motet text has seventy-two syllables while Psalm 2 has virtually double the number of grammatical units, 145 words (144 if one follows Jerome and omits 'iusta' in v. 12).

the *roman* and MS fr. 146 as a whole, kingship. It is squarely congruent with the political theology of the later Capetian monarchs, and that was forcefully articulated during the reign of Philippe le Bel.[82] This is an ideology of kingship that saw the Capetian lineage as the successor to the kings of biblical Israel, and especially David and Solomon. The king is God's chosen one to be the steward of Christ's kingdom on earth. His authority derived from Christ's kingship. Capetian kingship was intrinsically saintly; we have already seen aspects of that in the brief consideration of Louis IX and the Franciscans, in Part II, above. That sanctity derived from the virtues of good rule and just dealing, from wise and prudent administration of the realm. This royal ideology informs, if in different ways, the *Fauvel* motets addressed to Philippe le Bel's two immediate successors, *Rex beatus confessor domini/Se ceurs ioians/Ave* (p.mus. 32, to Louis X) and *O Philippe prelustrus francorum/Servant regem misericordia/Rex regum et dominus dominancium* (p.mus. 33, to Philip V in its *Fauvel* context, but possibly addressed to St Louis in an earlier state of the work).[83] Supported by its exegetical tradition, Psalm 2 provided a scriptural foundation for this theology of kingship.

Philippe le Bel's sainted grandfather Louis IX was the quintessential example of this holy kingship in action. The sanctity of Louis's kingship dominates his proper Office, *Ludovicus decus reg-*

[82] Regarding the late Capetians specifically, see J. R. Strayer, 'France: The Holy Land, the Chosen People, and the Most Christian King', in his *Medieval Statecraft and the Perspectives of History*, ed. J. F. Benton and T. N. Bisson (Princeton, 1971), pp. 300–14; E. A. R. Brown, 'The Prince is the Father of the King: The Character and Childhood of Philip the Fair of France', *Mediaeval Studies*, 49 (1987), pp. 282–334; ead., 'Persona et Gesta: The Images and Deeds of the Thirteenth-Century Capetians, the Case of Philip the Fair', *Viator*, 19 (1988), pp. 219–46; ead., 'Kings Like Semi-Gods: The Case of Louis X of France', *Majestas*, 1 (1993), pp. 5–37; ead., 'The Religion of Royalty: From Saint Louis to Henry IV, 1226–1589', in *Creating French Culture: Treasures from the Bibliothèque nationale de France*, ed. M.-H. Tesnière and P. Gifford (New Haven, 1995), pp. 131–48; A. W. Lewis, *Royal Succession in Capetian France: Studies in Familial Order and the State* (Harvard Historical Monographs, 100; Cambridge, Mass., 1981), pp. 122–49; the essays collected in W. C. Jordan, *Ideology and Royal Power in Medieval France: Kingship, Crusades and the Jews* (Variorum Collected Studies Series, 705; Aldershot, 2001); and, most recently, Gaposchkin, 'Sanctification and Memorialization', esp. ch. 3, 'Ideology, Kingship and Sanctity'. The present discussion is heavily indebted to Professor Gaposchkin's dissertation and to her '*Ludovicus decus regnantium*'.

[83] Regarding these two works see Brown, '*Rex ioians, ionnes, iolis*' and E. Dillon, 'The Profile of Philip V in the Music of *Fauvel*', in *Fauvel Studies*, pp. 215–31. On the relationship of *O Philippe prelustrus francorum* to Louis IX see Wathey, 'The Marriage of Edward III'. This theology of sacred kingship is also to be seen in the stained glass of the Sainte-Chapelle; see A. A. Jordan, *Visualizing Kingship in the Windows of the Sainte-Chapelle* (Turnhout, 2002).

nantium, perhaps composed in 1298 for Philippe le Bel in conformity with the court's ideology.[84] Significantly, the second psalm in the Matins liturgy is Psalm 2, *Quare fremuerunt*, introduced by an antiphon, *Regni sedem consectus*, that is itself a paraphrase of verse 6 of the psalm:

Ant. Having obtained the seat of the kingdom, he [Louis] surrendered himself to humility and, appointed in Sion, he shone in service to the Lord.

Regni sedem consectus humilem se prebuit, et in Syon constitutus cultu Dei claruit.

Ps. 2: 6. I am appointed king by him over Sion his holy mountain, preaching his commandments.

Ego autem constitutus sum rex ab eo super Syon, montem sanctum eius praedicans praeceptum eius.

Louis (and, with him, those of his line who followed him on the throne) is the new David. (In the Benedictus antiphon sung at Lauds in *Ludovicus decus regnantium*, Louis is said to be David's 'twin in virtue'.)[85] David was the prefiguration of Christ; Louis, the anointed king, reigned in the image of Christ. Sion, understood to connote Jerusalem and Israel, has become France. This has its immediate resonance in *Fauvel*, and nowhere more strikingly so than in the *vers, Ha Parisius civitas regis magni* (p.mus. 73), on fol. 30^{v} of MS fr. 146.[86] The text is a paraphrase of Psalm 47: 3: 'Fundatur exultatione universae terrae montes Sion latera Aquilonis civitas regis magni' ('With the joy of the whole earth is mount Sion founded, on the sides of the north, the city of the great king'). Sion has become not only France but even Paris; the picture that follows this piece depicts the Palais, and the chant that follows that image (p.mus. 74) is taken from the Feast of Relics at the Sainte-Chapelle, the royal reliquary built by Louis IX and emblematic of the sanctity of the Capetian lineage. The adjoining *roman* text describes Paris, the royal palace on the Seine, and the relics in the Sainte-Chapelle, declaring that Fauvel will be married there (La. add. vv. 28–52). This would seem to be the ultimate manifestation of the rebellion described in Psalm 2.

[84] The most readily available edn of this office is in M. Epstein, '*Ludovicus decus regnantium*: Perspectives on the Rhymed Office', *Speculum*, 53 (1978), pp. 283–334.

[85] 'hic virtute geminus'; see M. C. Gaposchkin, 'Philip the Fair, the Dominicans, and the Liturgical Office for Louis IX' (forthcoming).

[86] On this and the following piece, see Rankin, 'The "*Alleluyes, antenes, respons, ygnes et verssez*"', pp. 431–3; and ead., 'The Divine Truth of Scripture: Chant in the *Roman de Fauvel*', *Journal of the American Musicological Society*, 47 (1994), p. 227.

Implicit in the ideology of sacred kingship is the idea that royal sanctity resided in proper rule, in stewardship. The measure of sacred kingship, as defined in *Ludovicus decus regnantium*, is the well-being of the king's lands and subjects. Preserving the kingdom against evil, favouring justice over the other primary royal attribute, mercy, rewarding good with peace, and scattering evil were the foundations of good kingship for writers from Augustine on. Scriptural authority for all this is provided by Psalm 2. Verse 9 of the psalm evokes an important symbol of royal justice and authority, the sceptre or rod (*virga*) with which the king will rule his subjects.[87] The image is a triumphant and militant one, connoting battle and victory. It figured prominently in the coronation liturgy as part of the king's investment with the symbols of authority. In the *ordo* probably used for the coronation of Philippe le Bel, one of the prayers, drawing on text from numerous earlier coronation rituals, reads: 'take the sceptre [*sceptrum*] as the symbol of royal power [*potestatis*], the lawful sceptre [*virgam rectam*] of the kingdom, the sceptre of power [*virgam virtutis*] by which you may rule yourself well, and defend with royal power the Church and Christian people entrusted to you against the wicked, correct the corrupt, bring peace to the righteous . . .'.[88] It is noteworthy that 'virgam virtutis' connotes both power and virtue; this is wholly consistent with the commentary on Psalm 2 by Aquinas cited earlier. Royal virtue and royal power/authority are one and the

[87] Discussed in Gaposchkin, 'Philip the Fair, the Dominicans, and the Liturgical Office for Louis IX'.

[88] 'Accipe sceptrum regie potestatis insigne, virgam scilicet regni rectam, virgam virtutis qua te ipsam bene regas, sanctam ecclesiam populumque videlicet christianum tibi a Deo commissum regia virtute ab improbis defendas, pravos corrigas, rectos pacifices, et, ut viam rectam tenere possint tuo iuvamine dirigas, quatinus de temporali regno ad eternum regnum pervenias'; Jackson, *Ordines coronationis Franciae*, ii, p. 399; see commentary in Gaposchkin, 'Philip the Fair, the Dominicans, and the Liturgical Office for Louis IX'. Although much of the spirit of Psalm 2 is echoed in the Frankish and Capetian coronation texts, the psalm itself did not find any specific use there. However, Psalm 2 was sung within the weekly *cursus*, as in the proper Office for St Louis, in Sunday Matins as the second psalm. Coronation Ordo XXIIa, the so-called Last Capetian Ordo, describes the activity of the king-to-be and the clergy on 'Sabbato precedente diem dominicum in qua rex est consecrandus et coronandus', stating that after Compline, 'Matutine more solito decantantur'; Jackson, *Ordines*, ii, pp. 380–1 (cf. the fourteenth-century French translation, Ordo XXIIb: 'Matines doivent estre chantees selon la maniere acoustomee'; *ibid.*, pp. 424–5). If this is a reference to Sunday Matins, as the *ordo* implies, Psalm 2 would indeed have been sung in the context of the coronation, if not during the ceremony itself. See also Ordo XXV, for Charles VIII; *ibid.*, p. 573. I am grateful to Professor Jackson for sharing his thoughts on this question with me.

same. Fauvel and the 'reges et reguli' who follow him in *Quare fremuerunt* possess neither. The admonition to the new king, Philip V, is clear.

In addition to *Quare fremuerunt*, two important political essays written in the early fourteenth century draw on Psalm 2, a measure of its relevance for the theory of kingship in the Middle Ages. John of Paris's *De potestate regia et papali*, written *c.*1302–3 in support of the French position in the struggles between Philippe le Bel and Boniface VIII,[89] rejects the thesis that the 'Christus' of verse 2 should be understood to be the Pope, who, it is proposed, as Vicar of Christ has power over kings, countering that the psalm should be interpreted from a moral standpoint, as concerning 'the persecution of Christ sustained at present in his members through evil-doers, and his rulership in his members in the future, when . . . all things will be subject to him in heaven'.[90] This is in line with Aquinas. Dante's *Monarchia*, probably written between 1316 and 1318 (and therefore exactly contemporaneous with the production of MS fr. 146),[91] on the government of the world by a single monarch, opens Book 2 with a quotation of Psalm 2: 1–3.[92] Dante uses the text sermon-like for his own ends; thus, God's Anointed becomes the Roman Emperor, against whom enemies plotted in vain.[93] He draws on it a second time later in Book 2, at a major point of division in his presentation. Dante writes that 'those who claim to be zealous for the Christian faith are the ones who "raged" and "meditated vain things" against the Roman ruler. And yet they are not moved to pity Christ's poor, who are defrauded of the income of churches but also daily have the income of their very patrimonies snatched away from them. Thus the Church is impoverished while those who pretend to be just refuse to acknowledge him who is the executor of justice. Furthermore, such impoverishment cannot be done without incurring God's judgement. . . . What do [these so-called Christians] care if the wealth of the Church is dispersed, so long as the property of their

[89] John of Paris, *On Royal and Papal Power*; trans. J. A. Watt (Toronto, 1971).
[90] *Ibid.*, pp. 138–9 and 203–4.
[91] On the dating, see the summary in *Dante's* Monarchia, ed. and trans. R. Kay (Studies and Texts, 131; Toronto, 1998), pp. xx–xxxv.
[92] *Monarchia*, trans. Kay, 2.1.
[93] *Monarchia*, 2.1.5; see also p. 90, n. 1.

relatives is increased?'[94] The parallels with *Quare fremuerunt* (those who care only for their own enrichment, not for the welfare of the people under their protection) and *Favellandi vicium* (greed, corruption and hypocrisy) are striking – as is the eventual calling to account, also implied by John of Paris.

'I send you out as lambs in the midst of wolves'

Quare fremuerunt has twelve lines of text, with six syllables to a line, seventy-two in all. It presents its text over a span of seventy-two breve *tempora*. The composer does not set the text one syllable to a *tempus* unit, however, but instead utilises the full range of available rhythmic values, longs, breves, *recta* semibreves and semibreves *minimae* as syllable carriers. The motet unfolds in a series of short bursts of rhythmic activity, each leading to a point of stasis lasting a perfect long. The result is a remarkably symmetrical design, but one that does not always correlate perfectly with the unfolding content of the poem (L = long; B = breve):

music	A (24B)			A′ (24B)			B (24B)				
	L-6B-L	9B-L	//	L-6B-L	9B-L	//	6B-L	4B	5B	3B-L	
vv.	1–2	3–4		5–6	7–8		9	10	11	12	

These features suggest that the correlation between the number of syllables, the number of breve units, and the overall design of the piece is deliberate and consequently significant – that the number 72 has something to do with the content of the motet, and that this is reflected in its structure.[95] The key to that significance is found, once again, in Scripture.

To medieval readers familiar with the symbolism inherent in numbers, 72 was rich in connotations. Perhaps the most immediate association that would have been drawn is with the descendants of Noah, described in chapter 10 of Genesis. Noah's three

[94] *Monarchia* 2.10.1.

[95] Cf. the use of 72 by Dante, discussed in M. Hardt, *Die Zahl in der Divina Commedia* (Linguistica et Litteraria, 13; Frankfurt am Main, 1973), pp. 53–5 and 68–70. On the symbolic meaning of 72 see H. Meyer and R. Suntrup, *Lexikon der mittelalterlichen Zahlenbedeutungen* (Münstersche Mittelalter-Schriften, 56; Munich, 1987), cols. 760–4; M. Steinschneider, 'Die kanonischen Zahlen 70–73', *Zeitschrift der Deutschen Morgenländischen Gesellschaft*, 57 (1903), pp. 474–507; and V. F. Hopper, *Medieval Number Symbolism: Its Sources, Meaning, and Influence on Thought and Expression* (Columbia University Studies in English and Comparative Literature, 132; New York, 1938), pp. 70–1.

sons had a total of seventy-two male offspring. 'These are the families of Noah, according to their peoples [*populos*] and nations [*nationes*]. From these the nations [*gentes*] spread abroad on the earth after the flood' (Gen. 10: 32). Several texts quoted in the discussion to follow refer to this association. The significance of these seventy-two 'nations' for understanding the meaning of the 'gentes et poppuli' of *Quare fremuerunt* is obvious: *all* the nations of the earth are raging. By extension, the immediately following scriptural passage, Genesis 11: 1–9, describing the Tower of Babel, was construed as implying that these seventy-two nations spoke seventy-two different languages.[96] To Honorius of Autun, among many others, the number also suggested the seventy-two books of the Bible.[97] Whatever specific connotations 72 had, it stood symbolically for inclusiveness – all the races, all the languages. This is formulated in concise terms by Isidore of Seville in his *De ecclesiasticis officiis*:[98]

There are the seventy-two canonical books, and owing to this Moses selected seventy priests to prophesy, and owing to this Jesus our Lord charged seventy-two disciples to preach, and since seventy-two tongues were spread abroad in this world, the Holy Spirit accordingly made provision that there might be created as many books as there were nations, whose peoples and races might understand thanks to faith.

Hii sunt libri canonici LXXII, et ob hoc Moyses LXX elegit presbiteros qui prophetarent, ob hoc et Iesus dominus noster LXXII discipulos praedicare mandauit; et quoniam LXXII linguae in hoc mundo erant diffusae, congrue prouidit spiritus sanctus, ut tot libri essent quot nationes quibus populi et gentes ad percipiendam fidei gratiam aedificarentur.

Most medieval theologians concurred that these various connotations were interrelated; thus Alcuin: 'gentes septuaginta duae, inter quas misit Dominus discipulos septuaginta duos' ('the seventy-two races among which the Lord sent the seventy-two disciples').[99] Isidore's reference to Moses' priests concerns the seventy who attended him on Sinai (Exod. 24: 1–9), and also

[96] See, for example, Honorius of Autun, *Gemma animae sive de divinis officiis et antiquo ritu missarum deque horis canonicis et totius annis solemnitatibus*, in PL 172, cols. 560d–61a.

[97] *Ibid.*, col. 613a.

[98] Isidore, *De ecclesiasticis officiis*, ed. C. M. Lawson (CCSL 113; Turnhout, 1989), p. 11. On the continuing influence of writers such as Isidore on later authors, see, among much other literature, B. Smalley, *The Gospels in the Schools, 1100–c. 1280* (London, 1985), p. 246.

[99] Alcuin, *Opusculum primum interrogationes et responsiones in Genesin*, in PL 100, cols. 532c–533a; cf. the pseudo-Augustinian *De mirabilibus sacrae scripturae libri tres*, in PL 35, cols. 2160–1.

the seventy elders and officials of Israel ('whom you know to be elders and officers of the people [*senes populi . . . ac magistri*]') whom Moses gathered together at God's command, and who encountered God and spoke prophetically (Num. 11: 16–25). The number 70 had a range of connotations of its own, but it could also stand in for 72, or be symbolically equivalent to it, especially once the two elders who stayed behind in the Israelite camp were added to the tally of 70 (see Num. 11: 26).[100] Jesus' seventy-two disciples, described in the Gospel of Luke, were prefigured by the elders.[101]

It is the image of the seventy-two disciples of Christ that is crucial for our understanding of *Quare fremuerunt*. The narrative of the disciples' mission occurs in Luke 10: 1–24; it will be useful to quote verses 1–19 *in extenso*:

1 After this the Lord appointed seventy-two others, and sent them on ahead of him, two by two, into every town and place where he himself was about to come. 2 And he said to them: 'The harvest is plentiful, but the laborers [*operarii*] are few; pray therefore the Lord of the harvest to send out laborers into his harvest. 3 Go your way; behold, I send you out as lambs in the midst of wolves [*sicut agnos inter lupos*]. 4 Carry no purse, no bag, no sandals; and salute no one on the road. 5 Whatever house you enter, first say, "Peace be to this house!" 6 And if a son of peace is there, your peace shall rest upon him; but if not, it shall return to you. 7 And remain in the same house, eating and drinking what they provide, for the laborer deserves his wages; do not go from house to house. 8 Whenever you enter a town and they receive you, eat and drink what is set before you; 9 heal the sick in it, and say to them, "The kingdom of God is come near to you". 10 But whenever you enter a town and they do not receive you, go into its streets and say, 11 "Even the dust of your town that clings to our feet, we wipe off against you; nevertheless know this, that the kingdom of God has come near". 12 I tell you, it shall be more tolerable on that day for Sodom than for that town. 13 Woe to you, Chorazin! woe to you, Bethsaida! for if the mighty works [*virtutos*] done in you had been done in Tyre and Sidon, they would have repented long ago, sitting in sackcloth and ashes. 14 But it shall be more tolerable in the judgement [*in iudicio*] for Tyre and Sidon than for you. 15 And you, Capernaum, will you be exalted to heaven? You shall be brought down to Hades [*ad infernum*]. 16 He who hears you hears me, and he who rejects you rejects me, and he who rejects me

[100] Meyer and Suntrup, *Lexikon*, cols. 756, 758. Several of the sources for Isidore's *De ecclesiasticis officiis* read the number of Moses' priests as seventy-two. Isidore himself elsewhere reports the number of elders as seventy-two; see his *Allegoriae quaedam sacrae scripturae* [= *De nominibus legis*], in PL 83, cols. 109–10. So also does the pseudo-Augustinian *De mirabilibus sacrae scripturae*, col. 2192, where it is stated, 'Dum enim Moysi spiritus in septuaginta duos consiliarios distribuitur'.

[101] See Augustine, *De heresibus ad quod vult deum liber unus*, in PL 42, col. 38; pseudo-Augustine, *De mirabilibus*, cols. 2160–1; Honorius, *Gemma animae*, col. 550b. Whether the correct number is seventy-two or seventy remains unsettled; see B. M. Metzger, 'Seventy or Seventy-Two Disciples', *New Testament Studies*, 5 (1958–9), pp. 299–306. The medieval tradition is virtually unanimous in accepting 72.

rejects him who sent me.' 17 The seventy-two returned [*reversi sunt*] with joy, saying, 'Lord, even the demons are subject to us in your name!' 18 And he said to then, 'I saw Satan fall like lightening from heaven. 19 Behold, I have given you authority to tread upon serpents and scorpions, and over all the power [*omnem virtutem*] of the enemy; and nothing shall hurt you.'

Luke's narrative, which is without obvious parallels in the other Gospels, sets the disciples' mission at the beginning of the mission that would take Jesus to the royal capital, Jerusalem, a journey that would reach a climax in his triumphal entry into Sion, and then culminate in his crucifixion and resurrection. The 'harvest' is the spreading of the Word; the fact that Jesus sent seventy-two disciples suggests that the harvest is the entire world (or, at least, all of Israel, David's kingdom; it follows the earlier, more modest mission of the twelve apostles recounted in Luke 9: 1–10).[102] There is a sense of urgency in Jesus' injunctions to the disciples: they are his heralds, announcing that his kingdom is immediately at hand. There is a clear judgmental tone to Jesus' injunction to inform those whom they meet that 'the kingdom of God is come near', followed as it is by his malediction upon the disbelieving Galilean cities that had previously rejected him, comparing their fate with that of Sodom after its citizens attacked the two (!) angel messengers (Gen. 19). The disciples are not only enjoined to bear witness and teach, as in the other Gospels; they are also authorised to pass judgement. The judgement is to be public, declared in the streets. The seventy-two return joyous from their mission, having driven out demons in the name of Jesus. (This looks ahead to Jesus' own casting out of Beelzebub in Luke 11: 14–23.) In a visionary remark Jesus, responding to the story of their exorcisms, sees in their work the fall of Satan from his high place.[103] The disciples can destroy evil creatures in the name of the King.

[102] It would seem that the mission was to the Jews specifically; see H. L. Egelkraut, *Jesus' Mission to Jerusalem: A Redaction Critical Study of the Travel Narrative in the Gospel of Luke, Lk 9:51–19:48* (Europäische Hochschulschriften, XXIII/80; Frankfurt am Main, 1976), pp. 144–8. Augustine, *Sermo CI*, in PL 38, cols. 605–6, distinguishes between the metaphoric 'harvest' (among the Jews) and 'planting' (among the *gentes*). Bede, *In Lucae evangelium expositio*, ed. D. Hurst (CCSL 120; Turnhout, 1960), p. 214, states that the seventy-two were sent out to preach the Gospel into the whole gentile world, just as the twelve apostles had gone to the twelve tribes of Israel; see also the remarks of Isidore of Seville cited in n. 106, below.

[103] See Egelkraut, *Jesus' Mission*, esp. pp. 142–52; and D. P. Moessner, *The Lord of the Banquet: The Literary and Theological Significance of the Lukan Travel Narrative* (Philadelphia, 1998), *passim*.

Throughout Luke's account, those evil beings are couched in animal imagery – wolves, serpents, scorpions.

The relevance of the topos of the seventy-two disciples to *Quare fremuerunt* is clear. In the midst of the awful situation described in the motet, a wrecked country without her anointed king, her 'Christ' ruling after his scriptural model, the king's disciples are spreading the word of his imminent arrival. They are present in the very bricks and mortar of the motet, its seventy-two verbal and temporal elements. The seventy-two disciples speak out, crush evil creatures, cast out demons; they rebuke and cast out the demon Fauvel and his corrupt *fasuli*. Thus there are two scriptural authorities, one psalmic, the other an Evangelist, informing *Quare fremuerunt* and projecting its underlying message, the advent of the Anointed King and the end of Fauvel.

The linkage of Psalm 2 with the disciples of Christ is given a scriptural foundation of its own through an incident in New Testament history recorded in Acts. Peter addresses the throng in the Temple after he and John have healed a lame man, remonstrating with them, 'brethren I know that you acted in ignorance, as did your rulers [when you denied Christ and delivered him up to be crucified]. . . . Repent, therefore, and turn again, that your sins may be blotted out, that times of refreshing may come from the presence of the Lord, and that he may send the Christ appointed for you, Jesus' (3: 17–21). The next morning, 'the rulers and elders and scribes were gathered together in Jerusalem' (4: 5) to question Peter and John, after which they 'conferred with one another' (4: 15) and then warned the two apostles not to speak further in the name of Jesus. Peter replied, 'we cannot but speak of what we have seen and heard' (4: 20). When the two reported these happenings to their brethren, the community responded, quoting verses 1–2 of Psalm 2, 'why did the Gentiles rage, and the peoples imagine vain things? The kings of the earth set themselves in array, and the rulers were gathered together, against the Lord, and against his Anointed' (4: 25–6), then continuing, 'for truly in this city there were gathered together against thy holy servant Jesus, whom thou didst anoint, both Herod and Pontius Pilate, with the Gentiles and the peoples of Israel, to do whatever thy hand and thy plan had predestined to take place. And now, Lord, look upon their threats, and grant to thy servants to speak thy word with all boldness, while thou stretchest out thy hand to heal, and signs and wonders are performed through the name of thy holy servant Jesus' (4: 27–30). The company was greatly heartened, and 'with great power the apostles gave their testimony to the resurrection of the Lord Jesus' (4: 33).

The identification of the *nationes* and *populi* with the Gentiles and the people of Israel, and the rulers with Herod, Pilate and the dignitaries of the Temple; the rulers sitting in council, conferring against Christ, in effect conspiring to escape the law of God; Peter's remark that they had acted in ignorance but can gain understanding; the admonition to repent; the connotations of sanctified kingship seated in a royal capital: all these derive from Psalm 2 and are reflected in its exegetical tradition. The preaching of the apostles and the ecstatic words of the early Christians at the close of the passage put this psalmic material into the context of the disciples spreading the Word and doing their work. This relationship cannot have escaped either the *Fauvel* poet/composer or the reader of MS fr. 146 when he encountered *Quare fremuerunt*. The 'signs and wonders' worked in Christ's name, paralleled in the disciples' casting out of demons, have their counterparts, perhaps ironically, in the portents of *Quare fremuerunt*.

The theme of speaking out against the mischief-makers, present in Psalm 2 and in the passages from both Luke and Acts and important to *Quare fremuerunt*, is central to *Favellandi vicium*. Also linking the two motets is the motif of Christ's disciples labouring in the harvest: this recalls the allusion to the same text in *De gravi seminio*, the Latin motet source for *Favellandi vicium* across the page ('From the fertile stock that the Father sowed among his labourers . . . waxed the fruit of the bountiful harvest'; see Part II, above). Just as the psalmic backgrounds of the two motets complement each other, so this Lucan text links them, imparting yet another element of coherence to an already tight-knit page.

Further relating *Quare fremuerunt* to its scriptural sources is the medieval understanding of what the 'wolves' were, among whom the disciples laboured. Bede understands 'wolves' to be 'scribas et Pharisaeos . . . qui sunt clerici Iudaeorum'.[104] These are the very

[104] *Bede, In Lucae evangelium expositio*, p. 215; and *ibid.*, p. 216 for his thoughts on serpents and scorpions.

figures who, according to the commentators on Psalm 2, rose up against God's anointed king. In Luke's narrative, that king, Jesus, is making his way towards his capital, Jerusalem, and the seventy-two disciples are heralding his way and judging those very people who foment against him. Again, Old and New Testament themes are combined in *Quare fremuerunt*.

Another aspect of the wolf can be seen in Acts 20: 29–30. There, 'wolves' refers not to Jews hostile to the Christian doctrine, as in Isidore and elsewhere in Acts, but rather to those who teach a false Christian doctrine: 'I know that after my departure fierce wolves [*lupi rapaces*] will come in among you, not sparing the flock; and from among your own selves will arise men speaking perverse things, to draw away the disciples after them.' The link between these wolves and those in Luke 10: 3 is made explicit by Matthew 7: 15: 'Beware of false prophets, who come to you in sheep's clothing [*in vestimentis ovium*] but inwardly are ravenous wolves [*lupi rapaces*].' These threads are taken up by Alanus of Lille in his *Liber in distinctionibus dictionum theologicalium*:

> [*Lupus*] is said to be the Devil, whence in the Gospel: the wolf ravages and scatters the sheep, the wolf comes and the servant flees; for as the Devil rises up, the false shepherd is not attentive to the disquiet. . . . It is called the predator, whence the Prophet: the wolf dwells with the lamb. It is called a tyrant hounding God's Church, whence in the Gospel: seeing the wolf come, the servant, he who is not the shepherd, flees. It is called the persecutor of Christians, whence in the Gospel: behold, I send you as lambs in the midst of wolves. It is said to be the hypocrite, who deceives others with false doctrines.
>
> Dicitur diabolus; unde in Evangelio: Lupus rapit et dispersit oves, lupus venit et mercenarius fugit; quia, cum diabolus surgit, falsus pastor curam sollicitudinis non habet. . . . Dicitur raptor, unde propheta: Habitabit lupus cum agno. . . . Dicitur tyrannus persequens Ecclesiam Dei, unde in Evangelio: Mercenarius et qui non est pastor, videns lupum venientem, fugit. Dicitur persequens Christianum, unde in Evangelio: Ecce ego mitto vos, sicut oves in medio luporum. Dicitur hypocrita qui alios decipit falsa religione, unde in Evangelio: Attendite a falsis prophetis, etc., lupi rapacis.[105]

Alanus's *lupus* bears a tantalising resemblance to the figure of Fauvel himself (the horse of hypocrisy and the 'faus vel' ('veil of deceit'); La. vv. 241–2).

[105] In PL 210, col. 843b–c. Cf. Alanus' *Contra haereticos*, in PL 210, cols. 377c–380c. His language bears a striking resemblance to the rhetoric in the closing motet in the *Fauvel* collection, *In nova fert*, discussed in Part V, below.

The number 72 influenced the design and content of *Quare fremuerunt* in ways that reach beyond the symbolism that this number considered as an integer brings to the motet. Isidore of Seville, writing of the 'apostles' number', 12, states, 'Hic duodenarius numerus sexies multiplicatus facit septuaginta duos discipulos, qui missi sunt ad praedicandum per totum mundum in septuaginta duabus linguis divisum' ('this number 12 multiplied by 6 yields seventy-two disciples, who were sent to preach through all the world divided into seventy-two tongues').[106] The factoring of 72 into 12 × 6 is reflected in the motet poem, with its twelve six-syllable lines, and also to a considerable extent in the musical setting, which accords twelve *tempora* for each of the first four pairs of lines, while the last two pairs are off by one *tempus* each (13 and 11 *tempora* for vv. 9–10 and 11–12, respectively; see above), the disruption of the pattern occurring, not surprisingly, at the junction of the old and the new text.

A deployment of the number 72 with a different symbolic connotation can be inferred from the manner in which *Quare fremuerunt* unfolds, in its bursts of semibreve activity punctuated by points of stasis where the two voices dwell together on a perfect long. There are eight of these points of stasis distributed over the course of the piece, for a total of twenty-four *tempora*, one-third of the overall length of the motet. As the composition proceeds, its tripartite structure also results in blocks of music that each extend for twenty-four (this time, contiguous) *tempora*. If one admits the presence of number symbolism in this motet, the threefold aspect of its temporal planning can be seen as imparting a layer of allegory suggestive of the Trinity.[107] But it can be understood as connoting something else in addition: 72 is the number of hours (three days of twenty-four hours each) that Christ lay in the grave before his resurrection; thus the layout of the motet suggests the resurrection itself,[108] and by extension may even connote the rebirth of an orderly and sanctified France. (24 is the number of hours in the day, hence its musical exploitation suggests the dawning of a new

[106] Isidore, *Liber numerorum qui in sanctis scripturis occurrunt*, in PL 83, cols. 192c–193b.

[107] See the various explanations of Augustine, *Quaestionum evangeliorum libri duo*, in PL 35, col. 1339, Bede, *De tabernaculo*, ed. D. Hurst (CCSL 119a; Turnhout, 1969), pp. 111–13; and Honorius of Autun, *Gemma animae*, cols. 560d–561a.

[108] See Honorius of Autun, *Gemma animae*, col. 665c–d, quoted in Part V, below.

day.) In this regard, the eight points of rhythmic stasis mentioned above can be seen from the perspective of resurrection allegory: 8 connotes the day from the Sabbath to the next Sunday, the weekly octave, hence renewal and rebirth.[109] We shall return briefly to these themes when we examine *Adesto sancta trinitas* in Part V, below.

'ad te clamamus exsules filii Hevae'

There is still more to be said about *Quare fremuerunt*. Lorenz Welker has drawn attention to an extraordinary but hitherto unnoticed aspect of the motet, the fact that the music of the 'B' section, setting verses 9–12 of the motet poem, is based on a snippet of plainchant, the opening phrases of the Marian antiphon *Salve regina*.[110] Indeed, despite the melodic decoration with which it is festooned, the distinctive melodic profile of this celebrated chant is clearly evident, first in the motetus and then in the tenor, precipitating an abrupt shift in the tessitura and ambitus of the polyphonic complex, among other things (see Example 3). Welker speculates on the reason for the introduction of the chant melody, suggesting that perhaps 'the composer wished to exploit the salutation to the Queen of Heaven as a play on the reference to "reges" and "reguli"' in verse 10 of the poem'. Indeed: such an ironic counterpointing of images and ideas would be consistent with what we have already suggested about this motet and the other works on fol. 1^{r}. Moreover, the musical parallels between the two halves of the borrowed chant fragment serve as yet another element that relates verses 11–12, attributing the mischief running through the world to Fauvel and his gang, directly to the self-serving activity of the 'reges et reguli' in verses 9–10. The focus of the motet is thereby directed even more forcefully towards kingship, good and bad, sanctified and unholy.

But the presence of the antiphon melody in *Quare fremuerunt* has a deeper connotation. To appreciate it, it will be helpful to examine the full text of the antiphon, since surely the quotation of its opening would have triggered memory of the complete chant, text

[109] Meyer and Suntrup, *Lexikon*, col. 762.

[110] Welker, 'Polyphonic Reworkings', pp. 626–7. The antiphon is published, among other places, in *Antiphonale monasticum*, pp. 176–7, there assigned to Second Vespers from Trinity to Advent.

Example 3 *Salve regina* (beginning) and *Quare fremuerunt* (conclusion)

as well as music, just as the citation of the beginning of Psalm 2 must have evoked the psalm in its entirety.

Salve regina mater misericordia,	Hail, Queen, mother of mercy,
vita dulcedo et spes nostra salve.	our life, our sweetness, and our hope, hail.
Ad te clamamus exsules filii Hevae.	To you we cry, the banished children of Eve.
Ad te suspiramus gementes	To you we send our sighs, mourning
et flentes in hac lacrimarum valle.	and weeping, in this vale of tears.
Eia ergo advocata nostra illos tuos	Come, therefore, our advocate, turn your
misericordes oculos ad nos converte.	merciful eyes towards us.
Et Jesum benedictum fructum ventris	And after this, our exile, show us the
tui nobis post hoc exsilium ostende.	blessed fruit of thy womb, Jesus,
O clemens o pia o dulcis virgo Maria.	O clement, o loving, o sweet Virgin Mary.

In the immediate context of fol. 1r this petition to the Queen of Heaven complements the petition to God that ends *Favellandi vicium* across the page. Mary is the advocate to Christ on behalf of suffering and sinful humanity, wretched in its 'exile', its 'banishment' owing to the sin of Eve, and miserable in 'this vale of tears'. This 'vale' is the racked kingdom described in *Quare fremuerunt*, and indeed in all three motets on fol. 1^r. As seen in *Mundus a mundicia*, it is a filthy world dominated by Fauvel, the harlot queen, the First Eve, the antithesis of the antiphon's New Eve. The two motets that occupy column c of fol. 1^r are thus linked by a dialectic between the glancing allusions to these two 'Eves'.

Beyond this, in the immediate milieu that produced (and received) MS fr. 146, the citation of *Salve regina* would have evoked a more specific image, the cathedral dedicated to her and devoted overwhelmingly to her veneration, Notre-Dame of Paris, only a few steps from the Palais where Fauvel is said to have taken up residence and where our manuscript originated. The role of Mary in the scheme of salvation in Paris specifically is succinctly articulated by Rebecca Baltzer thus:

> the clergy of Notre-Dame of Paris asserted a special role – one closely tied to the Virgin – for their church in their world . . . [Mary] was the Mother of God, and through her, in *this* cathedral church built in her honor, salvation could best be found. Although Mary was first and foremost the Mother of God, from this role followed her other great position, that of the Queen of Heaven, crowned and seated on the right hand of Christ. But . . . Mary was also seen as a type of the Church, as the restorer of salvation (the new Eve), as intercessor to Christ in Judgement, and as the supreme mediatrix between heaven and earth. . . . [The] Virgin was, simply put, the sinner's best avenue to salvation. But she was also the Church, and it was through the Church, inside the *templum deitatis*, that she became accessible.[111]

Fauvel and his *fasuli* dominate the 'reges et reguli' and the 'palais Roial'; we shall learn later in the *roman* that Fauvel has even infected the Sainte-Chapelle, the king's chapel in the Palais. With the introduction of the *Salve regina*, the author, speaking with the collective voice of the seventy-two disciples heralding the coming of Christ, directs us for refuge from the scourge to another sacred house in Paris, the cathedral, and more specifically to its

[111] R. A. Baltzer, 'The Little Office of the Virgin and Mary's Role at Paris', in M. E. Fassler and R. A. Baltzer (eds.), *The Divine Office in the Latin Middle Ages: Methodology and Source Studies, Regional Developments, Hagiography, Written in Honor of Professor Ruth Steiner* (New York, 2000), pp. 470–1. On Mary as symbolising the Church itself see also C. Wright, 'Dufay's *Nuper rosarum flores*: King Solomon's Temple and the Veneration of the Virgin', *Journal of the American Musicological Society*, 47 (1994), pp. 396–441. Among much else see also H. Graef, *Mary: A History of Doctrine and Devotion* (Westminster, Md., 1985); M. Thurian, *Mary: Mother of the Lord, Figure of the Church*, trans. N. B. Cryer (London, 1985); D. Spivey Ellington, *From Sacred Body to Angelic Soul: Understanding Mary in Late Medieval and Early Modern Europe* (Washington, DC, 2001); M. O'Carroll, *Theotokos: Theological Encyclopedia of the Blessed Virgin* (Wilmington, Del., 1982); and D. Iogna-Pratt, E. Palazzo and D. Russo (eds.), *Marie: le culte de la Vierge dans la société médiévale* (Paris, 1996).

patroness, Mary.[112] (It may also conjure up the image of another cathedral, Notre-Dame of Reims, where the king of France was anointed and crowned.)[113] Mary is the mother not only of Christ passing the judgement called for in our motets, but also the mother of the Christ of Psalm 2, God's true king, represented on earth by the wise and holy king who comes to sit on the throne of France. [See the Postscript following this article.]

V

'Quomodo cantabimus?'

Quare fremuerunt is not the only musical work in the *Fauvel* collection to make significant symbolic and structural use of the number 72. Another such is the motet *Quomodo cantabimus/Thalamus puerpere*/[Tenor] (p.mus. 78, Schrade no. 26). *Quomodo cantabimus* appears on fol. 32r, where it is introduced as being sung by the Virtues as part of their ominous commentary on the unholy celebration unfolding at Fauvel's wedding feast (La. add. vv. 382–4). Like *Quare fremuerunt* it deploys the new compositional idiom but draws on material from the thirteenth century. Like *Quare fremuerunt*, again, the text is rooted in Scripture, this time taking its point of departure from Psalm 136: 4 ('Quomodo cantabimus canticum Domini in terra aliena?' – 'How shall we sing the song of the Lord in a strange land?'). Like *Mundus a mundicia*, *Quomodo cantabimus* is based on a conductus (a monophonic one) by Philip the Chancellor.[114] Unlike *Mundus a mundicia* but like *Quare*

[112] By analogy with the seventy-two disciples, some cathedrals had seventy-two canons. One such was Santiago de Compostela, which increased the total number to seventy-two under Bishop Gelmírez early in the twelfth century; see R. A. Fletcher, *Saint James's Catapult: The Life and Times of Diego Gelmírez of Santiago de Compostela* (Cambridge, 1984), 166. Notre-Dame of Paris had fifty-one canons in addition to a large number of other senior clergy; see C. Wright, *Music and Ceremony at Notre Dame of Paris, 500–1550* (Cambridge, 1989), pp. 18–27.

[113] Notre-Dame of Reims had seventy-two canons in the early fourteenth century, the number increasing to seventy-four in 1313, when Pope Clement V authorised the division of two prebends into four; see A. Walters Robertson, *Guillaume de Machaut and Reims: Context and Meaning in His Musical Works* (Cambridge, 2002), p. 33. I am grateful to Professor Robertson for sharing her work with me prior to its publication.

[114] F, fols. 425v–426r; Wolfenbüttel, Herzog August Bibliothek, cod. Guelf. 628 Helmstad. [W_1], fol. 185r (beginning lost); Da, fol. 4r (text of str. 1 only, attributed to Philip the Chancellor). Edited in *1pt Conductus*, ed. Anderson, pp. 37 and XLI.

fremuerunt it borrows only the text, not Philip's musical setting. Unlike both of these motets, its text has not been 'Fauvelised', provided with additional lines to link it more immediately to the topic of Fauvel. The *Fauvel* version, unique to MS fr. 146, uses the first two of Philip's three strophes, presenting them simultaneously, one in each of the two upper voices, and providing a newly composed tenor as a foundation and accompaniment.[115]

The text of this motet, particularly that of the first strophe, bears a striking relationship to the poem of *Quare fremuerunt*. Thus, in the motetus: 'Quomodo cantabimus / sub iniqua lege? / oves quid attendimus? / lupus est in grege / . . . o quando discuciet / spelunca latronum? / quam tremendus veniet / deus ulcionum' (verses 1–4, 11–14: 'How shall we sing under the weight of an unjust law? O sheep, why do we wait? The wolf is in the flock. . . . O when will He scatter this den of thieves? How fearful will the god of vengeance be when He comes'). The triplum speaks of the Church, equated with the very womb of the Virgin (the 'thalamus puerpere'), and of the Throne as beset by adversity, concluding that 'iustus germinabit' ('the just shall flourish', verse 14).

In view of links such as these, it is surely not without significance that each of Philip's strophes in the upper voices has thirty-six words in its text, for a total of seventy-two. (The unused third strophe, strongly Marian in content, has thirty-three.) The tenor *color*, apparently freely invented, has forty-eight notes and is stated twice (the second time the antepenultimate note is repeated thrice as part of a cadential slowdown, for a total of ninety-nine notes). The *color* is arranged according to an interesting symmetrical repetition scheme, thus: a (twelve longs) b (six longs) b (six longs) a (twelve longs), for a total of thirty-six perfections. This is stated twice, as just mentioned, but with the second statement extended by five longs because of the cadential slowdown. (In both upper voices the text at the slowdown consists of a melisma on the penultimate syllable of the strophe; the presentation of the text has effectively concluded, and the cadential extension is superfluous from the standpoint of text delivery.) Without the extension, that is, taking into account only the two statements of the *color* proper,

[115] The tenor melody spans a hexachord; it is the hexachord *g–e*, systematically avoiding the 'Fauvel' pitch *f*. Cf. the discussion of *In nova fert* and *Mundus a mundicia*, below. Clark, '*Concordare cum materia*', p. 124 states that the tenor has its source in a 'secular song'.

the motet extends for seventy-two perfections. Once again, the voices of the disciples of Christ are heard in judgment, this time embodied in the Virtues, and, what is more, arranged in a palindrome and thus suggestive of Fortune's wheel, informing the message of the motet and the *roman* in words and music alike, just as they did in *Quare fremuerunt*. In effect they drive out demons; they ensure the destruction of Fauvel and his crew at what would seem to be one of his moments of triumph, his (hollow) marriage to Vaine Gloire.

'In nova fert animus mutatas dicere formas corpora'

On fols. 42v–44v of MS fr. 146 the second *Livre de Fauvel* draws towards its conclusion with a series of prayers to the Virgin, God the Father and the Trinity, and Christ for deliverance from Fauvel and 'sa mesnie toute' (La. add. vv. 1653–1798),[116] ending with an exhortation to 'douz Jhesucrist' to imprison them, and another to the 'trez douz lis de virginite' to safeguard the Virtues, who protect 'le lis et le jardin de France' (La. add. vv. 1786–98), as they had done in their tournament with Fauvel's Vices a few pages before.[117] The remainder of fol. 44v is taken up by the motet *In*

[116] The prayers follow the author's complaint to Fortune about her permitting Fauvel to flourish, fol. 42v, col. a, bottom (introduced by a picture of the author addressing Fortune) to col. b, top. Each prayer is something of an independent unit, completely filling as it does a group of discrete columns in the manuscript. The prayer to the Virgin, La. add. vv. 1653–60, occupies all but the very top of fol. 42v, col. b, where it is capped by a picture of the author kneeling before the Mother and Child, and followed, at the bottom of the column and in all of col. c, by a motet. The strongly Trinitarian prayer to God the Father, La. add. vv. 1661–1784, occupies col. b of fol. 43r, where it is also capped by a miniature (the author kneeling before the Trinity) and surrounded on the other three sides by polyphony, all of col. b of fol. 43v, with music in cols. a and c, and col. a of fol. 44r, footed again by music and followed by polyphony in cols. b and c. This prayer is a set piece, not only because of its position in the manuscript, but also because of the text itself, since most of it is taken directly from Jean Maillart's *Roman du Comte d'Anjou* of 1316 (La. add. vv. 1661–1764, with one additional word in v. 1765 = *Anjou* vv. 877–944, 947–54 and 978–1008). The Maillart text effectively breaks off after the twentieth line in the column, exactly halfway down the page on fol. 44r; this is the point, La. add. vv. 1764–7, at which Fauvel is (re)introduced. Remarkably, much of this borrowed prayer touches on the theme of Christ's betrayal, suffering, death and resurrection in terms not unlike the exegetical tradition surrounding Psalm 2 explored in Part IV, above. The prayer to Christ, La. add. vv. 1785–98, occupies fol. 44v, the tops of cols. a–c, where it serves as a header for the motet *In nova fert* beneath.

[117] That these lines mark the end of the *roman* proper is evident from the way the material is presented in the manuscript: the scribe was obliged to write the last several lines in col. c of fol. 44v as though they were prose, so that they would fall where they do and so the final lines, expressing the hope that Fauvel will someday perish, and the explicit would fall at the top of fol. 45r.

nova fert/Garrit gallus/Neuma (p.mus.129, Schrade no. 33).[118] The following page, fol. 45ʳ, is largely a wrap-up: a few gloomy lines strategically placed at the top of this final page in the *roman*, hoping for the eventual end of Fauvel 'car touz iours vivre / ne pourra pas' (La. add. vv. 1799–1806), followed by a closing gesture (La. add. vv. 1806–8) and a formal explicit in Latin in a more formal script (+ 18), all this encircled on three sides by a little three-voice motet (p.mus. 130) and a refrain (ref. 15), the close, explicit, and musical works all on the theme of drinking and wine.[119]

In nova fert is justly famous as a technical tour de force, in every respect a fitting capstone to the *Fauvel* compilation.[120] Its text offers a virtuoso blend of imagery drawn from the *Renart* tradition and other animal fables, the Old and New Testaments, and Classical authors. The thrust of the motet as a whole is established at the very beginning of the motetus with a quotation from the opening of Ovid's *Metamorphoses.* This passage serves as a motto that echoes one of the principal themes of the *roman* itself, that man is become as beast: 'In nova fert animus mutatas dicere formas / [corpora]' (lib. 1, vv. 1–2; 'My mind turns to speak of forms changed into new [bodies]'). Transformation takes many guises in this motet, but at the centre is the metamorphosis of the red dragon of the Apocalypse (Rev. 12: 3–17; motetus verse 2: 'draco nequam', the 'worthless dragon') into a horrific Renart figure, a fox who deceives (blinds) and dominates the lion and ravages his kingdom (motetus verses 9–11: 'vivit in vulpem mutatus / cauda cuius lumine privatus / leo vulpe imperante paret' – 'it lives, transformed into a fox, the fox ruling the lion who, deprived of sight, is in thrall at his tail'; see also triplum verses 5–8 and 19–20).[121]

[118] A superior edition is *Anthology of Medieval Music*, ed. R. H. Hoppin (New York, 1978), no. 59. Also transmitted in Paris, BNF Collection de Picardie, MS 67, fol. 67ʳ, no. 2 (rotulus). Cited in the *Ars nova* attributed to Philippe de Vitry, the *Quatuor principalia* and the treatise of (pseudo) Theodoricus de Campo.

[119] Emma Dillon argues, in *Medieval Music-Making*, pp. 201–15, that these closing items on the theme of drinking are more than a whimsical packet of explicit material, that they are directly related to the themes of the preceding pages and to the organisation of the manuscript as a whole.

[120] This article will consider *In nova fert* and the other Marigny motets from only a limited perspective; a future study by Margaret Bent promises to afford these works the detailed examination that they deserve.

[121] This passage is not without its textual problems. MS fr. 146 reads 'draco nequam . . . russus vivit' ('the worthless dragon . . ., red, lives'); Picardie 67 reads 'rursus' ('lives again'). Both manuscripts read 'cauda', which Dahnk would emend to 'caude'; in keep-

It has long been recognised that this 'fox' is a grotesque but thinly veiled caricature of Philippe le Bel's chamberlain, Enguerran de Marigny.[122]

The Ovidian topos of *mutatio/mutabilitas* that is developed in *In nova fert* carried strong moral connotations in the Scholastic and Christian milieu that engendered *Fauvel*. Metamorphosis was viewed with suspicion from the standpoint of natural philosophy because of its apparent incompatibility with the Aristotelian categories and their predicate, the notion of inviolability of species; and it was considered well-nigh blasphemous and heretical by theologians, who saw it as contrary to the essential integrity of the body and soul, and to the survival of the individual *virtus* at the End of Time.[123] From Ovid to the present day, the most frequently reported sort of such body hopping is lycanthropy.[124] Most writers followed Augustine in holding that the metamorphosis of human beings into animals is impossible; when it is seen to occur, it is an illusion, a phantom, something concocted by demons as a snare.[125] These various speculative and moral threads find resonance throughout the motet's apocalyptic vision, and link it not only with its ostensible subject, Marigny, but also, and particularly

ing with triplum l. 20 ('fraudi paret vulpis'), Becker, *Fauvel und Fauvelliana*, p. 37, would emend 'cauda' to 'fraudi' ('fraud'), a reading adopted by most subsequent scholars. A slightly less literal rendering of the opening line might be, 'I shall speak of metamorphosis into new and strange things'. In the motet, 'corpora' is omitted, so that 'in nova . . . mutatus . . . formas' is followed by the subject of the motet, the 'draco nequam'.

[122] The relationship to Marigny was first systematically explored in Becker, *Fauvel und Fauvelliana*, pp. 36–41. Marigny was known for his overweening pride; it is noteworthy, therefore, that Ovid uses this phrase again in the *Metamorphoses*, 1. 775, putting it into the mouth of Phaethon's mother as her son's pride takes over his reason ('Si modo fert animus, gradere et scitabere ab ipso!' – 'If your mind is so inclined, go and inquire of him [the Sun] himself!'). This links *In nova fert* with another extraordinary Marigny motet in *Fauvel*, *Heu Fortuna subdola* (see n. 15, above), in a tantalising way that cannot be explored here.

[123] See, most recently, C. Walker Bynum, *Metamorphosis and Identity* (New York, 2001), esp. ch. 2, 'Metamorphosis, or Gerald and the Werewolf', rev. from her article in *Speculum*, 73 (1998), pp. 987–1013.

[124] See, among much other literature, D. M. Kratz, 'Fictus lupus: The Werewolf in Christian Thought', *Classical Folia: Studies in the Christian Perpetuation of the Classics*, 30 (1976), pp. 57–79. Ovid remarked of Lycaon, 'he became a wolf, and yet retained traces of his old form [*veteris vestigia formae*]'; *Metamorphoses*, 1. 237. Johannes de Garlandia read this passage as moral allegory, seeing Lycaon's transformation as a moral decline into wolfishness; see Bynum, *Metamorphosis*, 100. Ovid's account of Lycaon's behaviour (*Metamorphoses*, 1. 64–239) finds strong echoes in the text of *In nova fert*.

[125] *Sancti Aurelii Augustini de civitate Dei*, ed. B. Dombard and A. Kalb, 2 vols. (CCSL 47–8; Turnhout, 1954–5), lib. 18, ch. 18 (but see also chs. 16–17); ii, pp. 606–10.

effectively, with the subject of the *roman* into which the motet is inserted, Fauvel. Thus, compare the intrinsic falseness of the metamorphosis with the *roman*'s derivation of 'Fauvel' from 'faus vel'. Note the abiding nature of the dragon regardless of the *figura* in which he is cloaked (motetus, verse 16). Consider the motet's allusions to lycanthropy: the dragon is 'mox lupinis dentibus armatus' (motetus, verse 7: 'now armed with a wolf's teeth'; cf. the scriptural motif of the 'wolf in sheep's clothing' and the image of the false pastor, mentioned in our discussion of *Quare fremuerunt*). The monster is 'vulpes quamquam vispilio / in Belial vigens astucia' (triplum, verses 5–6: 'the fox, albeit the most insignificant of worthless creatures, flourishing with the cunning of Belial').[126] As Belial/the dragon he is the biblical Satan, but the name Belial also conjures worthlessness (cf. Deut. 13: 13, 2 Cor. 6: 14–15, and Rev. 12: 9 and 12; motetus, verse 2: 'draco nequam', cf. the reference to Fauvel in *Mundus a mundicia*, verse 8: 'favelli nequicia'). As Satan/the Serpent (Rev. 12: 14–15) he is the 'sedutrix hominum' of *Mundus a mundicia* – Fauvel. According to Revelation 12: 4–5 the dragon sought to devour the Woman's (Israel's, also the Church's, also Mary's) new-born son (the Messiah, Christ), 'who is to rule all the nations with a rod of iron'; this unmistakable allusion to Psalm 2 links the beast of *In nova fert* with the 'raging' rebels of *Quare fremuerunt*. (The appearance of the dragon in Revelation follows the seventh trumpet call, when 'the kingdom of the world has become the kingdom of our Lord and of his Christ', Rev. 11: 15.) As the creature who has taken the rightful place of the king, he embodies the 'favellandi vicium et fex avaricie' that now occupy the throne and the highest position in the court. Thus Fauvel's corruption in the highest places that had been decried in the first words of the very first work in the collection are given the exemplum of Marigny in the last work in the collection proper.

Enguerran de Marigny fell from power at the beginning of 1315 and after the death of Philippe le Bel, and was executed on 30 April of that year. He thus provides a vivid illustration drawn from recent history of the *mutatio* theme. The musical setting of *In nova fert* develops the idea of *mutatio* and the labile world of the motet

[126] In this context 'vispilio' could also connote a robber who stalks by night, perhaps a ghoul; see R. E. Latham, *Revised Medieval Latin Word-List, from British and Irish Sources* (London, 1965).

poem through its shifts back and forth between perfect and imperfect *modus*, the palindrome structure of its tenor rhythmic *ordo*, and the staggered isoperiodicity of its upper voices.[127] The motet is ordinarily dated 1313–14 on the basis of its description of a thriving Marigny. Margaret Bent has suggested on the other hand that there is no reason not to suppose that it was composed specifically for the *Fauvel* in MS fr. 146, that is, perhaps as late as 1316–17 or even 1318.[128] Our assessment of the poet's use of the *mutatio* topos lends support to that hypothesis. So also does the brief look at the design of the motet that follows here.

The tenor of *In nova fert* is based on a plainchant formula used to identify and characterise the fifth mode.[129] It carries no text of its own, but only the generic designation 'Neuma', although in the theoretical sources of the period this formula might be found with the stock texts 'amen' or 'alleluia'. It is one of a very few tenors in the *Fauvel* motets based on already existing material that does not carry an explicit scriptural, liturgical, or moral message – unless one wants to suppose that a reader would have associated it with 'amen', implying closure, or 'alleluia', implying jubilation, perhaps in anticipation of the death of Fauvel that is foreseen on the following page, perhaps at the completion of the *Fauvel* edition. (To the extent that *Fauvel* and the *Chronique métrique* are texts to be considered in tandem, with the other items in the manuscript understood as supplementary to them, the end of *Fauvel* on fol. 45^r does indeed mark the conclusion of the collection as a whole.) Nonetheless, a closer look suggests that the choice of tenor melody does in fact have something to do with Fauvel. Pitched on fa, *f*, it may be one more example of 'F' being thrown into relief as emblematic of Fauvel. Furthermore, the tenor *color* spans a hexachord, *f* to *d*, from *fa-ut* to *la* (*re-sol*), outlining the name of Fauvel

[127] See the description of the motet's design in E. H. Sanders, 'The Early Motets of Philippe de Vitry', *Journal of the American Musicological Society*, 28 (1975), pp. 26–7.

[128] Bent, 'Fauvel and Marigny'. This hypothesis is in line with the issue of authorship raised at the beginning of this article; see n. 4, above.

[129] For examples, see *Petrus de Cruce tractatus de tonis*, ed. D. Harbinson (Corpus Scriptorum de Musica, 29; American Institute of Musicology, 1976), p. xvii f.; and *Iacobi Leodiensis speculum musicae*, ed. R. Bragard, 7 vols. (Corpus Scriptorum de Musica, 3; American Institute of Musicology, 1955–73), vi, p. 231. The author, in *Petrus de Cruce tractatus*, p. vii, remarks on the diversity of usage exhibited by these formulae.

and even including the same number of elements, six.[130] (The tenor of *Mundus a mundicia* is also pitched on *f*, and it exceeds the range of the hexachord *f–d* only once, and then only in a structurally weak position and possibly for the sake of text painting – on 'con*tra*ria' in verse 2.) Finally, and most importantly, there is the length of the tenor melody, thirty-six notes. This *color* is stated twice, yielding a total of seventy-two notes. Now the melody of the tenor *neuma* does not correspond closely to any known form of the plainchant formula, let alone match it exactly. For one, the intonation ordinarily includes the pitch *e*, avoided in the tenor; for another, it does not unfold in the double melodic cursus found in the motet. Example 4 compares the tenor *color* with the form of the *neuma* found on fol. 9v of the manuscript Ivrea, Biblioteca capitolare, MS 115, the most important of all witnesses to the musical activity of Philippe de Vitry (but most likely copied in Savoy or Ivrea itself, not in France).[131] The divergences between the *neuma* and the motet tenor suggest that the formula was adjusted and extended to achieve the desired melodic profile and number of notes.[132] Supporting this hypothesis is the fact that each

[130] Moreover, this hexachord is the same pitch-letter sequence as that employed to organise the Lescurel songs, although there the texts are arranged in alphabetical order rather than following the pitch sequence (the Lescurel works proceed from A to D, skip E, then continue with F and G).

[131] See K. Kügle, *The Manuscript Ivrea, Biblioteca capitolare 115: Studies in the Transmission and Composition of Ars nova Polyphony* (Musicological Studies, 69; Ottawa, 1997), pp. 234–5.

[132] In the identical melodic form, the *neuma* is used in the tenor of another three-voice Ars nova motet, *Florens vigor/Floret cum vana gloria*/Neuma quinti toni, transmitted in the rotulus Brussels, Bibliothèque royale Albert Ier, MS 19606, no. 6 (preserving a repertory with significant ties to the *Fauvel* collection) and Cambrai, Médiathèque municipale, MS 1328 (fragmentary). In *Florens vigor* the number of notes in the *color* is thirty-seven, not thirty-six; the difference results from a repeat of the penultimate note in the second cursus. Since the two pitches together have the same duration as the single pitch in the first cursus, however, the total number of notes is effectively still thirty-six. The triplum alone is used in MS fr. 146 with the text *Carnalitas Luxuria in favelli palacio presunt* (p.mus. 36, called a 'prose' in the index to the collection; ed. in Sanders, 'Early Motets', pp. 37–45), placed on fol. 12r–v, near the beginning of Book 2, where it comments on the Vices attending the enthroned Fauvel. For the most recent discussion of this motet, see A. V. Clark, 'The Flowering of Charnalité and the Marriage of Fauvel', in *Fauvel Studies*, pp. 175–86 (the two tenors are compared on p. 177). Whatever the reasons for the composition of *Florens vigor* in the first place, whether it was initially intended for use in *Fauvel* or not, the triplum was most likely chosen for deployment in MS fr. 146 because it was informed with the 'content' (that is, the 'message') of the discarded tenor, a message that has everything to do with Fauvel, on one hand, and the symbolic meaning of the number 72, on the other. (Particularly intriguing is the possibility that *Florens vigor* was initially intended for fol. 45v, the page following the present close of *Fauvel* in MS fr. 146, a page that remained blank but that had been ruled for a large-scale three-voice motet. Should

Example 4 The tenor *color* of *In nova fert* (as given in MS fr. 146) and the *Neuma quinti toni* (as given in Ivrea MS 115)

statement of the *color*, with thirty-six notes, extends for seventy-two breve *tempora*. The two *colores* are separated by a perfect long rest, resulting in an overall design of 72 + 3 + 72 *tempora*, another layer of palindrome. Thus 72 controls both the number of tenor pitches and the extent of each limb of the palindromic arch. The motet thus parallels, if in a more complex fashion commensurate with its isorhythmic idiom, *Quare fremuerunt*, which uses 72 for both the number of words in the poem and the number of breve *tempora*. That is, the same underlying structural principle that informs

this prove to be the case, it would raise a host of questions about possible exemplars from which the *Fauvel* compilers may have drawn their repertory, and about the relationship between MS fr. 146 and other sources. In an as yet unpublished paper, Karl Kügle argues that the Brussels rotulus was prepared a decade or so later than MS fr. 146, and in a monastic setting, perhaps in the Empire near the north-eastern border with France. (I am grateful to Professor Kügle for sharing his work with me.) On the Cambrai fragments see I. Lerch, *Fragmente aus Cambrai: Ein Beitrag zur Rekonstruktion einer Handschrift mit spätmittelalterlicher Polyphonie*, 2 vols. (Göttinger musikwissenschaftliche Arbeiten, 11; Kassel, 1987), esp. i, pp. 205–15. The version of this *neuma* in Ivrea 115 is much closer to the tenor in Philippe de Vitry's motet *Douce playsence/Garison selon nature*/Neuma quinti toni, in the same manuscript, fols. 23^{v}–24^{r}, a work that, like *In nova fert*, may date from before 1320; see Sanders, 'Early Motets', p. 30. On the relationship of tenor *colores* to their plainchant sources, see Clark, '*Concordare cum materia*', pp. 25–54.

Quare fremuerunt, on the first page of *Fauvel*, and *Quomodo cantabimus*, in the middle of the *roman*, also informs this motet at the conclusion of the work.

Reading *In nova fert* in the light of these earlier motets, I suggest that implicit in its use of 72 as a structuring principle is the message that the followers of the anointed king, Christ, are on the scene, proclaiming the new king, speaking out, speaking the truth against the falsehood that is around them. They are 'labouring in the midst of wolves', in the den of the dragon/fox/wolf, the deceiver ruling in the king's stead. They are casting out the demon Belial/Fauvel that they find there. Their triumph in the struggle with the dragon has apocalyptic authority: 'And they have conquered [the dragon] with the blood of the Lamb and by the word of their testimony, for they loved not their lives even unto death' (Rev. 12: 11).[133] The 72 permeate the motet through the substructure of its tenor; like a virus, in effect, they invade, infect Fauvel at the height of his power. Their message complements the ominous shadow of Fortune that has hung over Fauvel from fol. 1^{r} on, symbolised musically in this motet by the palindrome design of the tenor *ordo* and the shifts in mensuration, both suggestive of her wheel and its instability. Both motetus and triplum close with the thought that the beast shall (or should) meet his end; this is also voiced in the *roman* text immediately before and after the motet. Through its design the tenor sends the same message. The tenor melody may represent Fauvel, but the creature thus symbolised is a doomed one.

'subito suo ruere merito in mortem privatam bonis'

In the tournanent that is the climax of the festivities that celebrate Fauvel's marriage to Vaine Gloire in MS fr. 146, the Virtues roundly defeat Fauvel's Vices, and the humiliated beast and his bride retire to their palace (the Palais de la Cité) with their retinue in tow while the populace (of Paris) rejoices (La. add. vv. 1401–1542). The jubilation is premature, however, for Fauvel prospers; he and Vaine Gloire spawn a swarm of 'Fauveaus nouveaus' who overrun 'li jardin de douce France', and a fetid Fountain

[133] It is noteworthy that the motet is dominated by the symbolism of 72, rather than drawing on the numerous opportunities for number allegory offered by Rev. 12, and specifically by its description of the dragon.

of Youth keeps them perpetually rejuvenated (La. add. vv. 1543–1642). On fols. 41^{v}–42^{r}, accompanying the description of the unholy fountain and the famous miniature that depicts it, is the motet *Quoniam secta latronum/Tribum que non abhorruit/Merito hec patimur* (p.mus. 120, Schrade no. 27).[134]

Quoniam secta latronum, like *In nova fert*, takes the example of Marigny as its subject, recounting how the fox who once ruled the (now deceased) lion has been brought to justice along with his 'tribe'; they have been cast out from the society they had polluted and their leader delivered to the gallows (as Marigny had been in 1315). Although clearly conceived as a companion piece to *In nova fert*, it has none of the latter's apocalyptic imagery. Instead of a final struggle with the forces of Heaven, it is the angry whim of Fortune that brings down the fox and his tribe (the presence of Fortune is suggested in the music of *In nova fert*, but she is not mentioned in the text).

The tenor of *Quoniam secta latronum* presents its liturgical melody in alternating short and long rhythmic values reminiscent of the second rhythmic mode in the *ars vetus*. It unfolds not in the breves and longs of the older tradition, however, but in longs and maximae; it is, therefore, an early example of augmentation, and thus is as remarkable in its fashion as the tenor of its companion, *In nova fert*. Its *color*, eighteen notes long, is repeated for a total of thirty-six notes, the number of notes in the *color* of *In nova fert*. These are laid out over a span of seventy-two imperfect longs. (This count includes the two longs of rest that theoretically conclude the final *ordo*, if we view the tenor rhythm as indeed being in the second mode. Seventy-two longs are 144 *tempora*, the same number as appear in *In nova fert* when the 'non-modal' rests at the end of the two *color* statements are *not* taken into account.) The seventy-two longs of tenor activity are preceded by one full *ordo*'s worth of tenor silence, six longs in all. During this prologue to the entrance of the tenor the triplum introduces the 'tribum que non abhorruit indecenter ascendere' (v. 1: 'the tribe that did

[134] Also transmitted in Brussels, Bibliothèque royale Albert Ier, MS 19696, no. 3; Munich, Bayerische Staatsbibliothek, clm 29775/10; Rostock, Universitätsbibliothek, MS 100, fol. 43^{r} (motetus and tenor only); Strasbourg, Bibliothèque municipale, MS Sm 222, fol. 71^{v} (destroyed); and London, BL Add. MS 28550, fol. 44^{r-v} (keyboard arrangement). It is also cited in the Wolf Anonymous and the *Tractatus figurarum*.

not shrink from ascending brazenly'), waiting for the tenor to enter before it tells us what has happened to the gang; and the motetus remarks that 'quoniam secta latronum' (v. 1: 'since the band of thieves . . .'.), singing this against the triplum's 'indecenter ascendere'. The entrance of the tenor, the work's foundation, spanning seventy-two longs, marks the arrival of the seventy-two disciples spreading the word, speaking out and casting out demons. The disciples are thus introduced after, and surely in ironic response to the 'gang' (or 'tribe') of Fauvel's followers (the *fasuli* of *Quare fremuerunt*). The irony is twofold: through the numerical symbolism of its design the tenor evokes the disciples of Christ and their work, but the very text to which the tenor is sung, 'We deserve to suffer these things', is surely to be read as the voice of the fallen and expelled 'tribe', heard against the moralising account of their fall in the upper voices.[135]

'Adesto sancta trinitas musice modulantibus'

Quoniam secta latronum is the first work in a veritable explosion of polyphonic music that extends from fol. 42^r to the *roman*'s explicit on fol. 45^r; these four folios proffer no fewer than eight of the collection's thirty-four motets (in addition to three monophonic 'verssez'[136] and the final one-line musical explicit). Apart from *Quoniam secta latronum* and *In nova fert*, the motets are all explicitly prayers addressed by 'nos' – that is, the author – to the Virgin, to 'omnipotens dominus' and the Trinity, and to Christ, the progression following the sequence of prayers in the surrounding *roman* text. In one way or another, all these musical prayers ask for deliverance from Fauvel. Several use liturgical texts in their

[135] See the discussion of this motet in Bent, 'Polyphony of Texts and Music', pp. 82–103. Enhancing the irony is the fact that the text of this liturgical melody is drawn from Gen. 42: 21, an episode from the story of the exiled Joseph. Joseph, risen to a position of authority, accuses his brothers of espionage and threatens them with imprisonment and death. The brothers (including Joseph, twelve in number!), who do not recognise Joseph, speak the words sung in the motet tenor among themselves as they acknowledge their guilt. The chant is a responsory sung at Matins on the Third Sunday in Quadragesima; interestingly, the Gospel reading for the Mass that day was Luke 11: 14–28, an account of Jesus driving out an unclean spirit.

[136] Two of the 'verssez' are new compositions; the other is an adaptation of a liturgical recitation formula, but in all likelihood this is a later addition put in to fill in empty space. On these pieces see Rankin, 'The "*Alleluyes, antenes, respons, ygnes et verssez*"', pp. 462–6.

upper voices, but only one deploys a plainchant melody or a liturgical or scriptural text in its tenor.[137]

The second of the motets that gloss the Trinitarian prayer on fol. 43^{r-v}, *Adesto sancta trinitas/Firmissime fidem teneamus/Alleluia Benedictus* 'et cetera' (p.mus. 124, Schrade no. 24),[138] brings the 72 into view again. *Adesto sancta trinitas* calls for devotion to Christ the Son (i.e., the True King, the model of Capetian royalty) as well as to the Father and the Holy Spirit. It is another compositional tour de force, another demonstration of *ars nova* virtuosity. The motetus text is a line-by-line gloss of the first stanza of a celebrated Trinitarian hymn, and the tenor *color* is the 'Alleluya' section of a proper alleluia for Trinity Sunday, clearly identified as such by the rubric, 'Benedictus et cetera', the 'et cetera' indicating that the reader contemplating the motet should have in mind not only the 'Alleluya' refrain that is being sung but indeed the complete text of the verse.[139] That text, 'Benedictus es domine deus patrum nostrorum et laudibilis in secula' ('Blessed art thou, o Lord the God of our fathers, and for ever worthy to be praised') is drawn from the beginning of Dan. 3: 52–90, the canticle of the three youths in the furnace, proclaiming their faith in the face of Nebuchadnezzar's murderous wrath. This choice of tenor is significant not only because of its associations with the Trinity liturgy, and hence with the *roman*'s Trinitarian prayer, but also because of its scriptural analogue to what we identify as one of the themes in the *Fauvel* compilation, the idea of disciples (or youths) – in this instance, numbering three, like the Trinity itself – speaking out in the midst of disbelievers and in the face of imminent danger. But its relevance to Fauvel reaches further: like the tenor of *In nova fert*, it is in mode 5, and the note *f* is the dominant pitch,

[137] Only two of them have texts of any sort in their tenors, *Celi domina/O Maria/Porchier* (p.mus. 122), fol. 42^{v}, based on a *Fauvel* rondeau that also appears near the end of Book 1, and *Omnipotens domine/Flagellaverunt Galliam et ortum eius inquinaverunt* (p.mus. 123), fol. 43^{r}. On the former, see N. F. Regalado, 'Le Porcher au palais: *Kalila et Dimna*, *Le Roman de Fauvel*, Machaut, et Boccace', *Études littéraires*, 31 (1999), pp. 119–32.

[138] Also transmitted in Brussels, Bibliothèque royale Albert Ier, no. 4; and London, BL Add. MS 28550, fols. 43^{v}–44^{r} (keyboard arrangement). Triplum text alone in Darmstadt, Hessische Landes- und Universitätsbibliothek, MS 521, fol. 228^{r}. Cited in the *Ars nova* attributed to Philippe de Vitry and the Wolf Anonymous.

[139] This practice holds for other chant texts in the *Fauvel* collection that follow the incipit with 'etc.'; see, for example, the incomplete quotation of *Alleluia veni sancte spiritus* 'etc.' (p.mus. 31), on fol. 10^{r}, placed towards the end of Book 1 in a position that is approximately parallel to that of *Adesto sancta trinitas* in Book 2.

occurring fourteen times out of a total of forty notes (five of the eight tenor *ordines* end on *f*, the other three on *a*; *f-a* for Fauvel).

Like *Quoniam secta latronum* and *In nova fert*, *Adesto sancta trinitas* presents its tenor in a remarkable display of mensural ingenuity: laid out in the second rhythmic mode, like *Quoniam secta latronum*, this tenor employs augmentation for the first of the two statements of its *color*, so that the melody moves in longs and duplex longs, then diminution for the second statement, with the movement entirely in equal breves. (*Maximodus* is perfect, as in *Quoniam secta latronum*, but *modus* and *tempus* are imperfect, hence the equal breves of the passage in diminution.) In the first statement of the *color* there are seventy-two (imperfect) long units; in the second there are twenty-four. This is but one of the numerous ways in which the motet is shaped by the three-in-one idea of the Trinity.[140]

It is noteworthy that the composer of *Adesto sancta trinitas* chose 72 to symbolise the Trinity. As the product of 24 (hours in the day) and 3 (illuminations of the earth by the sun), 72 was emblematic of the proclamation of faith in the Trinity. Thus, Bede, commenting on the seventy-two pomegranates and bells that were thought to adorn Aaron's priestly tunic (Exod. 28: 33–5), sees them as signifying the disciples sent forth by Christ and the lesser clergy of the Church, but adds that:

[Aaron] bore seventy-two golden bells and an equal number of pomegranates so that he might show mystically that the same faith and working of righteousness would lead the whole world from the darkness of error into the true light. For seventy-two hours comprise three days and nights, and because over the course of seventy-two hours this visible sun circles every part of the world three times as it sheds its light above and below, aptly was this number used . . ., teaching figuratively that Christ's sun of righteousness would illuminate the entire world and give it the gift of true faith, which is in the acknowledgement and confession of the Trinity, and also the gift of good works, found in the flowering and splendour of the virtues.

Portabat et septuaginta duo tintinnabula aurea cum totidem malis punicis ut ostenderet mystice quod eadem fides et operatio iustitiae uniuersum esset mundum ab errorum tenebris ad ueram lucem perductura. Tres namque dies ac noctes habent horas septuaginta duas, et quia sol iste uisibilis omnes mundi partes in septuaginta duabus horis supra infraque lustrando tribus uicibus circuit apte hic numerus . . . . inditus est ad docendum figurate quod sol iustitiae Christus orbem esset illuminaturus uniuersum eique donum praebiturus et uerae

[140] See esp. A. W. Robertson, 'Which Vitry? The Witness of the Trinity Motet from the *Roman de Fauvel*', in Pesce (ed.), *Hearing the Motet*, pp. 52–81.

fidei quae est in agnitione et confessione sanctae trinitatis et bonae operationis quae in uariarum est flore ac splendore uirtutum.[141]

The number also signified the length of time, three days, that Christ's body lay in the tomb before his resurrection. Thus, Honorius of Autun, in a passage that links the themes of the Resurrection and the seventy-two disciples:

We celebrate the three days of the Lord's entombment. Three days and nights we calculate as seventy-two hours. And therefore we put out all light, because we mourn on these days the extinguished true light, and replicate the sorrow of the seventy-two disciples.

His tribus diebus sepulturam Domini celebramus. Tres autem dies et noctes septuaginta duabus horis computamus. Et ideo totidem lumina exstinguimus, quia lumen verum his diebus exstinctum lugemus; et septuaginta duorum discipulorum tristitiam exprimimus.[142]

It was during this interval that Christ harrowed Hell; it is striking and perhaps no coincidence that the prayer glossed by *Adesto sancta trinitas* speaks at length of the Harrowing (La. add. vv. 1737–56). This use in common of that theme may suggest that the motet was composed specifically for MS fr. 146 and its *Fauvel* edition.

The three motets at the end of the *Fauvel* collection that we have just considered, the only works in the final group that are composed in the *ars nova*, all use the number 72 as a structuring principle. In its deployment of 72, *Adesto sancta trinitas* adds another strand of symbolic meaning to those underpinning *Quoniam secta latronum* and *In nova fert*. In retrospect its use of the three-in-one idea also lends weight, if only indirectly, to the suggestion of a Trinitarian subtext to *Quare fremuerunt* that we mentioned in passing in Part IV, above. All this further enriches the network of associations in which the *roman* is cloaked.

VI

We return, finally, to fol. 1r of MS fr. 146 and to the first item on the page, the motet *Favellandi vicium*. We remarked in Part II that this motet has an overall duration of seventy perfect longs in the transcription by Leo Schrade, with the *tractus* following the first

[141] Bede, *De tabernaculo*, in CCSL 119a, 112.
[142] Honorius of Autun, *Gemma animae*, in PL 172, col. 665c.

sentence rendered as a double bar rather than a pause of a given duration. If the stroke is read as written, as a perfect long rest, however, the total length increases to seventy-one longs. We suggested that this *tractus* acts to set the crucial opening sentence apart motto-like from the rest of the motet. We also noted the unusual rhythmic treatment of the equally crucial final thought, throwing into relief the 'here and now' thought that comes to the fore in the text. If we see this striking passage as concluding, at least conceptually, with a perfect long rest analogous to the one following the motto opening, then the motet is seventy-two longs in duration.[143] Considered in the light of what we have observed elsewhere in the *Fauvel* collection, including what we have found in what has emerged as the ideological parallel to this motet, *Quare fremuerunt*, either number, 70 or 72, should catch our attention. The scriptural sources are divided as to whether there were seventy-two or seventy disciples; the tally of Moses' elders exhibits a similar lack of consistency: the two numbers were well-nigh interchangeable in medieval number allegory.[144] If 72/70 is indeed a significant element in the 'text' of *Favellandi vicium*, when the author beseeches God, 'apply here [your] counsel!' the fact is that He has already done so: His seventy-two are already there, in the temporal bricks out of which the work is built. This scriptural undercurrent is found again in the temporal plan of *Mundus a mundicia*, but there it manifests itself in a somewhat different way. The music and text added to Philip the Chancellor's original conductus, which affirm the dominance of the harlot beast Fauvel

[143] In theoretical terms, the end of the piece, moving in Franco's second rhythmic mode, could indeed have concluded its rhythmic *ordo* with a perfect long rest. (This mode moves in alternating breves and longs or/and in all longs, in a manner similar to Franco's first mode; for confirmation see the examples in some of the manuscripts preserving the treatise, in *Franconis de Colonia ars cantus mensurabilis*, ed. G. Reaney and A. Gilles (Corpus Scriptorum de Musica, 18; American Institute of Musicology, 1974), p. 27, apparatus.) The tenor of *Quoniam secta latronum*, in the second rhythmic mode (in augmentation), extends for seventy-two longs when the rest that concludes the final *ordo* is taken into account. The same is true of the tenor *color* of *Adesto sancta trinitas*, also in the second mode, also moving in augmentation. On the other hand, the rest that concludes each of the two *colores* of *In nova fert* does not figure in the symbolic numerical count. The same is true of *Quare fremuerunt* and *Quomodo cantabimus*. The tenors of these three motets do not manifest a rhythmic flow conceived in 'modal' terms.

[144] See nn. 101 and 100, above. 70 also symbolises the number of years of the Babylonian Captivity (e.g. 2 Chron. 36: 21 and Jer. 25: 11), and evokes Septuagesima, the beginning of the liturgical progression towards Lent and Easter – that is, the very progression heralded by the Lucan disciples; see Meyer and Suntrup, *Lexikon*, cols. 755–9.

over the world, extend for twelve longs, thirty-six breves. If both voices are taken into account, the total is, again, 72 (this time, breves). (The disciples went forth in pairs, not unlike the two angel messengers who visited Sodom to warn of its impending destruction.)[145] In *Quare fremuerunt*, the usage is different again. The motet is seventy-two breves in length, and its text numbers seventy-two syllables. The disciples inform not only the duration of the motet, but also the organisation of the very words through which its message is articulated.

Thus the voice of the author, couched symbolically as the collective voice of the disciples of Christ 'labouring in the midst of wolves', is heard figuratively at the outset of the *Livres de Fauvel* to set the tone, to establish an allegorical and moral platform on which the edifice as a whole would be built. One or another aspect of that platform can be discerned from time to time as the *Fauvel* edition unfolds. At the close of *Fauvel* it is only the motets in the 'new' style that reveal the presence of the 72; there the voice of the disciples is heard in all three *ars nova* motets. Each uses the figure of the 72 as a structuring premise, but, as on fol. 1^r, each does so in a somewhat individual way. The three motets share many external features. They alone among the eight motets in the closing group are based on plainchant. They are the only pieces in the closing group that are not unique to MS fr. 146. Moreover, they have much in common stylistically. Taken together, these circumstances suggest with some degree of probability that they were written as a set, and specifically for *Fauvel*. Or, alternatively, one of them could have served as a model for the other two, the new works fashioned by a composer who understood the 'subtext'

[145] Gen. 19: 1. Moreover, the 12 (longs) can be seen as emblematic of the twelve apostles, the 'first' group of heralds dispatched to proclaim the coming of the King. Bede, commenting on the priestly vestments worn by Aaron, remarks (*De tabernaculo*, 112): 'ut sicut in umero ac pectore apostolicum ferre numerum iussus est ita etiam discipulorum septuaginta duorum circa pedes numerum assignatum haberet. Constat enim quod sicut duodenarius apostolorum numerus episcopalis gradum dignitatis inchoauit sic discipuli septuaginta duo qui et ipsi ad praedicandum uerbum sunt missi a domino gradum sacerdotii minoris' ('so that just as he [Aaron] was commanded to bear the apostolic number on his shoulder and breast, he might have the number of the seventy-two disciples put around his feet. For just as the number of the twelve apostles instituted the rank of the episcopal dignity, it is evident that the seventy-two disciples, who were also sent out by the Lord to preach, signify in their selection the lesser rank of the priesthood'). See the numerous other citations from Scripture and the exegetical literature given in Meyer and Suntrup, *Lexikon*, cols. 619–46.

encoded in his model.[146] (In fact, this hypothesis does not rule out the previous one; the two procedures are not mutually exclusive.) These three motets are precisely the *Fauvel* works that have the strongest claims to the authorship of Philippe de Vitry.[147] Were the relatively simple works on fol. 1^r^ also composed by this musician, Philippe or someone else, *pace* the seeming differences in style between *Favellandi vicium* and *Mundus a mundicia*, on one hand, and *Quare fremuerunt*, on the other, and between all three of these technically unassuming works and the three highly complex 'Vitry' motets? It seems reasonable to propose this hypothesis. If they were not all the work of this composer, they were in any event fashioned by someone who was privy to the message embedded in his compositions. Alternatively, were the complex works at the end of the *roman* written in response to the simpler ones on fol. 1^r^, and is this also the case with *Quomodo cantabimus* on fol. 32^r^, and possibly others still to be identified? Or is this the wrong way to put the question – ought we rather to be asking whether the person responsible for the music in the *Fauvel* collection decided on an allegorical topos that he or his composer(s) could develop in various but related ways? All these scenarios are interesting: if these pieces were indeed all written for *Fauvel*, as the arrangements on fol. 1^r^ surely were and as Margaret Bent has suggested is the case with the 'Vitry' motets,[148] then there is a strong possibility that one or another of them was at work.

[146] On 'imitation' and other forms of modelling, see most recently J. Ziolkowski, 'The Highest Form of Compliment: *Imitatio* in Medieval Latin Culture', in J. Marenbon (ed.), *Poetry and Philosophy in the Middle Ages: A Festschrift for Peter Dronke* (Leiden, 2001), pp. 293–307.

[147] For the most recent discussion of the vexed question of what works can be ascribed to Philippe de Vitry, see A. Wathey, 'Vitry, Philippe de [Vitriaco, Vittriaco]', in *New Grove II*. Briefly stated, no work in MS fr. 146 can be attributed to Philippe de Vitry on external grounds. There is, however, evidence to suggest that he at least knew one (and possibly more) of the *Fauvel* motets, *Quoniam secta latronum*, two decades after the preparation of MS fr. 146; see Wathey, 'Myth and Mythography in the Motets of Philippe de Vitry', *Musica e storia*, 6 (1998), pp. 95–6. This is not to say that he did not write some or even many of them, including all those under discussion here, only that our analytical tools are not yet sharp enough to be reliable, and that we may sometimes find significance in the wrong sorts of data, leading us to unsupportable conclusions. Until we are better equipped and can frame the questions more cogently, it would seem better to err on the side of restraint, a policy that few would reject when studying, say, the music of the fifteenth century. The possibility that Philippe de Vitry was the musician involved in the production of MS fr. 146 is very attractive, the lack of hard evidence notwithstanding; if it should prove to be true, this manuscript would represent the closest thing to a composer's autograph to survive from the Middle Ages.

[148] Bent, 'Fauvel and Marigny'.

All this raises tantalising questions, not only about the oeuvre of Philippe de Vitry but also about the role he might have played in the preparation of MS fr. 146, perhaps as its music scribe, perhaps as someone whose involvement in the production of its *Fauvel* was even more central. It also suggests the need for further enquiry into the difference between 'old' and 'new' musical idioms at the dawn of the Ars nova, about whether we know what those differences actually consisted of and how (if at all) they relate to the notions of 'simple' and 'complex' that we have just used to characterise those idioms, about how deep-seated those distinctions are in fact, and about their relevance in discussions of attribution and chronology.[149]

This study has concentrated on a single page, fol. 1^{r}, but similar sorts of observations could be made regarding many other pages and groups of pages in MS fr. 146. The version of *Fauvel* in this book can be understood as behaving like a giant motet, as a huge assemblage of different elements, textual, musical, illustrative, all brought together on the page in an intricate web of intertextual relationships that transcends language, genre and medium.[150] On

[149] Among other recent work on these questions, cf. D. Leech-Wilkinson, 'The Emergence of *Ars nova*', *Journal of Musicology*, 13 (1995), pp. 285–317; Bent, 'Fauvel and Marigny'; ead., 'Polyphony of Texts and Music'; ead., 'Early Papal Motets', in R. Sherr (ed.), *Papal Music and Musicians in Late Medieval and Renaissance Rome* (Oxford, 1998), pp. 5–43; and Robertson, 'Which Vitry?' See also the reviews of *Fauvel Studies* by L. M. Earp, in *Plainsong and Medieval Music*, 9 (2000), pp. 185–202, and D. Leech-Wilkinson, in *Journal of the American Musicological Society*, 53 (2000), pp. 152–9.

[150] 'War er's nicht, der meint', ich ging zu weit? . . . Und blieb ich nicht im Geleise, war's nicht auf seine Weise? Doch war's vielleicht auch Eitelkeit?' (Veit Pogner). Has recent research on *Fauvel* gone too far, reading too much into what can be found in MS fr. 146 in its pursuit of the game at the expense of common sense? I do not share the concerns in this regard voiced by Leech-Wilkinson in his review of *Fauvel Studies* (see n. 149, above). My own experience with the manuscript convinces me that it is a highly cohesive artefact, the parts of which inform each other, often in subtle ways, at every turn and over large spans. Despite, or perhaps because of, the fact that the collection achieved its final form (indeed, perhaps its very form) only as it was being produced, it shows many signs of the planning that went into its production, and it reveals a close and subtle interaction between the book as an artefact and the book as a repository of texts. MS fr. 146 is not alone in this regard, of course: for another striking example see K. A. Duys, 'Books Shaped by Song: Early Literary Literacy in the *Miracles de Nostre Dame* of Gautier de Coinci' (Ph.D. diss., New York University, 1997); and, among numerous other studies of late medieval illuminated psalters and books of hours, see the forthcoming monograph by K. A. Smith, *Three Women and their Books of Hours: Art and Devotion in Early Fourteenth-Century England* (The British Library Publications). See also Dillon, *Medieval Music-Making*, esp. ch. 1. What sets MS fr. 146 apart from comparable volumes may be the fact that much of the evidence lies so close to the surface, and hence is easily discovered.

fol. 1r the material added to the original text, and above all the added music, sets in motion a dialectic that will continue off and on throughout the *roman*. The three motets underscore and focus the *roman*'s picture of a monarchy degraded by unworthiness and vice, but at the same time they promise salvation, relief from Fauvel and the evil he represents – salvation that is to come from within the institution of kingship itself. Fauvel appears on the surface to be omnipotent; the interpolated Fountain of Youth passage late in the narrative suggests that he and his like might continue to reign for ever. But the attentive reader has known otherwise from the outset, from fol. 1r. The Lucan and psalmic references that drive much of the music on that page tell us this, and tell us why that is so. The text at the very end of the *roman*, on fol. 45r, says that Fauvel 'will meet his end, for he cannot live for ever'; the motets on fol. 1r suggest a less literal rendering of the French, 'for eternal life is not granted him'. The reappearance of the 72 later in the *roman* reminds us of the prophecy that imbues the first page. The disciples tell us as surely as the fact that it was Fortune who perched the tethered Fauvel on high, that the creature will perish. Damnation, not eternal life, is for him. The 'author', the creative genius behind the enterprise that is MS fr. 146, proclaims this and the coming of the True King with biblical *auctoritas*, with the voice of those 'labouring in the midst of wolves'.

The year 1314 saw the execution of Jacques de Molay on 18 March at the hands of Philippe le Bel, and then the deaths of the two major players in the suppression of the Templars, Pope Clement V (20 April) and Philippe le Bel himself (29 November). Philippe's last year was marked by widespread unrest over his fiscal policies and, breaking out in mid-April, the adultery scandal that engulfed the wives of his three sons, throwing into question the legitimacy of the royal succession. Jeanne, the wife of the future Philip V, was eventually cleared of the allegation of complicity that had been brought against her, but the other two spouses were evidently guilty. Marguerite of Burgundy, the notorious wife of Louis X, died in prison under suspicious circumstances in late April 1315; a few days later, on 30 April, Philippe's chamberlain Enguerran de Marigny was hanged after a show trial. Louis X did not compare favourably with his sainted great-grandfather and namesake, Louis IX, and his premature courtship (initiated months before Marguerite's death) and hasty marriage (31 July 1315) to Clementia of Hungary perpetuated the cloud of scandal that hung over the Throne of France. His own sudden death on 5 June 1316, leaving behind a pregnant queen, precipitated uncertainty over the succession that was not resolved until the death of the newborn Jean I in mid-November of that year. The advent to the throne of Philip V at the beginning of 1317 settled the question of succession; it also held out the hope that Holy France would once again prosper under proper rule.

Proper kingship as embodied in the new king Philip V is the subject of MS fr. 146. The theme of the king anointed by God and presiding in virtue, prevailing over evildoers who would set aside his rule and God's law, is one of the principal ideas running through its *Fauvel* edition. Implicitly, the newly crowned Philip V is an exemplum of good kingship – indeed, it seems reasonable to suppose that his advent to the throne was the catalyst for the *Livres de Fauvel* and the compilation as a whole. It is not known whether Philip ever saw the book, or whether in fact it was even intended for his eyes, either in public or in private: its composition as an *admonitio* on kingship tells us nothing about who commissioned it or why, or its *destinataire*.[151] We should be equally circumspect about concluding that the reign of Fauvel that is excoriated so stridently was meant to be understood as the reigns of Philip's immediate predecessors, Philippe le Bel and Louis X. The examples that those reigns provided were convenient and vivid cases in point on the pitfalls of monarchy, and they could make the ascent of the new king appear all the more climactic and meaningful. They are rhetorical ploys that help situate the theme of good kingship and the new king who exemplifies it, but not necessarily more than that.

Form and content interact in MS fr. 146 to promote its message. The message is launched on the first page of *Fauvel* with

[151] We must conclude that the makers – the scribes and decorators – of MS fr. 146 were themselves responsible for shaping the final form of much if not all its content, if not necessarily for its overall thrust. They are certainly not unique in this regard: in a forthcoming monograph on the books produced for the Bohun family in the second half of the fourteenth century, Lucy Freeman Sandler shows that the Bohun artists, working as an integral part of the household over an extended period of time, articulated the political and dynastic aspirations of the family with considerable originality and independence of thought.

an Old Testament foundation congruent with Capetian political ideology, and proclaimed by New Testament heralds out in a world infested by devils. Scriptural allegory is deployed as a rhetorical tactic that both articulates the theme of kingship and shapes it. There are many threads woven into *Fauvel*, but those discussed here are surely among the more prominent ones unifying and colouring this complex tapestry.

New York University

Postscript. In our discussion of *Quare fremuerunt* in Part IV we suggested that the *Salve regina* melody embedded in the motet served to direct the reader to the Virgin and the cathedral dedicated to her Assumption, Notre-Dame of Paris, as refuges from Fauvel. Now in its essay on the Assumption, the *Legenda aurea* of Jacobus de Voragine reports the following: 'Et, secundum quod ait Epiphanius, XXIV annis post ascensionem filii sui superuixit. Refert ergo quod beata uirgo quando Christum concepit erat annorum XIV et in XV ipsum peperit et mansit cum eo annis XXXIII et post mortem Christi superuixit annis XXIV et secundum hoc quando obiit erat annorum LXXII' ('According to the statement of Epiphanius, she lived for 24 years after her son's Ascension. He figures, then, that the Blessed Virgin was 14 years of age when she conceived Christ, and she gave birth in the 15th [year], and she lived with him for 33 years, and she lived after the death of Christ for 24 years, and, so it follows, she was 72 years of age when she died'); Iacopo da Varazze, *Legenda aurea, edizione critica*, ed. G. P. Maggioni, 2nd edn, 2 vols. (Florence, 1998), ii, p. 779 (Jacobus probably drew directly or indirectly on the Latin version of the apocryphal life of the Virgin by the Byzantine monk Epiphanius, ed. as *Historia auct. Epiphanio mon., interprete Paschali Romano*, in E. Franceschini, *Studi e note di filologia medievale* (Pubblicazioni della Università Cattolica del Sacro Cuore, IV, 30; Milan, 1938), esp. pp. 115, 123–4). The passage is retained in the French translation by Jean de Vignay; see Jacques de Voragine, *La légende dorée, édition critique dans la révision de 1476 par Jean Bataillier, d'après la traduction de Jean de Vignay (1333–1348) de la* Legenda aurea *(c. 1262–1266)*, ed. B. Dunn-Lardeau (Paris, 1997), p. 739. Guillaume Durand presents the same information in very similar words in his *Rationale divinorum officiorum; Guillelmi Duranti rationale divinorum officiorum*, ed.

A. Davril and T. M. Thibodeau, 3 vols. (Corpus christianorum continuatio mediaevalis, 140, 140A–B; Turnhout, 1995, 2000), ii, p. 70. Both authors go on to question Epiphanius' account, but the very fact that these widely read works of the later thirteenth century associate the Assumption with the number 72 has significance for our reading of *Quare fremuerunt*: it strengthens the association of the motet's Marian aspect with Notre-Dame specifically, and links that Marian aspect to the other connotations of 72, the numerical *res* determining structure and meaning in the motet.

Early Music History (2003) Volume 22. © *Cambridge University Press*
DOI:10.1017/S026112790300305X Printed in the United Kingdom

PETER WRIGHT

WATERMARKS AND MUSICOLOGY: THE GENESIS OF JOHANNES WISER'S COLLECTION

I. INTRODUCTION

The twin questions of the origin and purpose of Trent 88–91, the four celebrated codices compiled by Johannes Wiser during the third quarter of the fifteenth century, have continued to puzzle musicologists ever since the manuscripts were rediscovered more than a hundred years ago. Adler and Koller, whose pioneering study of the Trent Codices, published in 1900, still retains so much of its original force, saw Wiser's collection as having been compiled 'in and for Trent' under the humanistic influence of Johannes Hinderbach, provost of the cathedral from 1455 and prince-bishop of the city and region from 1465.[1] At the time of writing, next to nothing was known about the life of the obscure priest who had been responsible for the most important musical collection of the fifteenth century, and it was not until nearly thirty years later that

I am grateful to Margaret Bent, Rudolf Flotzinger, John Morehen, Joshua Rifkin, Reinhard Strohm and Lorenz Welker for having read and commented on this article, and to the following for advice and practical assistance in its preparation: Emanuele Curzel, Marco Gozzi, Reinhard Höppl, Franz Körndle, Dietrich Kudorfer, Sabine Kurth, Jake Matchett, Daniela Rando, Manfred Rupert and Bernhold Schmid. The research for this study was funded by grants from the British Academy and the Arts and Humanities Research Board, and would not have been possible without the generous cooperation of the following libraries and archives (here listed with abbreviations): Innsbruck, Tiroler Landesarchiv (ITL); Innsbruck, Universitätsbibliothek (IU); Munich, Bayerisches Hauptstaatsarchiv (MBH); Munich, Bayerische Staatsbibliothek (MBS); Munich, Stadtarchiv (MS); Stuttgart, Hauptstaatsarchiv; Trent, Archivio Capitolare (TAC); Trent, Archivio di Stato (TAS); Trent, Castello del Buonconsiglio, Monumenti e Collezioni Provinciali. The following abbreviations are used for the Trent Codices: Trent 87–92 (Trent, Castello del Buonconsiglio, Monumenti e Collezioni Provinciali, MSS 1374–1379, formerly 87–92), Trent 93 (Trent, Biblioteca del Archivio Capitolare, MS 93, formerly 'B.L.').

[1] *Sechs Trienter Codices: Geistliche und weltliche Compositionen des XV. Jahrhunderts, erste Auswahl*, ed. G. Adler and O. Koller (Denkmäler der Tonkunst in Österreich, Jg. vii, 14–15; Vienna, 1900), pp. xvi and xx.

the Trentino scholar Renato Lunelli published his crucial discovery showing that Wiser was employed as schoolmaster at the cathedral school in Trent during the very period when he must have been busy assembling his great collection.[2] The article in question was written partly in response to a highly polemical and largely unsubstantiated piece that had been published by the Austrian historian Rudolf Wolkan a few years earlier.[3] Wolkan had rejected the idea of a Tridentine origin for the codices, arguing that there was literally no evidence of any form of musical activity in Trent prior to Hinderbach's time, and that the reign of his predecessor, Georg Hack (1444–65), which Adler and Koller had defined as the period during which most of the copying must have taken place, would not have been conducive to so large-scale an artistic enterprise, owing to Hack's strained relations with the city over which he presided. Instead, Wolkan maintained that the codices had been compiled in Vienna, where they might have formed part of Hinderbach's library, and suggested that it could have been under his auspices that they eventually reached Trent.

Whilst there may have been some validity to Wolkan's points in relation to Hack, his statement about the lack of musical life in Trent was, of course, completely unfounded, as Lunelli and others have subsequently shown, and his proposal of a Viennese origin for the codices little more than wishful thinking. This latter theory was dealt a severe blow by Lunelli's discovery, which, through its implicit linking of the later codices to the institution for which their compiler worked,[4] provided a powerful endorsement of the 'in and for Trent' position originally postulated by Adler and Koller. At the same time Lunelli was brusquely dismissive of the possibility that Hinderbach might have had any role in the formation of the collection, and thus showed something of the same lack of objectivity of which Wolkan himself had been guilty. That both men should have adopted such partisan viewpoints is hardly surprising in the light of the background circumstances: Italy, following the Allied victory, had taken over from Austria the entire

[2] R. Lunelli, 'La patria dei codici musicali tridentini', *Note d'Archivio per la Storia Musicale*, 4 (1927), pp. 116–28.

[3] R. Wolkan, 'Die Heimat der Trienter Musikhandschriften', *Studien zur Musikwissenschaft*, 8 (1921), pp. 5–8.

[4] Lunelli never goes quite as far as to state that the codices were compiled for the cathedral school, although this is the clear implication of the facts as he presents them.

region comprising the south Tyrol and the Trentino,[5] including the city of Trent, and in accordance with the terms of the Treaty of St Germain (1919) it had been decided that the musical codices were the property of the Italian state and should therefore be returned to their presumed city of origin.[6] Feelings about the manuscripts' destiny inevitably were running high.

Much of the ensuing debate about the origin and purpose of the codices was coloured by these nationalistically oriented theories, as Adelyn Peck Leverett has usefully shown,[7] but in due course a degree of consensus emerged. It came to be widely accepted, for instance, that Trent, not Vienna, must have been the place where most of the copying was carried out. And the idea, first formulated by Adler and Koller, that Hinderbach was in some sense the moving force behind the collection became a leitmotiv in the writings of scholars of all nationalities. The focus on Hinderbach sometimes tended, however, to be at the expense of a proper consideration of the contexts in which the manuscripts and their repertories are likely to have been used,[8] and it was not until relatively recently that this aspect of the codices' history began to be seriously addressed.

Over the past twenty years or so, a number of studies have appeared that focus on local musical and liturgical practices, and on the institutions and individuals that helped sustain them.[9] As

[5] This region is now known as 'Trentino–Alto Adige'. Historically, it represents the area of the medieval ecclesiastical principalities of Trento (Trent) and Bressanone (Brixen). For present purposes the northern part of the region, the Alto Adige, is referred to by its alternative designation of 'south Tyrol'.

[6] At that stage Trent 87–92 were in Vienna. For further details see A. P. Leverett, 'A Paleographical and Repertorial Study of the Manuscript Trento, Castello del Buonconsiglio, 91 (1378)' (Ph.D. diss., Princeton University, 1990), pp. 6–7.

[7] *Ibid.*, pp. 13–31.

[8] Even as searching and thought-provoking a study as Martin Staehelin's attempt to explain aspects of the later codices in terms of humanist thought and practice makes virtually no reference to Wiser's working environment. See M. Staehelin, 'Trienter Codices und Humanismus', in N. Pirrotta and D. Curti (eds.), *I codici musicali trentini a cento anni dalla loro riscoperta* (Trent, 1986) [henceforth *I codici musicali trentini 1986*], pp. 158–69.

[9] See, in particular, the following musicological studies: G. Spilsted, 'The Paleography and Musical Repertory of Codex Tridentinus 93' (Ph.D. diss., Harvard University, 1982); P. Wright, 'On the Origins of Trent 87_1 and 92_2', *Early Music History*, 6 (1986), pp. 245–70; S. E. Saunders, *The Dating of the Trent Codices from their Watermarks, with a Study of the Local Liturgy of Trent in the Fifteenth Century* (New York, 1989); R. Dalmonte (ed.), *Musica e società nella storia trentina* (Trent, 1994); Leverett, 'A Paleographical and Repertorial Study'; M. Gozzi, 'I codici più recenti nel loro contesto storico-liturgico: i contrafacta', in P. Wright (ed.), *I codici musicali trentini: nuove scoperte e nuovi orientamenti della ricerca* (Trent,

a result, we now have a fuller picture of the musical environment of fifteenth-century Trent and the surrounding area than might once have been imagined possible, although it remains a very incomplete one. There is still little evidence of the kinds of musical resources that might help explain the existence or configuration of a collection of the scale and character of Johannes Wiser's, and there is no documented proof of a direct link between his codices and the cathedral school.[10] Leverett even goes as far as to propose a severance of any possible connection between the two. Instead she advances a modified version of what she terms the 'Austrian hypothesis', on the one hand accepting the view that the codices reflect 'primarily the musical life of Vienna and of the nearby Court', while on the other suggesting that they may have been produced by and for an amateur circle closely associated with Hinderbach.[11]

Through a series of important studies published over two decades Reinhard Strohm has reached a view of the later Trent Codices that uniquely embraces and develops a number of different perspectives on the manuscripts' origin and purpose.[12] On the

1996) [henceforth *I codici musicali trentini 1996*], pp. 55–88; id., 'I manoscritti liturgici quattrocenteschi con notazione della Biblioteca comunale di Trento', *Fonti Musicali Italiane*, 3 (1998), pp. 7–64. On the history of the cathedral chapter, see E. Curzel, *I canonici e il Capitolo della cattedrale di Trento dal XII al XV secolo* (Bologna, 2001).

[10] Moreover doubts have been expressed, both in the context of specific discussions of the codices and as part of a wider debate, as to whether small-format manuscripts of this type, with their problems of decipherment and copious errors, were intended to be performed from at all. With respect to the Trent Codices, see in particular C. Hamm, 'Interrelationships between Manuscript and Printed Sources of Polyphonic Music in the Early Sixteenth Century – An Overview', in L. Finscher (ed.), *Quellenstudien zur Musik der Renaissance,* ii: *Datierung und Filiation von Musikhandschriften der Josquin-Zeit* (Wolfenbütteler Forschungen, 26; Wiesbaden, 1983), pp. 1–13, esp. pp. 1–2, and Staehelin, 'Trienter Codices und Humanismus', pp. 158–60. For arguments in support of the idea that the codices were used in performance, see M. Bent, 'Trent 93 and Trent 90: Johannes Wiser at Work', in *I codici musicali trentini 1986*, pp. 84–111, and Gozzi, 'I codici più recenti', pp. 55–88.

[11] Leverett, 'A Paleographical and Repertorial Study', pp. 24–31.

[12] Of the many studies by Strohm dealing with aspects of the Trent Codices, those most directly concerned with the origin and purpose of the later manuscripts are (in order of publication): 'Native and Foreign Polyphony in Late Medieval Austria', *Musica Disciplina*, 38 (1984), pp. 205–30, esp. pp. 221–3; The *Rise of European Music, 1380–1500* (Cambridge, 1993), pp. 509–11; 'European Cathedral Music and the Trent Codices', *I codici musicali trentini 1996*, pp. 15–29, esp. pp. 26–7; 'Zur Entstehung der Trienter Codices: Philologie und Kulturgeschichte', in M. Staehelin (ed.), *Gestalt und Entstehung musikalischer Quellen im 15. und 16. Jahrhundert* (Wolfenbütteler Forschungen, 83; Wiesbaden, 1998), pp. 11–20, at p. 18; 'Trienter Codices', *Die Musik in Geschichte und Gegenwart*[2], ed. L. Finscher (Kassel, 1994–): *Sachteil*, viii (1998), cols. 801–12, esp. cols. 804–6.

one hand he endorses Adler's and Koller's view that Hinderbach must have been responsible, directly or indirectly, for the transfer of the music to Trent Cathedral, and argues that parts of the repertory must have originally served the imperial chapel.[13] On the other hand he offers what is arguably the most convincing attempt so far to provide a context for Wiser's manuscripts, which he sees as belonging to a tradition, already well established by the middle of the century, of sources written for the *Kantorei* or choir school – a term that, like 'choir' or 'chapel', referred both to a musical group (in this case an ensemble comprising boys, adolescents and a singing-master) and to the building (in this instance the cathedral school) where they rehearsed and carried out some of their performances.[14] Strohm sees the physical status of the codices and their musical contents as matching the needs of a *Kantorei*, the functions of whose repertoire would have included music for endowed masses in guild chapels, masses for civic ceremonies, private services for visiting nobility, endowed ceremonies including civic processions, Vespers and 'Salve' services, and the celebration of particular political events.[15]

Taking as a model the well-documented parish school of the nearby town of Bolzano, an establishment where there seems to have been continual music-making,[16] Strohm apparently finds no difficulty with the lack of comparable documentation at Trent, arguing that the school there must have been famous, since the Innsbruck cantor Nikolaus Kromsdorfer would not otherwise have hired two of its choirboys for use at the Tyrolean court in 1466.[17] The new and vivid context he provides for the Wiser codices is a very persuasive one, and it may be, as he seems to imply, that we need be less concerned by the relative lack of documentation than we have been hitherto.[18]

[13] Strohm, 'Native and Foreign Polyphony', p. 222.

[14] Strohm, *The Rise of European Music*, pp. 287–91. On the *Kantorei* of the collegiate church of St Stephen's in Vienna see id., 'Music and Urban Culture in Austria: Comparing Profiles', in F. Kisby (ed.), *Music and Musicians in Renaissance Cities and Towns* (Cambridge, 2001), pp. 14–27, at p. 17.

[15] Strohm, *The Rise of European Music*, p. 510.

[16] Strohm, 'Music and Urban Culture', pp. 24–7; further details are given in M. Gozzi and D. Curti, 'Musica e musicisti nei secoli XIV e XV: contributo per una storia', in Dalmonte (ed.), *Musica e società nella storia trentina*, pp. 88–90.

[17] Strohm, 'European Cathedral Music', p. 27.

[18] For the period of the codices' compilation, and indeed for most of the fifteenth century, there appears to be very little documentation that could be construed as referring to

Central to Strohm's thinking is the important notion of music copying as a means by which a scribe could build a career for himself, and this is one reason why, in Wiser's case, the question of the precise copying dates of his manuscripts proves to be particularly crucial. For a long time a chapter record of 1459 describing Wiser as master and rector of the cathedral school[19] was the earliest known archival reference to him, and on the basis of this it came to be widely assumed that he had arrived in Trent only recently and was at that point just starting work on his collection. But in the early 1980s two important discoveries were made that led to a modification of this view. One was the uncovering of watermark evidence suggesting that work on Trent 90, the first of the Wiser codices, and Trent 93, the source that served as its chief exemplar,[20] must have begun several years earlier than previously

musicians or musical performance (none of the cathedral account books, for example, survives). An exception is the accounts of the church of S. Pietro in Trent, which were administered by Hinderbach during the 1470s and 1480s. These include payments to a group comprising the *magister scolarum*, the *scolares* and the *organista*, which probably performed polyphony (see F. Ghetta, 'Johannes Hinderbach, amministratore: i registri delle offerte della chiesa di S. Pietro a Trento', in I. Rogger and M. Bellabarba (eds.), *Il principe vescovo Johannes Hinderbach (1465–1486): fra tardo Medioevo e Umanesimo* (Trent, 1992), pp. 193–252, at p. 213, no. 26 and p. 214, no. 33). For the early sixteenth century the situation is somewhat better. The following notes taken from a document of 1508–14 headed 'Quaedam adnotationes pro reformatione chori et capituli tridentini' furnish details probably not dissimilar to what one might have expected to find fifty years earlier: 'Habeatur bonus magister schole qui sit doctus in gramatica et musica, saltem baccalaureatus alicuius universitatis; habeat bonum salarium pro laboribus chori' (13°); 'Curandum habere scolares plures quia bona scola bonum chorum facit' (15°); 'Mansionarii duo sint boni cantores et bene vociferati in vocalibus concordantes' (20°), an apparent reference to vocal polyphony (TAS, APV, Sezione Latina, Capsa 44, no. 46; transcription taken from F. Ghetta and R. Stenico, *Archivi principatus tridentini regesta, sezione latina: Guida*, 2 vols. (Trent, 2001), i, p. 675.

19 'honestus et discretus iuvenis dominus Johannes Wisser de Monaco Frisingensis diocesis magister et rector scolarum' (TAC, Instrumenta Capitularia IX, fols. 19v–20r, at fol. 19v (3 June 1459); summarised in L. Santifaller, *Urkunden und Forschungen zur Geschichte des Trientner Domkapitels im Mittelalter*, i: *Urkunden zur Geschichte des Trientner Domkapitels 1147–1500* (Veröffentlichungen des Instituts für Österreichische Geschichtsforschung, 6; Vienna, 1948), p. 363, no. 486). Wiser, in contrast to his predecessor, had the title of 'rector' as well as that of 'magister'; it is thought that this term could indicate a substitute for the senior position of 'scolasticus' at the cathedral: see E. Curzel, 'Scolastici e *scolares* nella cattedrale di Trento (secoli XII–XV)', *Annali di storia dell'educazione e delle istituzioni scolastiche* (in press; I am grateful to dott. Curzel for providing me with a copy of his article in advance of its publication).

20 Until as late as the 1970s, Trent 93, which like Trent 87 and 92 is essentially a non-Wiser manuscript, was believed to be a copy of Trent 90 rather than its main exemplar. The correct relationship between the two manuscripts was first recognised by Margaret Bent, who reported it in her edition *Fifteenth-Century Liturgical Music*, ii: *Four Anonymous Masses* (Early English Church Music, 22; London, 1979), pp. x–xi and Critical Commentary, and subsequently made it the subject of a detailed study (see 'Trent 93 and Trent 90', pp. 84–111, esp. pp. 92–9).

supposed.[21] The other was the discovery that Wiser was already in post in Trent as early as July 1455, not as schoolmaster, but as succentor to the then schoolmaster, Johannes Prenner.[22]

The year 1455 emerges from Strohm's writings as a critical one in the history of the later codices, prior to which, he suggests, 'hardly any large-scale enterprise had been possible due to the Episcopal schism' (a reference to the instabilities of Bishop Hack's reign). It was then, he argues, that a 'comprehensive re-orientation' took place in Trent, signalled by 'the arrival of the new provost, Johannes Hinderbach, the new schoolmaster, Johannes Prenner, and the new *succentor*, Johannes Wiser' – a reorientation that was 'favoured by the newly crowned Emperor Frederick and tolerated by the new Pope Calixt III'.[23] This, he suggests, was the point when Trent 93 was 'transferred to Trent Cathedral' and the copying of its main layer into Trent 90 begun. Wiser, he proposes, must have undertaken this task in the expectation of having to leave Trent to pursue his career elsewhere, but in the hope that doing so might help him secure a position as schoolmaster,[24] a goal that he eventually attained in Trent itself, some time between December 1457 and March 1458.[25]

Strohm's hypothesis is a compelling one: it provides an explanation for the puzzling fact that Trent 93, chief exemplar of one

[21] S. E. Saunders, 'The Dating of Trent 93 and Trent 90', in *I codici musicali trentini 1986*, pp. 60–83, and ead., *The Dating of the Trent Codices*, pp. 80–3.

[22] The document recording his presence was first reported in P. Wright, 'On the Origins of Trent 87_1 and 92_2', *Early Music History*, 6 (1986), pp. 245–70, at p. 261, n. 42, but with a misreading of two words, the first of which is especially hard to decipher. Marco Gozzi's interpretation of this passage as 'succentor scolarum' makes excellent sense; the full citation reads: 'Johannes Wissar, succentor scolarum in dicta civitate' (see M. Gozzi, *Il manoscritto Trento, Museo Provinciale d'Arte, cod. 1377 (Tr 90), con un'analisi del repertorio non derivato da Tr 93*, 2 vols. (Cremona, 1992), i, p. 9). For a summary of the document see E. Curzel, 'Ricerche sul Capitolo della Cattedrale di Trento alla metà del Quattrocento: aspetti istituzionali e socio-economici, con un appendice di 606 regesti di documenti (1436–1458)' (Tesi di laurea, University of Trent, 1989–90), Appendix III, no. 405 (Curzel does not offer a reading of the word 'succentor'); see also Santifaller, *Urkunden und Forschungen*, p. 348, no. 477.

[23] Strohm, 'European Cathedral Music', p. 26.

[24] *Ibid.*, p. 27. This view is essentially reiterated, with varied nuancing, in Strohm, 'Zur Entstehung der Trienter Codices', p. 18, and id., 'Trienter Codices', col. 805.

[25] Wiser must have succeeded Prenner between 13 December 1457, the last occasion on which the latter is described as schoolmaster (TAC, Instrumenta Capitularia IX, fols. 325^{v}–326^{v}, at fol. 325^{v}), and 3 March 1458, the first on which Wiser is referred to as occupying this position (*ibid.*, fol. 333^{r-v}, at fol. 333^{r}). A summary of each of these documents is given in Curzel, 'Ricerche sul Capitolo della Cattedrale', Appendix III, nos. 465 and 473.

of the other codices, should form part of the collection at all; it offers a *raison d'être* for Trent 90 as well as a time frame for its execution that realistically allows for the substantial developments manifested in Wiser's work; and it suggests a causal link between changes within the church establishment at Trent and the initiation of the collection. But just how sustainable is it?

A large part of Strohm's argument hangs on the question of the precise dates of copying. According to Suparmi Saunders, on whose watermark evidence the revised dating of Trent 93 and Trent 90 was based, the two manuscripts were copied *c.*1450–6 and *c.*1452–9 respectively. On the basis of this she suggests that Wiser was working in Trent 'from 1452 onwards',[26] a conclusion that is, of course, incompatible with Strohm's theory, although Saunders's dates, as we shall see, are sometimes less than secure.

No less important for Strohm's theory is the question of the starting dates of the three appointments that he cites as evidence of a 're-orientation' at Trent. While it may well be that Prenner's and Wiser's appointments took effect on or shortly before 30 July 1455, the date of the document in which the two men are respectively cited as schoolmaster and succentor, this is by no means certain.[27] What is clear is that whenever Prenner and Wiser took up their appointments, it must have been at least two months before the provostship was assigned to Hinderbach on 5 October.[28]

[26] Saunders, *The Dating of the Trent Codices*, pp. 82–3.

[27] This document (TAC, Instrumenta Capitularia IX, fol. 284^{r-v}) contains the earliest known reference to each of these men. Its purpose was to record the assignment of the altar of S. Caterina in Trent Cathedral to 'Johannes Prenner de tridento artium grammatice professor', following the death of the previous incumbent, Andrea Augenlicz. The name of Prenner's predecessor as schoolmaster is not known; we may only speculate that it was Augenlicz, who died between 8 May and 30 July 1455 (see Gozzi and Curti, 'Musica e musicisti', p. 111; I have found no evidence to support their claim (*ibid.*) that he held the post of 'rector scolarum'). It is possible that a period of several months or more separated Prenner's appointment as schoolmaster and his subsequent installation as a cathedral chaplain (in Wiser's case there was a separation of over a year). Were Prenner to have taken up his new post in 1454, this could imply that Wiser did the same, since apparently it was common for the appointment of a new succentor (or 'Junkmeister') to coincide with that of a new schoolmaster (see Strohm, *The Rise of European Music*, p. 509, n. 397).

[28] On the same day he was also assigned a canonry at Trent and another at Passau. For details of Hinderbach's career, and in particular the provostship, see L. Santifaller, *Das Trientner Domkapitel in seiner persönlichen Zusammensetzung im späten Mittelalter (Mitte 14. Jahrhundert bis 1500)* (Veröffentlichungen des Südtiroler Landesarchivs, 9; Bolzano, 2000), pp. 92–3, and A. Strnad, 'Personalità, famiglia, carriera ecclesiastica di Johannes Hinderbach prima dell'Episcopato', in Rogger and Bellabarba (eds.), *Il principe vescovo Johannes Hinderbach*, pp. 1–63, at pp. 22–3.

More importantly, the post of provost was a largely titular one that was held *in absentia*;[29] as yet there is no firm evidence that Hinderbach was present in Trent prior to his formal entry in the diocese in 1466 (although there has been an assumption in a number of musicological writings that he actually 'arrived' there eleven years previously). Thus while it remains quite possible that Hinderbach was at some level influential in relation to the musical enterprise at Trent, this has yet to be proved: so far there is no evidence of any link between his appointment and that of either Wiser or Prenner.[30]

According to an alternative hypothesis advanced by the present writer several years ago, Wiser must indeed have arrived in Trent in the first half of 1455, or possibly even the previous year, but having begun Trent 90 elsewhere.[31] The fact that he came from Munich, and that several of the papers he used were then current in southern Bavaria, suggested that it might have been in or near his home city that he embarked on his project. This theory, the development of which is central to the present study, was initially based on only a small range of evidence and was therefore necessarily couched in cautious terms. It nevertheless soon received support from several quarters,[32] although Strohm has

[29] Curzel, 'Ricerche sul Capitolo della Cattedrale', p. 275.

[30] Daniela Rando, who has generously shared with me some of the findings of her forthcoming study of Hinderbach's marginal annotations, confirms the lack of any firm evidence of his presence in Trent as provost. She points out, however, that in one of his annotations (TAS, APV, Sezione Latina, Cod. 3, fol. 11v), written some time after September 1466, Hinderbach indicates that his predecessor as bishop, Georg Hack, had wanted him as his assistant and eventual successor, and suggests that on the basis of this a presence in Trent might be 'imagined'. Dott.ssa Rando also observes that Hinderbach had the intention, after his appointment as provost, of taking a Marian office with him to Trent, as is evident from his note of ownership in Trent, Biblioteca comunale, MS 1785: see *'Pro biblioteca erigenda': manoscritti e incunabili del vescovo di Trento Iohannes Hinderbach (1465–1486)* (Trent, 1989), pp. 60–2. She believes it unlikely that at this stage Hinderbach had the power to take important decisions, or that he would have been in a position to influence appointments such as Wiser's (the provostship, which since the inception of the post in 1425 had been a bone of contention, continued to be contested throughout the period of Hinderbach's tenure; see Santifaller, *Das Trientner Domkapitel*, p. 93).

[31] Wright, 'Johannes Wiser's Paper', *I codici musicali trentini 1996*, pp. 31–53, at pp. 43–4.

[32] See D. Fallows, 'Ockeghem as a Song Composer: Hints towards a Chronology', in P. Vendrix (ed.), *Johannes Ockeghem: Actes du XLe Colloque international d'études humanistes* (Paris, 1998), pp. 301–16, at p. 305 (though Fallows inadvertently credits me with making the case for Trent 93 instead of Trent 90); and N. Schwindt, 'Die weltlichen deutschen Lieder der Trienter Codices — ein "französisches" Experiment?', *Neues Musikwissenschaftliches Jahrbuch*, 8 (1999), pp. 33–72, esp. pp. 43–5.

continued to maintain his original position, arguing that paper used in Bavaria could either have travelled south and been acquired there by Wiser or else have been brought to Trent by him prior to being inscribed with music.[33]

The problems of the date of Trent 90, its place of origin and the purpose behind its copying are thus connected in a particularly intimate way, and are in turn closely bound up with similar issues pertaining to Trent 93, to the nature of its relationship with Trent 90, and to the time lag between their respective compilations. The present study, while making no claims to a definitive solution to these problems, offers a detailed assessment of the delicate balance of probabilities they entail, in an attempt to gain a fuller understanding of the complex questions at issue. Central to it is a rich quantity of new watermark evidence, here evaluated in the belief that such evidence, if properly considered in conjunction with other types of evidence, can substantially advance our understanding of important musicological questions.[34]

II. METHODOLOGY AND SOURCE MATERIALS

For most of the twentieth century, scholars had only a very imprecise idea of when the later Trent Codices were actually copied. Adler and Koller considered the reign of Georg Hack (1444–65) as the period during which Wiser must have gathered and copied most of his repertoire, and that of his successor, Johannes Hinderbach (1465–86), as the period during which he completed the task. But beyond a handful of references to local events or personages found in several of the codices' texts, they had little on which to base their assessment. Following Lunelli's discovery that Wiser was in post at the cathedral school in 1459, it became common, as has been noted, for this to be seen as the year in or around which he embarked upon his collection, beginning with Trent 90.

[33] Strohm, 'Trienter Codices', col. 805.

[34] The first part of the title of the present article is an allusion to Jan LaRue's 'Watermarks and Musicology', *Acta Musicologica*, 33 (1961), pp. 120–46, a seminal study that did much to increase general awareness of the potential value of paper as evidence. LaRue's simple observation (p. 121) that 'filigranological and papyrological evidence increases in value in direct proportion to the total accumulation of data' is especially relevant here.

It was not until the 1980s, when modern techniques of watermark study began to be systematically applied to the codices, chiefly through the work of Saunders, that a set of copying dates was established that had some scientific basis. Altogether more precise than any hitherto suggested, these dates offered a substantial refinement of previous estimates, and included the proposal that Trent 90 and 93, rather than having been begun at the end of the 1450s, were compiled *during* that decade.

Given the sheer significance of the later Trent Codices in terms of the quantity of important music they uniquely preserve, and the difficulties of assigning even approximate compositional dates to a repertoire that is largely anonymous, it was natural that a new set of copying dates grounded in modern methodology should have been readily and widely embraced. While Saunders's results may have been greeted with a measure of caution or scepticism in some quarters,[35] they nevertheless gained widespread general acceptance; and not without some justification, since there can be little doubt that many of the newly proposed dates are broadly correct and represent a significant advance on previous estimates. Yet subsequent investigation of some of the Trent watermarks has shown that a number of the findings of this study are in need of revision, and that the foundations on which they rest are in fact a good deal less secure than has been generally recognised.[36] If real progress on the seemingly intractable questions pertaining to the genesis of Wiser's collection is to be made, then some reassessment of Saunders's methodology is certainly called for.

The starting point for her investigation is a series of reproductions of the Trent watermarks, most of which are based on her tracings of the marks, although a small number are presented in photographic form. Each of the main types, or designs, of watermark found in the codices is reproduced, together with a brief

[35] G. Montagna, 'Johannes Pullois in Context of his Era', *Revue Belge de Musicologie*, 42 (1988), pp. 83–117, at p. 86, wrote of Saunders's work that 'it is too early to grant the watermark evidence the finality which it claims. The study of archival equivalents is one of the most difficult fields of research, and the methodology behind such sweeping proposals requires careful examination before credibility can be granted. Saunders' work has just reached print and is only now receiving critical attention. Since other scholars are currently investigating the origin of the Trent codices, it is probably best to await their detailed evaluation of Saunders' proposal.' See also the review by Gareth Curtis in *Music & Letters*, 73 (1992), pp. 322–4.

[36] Leverett, 'A Paleographical and Repertorial Study', p. 19, n. 36; p. 36, n. 61; p. 43, n. 75.

accompanying description. The manual reproductions usefully include numbered, attendant chain-lines and a note of the height of a mark and its position on the mould, yet they are reduced from their original size[37] and like all manually reproduced watermark images are inherently inaccurate and thus potentially misleading. Unfortunately Saunders usually reproduces just one member of a pair of marks,[38] thereby providing us with only an incomplete picture of most papers. Many of the marks, moreover, are reproduced 'in reverse', as a result of having been viewed from the felt-side of a sheet rather than from the mould-side, which is the practice commonly recommended.[39] In several important respects, then, Saunders's data is less than complete or reliable.

Once assembled, this data was compared with examples published by the great paper scholar Gerhard Piccard in his series of 'Findbücher',[40] as well as with unpublished examples drawn from his vast collection of watermark reproductions.[41] On the basis of these comparisons a date or range of dates was arrived at for each paper.[42] While a number of the examples cited by Saunders provide quite convincing matches for the Trent marks, many turn out to be no more than approximations, some of them far from close.

Saunders, like many scholars, relies almost exclusively on Piccard for dated equivalents of the marks she is examining;[43] yet

[37] This is true only of Saunders's published work. The unpublished version of her dissertation ('The Dating of the Trent Codices from their Watermarks, with a Study of the Local Liturgy of Trent in the Fifteenth Century' (Ph.D. thesis, University of London, 1984)) reproduces the Trent watermarks at their original size.

[38] Watermarks from this period normally survive in pairs, as explained in A. Stevenson, 'Watermarks Are Twins', *Studies in Bibliography*, 4 (1951–2), pp. 57–91.

[39] By Stevenson (*The Problem of the Missale Speciale* (London, 1967), p. 38) and others. Although Saunders cites Stevenson's practice (*The Dating of the Trent Codices*, p. 33), it is unclear whether or not she intended to follow it.

[40] G. Piccard *et al.*, *Die Wasserzeichenkartei Piccard im Hauptstaatsarchiv Stuttgart: Findbücher I–XVII* (Stuttgart, 1961–97). Each Findbuch comprises a volume (or volumes) dedicated to a particular type of watermark, such as the anchor, the horn, the bull's head or the key.

[41] Stuttgart, Hauptstaatsarchiv, Wasserzeichungsammlung Piccard (Bestand J 340). It is from this archive that the watermark examples published in the Findbücher are drawn. Some 37,000 examples remain unpublished, however, and these are currently in the process of being made available in digital form, many of them on-line (see www.lad-bw.de/hstas).

[42] The data is summarised in Saunders, *The Dating of the Trent Codices*, pp. 203–4.

[43] Only once does she refer directly to an original source (the archival equivalent for Figure 32 is specified as TAS, APV, Sezione Latina, Capsa 26, no. 28: see *The Dating of the Trent* Codices, p. 203, and Appendix 2, below). It would seem that Saunders cannot have explored the city archives very fully, since, if she had, she would no doubt have soon

however great the value of Piccard's work as a reference tool – and it is enormous, as the countless source studies that depend on it testify – it inevitably has its limitations and shortcomings.

To begin with, Piccard's tracings, like all manual watermark reproductions, are incapable of indicating many of the finer nuances of a mark – the subtle divergences of contour and size that allow variant states or closely related versions of the same basic type to be distinguished. Then there is the fact that he, too, sometimes views a mark from the felt-side of a sheet rather than from the mould-side (in some cases apparently explaining the same occurrence in Saunders), or fails to recognise its twin status. Finally, there are the difficulties that can arise from the synoptic manner in which Piccard's data is published, as the following example shows.

The watermark design here is that of a bull's (or ox's) head surmounted by a seven-petalled flower on a two-line stem, a common type that exists in varying shapes and sizes, as can be seen from the relevant section of the published Ochsenkopf Findbücher.[44] Among the many examples of this variant that Piccard publishes are two, numbered XIII 246 and 247, that he considers to form a pair, and which Saunders equates with the pair of marks found in Trent 90, gatherings XXIX–XXX.[45] Piccard provides the following summary of his data for the pair:

a	h	b	c		
68	106–107	33–34	23	: 1450	Hall (Tirol), Innsbruck,
70–72	[106–107]	35–36	20–25	: 1457–1460	– Augsburg, Eichstätt, München,
68–71	110–116	[35–36]	18–19	: 1454–1457	Neuburg (Donau), Öhringen,
[68–71]	[110–116]	34–37	20–24	: 1452–1459	Pappenheim, Schrobenhausen, Wartenberg, – Breslau, Agram, – Marienburg (Wpr.)

encountered some of the many examples of the codices' papers that are to be found there. It appears, moreover, that she did not actually inspect the Piccard archive at first hand, but instead verified her findings through direct correspondence with Piccard himself (Saunders, *The Dating of the Trent Codices*, p. 35).

[44] Piccard, *Die Wasserzeichenkartei Piccard . . . Findbuch II (1–3): Die Ochsenkopf-Wasserzeichen* (Stuttgart, 1966), section XIII.

[45] Saunders, *The Dating of the Trent Codices*, pp. 187–8, 203 and 256–7 (Figures 28 and 29).

Each of the four sets of dimensions listed (or implied) comprises: the distance between attendant chain-lines (a); the overall height of the mark (h); the distance between the tips of the ears (b); and the distance between the tips of the horns (c). In the penultimate column each set is assigned a date or range of dates, and in the final column the provenances of the various sources are listed by region. There is no consistent alignment between dates and places, nor is any indication given of the archival sources from which this information derives.

Thus the two marks that Piccard numbers XIII 246 and 247 together represent a series of what might be called 'sub-variants' of a particular type. To the Trent 90 pair – designated 'Bull's head 5' (BH5) below – with which Saunders equates Piccard's pair she assigns the date range 1452–9. She is correct in doing so in the sense that the measurements of the Trent 90 twins clearly lie closer to the third and fourth sets of dimensions, with their respective date ranges of 1454–7 and 1452–9, than to the first or second sets, although whether she was equating them with one set or both sets is unclear. Examination of the individual analogues on which the above data is based, however, shows the situation to be less straightforward than the information published by Piccard suggests. No fewer than eighteen examples of this watermark type are to be found in the Piccard archive, ranging from 1450 to 1460, but in fact thirteen of these examples fall within the period 1454–7, and, of these, nine belong to the years 1454–5. Furthermore, only two of Piccard's examples, a pair of marks from 1454 (Augsburg), appear to be identical[46] to the Trent marks. It would seem, therefore, that Saunders's range of dates for this paper is somewhat overgenerous.[47]

Normally the published Findbücher do not provide any details

[46] Identity is taken to mean that two watermarks correspond precisely in terms of their essential shape and their dimensions. In the case of manual reproductions such as Piccard's, some allowance has to be made for slight vagaries of contour, and there is, of course, no means of determining identity of mould.

[47] Three of Piccard's examples are very similar, rather than identical, to one of the marks, 'BH5-A'. One of these is a document from Pappenheim (Mittelfranken, Bavaria) of 1459 (see Appendix 3). The fact that the date of this document lies well beyond the range of dates represented by the other equivalent or near-equivalent marks for BH5 suggests that it may be spurious or that the document may be a copy. It was presumably this example that formed the basis of Saunders's extension of the proposed date range for the BH5 paper, and hence for Trent 90 in its entirety, to as late as 1459.

of the source, or even the archive, from which a particular example is drawn. For information of this kind one must consult the original watermark drawing, housed in the Piccard archive, which usually contains a note of a document's archival location and (where known) its precise date and place of copying. Even then one cannot be certain, without reference to the actual source itself, of the reliability of these details, or of whether one is dealing with a copy rather than an original document.[48] Piccard provides us with an invaluable starting point, a preliminary guide to the 'documented life', or known period of usage, of a particular paper. But it is no more than that. If a more secure and refined estimate is needed, then nothing less than a direct examination of the relevant primary source materials will suffice.

It is precisely such an examination that underpins the present study, one based on a search of many hundreds of archival documents and several dozen manuscript books located in various Italian, German and Austrian archives and libraries. This search has brought to light more than sixty sources that employ the same paper as either or both Trent 90 and Trent 93 (see Appendices 1 and 2) – a significant body of new material that, when taken in conjunction with existing findings (Appendix 3), provides an altogether more solid basis for dating the manuscripts, and hence for addressing some of the wider issues pertaining to the genesis of Wiser's collection.

III. DATING THE PAPERS OF TRENT 93 AND TRENT 90

The distribution of papers in Trent 93 and Trent 90 is summarised in Table 1 below (p. 269), as are details of the gathering structure and musical contents of each source. It can be seen from this that there are ten main stocks of paper, three used for Trent 93 only, five for Trent 90 alone, and two for both manuscripts, in addition to which there is a half-leaf insert in Trent 90 (fol. 194b) drawn from a separate stock, bringing the total number of papers to eleven. For each manuscript the papers will be examined individ-

[48] In fact a check of some of the original documents cited by Piccard shows that a number are taken from *post facto* compilations (for example, the Lehenbücher of the Tiroler Landesarchiv: see Appendix 3, s.v. Bull's head 2, StAJ Lehenbücher), and that the dates given in these documents are therefore not necessarily the actual dates when the documents were drawn up.

ually, and in order of first appearance, before the combined evidence they yield is considered.

Trent 93 falls into two distinct parts: the first, 'Trent 93-1', essentially comprises the main layer of the manuscript, a large collection of mass music systematically ordered by liturgical type, while the second, 'Trent 93-2', consists of a miscellaneous collection including songs and contrafacta, apparently compiled separately from the main part of the volume.

The first of the Trent 93-1 papers, here referred to as the 'Cross' paper, is marked with a small cross on a base (Figure 1). Piccard

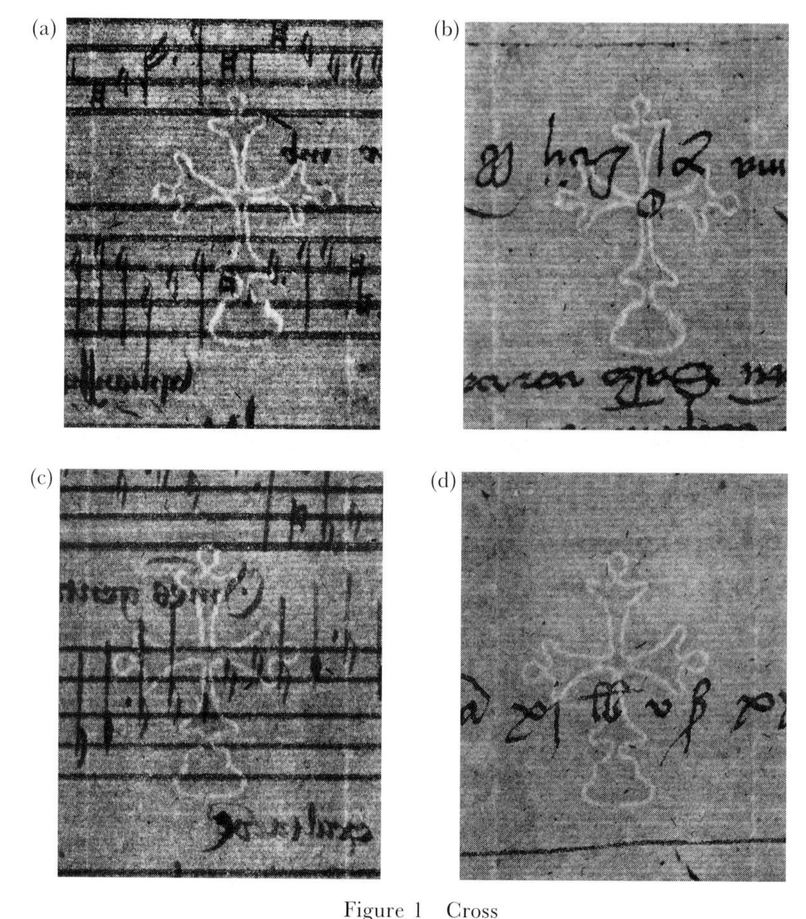

Figure 1 Cross
(a) Trent 93, fol. 63^{r}: A; (b) MS, Kamm. 1/60, fol. 67^{r}: A;
(c) Trent 93, fol. 29^{r}: B; (d) MS, Kamm. 1/60, fol. 55^{r}: B

actually publishes a pair of marks that corresponds exactly to the Trent pair,[49] the source of which dates from 1451 and provides the basis of Saunders's dating of this paper to the same year. His unpublished records include three further examples of the same type, one from 1450, the other two from 1451, but these turn out to be similar to rather than the same as the Trent marks. The present findings, while demonstrating that this paper was actually being manufactured as early as 1450, also show that it continued to be in use until as late as 1453.

Next is the first of six papers marked with the familiar motif of a bull's (or ox's) head, here designated 'BH1' to 'BH6' respectively.[50] For BH1 (Figure 2), which is distinguished from all the other BH variants by the absence of eyes, Saunders, following Piccard, offers a range of dates between 1450 and 1452 based on a small number of documents with varying degrees of congruence with the Trent marks. In fact eight documents containing equivalents of these marks have come to light during the present investigation, five of which date from 1450, two from 1451 and one from either 1452 or 1454.[51] Thus with one possible exception all of these examples fall within the narrow range of dates provided by Saunders.

The pattern of alternation between the Cross and BH1 papers in the first six gatherings of Trent 93, and their co-existence within a late gathering of the manuscript (gathering XXX), suggest that the compiler must have acquired these papers at the same time – an impression strongly reinforced by the degree of corresponding repertorial continuity. Each paper makes a further appearance later in the main layer, but for all except two of the remaining twenty-two gatherings of Trent 93-1 a different paper is used, one marked with a tall cross and three mounts (Figure 3). As with the

[49] These, in fact, are the marks published here as Figures 1b and 1d. Not only are they the same as the Trent 93 Cross marks, but they were also produced from the same pair of moulds. Throughout this study, 'identity' – where comparison is being made with actual watermarks rather than with reproductions – implies identity of mould as well as of mark unless otherwise indicated. All photographic illustrations of watermarks in this article reproduce the marks to within a millimetre of their original dimensions.

[50] The reader is warned that the numbering system used here is different from that employed in Wright, 'Johannes Wiser's Paper'.

[51] The scribe dated the document in question (MBH, KAA 1949) 1454, but may have meant to date it 1452. For details see the entry for this document in Appendix 2.

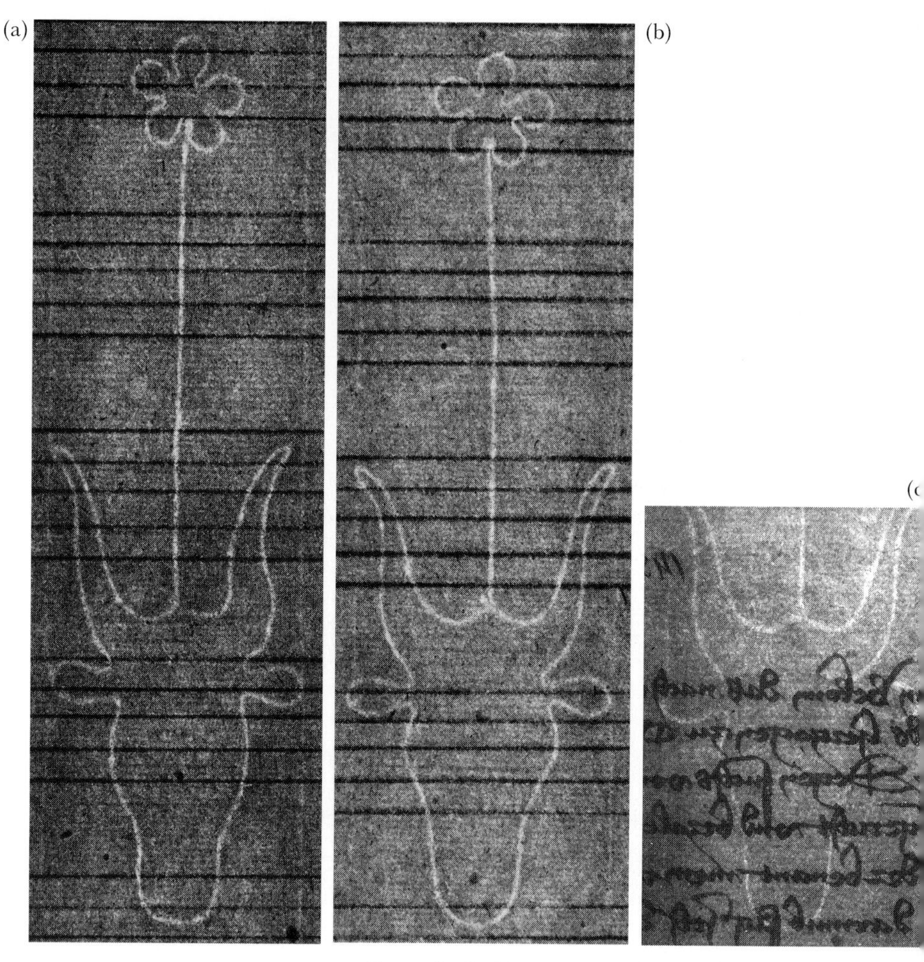

Figure 2 Bull's head 1
(a) Trent 93, fol. 43r: A1; (b) Trent 93, fol. 177r: A2;
(c) ITL, U. I 3719, verso: A2

Cross and BH1 papers, the new evidence for the 'Cross-on-mounts' paper[52] confirms and extends the established range of dates (1451–2). The seven newly discovered equivalents include four from 1451 and one each from 1450, 1452 and 1453, to which should

[52] This is a complex paper in that some of the marks contained in gatherings XIX–XXI and XXIX differ very slightly in shape and size from the prevailing pair of marks. So minute are these differences that it is hard to tell whether the marks in question represent variant states or variant marks. Therefore no attempt has been made to distinguish them formally, and for present purposes all of the Cross-on-mounts marks are considered to represent one paper.

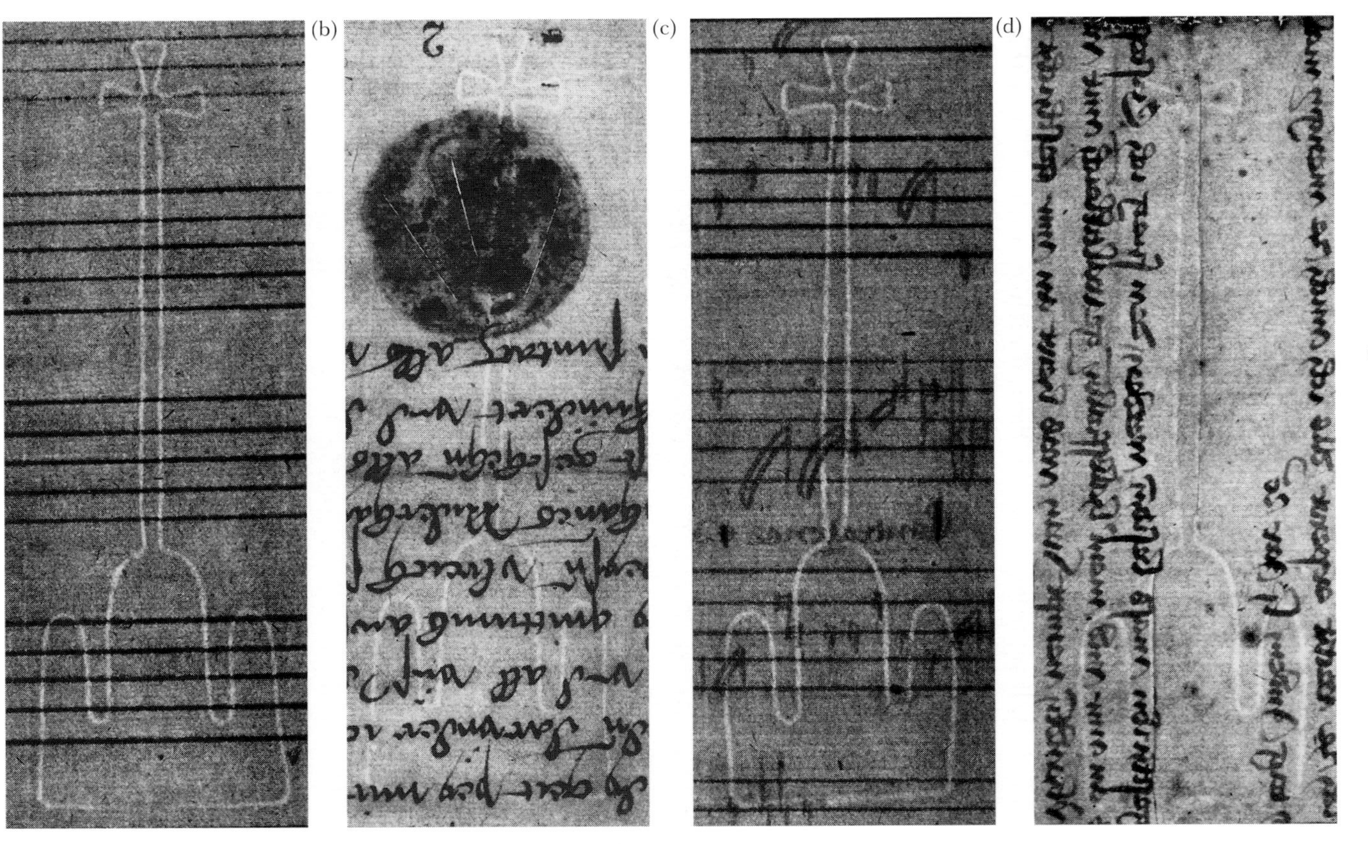

Figure 3 Cross-on-mounts

(a) Trent 93, fol. 342^{r}: A1; (b) MBH, AR 395, fol. 2^{r}: A1; (c) Trent 93, fol. 211^{v}: A2; (d) TAS, APV, s.t., Capsa misc. no. 9, verso: A2

be added two matches from the Piccard archive that Saunders apparently overlooked, one from 1454, the other from 1455.

Thus for the three Trent 93-1 papers combined no fewer than twenty-one new sources have been found, a sizeable total that affords a fuller context within which to assess this manuscript's date. Broadly speaking, they confirm the thrust of Saunders's findings, while inviting the possibility that the compiler of Trent 93-1 obtained these papers a year or two later than she allows for.

'BH2' (Figure 4), the first of the two papers employed for Trent 93-2, is well represented in the Piccard archive, with no fewer than twelve convincing matches, ranging from 1452 to 1455 (Saunders's dates), but with most concentrated in the years 1452–4. To these may be added three new examples, which turn out to be complementary to Piccard's: one each from the years 1452, 1454 and 1455. For the other paper used in Trent 93-2, 'BH3' (Figure 5), the opposite situation obtains, in that none of the many examples of this type provided by Piccard offers a convincing match, making it difficult to see what basis there is for Saunders's assignment to this paper of a range of dates from 1452 to 1456. Only two new sources of BH3 have come to light, one an undated copy of a document of 1450, the other a section of a manuscript completed in July 1454 and, as such, apparently the only firm dated equivalent for BH3 that we have so far.

As Table 1 shows, BH2 and BH3 not only conclude Trent 93 but also open Trent 90 (though in reverse order), a pattern of overlap that occurs twice more between successive codices[53] and that may be seen as a physical manifestation of the continuity of purpose that exists between individual volumes within the Trent complex. Any conclusions about the dates of BH2 and BH3 must therefore have an equal bearing upon both manuscripts.

The third paper to be used in Trent 90 is marked with a Tower (Figures 6a and 6d), one of the most common of fifteenth-century watermark designs, although the version found here is unusual in being simpler and less ornate than most marks of this type. Among the many versions published by Piccard, no more than a handful belong to this simpler variety, and, of these, only two are centred, like the Trent marks, between chain-lines rather than on a single chain. One of these provides an excellent match for Tower B, while

[53] Trent 88 opens with the same paper that concludes its predecessor (Trent 90), as does its successor, Trent 89.

(a)

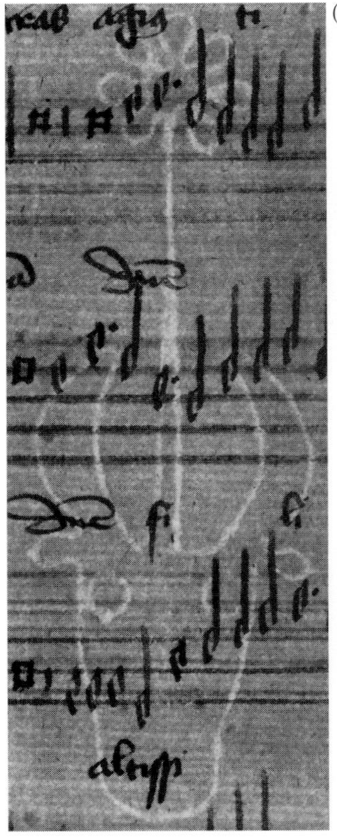

(b)

(c)

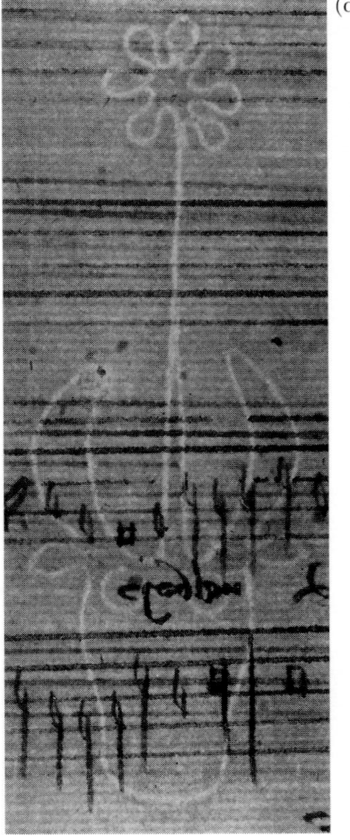

(d)

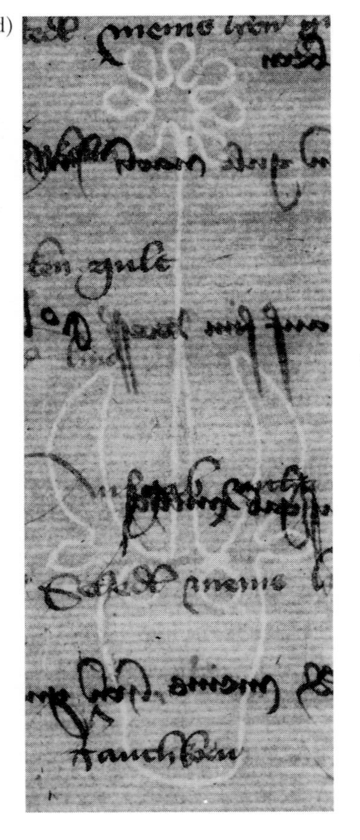

Figure 4 Bull's head 2

(a) Trent 90, fol. 114^{v}: A^{1}; (b) MBH, AR 270, fol. 226^{v}: A^{1}; (c) Trent 90, fol. 84^{v}: B^{1}; (d) MBH, AR 270, fol. 217^{r}: B^{1}

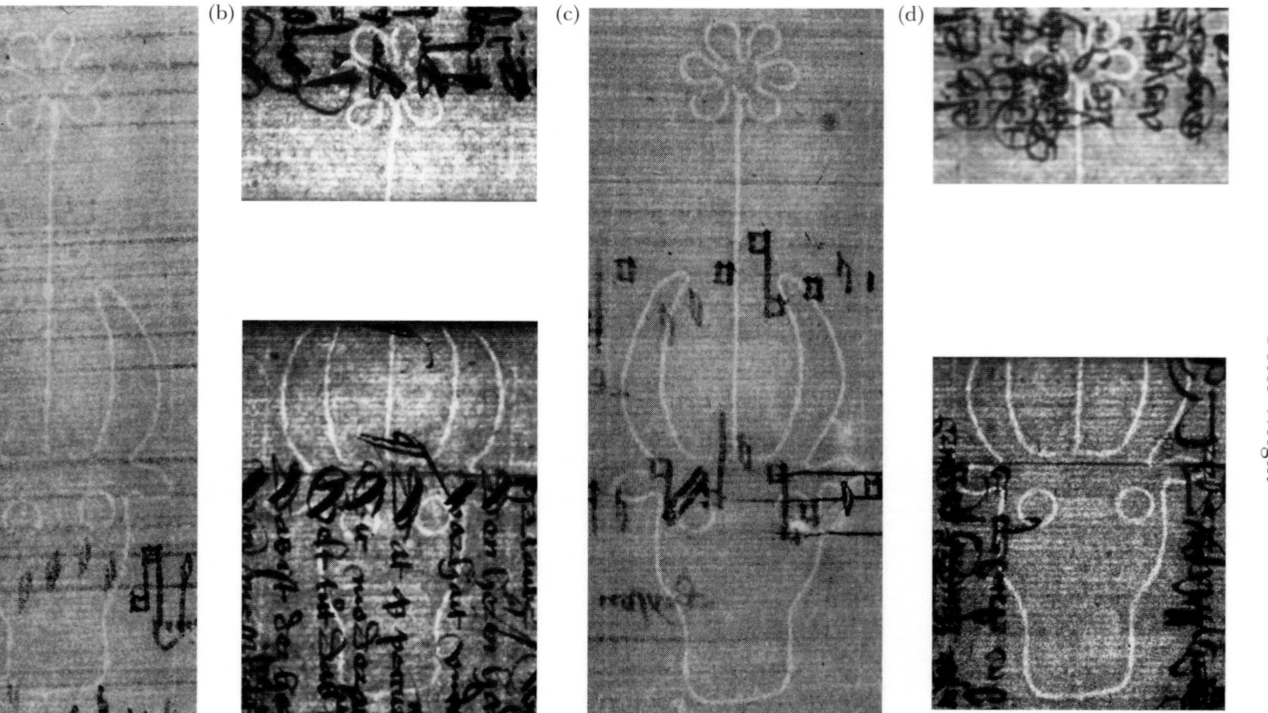

Figure 5 Bull's head 3

(a) Trent 90, fol. 21^{r}: A; (b) MBS, Cgm 379, fols. 21^{v} (upper) and 14^{r} (lower): A;
(c) Trent 90, fol. 74^{r}: B; (d) MBS, Cgm 379, fols. 110^{r} (upper) and 115^{v} (lower): B

Table 1 *Structure and contents of Trent 93 and Trent 90*

Gatherings	Folios	Paper	Main contents
Tr 93-1			
I^{11}	1–11	Cross	Antiphons
II^{12}	12–23	BH1	Introits
III^{10}	24–33	Cross	Introits
IV^{12}, V^{11}	34–56	BH1	Introits
VI^{12}	57–68	Cross	Introits
VII–XV^{12}	69–176	Cross-on-mounts	Introits, Kyries, Glorias
XVI^{12}	177–88	BH1	Glorias
XVII–XIX^{12}, XX^{11}	189–235	Cross-on-mounts	Glorias, sequences
XXI–XXII^{12}, XXIII^{13}	236–72	Cross-on-mounts	Credos
XXIV–XXVIII^{12}, XXIX^{11}	273–343	Cross-on-mounts	Credos, Sanctus, Agnus
XXX^{12}	344–55	BH1 (+ Cross)[a]	Sanctus, Agnus
Tr 93-2			
XXXI^{10}	356–65	BH2	Mixed
XXXII^{8}, XXXIII^{9}	366–82	BH3	Mixed, hymns
Tr 90			
I^{11}, II–VII^{12}	1–83	BH3	Introits, Kyries
VIII–XI^{12}	84–131	BH2	Kyries, Glorias
XII–XVIII^{12}	132–215	Tower (+ Crayfish)[b]	Glorias, Credos
XIX–XXIV^{12}	216–87	BH4	Credos, Sanctus, Agnus
XXV^{12}	288–99	Tower	Mixed
XXVI^{10}, XXVII–XXVIII^{12}	300–33	BH4	Mixed
XXIX–XXX^{12}	334–57	BH5	Mixed
XXXI–XXXIII^{12}	358–93	BH6	Mixed
XXXIV–XXXIX^{12}	394–465	Crescents	Ordinary cycles and sections

[a] Cross paper is used only in the outermost sheet of the gathering (344/355).
[b] Crayfish paper is used only for the inserted half-leaf numbered '194b'.

the other, though clearly of the same type as its twin, Tower A, provides only an approximation to it.

No fewer than nine new sources of the Tower paper have emerged, although this statement needs some qualification. It appears that this paper was produced from at least two closely related pairs of moulds, one pair, 'A*a*' and 'B*a*', representing the Trent marks (Figures 6a–b and 6d–e), the other, 'A*b*' and 'B*b*', a closely related pair (Figures 6c and 6f). So minute are the differ-

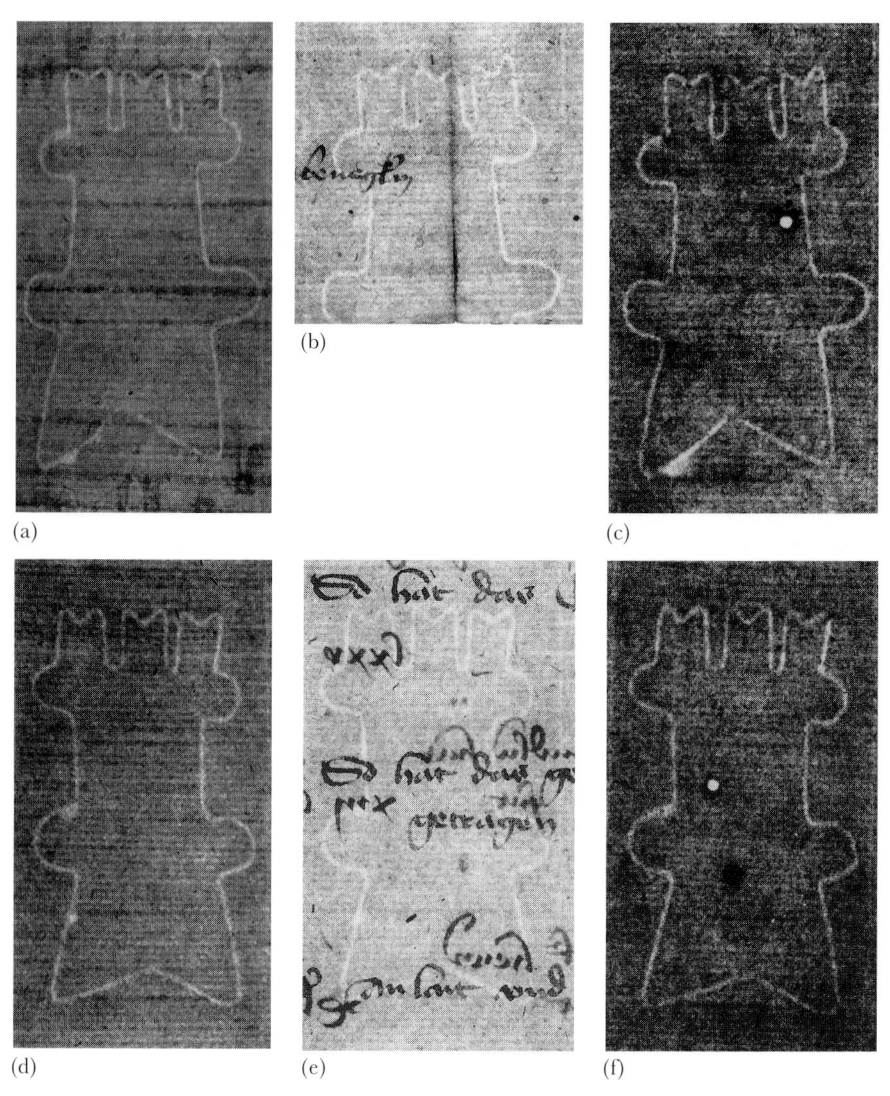

Figure 6 Tower
(a) Trent 90, fol. 161^{v}: A*a*; (b) MBH, KU 9753, verso: A*a*;
(c) MBS, Cgm 572, fol. 23^{r}: A*b*; (d) Trent 90, fol. 199^{r}: B*a*;
(e) MBH, AR 395, fol. 78^{r}: B*a*; (f) MBS, Cgm 572, fol. 24^{r}: B*b*

ences between the Trent twins and their relations as to deceive the naked eye, conveying the impression that one is dealing with two marks rather than four, but in fact close scrutiny of these marks reveals enough subtle variations in their dimensions and contours to confirm that they are not identical. From the patterns of distribution of the marks, however, it appears that the two pairs of moulds that produced them must have been in use at the same time, and so the paper they produced is considered as a single stock.[54] Seven of the nine new sources carry dates, all falling in either 1453 or 1454, while the only firm match provided by Piccard dates from January 1455. The documented life of the Tower paper is therefore at most two years.[55]

Inserted in the middle of one of the Tower gatherings (XVII, fols. 189–200) is a half-leaf, numbered '194b', containing part of the contratenor voice of the Credo from the *Missa sine nomine* variously attributed to Dunstaple, Power and Benet. This is in fact a corrected version of a section of music found on the next folio of the manuscript (fol. 195), which it is obviously intended to replace.[56] Both script and ink of the half-leaf correspond to those of the surrounding contents, indicating that they must be contemporary with this stage of the copying process. The half-leaf may have belonged to a paper supply that Wiser had just exhausted or was using or about to use for another purpose; its presence certainly invites speculation that he was involved in additional projects. Simply by virtue of having thus incorporated this scrap, Wiser unwittingly opened a fascinating window onto the history of his manuscript, for there is more to be learned about this paper than about any other.

[54] Tower B*b* appears to be the same as its Trent 90 counterpart (Tower B*a*), but about 2 mm taller, while its companion, Tower A*b*, is similarly closely related to its counterpart (Tower A*a*), but is about 1 mm taller. The situation whereby two pairs of moulds with closely related pairs of marks were used simultaneously at the same mill is known to have existed in the mid-fifteenth century: see Stevenson, *The Problem of the Missale Speciale*, pp. 121 and 127.

[55] Noting that several of the manuscripts that use Tower paper come from Augsburg, I searched the published catalogue of German medieval manuscripts held in the city's university library, which includes information on watermarks, for possible further evidence of this paper. One manuscript, numbered 'III.1.4° 42', is described in the catalogue as containing paper watermarked with the tower listed by Piccard as no. II 326, that is, Tower B*a*, although it has not been possible to see this source in order to verify the identification. The only dates given in the manuscript, 29 November 1453 (fol. 122ᵛ) and 1454 (fol. 226ᵛ), fall within the documented life of the Tower paper. See K. Schneider, *Deutsche mittelalterliche Handschriften der Universitätsbibliothek Augsburg: Die Signaturgruppen Cod.I.3. und Cod.III.1* (Wiesbaden, 1988), pp. 363–5.

[56] For details of the transmission of the Credo movement see *John Dunstable: Complete Works*, ed. M. F. Bukofzer (Musica Britannica, 8; London, 1953; rev. 2nd edn., 1970), no. 57, and P. Wright, *The Related Parts of Trent, Museo Provinciale d'Arte, MSS 87 (1374) and 92 (1379): A Paleographical and Text-Critical Study* (New York, 1989), pp. 253–4.

The watermark contained in the half-leaf represents a crayfish (Figure 7a), as can be seen from the shape of its body and the number of its legs (eight). Appended to its tail is a large letter 'S' – possibly a reference to the maker of the watermark or to its place of origin. Most of the mark is clearly visible, with only the bottom of the 'S' hidden from view as it disappears into the 'gutter'. Although the chain-lines are rather faint in the Trent 90 leaf, the pattern of laid-wires is reasonably clear and distinctive, thus facilitating the establishment of identity between sheets produced from the same mould.

The crayfish watermark is not a particularly familiar type. Briquet published an example that lies quite close to the Trent 90 mark,[57] and a further example, also similar, is included in a collection of watermarks from Brescia.[58] Several unpublished examples are to be found in the Piccard archive, including two that correspond to the Trent 90 mark; and the discovery of several references to a crayfish watermark in the catalogue of manuscripts of the Bayerische Staatsbibliothek raised the possibility of further equivalents. Subsequent examination of the manuscripts in question confirmed that they contained the very same crayfish mark found in Trent 90, and further searches among other sources revealed many additional examples: no fewer than twenty have so far come to light (see Appendix 1).

Together these sources provide a rich context for the Trent 90 crayfish. Through them, for instance, we learn of the existence of a twin mark closely comparable in shape and size. We also discover that, as with some of the other Trent papers, the twins are respectively located in the same half of a sheet (in this case the right half) rather than in different halves, as was the norm at this time.[59]

[57] C. M. Briquet, *Les filigranes: dictionnaire historique des marques du papier*, 2nd, rev. edn. (Hilversum, 1968), no. 5939. The mark is incomplete, since there is no 'S' and part of the tail is missing. It is taken from a document copied in Wal (Bavaria?) in 1454.

[58] L. Mazzoldi, *Filigrane di cartiere bresciane*, 2 vols. (Brescia, 1991), ii, p. 141, no. 851. This example, taken from a document copied in Brescia on 28 August 1453, is reduced in size but corresponds in its shape and in the disposition of its parts to the mark designated below as 'Crayfish B2^{1}'.

[59] It is unclear what significance, if any, there is in this phenomenon, although several writers have noted its existence: see T. Gerardy, *Datieren mit Hilfe von Wasserzeichen* (Bückeburg, 1964), p. 40, and Stevenson, *The Problem of the Missale Speciale*, p. 277, n. 16. Four of the Trent 93/90 papers (BH1, Cross-on-mounts, Crayfish, BH4) were produced from pairs of moulds in which the twin marks were placed at corresponding rather than opposite ends of their respective moulds. Whether one considers a mark as being located

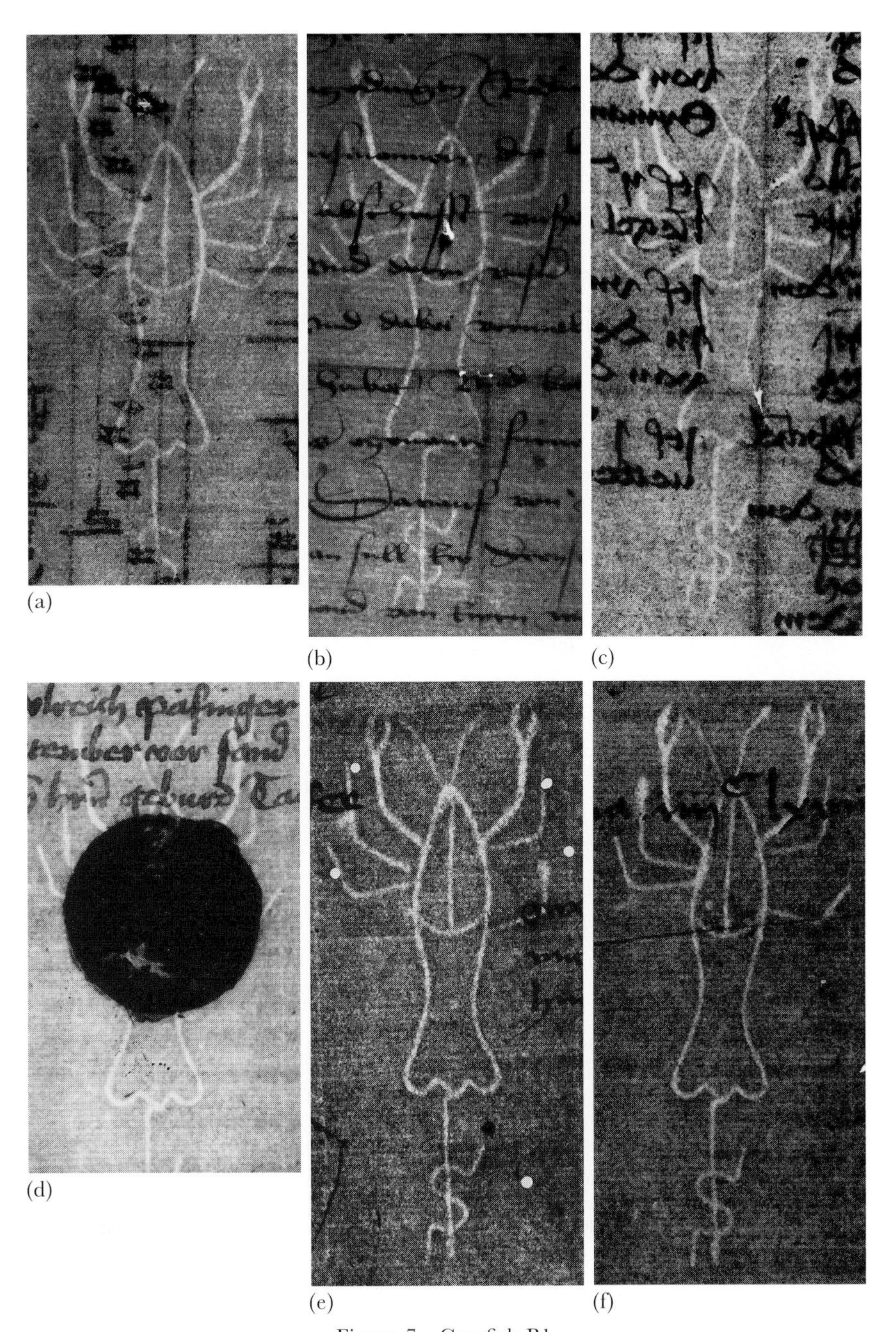

Figure 7 Crayfish B1
(a) Trent 90, fol. 194b^{r}: B1^{1}; (b) ITL, P1348/2, recto: B1^{1};
(c) MS, Kamm. 1/63: B1^{1}; (d) MBH, KU 18489, recto: B1^{2};
(e) MBS, Cgm 2153, p. 93: B1^{3}; (f) MS, Kamm. 1/64, fol. 54^{r}: B1^{4}

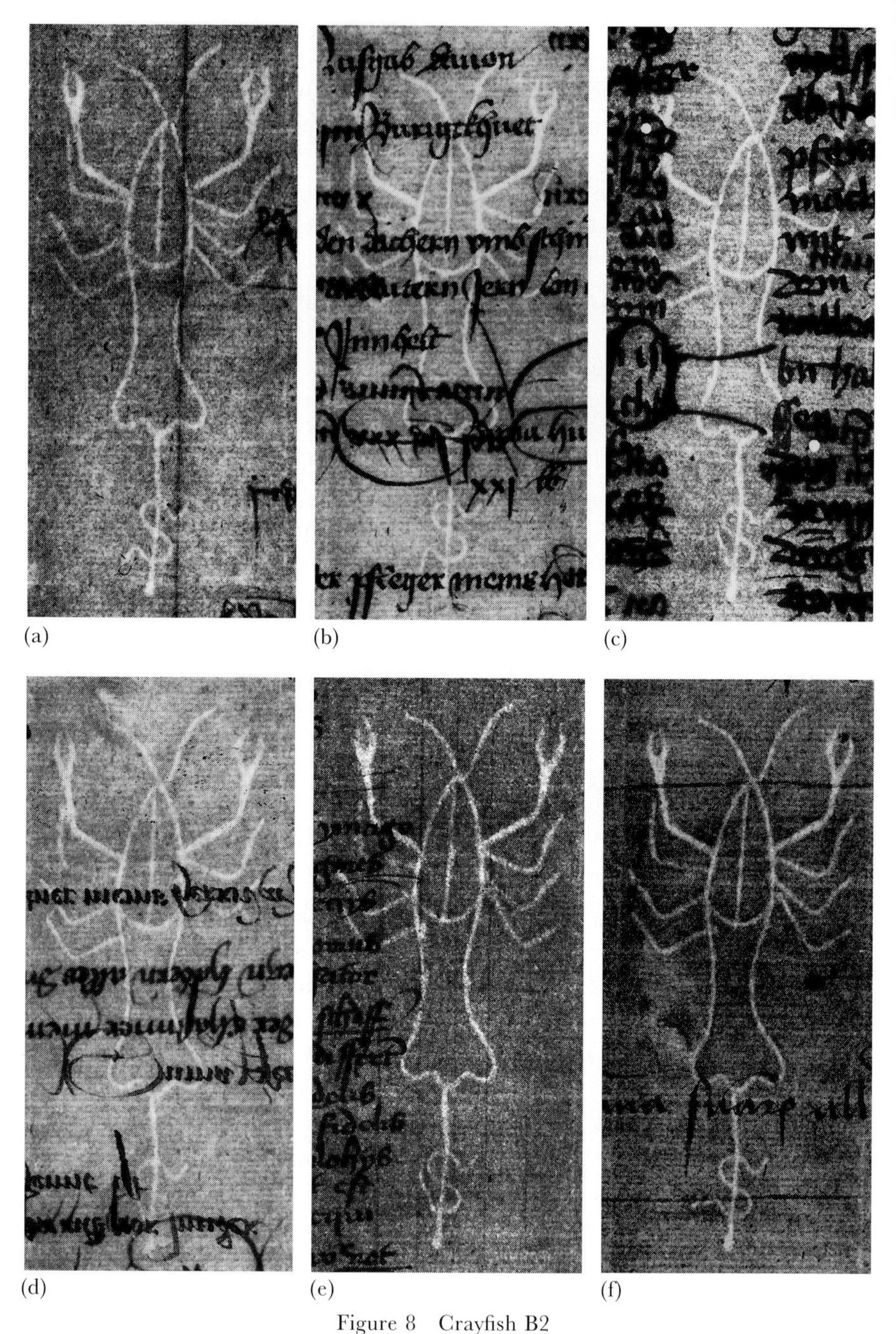

(d) (e) (f)

Figure 8 Crayfish B2
(a) MBH, AR 270, fol. 282*a*ʳ: B2[1]; (b) MBH, AR 396, fol. 49ʳ: B2[2]; (c) MBS, Cgm 2153, p. 73: B2[3]; (d) MBH, AR 396, fol. 23ᵛ: B2[3]; (e) MBS, Cgm 641, fol. 101ʳ: B2[4]; (f) MS, Kamm 1/64, fol. 21ᵛ: B2[5]

Most importantly, we see that each of the twins survives in more than one 'state', or identifiable stage of its history, a feature that sets these marks apart from nearly all of the others under consideration. The main reason for this is the precariousness of the design, and in particular the legs, which are prone to movement on the mould and at times even become severed from the body of the fish. The existence of different states allows us to posit a history for the Crayfish marks, although the task of doing so proves to be far from straightforward.

Let us begin with the Trent 90 mark, 'Crayfish B1'. Four states of this mark can be identified, the earliest of which, 'B1^{1}', appears to be that represented in Trent 90, here shown together with two equivalents as Figures 7a–c. That these do indeed represent the first known state is suggested by the fact that all eight legs are present, whereas in each of the other states one or two legs are missing. It could of course be countered that the latter are earlier states and that the state shown in Trent 90 represents a repaired version of the mark, but the pattern of deterioration and the freshness and clarity of the Trent mark argue against this.

Figure 7d shows the same mark as Trent 90, but with the lowest left leg missing (though this is a little hard to make out since much of the mark is obscured by the presence of a seal), suggesting that this represents a second state of the mark, 'B1^{2}'. Figures 7e and 7f show the two remaining states, 'B1^{3}' and 'B1^{4}', in each of which two legs are missing: the fourth one down on the left-hand side and the third one down on the right-hand side. The main difference between these last two states lies in the position of the fourth leg down on the right-hand side: in Figure 7e this leg is attached at a lower point from that seen in Figures 7a–d, whereas in Figure 7f it is attached at the same point. Although initially confusing, the situation becomes clearer on closer inspection: in state 'B1^{3}' (Figure 7e) the second leg down on the left has become detached from the body of the fish, whereas in state 'B1^{4}' (Figure 7f) the leg is secure; moreover additional sewing dots can be seen, both in this area and at the point where the fourth leg down on the right is attached to the body. It would therefore appear that

in the right or left half of a sheet depends on which way up one views it. Normally this is self-evident, but in the case of the Crayfish twins it is not, and so the decision to view these marks with the letter 'S' at the bottom is necessarily a subjective one.

B1^4 represents a repaired version of B1^3, but with two legs still missing, although the possibility that this is the reverse of what actually occurred cannot be completely discounted.

The history of 'Crayfish B2' is not dissimilar to that of its companion mark. Five different states can be distinguished on the basis of anatomical changes. Figure 8a illustrates what appears to be the earliest known state of the mark, 'B2^1', in which all eight legs are present (as in Crayfish B1^1) and the first and second legs on the left-hand side, in contrast to other states of the mark, are very close together. This is in fact the only significant difference between the second state, 'B2^2' (Figure 8b), and the first. In the third state, 'B2^3' (Figures 8c and 8d), one of the legs (the fourth down on the right) is missing and the lower part of the letter 'S' has become pinched. By the fourth state, 'B2^4' (Figure 8e), the missing leg has been reinstated, but is attached, rather loosely, to a different point of the fish's body, while the 'S' remains distorted. The fifth state, 'B2^5' (Figure 8f), is essentially identical to the fourth, but with the lower serif of the 'S' adjusted.

So much, then, for the physical characteristics of the Crayfish twins. But what of the sources containing these marks? Crayfish B1 survives in no fewer than a dozen dated sources, all from the years 1453–5. Table 2 shows that there exists a broad correlation between the dates of the sources and the order of states just defined. One of the two dated examples of state 1 dates from April 1453, the other from an unspecified point in 1454, while both examples of state 2 date from the latter year. Each of the two remaining states, however, spans the years 1454–5, but whereas the examples of state 3 are evenly divided between the two years, the examples of state 4 belong mainly to the latter. Clearly there are overlaps here of the kind produced by variations of timing in the supply, purchase and usage of a particular paper; yet there is nevertheless some sense of a correlation between states and dates, which may be summarised as follows:

B1^1	1453, 1454
B1^2	1454
B1^3	1454, 1455
B1^4	1454, 1455

If there are residual doubts about the correct sequence of states 3 and 4, then the pattern of dates shown in Table 2 could be seen as marginally reinforcing the order proposed here.

Table 2 *Crayfish B1*

State	Source	Date
$B1^{1}$	Trent 90	undated
	ITL, P 1348/2	18 April 1453
	MBS, Cgm 351	undated
	MS, Kamm. 1/63	1454
$B1^{2}$	MBH, KU 18489	19 September 1454
	MBS, Cgm 778	early 1454
$B1^{3}$	MBH, AR 396	1454
	MBS, Cgm 2153	completed 30 October 1454
	MBS, Cgm 667	completed 15 March 1455
	MBS, Cgm 781	1455
$B1^{4}$	MBS, Cgm 605	between 30 September and December 1454
	ITL, U. II 8396	21 July 1455
	MBH, KU 15064	17 September 1455
	MS, Kamm. 1/64	1455
	MBS, Cgm 641	undated
	MBS, Cgm 688	undated

Crayfish B2, the companion mark, is found in twelve dated sources, all but four of which are the same as those containing Crayfish B1 (see Table 3). It is therefore no surprise to discover a similar pattern here:

$B2^{1}$	1453, 1454
$B2^{2}$	1454
$B2^{3}$	1454, 1455
$B2^{4-5}$	1454, 1455

As Table 4 shows, the Crayfish twins are found together in as many as nine sources, seven of them dated, and from this some striking patterns emerge: $B1^{2}$ and $B2^{1}$ appear together only once; and $B1^{3}$ and $B2^{3}$ always appear in conjunction with one another, as do $B1^{4}$ and $B2^{4}$, with one exception.[60] The pattern of these sources may therefore be summarised as follows:

$B1^{2}$ + $B2^{1}$	early 1454
$B1^{3}$ + $B2^{3}$ (+ $B2^{2}$)	late 1454, 1455
$B1^{4}$ + $B2^{4}$	late 1454
$B1^{4}$ + $B2^{5}$	1455

[60] MS, Kammerrechnungen 1/64, in which $B1^{4}$ is accompanied by $B2^{5}$.

Table 3 *Crayfish B2*

State	Source	Date
$B2^{1}$	MBH, AR 270	1453
	MBH, AR 395	1453
	MBS, Cgm 778	early 1454
$B2^{2}$	MBH, AR 396	1454
$B2^{3}$	MBH, AR 396	1454
	MBS, Cgm 2153	completed 30 October 1454
	MBS, Cgm 667	completed 15 March 1455
	MBS, Cgm 781	1455
$B2^{4}$	MBS, Cgm 605	between 30 September and December 1454
	MBS, Cgm 641	undated
	MBS, Cgm 688	undated
$B2^{5}$	MBH, KU 9750	12 June 1454
	MBH, KU 29241	10 April 1455
	MS, Kamm. 1/64	1455

Table 4 *Crayfish B1 and B2*

State	Source	Date
$B1^{2} + B2^{1}$	MBS, Cgm 778	early 1454
$B1^{3} + B2^{3}$ $(+B2^{2})$	MBH, AR 396	1454
$B1^{3} + B2^{3}$	MBS, Cgm 2153	completed 30 October 1454
$B1^{3} + B2^{3}$	MBS, Cgm 781	1455
$B1^{3} + B2^{3}$	MBS, Cgm 667	completed 15 March 1455
$B1^{4} + B2^{4}$	MBS, Cgm 605	between 30 September and December 1454
$B1^{4} + B2^{4}$	MBS, Cgm 641	undated
$B1^{4} + B2^{4}$	MBS, Cgm 688	undated
$B1^{4} + B2^{5}$	MS, Kamm. 1/64	1455

Much else could be said about this fascinating pair of marks, but only at the risk of losing sight of the main object of the discussion, namely the dating of the little Trent 90 insert. What seems clear is that this must represent the earliest known surviving state of Crayfish B1, and that if more of this paper had been included in Trent 90 one would soon have encountered examples of its twin, most probably in its first known state. In all there are just five dated sources of $B1^1$ and $B2^1$: three from 1453, one from the early months of 1454 and one from an unspecified date in the same year. Whatever the fascination of the subsequent history of these marks, it is this evidence that is so critically important, since it indicates that the paper used by Wiser to revise part of a Credo he was copying into the main layer of his manuscript was already being manufactured by April 1453, and that it is more likely, on the basis of the available evidence, to have been acquired by him later that year or early the following one than at any subsequent stage. In this context it is worth recalling that the documented life of the Tower paper, within whose leaves the Crayfish half-leaf nestles, is 1453 to January 1455.

Wiser's next paper, BH4, has its own complexities. Interestingly its marks, like those of the Crayfish, are located in the same half of a sheet rather than in different halves, but whereas the Crayfish paper, surviving as it does in substantial quantities, was entirely produced from just one pair of moulds, the BH4 paper was produced from several, each pair bearing marks that while often closely related to one other are not quite the same. The two basic types, here designated 'B1' and 'B2', are illustrated in Figures 9 and 10. While less manifestly divergent than most pairs of marks, they can nevertheless be fairly readily distinguished by details in the disposition of their various parts and by their location between different pairs of chain-lines. What is initially confusing is the sheer degree of proximity between some of the marks belonging to the same type, conveying the impression that there are different states of a mark. Yet close examination of the details suggests that they are in fact different marks. It is impossible, in the absence of clearly visible sewing dots, to be completely certain about this, since it is conceivable that some of the marks are adaptations of existing marks, but this is the way in which they are interpreted here. The evidence is very intricate, and in several sources there are severe problems of decipherment, so the conclusions about these watermarks are necessarily slightly provisional. For present purposes the BH4 paper is considered as a single stock.

Four new sources have been found that use this paper, three of

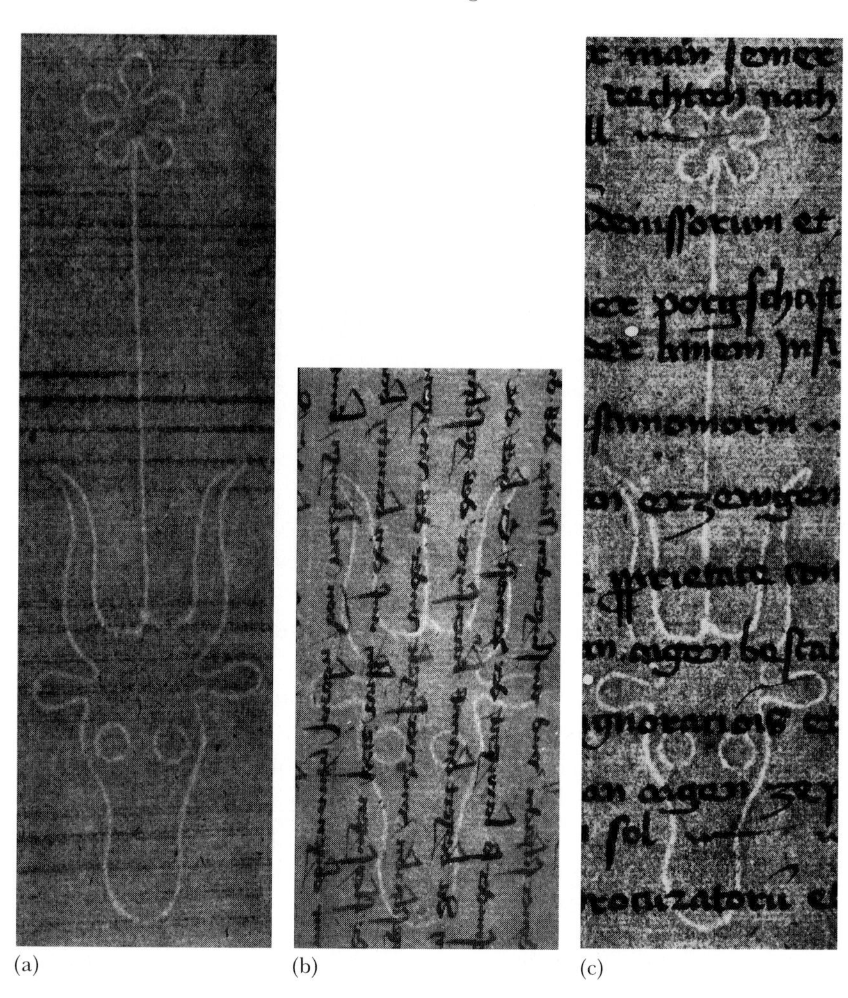

(a) (b) (c)

Figure 9 Bull's head 4-B1
(a) Trent 90, fol. 248^{r}: B1*a*; (b) ITL, P1080, verso: B1*a*;
(c) MBS, Cgm 2153, fol. II^{r}: B1*b*

them manuscripts from 1454 (two from the later part of the year), the fourth a document dated April 1455. One of the manuscripts (MBS, Cgm 775) uses just two leaves of BH4, while the other two (MBS, Cgm 605 and Cgm 2153) employ a substantial quantity of the paper, within which two or three versions of each twin may be found, here designated 'B1*a*', 'B1*b*', etc. The Trent 90 marks, 'B1*a*' and 'B2*a*', are in fact rarely found in these sources, and never

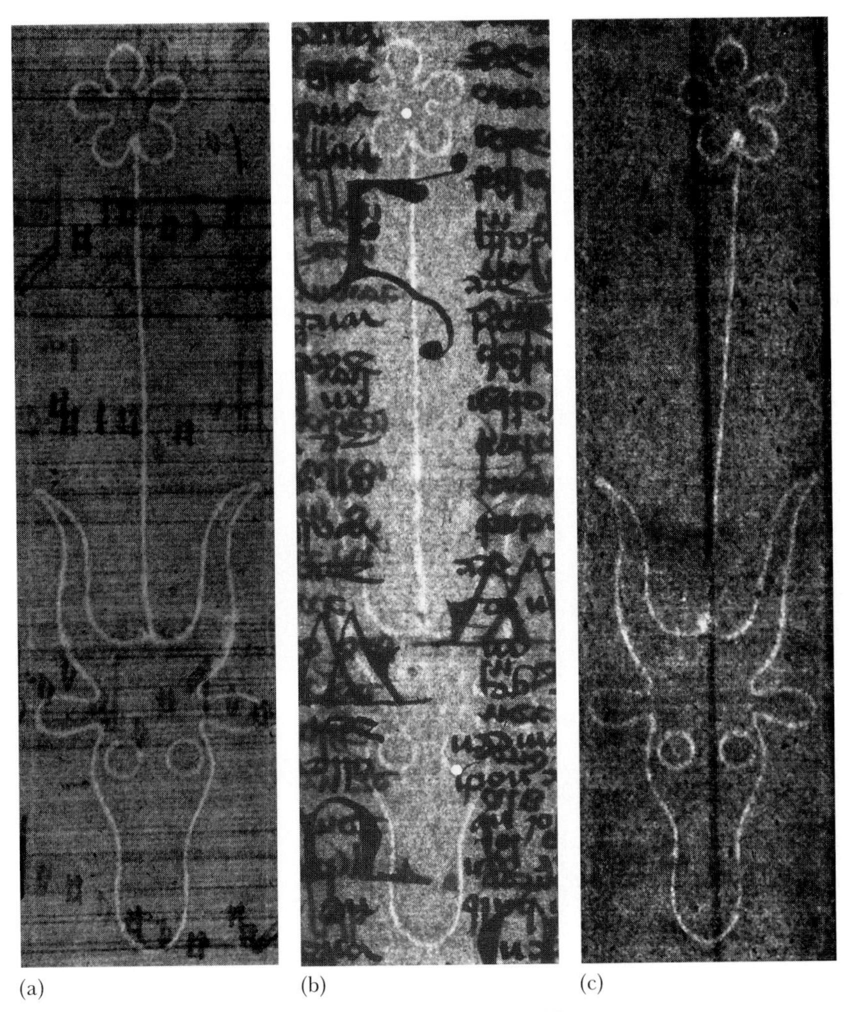

(a) (b) (c)

Figure 10 Bull's head 4-B2
(a) Trent 90, fol. 259r: B2*a*; (b) MBS, Cgm 2153, p. 24: B2*a*;
(c) MBS, Cgm 605, fol. 210^{v}: B2*b*

together, always occuring alongside other variants of this type. If the present interpretation of the BH4 paper is correct, then it appears that it must have been produced from two or three pairs of moulds that were in simultaneous use at the same mill.

The three remaining Trent 90 papers, BH5, BH6 and Crescents, are more easily dealt with. BH5 (Figure 11) belongs to a very common type that embraces many examples so closely related to one

Figure 11 Bull's head 5

(a) Trent 90, fol. 352v: A; (b) MBH, AR 313, fol. 1r: A; (c) Trent 90, fol. 339r: B; (d) MBH, AR 313, fol. 9r: B

another that establishing identity can prove difficult. Nevertheless five, possibly six, dated sources have come to light whose marks correspond with the Trent 90 pair, their dates ranging from 1454 to 1456 (a considerably smaller span than that suggested by Saunders).[61] Examination of Piccard's tracings shows that there are convincing matches from the same period.[62]

Identity is more easily established in the case of BH6 (Figure 12), since all of the known examples of this paper were produced from one pair of moulds only. Five firmly dated sources have been found, and, as with the BH5 paper, they range from 1454 to 1456. In addition, there are contemporary copies of three letters, one written in April and two in June 1456; both of the latter show BH6-B in a later state than elsewhere. Saunders offers a broader range of dates (1454–8), but the post-1456 examples of Piccard's on which she bases this range are in fact only loose approximations of the Trent 90 twins, and not true equivalents.

The final paper, here referred to as 'the Crescents' on account of the fact that it is marked with a pair of crescent moons (Figure 13), appears to be unknown from published sources. Its discovery in three sources, two of them dated, is thus of particular interest. And the fact that both of the dated sources belong to the same five-month period (May–October 1456) may be significant, in that it suggests a possible *terminus* not only for the completion of Trent 90 but also for the commencement of its successor, Trent 88, which opens with the same paper.

Table 5 summarises the evidence drawn both from newly discovered sources and from sources already known to Piccard, including those containing near as well as precise watermark equivalents. From the evidence of the precise matches it can be seen that the eight papers used for Trent 90 have a combined time span of just four to five years (1452–6), as against the seven to eight proposed by Saunders (1452–9), with a prevailing range of just three or four years (1453–6). For Trent 93-1 the overall range is 1450–5, with a prevailing range of 1450–3, while for Trent 93-2 the overall range is 1452–5. It must be emphasised, however, that each range of dates represents the period during which the papers it embraces

[61] One of these sources, MBS Cgm 521, was completed on 2 February 1457, but it appears that the BH5 paper must have been inscribed the previous year (see Appendix 2).

[62] See pp. 259–60 above.

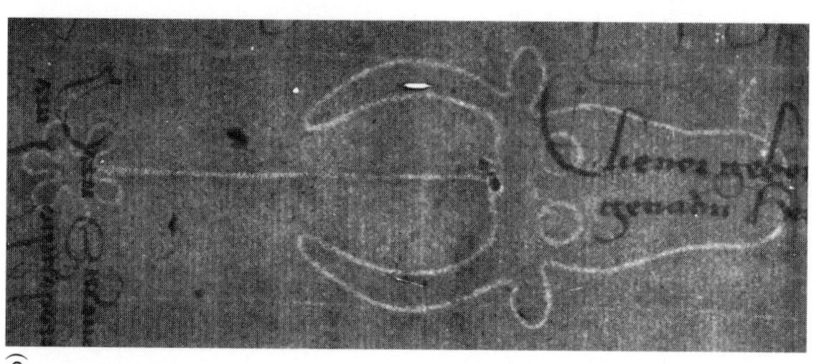

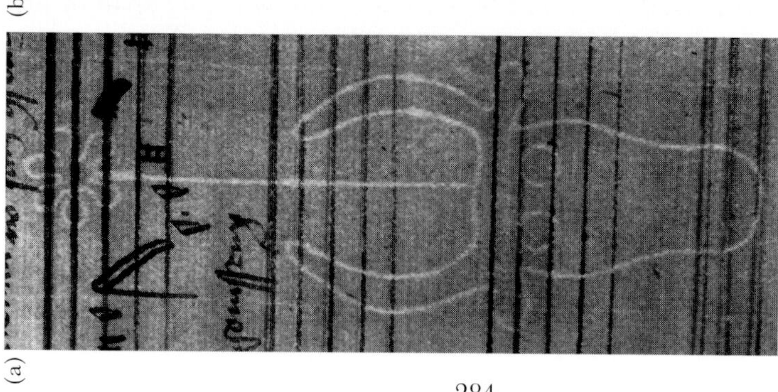

(a)

Figure 12 Bull's head 6
(a) Trent 90, fol. 386v: A; (b) ITL, U. I 5985/4, recto: A;
(c) Trent 90, fol. 384v: B1; (d) ITL, U. I 5984/2, verso: B1

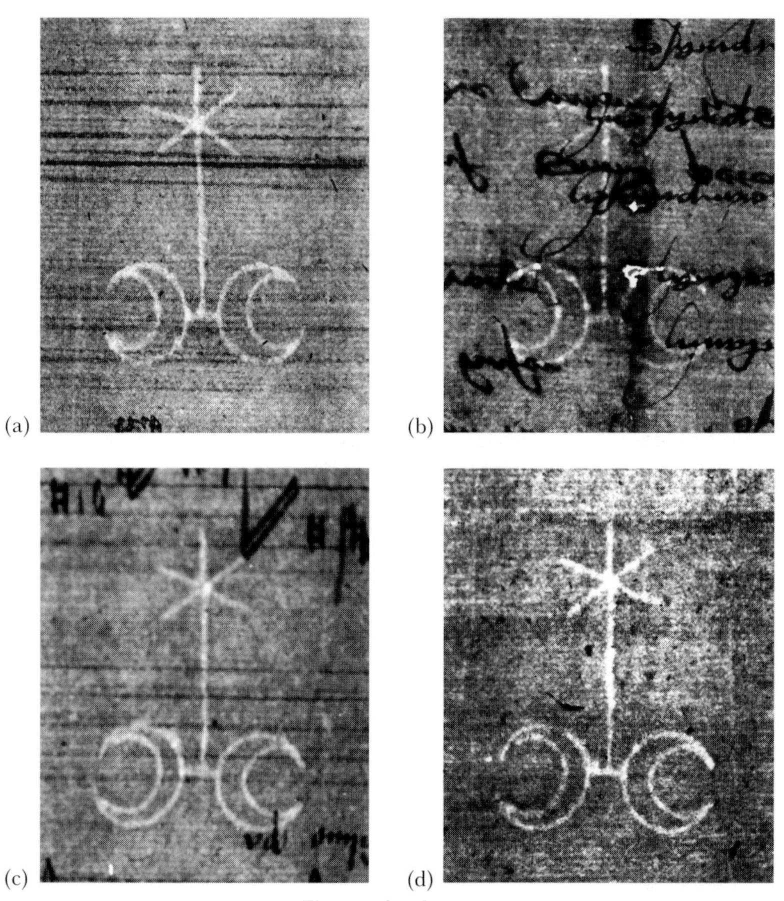

Figure 13 Crescents
(a) Trent 90, fol. 411r: A; (b) TAS, APV, s.t., Capsa 53.xx, [fol. 1r]: A;
(c) Trent 90, fol. 436v: B; (d) TAS, APV, s.l., Capsa 22/6, fol. 192r: B

are known to have been in use, and cannot automatically be presumed to correspond to the period during which the manuscript in question, or section thereof, was being copied. For present purposes a distinction between the two needs to be made.

IV. THE PROVENANCE OF TRENT 90 AND TRENT 93

Thus far, little attention has been paid to the actual sources on which the conclusions about the dating of the Trent 90/93 papers are based, but it is now time for this aspect to be addressed. As

Table 5 *Dates of Trent 93 and Trent 90 papers*

Dates in parentheses refer to sources whose watermarks represent near rather than precise equivalents of the Trent marks.

Paper	New sources	Piccard
Tr 93-1		
Cross	1450–3	1451 (1450–1)
BH1	1450–1, 1454/?52	1452 (1450–2)
Cross-on-mounts	1450–3	1454–5 (1451–52/53)
Tr 93-2		
BH2	1452, 1454–5	1452–5 (1452)
BH3	1454	—
Tr 90		
BH3	1454	—
BH2	1452, 1454–5	1452–5 (1452)
Tower	1453–4	1455
Crayfish	1453–5	1455 (1455)
BH4	1454–5	1454 (1455)
BH5	1454, 1455?, 1456	1454 (1455, 1459)
BH6	1454–6	1454–6
Crescents	1456	—

can be seen from Appendix 2, the vast majority of these sources are located in archives and libraries in Munich and Innsbruck, while the remainder are to be found in the Archivio di Stato in Trent. The latter in fact represent the tail end of a comprehensive search of the dated paper documents of the period 1450–80 found both in this archive and in the much smaller Archivio Capitolare, which was undertaken with the aim of establishing whether any of the papers used by Wiser and his colleagues for Trent 88–91, the four codices believed to have been compiled in the city of Trent, happened also to survive in contemporary Tridentine documents. Such information, it was realised, had the potential to assist with questions not only of dating and chronology but of provenance as well.

The search proved most fruitful in the case of the last of the codices to be compiled, Trent 91, where the discovery of a substantial body of new evidence (more than forty documents) led to a redating of the source, a rethinking of its chronology and a confirmation of its Tridentine provenance.[63] For the 'middle codices',

[63] P. Wright, 'Paper Evidence and the Dating of Trent 91', *Music & Letters*, 76 (1995), pp. 487–508.

Trent 88 and Trent 89, the evidence turned out to be far less copious (just nine sources came to light), yet sufficiently strong to confirm or refine earlier datings as well as reaffirm Trent's status as the manuscripts' likely place of origin.[64] For Trent 90, however, the evidence proved to be meagre by comparison: a mere four archival sources, three using Crescents paper, the fourth a sheet of BH5 (the antepenultimate paper in the manuscript). The investigation also brought to light two specimens of paper used in Trent 93-1.

It was the sharp contrast between, on the one hand, the survival of archival specimens of most of the papers used for Trent 88–91 and the later stages of Trent 90 and, on the other hand, the complete lack of comparable examples of any of the papers used for the earlier stages of Trent 90 that first raised doubts about the manuscript's presumed place of origin. Could it have been that the first of Wiser's music books, a source that ever since the debates of the early part of the last century had been accepted – more or less unquestioningly – as originating in Trent, was in fact only completed there, having been begun elsewhere, perhaps in or near its compiler's home city of Munich? And what of Trent 90's chief exemplar? If Trent 90 was begun somewhere other than Trent, would it not follow, given the nature of the relationship between the two manuscripts, that Trent 93, too, is unlikely to be of Tridentine origin? The possibility that paper evidence might lead to a better understanding of these intriguing questions seemed, at the very least, to be worth exploring.

The first step was to try and establish whether any of the papers used for Trent 90 or 93 were current in Bavaria, and in particular the southern part of the state (the regions surrounding Munich),[65] during the 1450s, the period when these sources must have been in the process of being copied. For this purpose the published volumes of the new and exemplary catalogues of manuscripts of the Bayerische Staatsbibliothek, in which all of the main types of watermark contained in each manuscript are listed by reference to the standard authorities (chiefly Piccard), provided

[64] Wright, 'Johannes Wiser's Paper' (above, n. 31).

[65] For present purposes it will be convenient to use 'Bavaria' to refer to the modern state of Bavaria, including Schwabia. Most of the places referred to here as being in Bavaria in fact formed part of this region as it was constituted in the fifteenth century.

an invaluable starting point.[66] All entries for dated manuscripts from the 1450s, and for good measure those from the late 1440s, were checked, as were all entries for fifteenth-century manuscripts of approximate date only. On the basis of this information a list was drawn up of all items of potential interest, which were then inspected at first hand. From this it became apparent that a number of the short-listed manuscripts contained watermarks that were no more than broadly similar in type to the Trent marks, and that these sources could therefore be eliminated from further consideration. Most of the manuscripts, however, contained marks that either matched the Trent marks exactly or else were so close to them, and distributed among them in such a fashion, as to indicate that the moulds from which they were produced must have been in use at the same time as the moulds from which their close relations were produced.

No fewer than eighteen of the Staatsbibliothek manuscripts, eleven of them dated, were found to use the same paper as Trent 90 and/or Trent 93. That all eighteen should be of Bavarian provenance may seem unsurprising in the light of the natural emphasis of the collection, yet it is a fact not without significance, since the Staatsbibliothek contains large numbers of manuscripts of non-Bavarian origin. Of the eighteen, the vast majority are known to have originated in the southernmost parts of the state, the present-day regions of Schwabia and Lower and Upper Bavaria. A number of the manuscripts are known or believed to be from Munich itself, whilst others emanate from cities and towns such as Augsburg, Polling, Schäftlarn and Tegernsee; several once belonged to famous monastery libraries. Of the eleven papers under consideration, seven are to be found within the leaves of these manuscripts, with the Tower, Crayfish, BH4 and BH5 papers especially well represented.

[66] The manuscripts of the Staatsbibliothek are principally divided into two classes, Latin and German, with a separate, multi-volume catalogue for each class. Two new catalogues are in progress, with the German series currently at a more advanced stage; both include watermark details. All the manuscripts found to have watermark correspondences with Trent 90/93 are German. See K. Schneider *et al.*, *Die deutschen Handschriften der Bayerischen Staatsbibliothek München* (Catalogus codicum manu scriptorum Bibliothecae Monacensis, 5; Wiesbaden, 1970–).

How widely, then, were these papers used in Bavaria? And what of those for which no equivalents had so far emerged? It was in response to these questions that the scope of the enquiry was broadened to include two of Munich's archives: the Bayerisches Hauptstaatsarchiv, principal archive of the region, and the Stadtarchiv, a small archive dedicated to the city itself.[67] Unfortunately the sheer quantity of material of potential interest in both archives – particularly the former – and the manner of its organisation meant that for practical reasons the searches conducted there had to be very selective.

The search of the Stadtarchiv was confined simply to the city account books, an extensive series of folio-size volumes dating back to the early fourteenth century.[68] Normally a single paper is used throughout a volume, and this was certainly the pattern found among the eight volumes surveyed, those dating from 1450 to 1457. Three of these were found to employ the same paper as Trent 90/93: the 1451 accounts book uses Cross paper, the 1455 book Crayfish paper, while the 1454 book has a sheet of the latter enclosed within the leaves of a different paper.[69]

In the Hauptstaatsarchiv a broader range of materials was surveyed. Most of the fifteenth-century materials are housed in the first of the archive's five main sections ('Ältere Bestände'), which is itself divided into many subsections, principally by region. Time constraints meant that any search had to be confined to materials relating to the region known as Kurbayern – essentially the Wittelsbach territories that comprise most of modern-day Bavaria. Three categories of material were examined: individual documents or 'Urkunden' (Kurbaiern: Urkunden), groups of documents, or 'Akten' (Äußeres Archiv), and account books (Ämterrechnungen).

This stage of the enquiry brought to light a further eighteen dated sources of Trent 90/93 paper – four account books and four-

[67] For a detailed overview of the Hauptstaatsarchiv, see *Die Staats- und Landesarchive in der Arbeitsgemeinschaft Alpenländer (Arge Alp): Archivführer und Inventar der grenzüberschreitenden Überlieferung* (Munich, 1995), pp. 18–62. A brief introduction to the Stadtarchiv may be found in *Archive in München*, ed. Stadtarchiv München (Munich, 1996), pp. 13–15.

[68] See F. v. Hössle, 'Wasserzeichen alter Papiere des Münchener Stadtarchivs', *Der Papier-Fabrikant*, 9 (1911), pp. 69–76. Hössle devotes most of his attention to fourteenth-century watermarks, dealing much more sketchily with those from the fifteenth century.

[69] It was only after I had inspected these volumes that I visited the Piccard watermark archive and became aware that Piccard's unpublished records included the watermarks contained in them.

teen documents[70] – which together with the three account books of the Stadtarchiv took the total number of archival sources to twenty-one. All but one of these items are of demonstrably Bavarian origin;[71] several are known or believed to come from Munich itself, while others emanate from towns such as Ingolstadt, Landshut and Starnberg that are located within roughly a sixty-mile radius of the city; a few come from further afield. These sources furnish us with additional specimens of Trent 90/93 papers already found to have been used in manuscripts of Bavarian origin, and with examples of papers that make no appearance in these manuscripts. Taking archival and library findings together, it transpires that during the period 1450–6 all but one of the eleven Trent 90/93 papers (the Crescents) were in use to some extent in southern Bavaria.

But just how widely were these papers being used elsewhere? Is the fact that relatively few of them survive in the Trent archives merely an accident of history, or is it an indication that most were never employed in the region? What has to be borne in mind here is that a far greater quantity of fifteenth-century material survives from Bavaria than from the Trentino, where only a few manuscripts and a relatively small number of paper documents from the 1450s can be shown to have originated. The libraries and archives of Trent and the surrounding region simply do not afford comparable opportunities – at least for the 1450s – for solid conclusions about paper to be drawn,[72] and as a result there is the

[70] The following gives some idea of the sheer quantity of material that had to be surveyed in order to yield these findings: all of the account books ('Ämterrechnungen') for the dukedom of Bavaria for the period 1450–7 (a total of thirty-three); all individual documents ('Kurbaiern, Urkunden') for the years 1452–5 (more than 300, the majority of which turned out to be written on parchment); and fifty-eight volumes of acts (Äußeres Archiv). While access to the account books was straightforward, dealing with the Urkunden was problematic owing to the fact that the card catalogue of this section of the archive normally gives no indication of the writing material used. This meant that establishing which documents are written on paper proved exceptionally laborious. With the Akten, there was a similar problem of locating the relevant materials. There are more than 4,000 volumes of acts in all, which are subdivided into forty groups (or 'Klassen') organised principally by place. Most of these volumes encompass a wide time span, and it is often unclear from the catalogue whether a particular volume includes the period under scrutiny. It thus became quickly apparent that a selective approach would be necessary, and so attention was focused on those volumes which appeared to emphasise the 1450s.

[71] MBH, KU 35960 appears to be from Upper Austria.

[72] Just three non-musical manuscripts from the period 1450–60 can be shown to have originated in the city of Trent: see *I manoscritti datati della Provincia di Trento*, ed. M. A. C.

risk of the evidence, or lack thereof, being over-interpreted. Having said that, it should be stressed that, whereas examples of just four of the eleven papers used in Trent 90 and 93 have come to light in the Trent archives, specimens of all but two of the nine papers used in Trent 88 and 89 have surfaced there, even though the number of dated documents for the period in which these manuscripts were compiled is not significantly greater than it is for the period in which Trent 90 and 93 were compiled.

It was with considerations such as these in mind that a decision was taken to broaden the enquiry to include the northern part of the Tyrol, the region that lies to the south of Bavaria. The principal archive for the region is the Tiroler Landesarchiv in the capital city of Innsbruck, which, like its Bavarian counterpart, is a potentially rich mine of information on fifteenth-century papers, not just for the north but also for the south Tyrol. The two main series of documents, Urkundenreihen I and II, were systematically examined for the years in question, as were several other potentially interesting sections of the archive – a search that resulted in the discovery of a further twenty-two sources of Trent 90/93 paper.[73] In addition, a study of unpublished watermark data relating to the dated manuscripts of the Universitätsbibliothek at Innsbruck was undertaken (the data forms part of the library's holdings), though this brought to light only one relevant source. Most of the new watermark equivalents are from sources copied in or near Innsbruck; a few originated elsewhere in the north Tyrol, and a handful in the more northerly parts of the south Tyrol. The result was the discovery of a further twenty-three

Mazzoli *et al.* (Manoscritti Datati d'Italia, 1; Florence, 1996), nos. 17, 20 and 52. For the same period (1450–9), just 157 dated documents, for example, are listed as belonging to the Sezione Latina, the principal section of the Archivio Principesco-Vescovile (see *Archivio di Stato di Trento: Archivio del Principato Vescovile; inventario* (Pubblicazioni degli Archivi di Stato, 4; Rome, 1951), pp. 174–5), although twenty-three of these are missing. For a period of less than half this time (1452–5), more than twice the number of documents are to be found in the section of the Bayerische Hauptstaatsarchiv headed 'Kurbayern: Urkunden' (see n. 70 above), although in fact most of these are on parchment.

[73] An overview of the archive can be found in *Die Staats- und Landesarchive der Arbeitsgemeinschaft Alpenländer*, pp. 160–94. Urkundenreihen I and II are listed as sections I.1.a and I.1.b. The other sections of the archive that were examined are as follows: Parteibriefe (I.1.c), Urbare (XXII.1), Inventare (XXII.2), Handschriften (XXIV.1), Rechnungsbücher (XXIV.1.2).

dated sources of papers used in the musical manuscripts, containing examples of all but two of these papers.[74]

What this part of the investigation shows is that all but two of the Trent 90/93 papers were in use in the north and south Tyrol, although in most cases only one or two examples survive. These findings are in no sense incompatible with the hypothesis that it was in Bavaria that most of the Trent 90/93 papers were primarily used, but they do slightly weaken it, and it is quite possible that further exploration of the archives of the region, in particular those located in towns lying between Innsbruck and Trent, such as Merano, Bolzano and Bressanone, could yield findings that would weaken it further. Be that as it may, the fact remains that of the sixty-seven sources listed in Appendix 2, no more than four can be shown to have originated in Trent itself or in the vicinity of the city.

So far in this discussion of provenance, consideration has only been given to 'newly discovered' sources – that is, sources that have been found, as part of the present investigation, to use the same paper as the musical codices. But there are also Piccard's own findings to be considered, the full details of which are unpublished. Appendix 3 includes a note of the provenance of each archival equivalent or near-equivalent cited, and while it is true that these include a number of documents from, for example, northern Germany and the Baltic coast, the fact is that more than half of these sources are from Bavaria and the Tyrol. This is a not insignificant finding, since Piccard spread his net very wide, with archival searches that extended throughout Germany as well as to many other parts of Europe, including north Italian cities such as Bologna, Brescia, Treviso, Turin and Udine. The fact that such wide-ranging enquiries should have produced such a high proportion of examples of the Trent 90/93 papers from Bavaria and the Tyrol seems to reinforce the impression that their usage in these regions was particularly extensive.[75]

[74] It needs to be borne in mind that, as in Munich, the quantity of relevant materials available in Innsbruck was far greater than in Trent: over 400 dated documents or groups of documents in the Tiroler Landesarchiv were surveyed for the period 1450–9 – roughly twice the number available for the same period in Trent.

[75] The question of where the various Trent 90/93 papers originated, as distinct from where they were used, is a difficult one. We know too little about the history of paper-making of this period to be able to offer an answer, yet there is evidence that by the middle of

Table 6 summarises the findings on the provenances of the various sources under consideration. These findings demonstrate a broad overall pattern of 'diminishing returns' as one travels south, although they need, as we have seen, to be interpreted with particular care. The evidence for Trent 93 is too ambiguous to allow any meaningful conclusions to be drawn, but in the case of Trent 90 it is altogether more clear-cut. Two important points in Table 6 need emphasising. The first concerns 'Trent 90*C*' – that part of Trent 90 (most of fols. 1–282) which is a copy of Trent 93: each of the five papers used for this copy (these are emboldened in the table) was in circulation in Bavaria, yet so far none has turned up in a document that originated in the Trentino.[76] The

Table 6 *Sources by region*

Numbers not in parentheses refer to new-found sources of the Trent 90/93 papers; numbers in parentheses refer to sources from the Piccard archive, with those in italics indicating sources whose watermarks represent near rather than precise equivalents of the Trent marks; the papers of Trent 90*C* (and Trent 93-2) are shown in bold type.

Paper	Bavaria	N. Tyrol	S. Tyrol	Trentino	Other
Cross (Tr 93-1)	5 (+*1*)	1	1	0	(*2*)
BH1 (Tr 93-1)	1	7 (+*2*)	0	0	(1+*2*)
Cross-on-mounts (Tr 93-1)	4 (+1+*1*)	1	1–2	0–1	(1+*3*)
BH2 (Tr 93-2, Tr 90)	**2 (+*1*)**	**1 (+2)**	**0 (+1)**	**0**	**(7)**
BH3 (Tr 93-2, Tr 90)	**1**	**1**	**0**	**0**	**0**
Tower (Tr 90)	**8**	**0**	**0 (+1)**	**0**	**1**
Crayfish (Tr 90)	**17 (+1+*1*)**	**2**	**1**	**0**	**1**
BH4 (Tr 90)	**3 (+ *1*)**	**0**	**1 (+1)**	**0**	**(*1*)**
BH5 (Tr 90)	7 (+1+*2*)	1	0	1	(*1*)
BH6 (Tr 90)	1	5	1–3	0–2	0
Crescents (Tr 90)	0	0	0	3	0
TOTAL	49 (+2+*7*)	19 (+2+*2*)	5–8 (+3)	4–7	(10+*9*)

the century paper was being manufactured in several parts of southern Germany. The paper specialist Friedrich von Hössle charted some of these developments by region in a series of studies undertaken in the early part of the last century: for a listing of some of his writings, see P. Pulsiano, 'A Checklist of Books and Articles Containing Reproductions of Watermarks', in S. Spector (ed.), *Essays in Paper Analysis* (London, 1987), pp. 115–53, at pp. 129–30.

[76] Five specimens of three of the papers are found, however, in documents from the south Tyrol: two examples of BH4 (one from Bressanone, the other from the same region), and one example each of the BH2, Tower and Crayfish papers (from Bressanone, Sterzing and Bolzano respectively).

second point is that conversely, no trace of the last paper in the manuscript, the Crescents, has yet surfaced in any document originating outside the Trentino, and that the penultimate paper, BH6, is chiefly represented in Tyrolean/?Trentino sources; the fact that Wiser must have acquired these papers around the time of his first recorded presence in Trent may therefore be significant.

There is, however, always the risk of over-interpreting evidence of this kind, and of forgetting that patterns of survival cannot necessarily be trusted to reflect fairly the original patterns of circulation and usage. If the balance of paper evidence seems to favour the idea that Trent 90 was begun in south Bavaria, the possibility that the manuscript originated in Trent cannot, on the basis of this evidence, be ruled out.[77]

V. THE COPYING OF THE MANUSCRIPTS; THE SCRIBES

Let us briefly take stock of the evidence gathered so far. A period of usage has been established for each of the Trent 90/93 papers that provides us with an overall range of dates running from 1450 to 1456, although on the basis of this information alone we cannot be sure of the exact years when the copying took place, or indeed whether all of it was actually carried out within this time frame. We know that at some point during this period, and certainly prior to 30 July 1455, Johannes Wiser must have left Munich and taken up the post of succentor at Trent Cathedral. And we have established as a reasonably strong possibility the idea that Trent 90 may have been begun in southern Bavaria and completed in Trent. Each of these three main strands of evidence carries with it various uncertainties, yet together they provide a basis for a new theory of the origins of Wiser's collection. It is now time to develop this theory further by exploring several aspects of the evidence more fully and considering them in conjunction with other kinds of evidence.

Surveying the pattern of dates for Trent 90 (Table 7), it can be seen that almost all of the dated or datable sources of its paper – a total of nearly seventy – belong to the years 1453–6. The only

[77] On reflection, my earlier conclusion that 'if one thing now seems reasonably certain, it is that [Trent 90's place of origin] cannot have been Trent' (Wright, 'Johannes Wiser's Paper', p. 44) was insufficiently supported by the evidence on which it was based.

Table 7 *Distribution of Trent 90 watermarks by year*

Numbers not in parentheses refer to new-found sources, those in parentheses to sources from the Piccard archive.

Watermark	1452	1453	1454	1455	1456	
BH3	0	0	1	0	0	Trent 90*C* papers
BH2	1 (3/4)	0 (2)	1 (4)	1 (2)	0	Trent 90*C* papers
Tower	0	2	6	0 (1)	0	Trent 90*C* papers
Crayfish	0	4	7	6 (1)	0	Trent 90*C* papers
BH4	0	0	3 (1)	1	0	Trent 90*C* papers
BH5	0	0	3/4 (1)	0/1	2	
BH6	0	0	1	2 (1)	3–5	
Crescents	0	0	0	0	2	
TOTAL	1 (3/4)	6 (2)	22/23 (6)	10/11 (5)	7–9	

exceptions are five sources of BH2 paper from 1452, and the date of one of these is suspect;[78] all the other examples of this paper date from later. Such is the weight of the evidence that it seems unlikely that the manuscript was begun any earlier than 1453, though it remains possible that it was begun as late as 1454, or even the early part of the following year.

Determining when the manuscript was completed, and the dates by which the different stages of the compilation had been accomplished, is, of course, much harder, owing to uncertainties of the kind that inevitably surround sources such as this one. We know little, for instance, about the speed at which scribes worked, the frequency and extent of lulls in the copying process, or the delays that occurred between the acquisition of a supply of paper and its actual usage. But in the case of Trent 90 there is evidence that may help shed light on some of these issues.

Had Wiser worked on his manuscript more or less continuously, it would probably have been physically possible for him to copy it in its entirety within as little as three months. There is certainly nothing in the paper evidence that conflicts with such a possibility: by the late months of 1454 all but the last of the papers he used were in circulation and could therefore theoretically have been purchased in one lot; and if further proof of the close con-

[78] This is the example of Piccard's given as 'StAJ Lehenbücher, liber fragm II 256' (Appendix 3), a *post facto* compilation. See n. 48 above.

temporaneousness of these papers were needed, one could point to the way in which two or even three of them occur, often contiguously, in the same source (Table 8). Yet while it is conceivable that parts of Trent 90 were copied at high speed, it seems unlikely that the entire manuscript was executed within a short space of time. The sheer degree of evolution in Wiser's script, from its hesitant beginnings to the much better formed, bolder and more confident hand of the later stages of the manuscript's compilation, suggests a process that would have required more than a couple of months in which to unfold.[79]

Trent 90 was probably not completed before 1456, the latest firm date of any of its papers, but the indications are that Trent 90*C*, the copy of the main layer of Trent 93, was finished well before then. Most specimens of the papers used for Trent 90*C* – BH3, BH2, Tower, Crayfish and BH4 – date from 1454, while a smaller number belong to the previous and the following years. According to Table 7, the numbers of watermark equivalents of these five papers for the years 1453, 1454 and 1455 (inclusive of Piccard examples) are eight, twenty-three and twelve respectively. But it needs to be remembered that the majority of examples of the Crayfish marks occur in later states than that found in Trent

Table 8 *Manuscripts using more than one Trent 90 paper*

The numbers in parentheses indicate the order of first appearance of each paper within a manuscript; numerically successive papers within a source are contiguous; Cgm = MBS, Cgm.

Trent 90 n.d.	Cgm 351 n.d.	Cgm 605 1454	Cgm 744 n.d.	Cgm 2153 1454	IU, Cod. 45 1455
BH3					
BH2					BH2 (1)
Tower	Tower (1)				
Crayfish	Crayfish (3)	Crayfish (2)		Crayfish (2)	
BH4		BH4 (1)		BH4 (1)	
BH5	BH5 (2)		BH5 (1)		
BH6			BH6 (2)		BH6 (2)
Crescents					

[79] R. Gerber, 'An Assessment of Johannes Wiser's Scribal Activities in the Trent Codices', *Musica Disciplina*, 46 (1991), pp. 1–18, at pp. 3–4, includes a brief but useful survey of Wiser's changing clef-forms. A full and systematic study of the development of his script is a task still waiting to be undertaken.

90. Once this is taken into account, the number of sources with corresponding marks for the year 1455 falls to just five, spanning the months from January to mid-June.[80] The latest of these sources contains BH2 paper, but, significantly, in distinctly later states than those found in Trent 90*C*. And two other sources, also of BH2 paper, are documents from the Baltic Coast that were apparently copied several hundred miles away from the region where their paper is likely to have originated or at least was mainly used. Thus only two sources from 1455 that were copied in the regions under consideration, one from January and the other from April, can be shown to contain paper in the same state in which it is found in Trent 90*C*. There is therefore little evidence from the findings on paper to suggest that work on the main layer was taking place as late as the early months of 1455, and none at all to support the idea that Wiser was engaged in copying this part of his manuscript in or beyond July, the month in which he is cited as succentor.

Taking paper evidence together with both palaeographical evidence and what little we know of Wiser's circumstances at the time, we may reasonably conclude that Trent 90 was begun no earlier than 1453 and was completed by 1456 or very shortly thereafter; that the main layer was executed some time during the period between 1453 and the early months of 1455; and, if the patterns of paper distribution are any guide, that it was in the year 1454 that the bulk of the copying of this layer – perhaps even all of it – is most likely to have fallen (see Table 9).

These conclusions are, of course, at odds with Strohm's view that Wiser did not embark on his collection until after he had been installed as succentor, an appointment he appears to believe occurred, along with that of Johannes Prenner as schoolmaster, in July 1455. According to Strohm, Wiser either acquired his main layer papers in Trent or else brought them there from his previous place of employment. The first proposition requires us to believe that Wiser acquired these papers in a place where there is little or no trace of their ever having been used, and – if we suppose, with Strohm, that this did not occur before July 1455 –

[80] They are: IU, Cod. 45 (Stams, near Innsbruck, completed 14 June 1455; BH2), ITL, P1080 (Bressanone region, 9 April 1455; BH4), StAK O.B.A.: Elblag, Poland (March 1455; BH2), StAK O.B.A.: Gdańsk (May 1455; BH2), StAK O.B.A. Sterzing (January 1455; Tower). Details of the first two examples are given in Appendix 2, details of the last three in Appendix 3.

Table 9 *Summary of proposed Trent 90 copying dates*

Section of MS / Folios	Papers	Proposed date of copying
Trent 90*C* (= 1–282 minus additions)	BH2, BH3, Tower, Crayfish, BH4	(?1453→) 1454 (?→1455) completed late 1454 / early 1455
'Appendix' (= 283–465)	BH4, BH5, Crescents	(?1454→) 1455–6
92ᵛ–93ʳ, 94ᵛ–96ʳ (later additions by Wiser) *		(?1454→) 1455 (?→1456)
1ʳ, 20ʳ, 58ʳ, 72ʳ (last additions by Wiser) *		1456 or later

* These additions are dated partly on the basis of their position within the chronology of Wiser's script.

that he acquired them after their documented life was over. The second proposition – that Wiser brought his supplies with him – requires us to suppose that he was hoarding paper in the general expectation of needing it, but with no specific purpose in mind.[81]

Yet Wiser, as we know, had a very definite purpose in mind, namely the replication of the main layer of Trent 93. What stage the manuscript had reached by the time he started copying from it is a difficult question, though it seems clear that it must still have been in the process of being compiled. After the two main scribes, A and B, copied the mass repertory that constitutes the main layer (most of Trent 93-1), a number of secondary scribes entered additional works, related and unrelated, in spare spaces of the manuscript. Nearly all of these pieces are absent from Trent 90*C*. While Wiser could have deliberately ignored them on the grounds that their inclusion would have undermined the integrity of the plan he was endeavouring to replicate, the fact that a number are repertorially integrated with their surrounding contents makes it altogether more likely that they had simply not yet been entered. More significant, however, is his non-inclusion of works that form part of the main layer of Trent 93, in particular

[81] This is a perfectly reasonable supposition. A scribe about to enter new employment might well have felt inclined to stock up with paper in advance. In this particular instance, however, there are circumstances that seem to militate against this possibility.

the sixteen sequences that occupy most of gatherings XVIII–XX (fols. 201–35).[82]

These gatherings form an interpolation to Trent 93, with the sequences having been inserted in their correct liturgical position between the Gloria and Credo settings after these works had been copied.[83] Their status as a late addition is indicated by their signatures, which duplicate those of the gatherings that now appear as XXI–XXIII; the present gatherings XXI–XXIII were the original XVIII–XX.[84] It may be, as Margaret Bent proposes, that the sequence gatherings represent 'a later continuation of the collaboration between scribes A and B that had been begun in the Mass Ordinaries';[85] if so, the fact that these gatherings have the same paper, layout, inks and patterns of scribal collaboration that are found throughout most of the remainder of the main layer suggests that any lull in this collaboration can have been only brief. As Bent notes, Wiser subsequently had access to these gatherings, since he copied one work (a Gloria) across the join of gatherings XVII–XVIII (fols. 199^{v}–201^{r}) and another (a textless fragment of a Credo) into gathering XX (fol. 234^{v}). What should also be mentioned is the fact that the script of these two added works is firmly contemporary with Wiser's script as it appears in Trent 90*C*. This is a crucial point, since it suggests that unless the sequences were incorporated into Trent 93 prior to Wiser having reached the corresponding point in his copy, but were deliberately suppressed by him,[86] these works are likely to have become

[82] The other works that Wiser did not copy are the two Kyrie settings on fols. 98^{v}–99^{r} and 119^{v}–120^{r}, and the incomplete Credo on fol. 254^{v}. Bent, 'Trent 93 and Trent 90', pp. 93–4, suggests that the first Kyrie may have been omitted inadvertently, but that the omission of the second Kyrie (an alternative version of which was entered by Wiser on Trent 90, fol. 125^{v}) and the Credo (which is self-evidently incomplete) was probably deliberate.

[83] Reinhard Strohm makes the interesting suggestion (private communication) that because the Mass Ordinary copies in Trent 93 were partly derived from exemplars in cyclic form, the Sanctus and Agnus sections would have been copied before the sequences were added.

[84] Bent, 'Trent 93 and Trent 90' (above, n. 10), p. 86.

[85] *Ibid.*

[86] It is difficult to imagine why Wiser should have omitted these works intentionally. Had he known at this stage that he was going to Trent, there would have been especially good reason for him to include them, since, according to Marco Gozzi (who has kindly shared with me his thoughts on this subject), there was a strong tradition in the Trent diocese at this time of including sequences in the Proper of the Mass (a tradition that practically disappears in contemporary Roman sources). Prof. Gozzi is of the view that the Trent 93 sequences would have been of particular interest to Wiser.

available to him *during* rather than *after* his copying of the main layer.[87]

The evidence relating to the sequence gatherings certainly suggests quite strongly that the main layer of Trent 93 was still in progress when Wiser began making his copy of it, which could mean either that gatherings were being assembled or that the copying was still being carried out. If this hypothesis is correct, then the year in which work on Trent 90 began – whether 1453, 1454 or even, at a stretch, early 1455 – must also have been a year in which work on Trent 93-1 was ongoing in some shape or form. By the same token, the place where Trent 90 was begun would also need to be considered as the place where this activity on Trent 93-1 was being conducted. The watermark evidence relating to Trent 93, as we have seen, allows alternative provenances to be postulated.

It is difficult to see why Wiser would have copied Trent 93 unless in the expectation that access to it would be limited. Such a situation has, however, proved hard to square with the fact that both copy and exemplar survive in the same place. According to Strohm, Wiser 'expected to leave his place of work (Trent) in order to pursue his career, and could not be sure that in a new position he would find all the music he wanted'. The possession of a large collection such as Trent 90, he argues, 'might in any case [have] increase[d] his chances of securing a position as schoolmaster in a cultural centre'.[88] The position he eventually secured was, of course, that of schoolmaster in Trent itself.

This thesis offers the best explanation to date for Wiser's duplication of the Trent 93 repertoire. Yet there is no reason why the motives Strohm ascribes to Wiser could not apply equally to his securing of the post of succentor, or why a scenario similar to the one he describes could not just as well have been enacted somewhere other than Trent. If indeed Trent 90 *was* begun in Munich, then its chief exemplar must have been present there too, if only for a limited period. This at once raises the possibility that Wiser

[87] Since the Gloria section of Trent 90 ends on the last full opening of one gathering (XIV: fols. 156–67) and the Credo section begins on the first full opening of the next gathering (XV: fols. 168–79), there would have been nothing to prevent Wiser from locating the sequences in their correct liturgical position, between the Glorias and the Credos, had they been available to him and had he wished to do so.

[88] Strohm, 'European Cathedral Music' (above, n. 12), p. 27.

not only expected to be, but actually was, parted from Trent 93, and this, in turn, raises the question of who, in such circumstances, could have been the agent of the manuscript's eventual transfer to Trent.

Strohm has already suggested that Johannes Prenner, whom Wiser served as succentor and soon after succeeded as schoolmaster, may have been responsible for Trent 93's transfer (from an unspecified location) and may even have had a hand in its compilation.[89] Nothing is known about Prenner prior to his installation as a cathedral chaplain, and pursuit of his early career is not helped by the fact that his name appears to have been a fairly common one in the fifteenth century.[90] The recent proposal by Rudolf Flotzinger that he is the 'Johannes Prenner de Prawnaw' (= Braunau, currently in Upper Austria but formerly part of Bavaria) who matriculated at the University of Vienna in 1447[91] has the merit of providing us with a candidate who was a student in a major musical centre at the time when the Trent 93 repertory was being collected, and who came from the same region (southern Bavaria) as Wiser.[92] The only difficulty with this proposal is that the schoolmaster Johannes Prenner is described in 1455 as being from Trent ('de Tridento').[93]

An alternative candidate is Petrus 'Schrot', or 'Sroch', the man who was to become Wiser's own succentor and eventually succeed him as schoolmaster (just as Wiser had succeeded Prenner).

[89] *Ibid.*, p. 26, and Strohm, 'Trienter Codices' (above, n. 12), col. 805.

[90] Of the various of bearers of this name that I have encountered in archival records, two are particularly worth mentioning. One is the man cited as a judge in Termeno ('richter zu Tramin'), a town near Bolzano in the Trent diocese, during the early 1450s (ITL, Urkundenreihe I, no. 5804 (21 August 1455), and TAS, APV, Sezione Tedesca, Capsa 27.p (1451–4)). The other is the man cited as a chaplain at the church of Stephen's in Vienna during the late 1440s and early 1450s (see A. Mayer *et al.*, *Quellen zur Geschichte der Stadt Wien*, 10 vols. (Vienna, 1895–1937), 2/ii (1900), p. 275, no. 3169; p. 288, no. 3230; p. 356, no. 3547). While any identification of the former (who was not an ecclesiastical figure) with the Trent schoolmaster can easily be discounted, the possibility that the latter and the chaplain of St Stephen's are one and the same person cannot yet be ruled out.

[91] R. Flotzinger, 'Auf der Suche nach Einheimischen in den Trienter Codices: Fakten und Hypothesen', paper given at the conference Manoscritti di Polifonia nel Quattrocento Europeo, Trent, October 2002. See *Die Matrikel der Universität Wien*, i: *1377–1450*, ed. F. Gall (Publikationen des Instituts für Österreichische Geschichtsforschung, ser. vi, 1/i; Graz and Cologne, 1956), p. 256, col. 2, no. 16.

[92] In this context it may be worth mentioning the existence of a document from the Anger Kloster in Munich, dated 24 April 1453 (MBH, München-Angerkloster Urk. 546), that records the presence of a witness by the name of 'Hanns Prennär'.

[93] See n. 27 above.

Although the only mention of him as succentor dates from 1460, his appointment probably took effect when Wiser became schoolmaster two or three years earlier.[94] He could well be the 'Petrus Schroff de Monaco' who matriculated at the University of Vienna in April 1451, just around the time when work on Trent 93 must have been beginning.[95] The ending 'f' is unknown in Italian; 'Sroch' and 'Schrot' could represent the attempts of the Italian scribes who recorded them to deal with an unfamiliar sound. Since the post of succentor tended to be in the schoolmaster's gift, it would have been natural for Wiser to turn to a respected and trusted former colleague when it came to making this appointment.

At this stage a crucial piece of palaeographical evidence needs to be considered. On fol. 261r of Trent 90, a mere twenty folios from the end of his copy of the main layer of Trent 93, Wiser, who hitherto had adhered so steadfastly to his task, suddenly and unexpectedly broke off work during a Sanctus setting. Having copied the first four of the work's five sections (fols. 260v–261r), he left the final section (fol. 261v) to an assistant, who then proceeded to complete Trent 90*C*. The possible significance of this event should not be underestimated. The task in which Wiser was engaged must have been one with which he wished to be personally identified; that he was keen to make his mark as a scribe is suggested by what appears to be an unwarranted attempt to append his name

[94] Schrot is cited as Wiser's succentor on 2 December 1460: 'Johannes Wisser artium gramatice professori et altariste altarii Sancte Dorathee et Sancti Nicholai in dicta ecclesie fundati et magistro Petro Sroch succentori predicti idem Johannem Wiser' (TAC, Instrumenta Capitularia X, fols. 65r–66r, at fol. 65r). A document of 8 June 1465 cites a certain Petrus as 'rector scolarium' and describes him as chaplain of the cathedral altar of S. Caterina, apparently incorrectly, since this chaplaincy was held by Prenner from 1455 until his death *c.*1483 (TAC, Instrumenta Capitularia XI, fols. 69v–70r, at fol. 69v; summarised in Santifaller, *Urkunden und Forschungen*, pp. 374–5, no. 499). That this 'Petrus' is indeed Schrot appears to be confirmed by a later document, of 26 August 1476, in which 'Petrus Schrot' is described as 'rector scolarum' (ITL, Urkundenreihe I, no. 5431; summarised in F. Schneller, 'Beiträge zur Geschichte des Bisthums Trient aus dem späteren Mittelalter', *Zeitschrift des Ferdinandeums für Tirol und Voralberg*, ser. iii, 39 (1895) [part 2], pp. 181–230, at p. 198, no. 825). This document is of additional interest on account of the fact that it cites all three members of the 'triumvirate' – Prenner, Schrot and Wiser – as witnesses.

[95] *Die Matrikel der Universität Wien*, ii: *1451–1518*, ed. W. Szaivert and F. Gall (Publikationen des Instituts für Österreichische Geschichtsforschung, ser. vi, 1/ii; Graz, Vienna and Cologne, 1967), p. 4, no. 236; Shroff matriculated on 14 April 1451 and is listed under 'Natio Renensium'. I have not yet had an opportunity to check the unpublished graduation records for his name.

to one of his contributions to Trent 93.[96] One can only guess at the possible reasons behind Wiser's sudden abandonment of a task to which he had so far dedicated himself with such single-mindedness, but it is precisely the kind of event likely to have been occasioned by some external change of circumstance.[97] It occurs towards the end of the first run of BH4 paper, which in turn follows the initial run of Tower paper, including, as it does, the inserted half-leaf of Crayfish paper (see Figure 14). Given the likelihood that Wiser had reached this point of the manuscript during the later part of 1454, or perhaps even the early months of the following year, it is difficult to resist the idea that it was the news of his appointment to the succentorship at Trent that prompted the interruption. But maybe this news was itself the catalyst for Trent 90*C*; perhaps Wiser found himself, for whatever reason, with no more than a few weeks in which to replicate the Trent 93 main layer, but not quite long enough to complete the task. Either way, this could explain the absence from Trent 90 of the sequences, which may have become available for copying too late to be included.

The person who did complete Trent 90*C*, whom we may designate 'scribe X', apparently had an especially close working relationship with Wiser. As well as being entrusted with this important task, he was the one scribe apart from Wiser who contributed to both manuscripts, and in the case of Trent 93-2 he actually used the same stocks of paper with which Wiser began Trent 90.[98] The fact that once he had completed Trent 90*C* scribe X made no fur-

[96] The work in question is the Kyrie on fol. 125v, which is followed by the inscription 'Scriptum notatum' (as in the *explicit* to Trent 90) and an indecipherable erasure where, presumably, Wiser's name once stood (see n. 82 above).

[97] One has only to think, for example, of the circumstances believed to have caused the abrupt and premature curtailment by the main scribe of the Old Hall Manuscript of his original compilation. This interruption was first diagnosed by Margaret Bent ('Initial Letters in the Old Hall Manuscript', *Music & Letters*, 47 (1966), pp. 225–38, esp. 234–8), and a convincing explanation for it subsequently offered by Roger Bowers ('Some Observations on the Life and Career of Lionel Power', *Proceedings of the Royal Musical Association*, 102 (1975–76), pp. 103–27, at pp. 109–10).

[98] Scribe X contributed two pieces to Trent 93-1, the Kyrie on fols. 107v–108r and the Gloria on fols. 210v–211r, and inscribed two of the three gatherings that make up Trent 93-2: XXXII (fols. 366–73; only fol. 366r is in a different hand) and XXXIII (fols. 374–82). Scribal analyses of Trent 93 and Trent 90 are given, respectively, in Wright, *The Related Parts*, pp. 304–5 (where scribe X is designated 'scribe C'), and id., 'Johannes Wiser's Paper', p. 35.

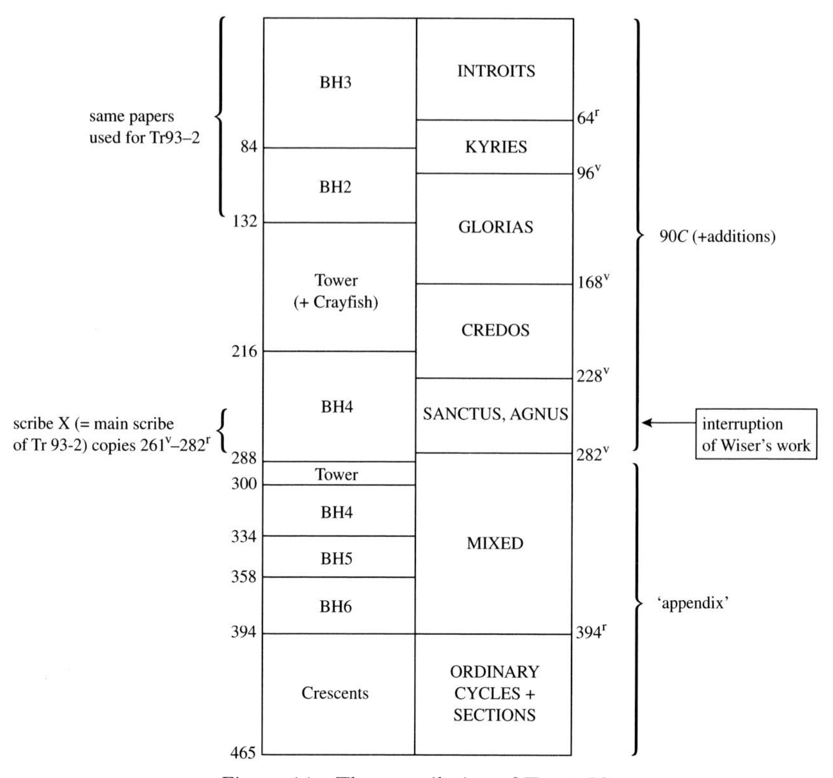

Figure 14 The compilation of Trent 90

ther contribution to this or any of the later codices would support the idea that the two men became separated around this time.

The news of Wiser's appointment at Trent Cathedral could have occurred suddenly and unexpectedly, necessitating a precipitate departure from Munich. Young musicians working in the *Kantorei* as assistants to the schoolmaster and succentor had to be prepared, as Strohm observes, 'to learn quickly and to take up jobs elsewhere at short notice like the travelling apprentices of other crafts and trades'.[99] Wiser could have delegated the task of completing the copy of the Trent 93 main layer to a colleague while he prepared himself for his departure, perhaps suspending his copying activities during the ensuing journey. At that stage he would presumably have had residues of the Tower and BH4 papers waiting to be

[99] Strohm, *The Rise of European Music*, p. 290.

inscribed, and perhaps also the BH5 paper, whereas the two papers that complete the volume, BH6 and Crescents, are more likely to have been purchased en route to Trent or on arrival there.

If indeed Wiser did begin work on Trent 90 in Munich, where might he have been employed? Arguably the most plausible context in the city for his early career is that provided by the church of St Peter, principal church of the diocese in the mid-fifteenth century and one renowned for its musical traditions.[100] With a foundation dating back to the origins of the city itself, St Peter's is regarded as being synonymous with the beginnings of music in Munich. From the thirteenth century it had its own school, where the boys received an education in the liberal arts and instruction in singing. While the records of musical activities may be sparse prior to the sixteenth century, we know, for instance, that from 1343 the boys of the choir school sang spiritual songs as part of the procession for Corpus Christi, and that in 1384 a nine-bellow organ was built for the church by Lorenz von Polling. The church had a cantor and its own school;[101] we even know the name of the schoolmaster who was in post at the time when Wiser would have been embarking on his scribal career.[102] Given the pattern of that career, it would seem that this is just the kind of background from which he is likely to have emerged: a church choir school where, as one of the schoolmaster's *Astanten* (assistants), he would have been engaged in copying music and helping with the training of the boys.[103]

At this stage of his career – the early 1450s – Wiser must have been in his early twenties; he had probably just completed, or was in the process of completing, his university education.[104] A birth

[100] For a brief outline of the early history of the musical activities of the church, see B. A. Wallner, 'Beiträge zur Geschichte der Kirchenmusik bei St. Peter in München bis Ende des 17. Jahrhunderts', *St. Peters-Kalender für das Jahr 1917* [Munich, 1917], pp. 52–7. Still the best historical overview of music in Munich is that given in O. Ursprung, *Münchens Musikalische Vergangenheit: Von der Frühzeit bis zu Richard Wagner* (Munich, 1927); see also the entry 'München' in *Die Musik in Geschichte und Gegenwart*^{2}: *Sachteil*, vi (1997), cols. 582–3.

[101] For mid-fifteenth-century references to the posts of cantor and schoolmaster, see M. J. Hufnagel and F. von Rehlingen, *Pfarrarchiv St. Peter in München: Urkunden* (Bayerische Archivinventare, 35; Neustadt an der Aisch, 1972), p. 47, no. 129; also p. 42, no. 119.

[102] *Ibid.*, p. 50, no. 138: the rector in 1453 was Johannes Wirtel.

[103] See Strohm, *The Rise of European Music*, pp. 289–90.

[104] It is not known where Wiser took his first degree. Staehelin, 'Trienter Codices und Humanismus', pp. 165–6, noting that there is no record of a Johannes Wiser having matriculated at the University of Vienna, suggests that he may have studied in Italy.

date of about 1430 seems very likely. This would be perfectly compatible with the fact that Wiser was apparently still alive as late as 1503,[105] and would fit comfortably with the knowledge that he was probably ordained a priest – for which the normal minimum age was twenty-four[106] – some time between July 1455 and March 1458.[107] Trent 90 thus seems almost certain to be the product of a man in his early or mid-twenties; the elementary nature of many of Wiser's mistakes, and the particularly pronounced script changes that occur in the course of the manuscript, suggest a scribe on a steep learning curve. To what extent his exceptional assiduity as a music copyist was self-motivated, and to what extent driven by external factors, is impossible to determine. But it may be that Wiser was in some sense perceived as a torch-bearer for the 'fourth man' in this nexus of Tridentine musicians, Johannes Lupi, compiler and owner of the two earliest Trent Codices.

Lupi's will, the autograph document that provides the key to his identity as the compiler and principal scribe of Trent 87 and 92,

Proposing Padua, Pavia, Ferrara and Bologna as possibilities, he reports a negative find in the case of Bologna (see G. Knod, *Deutsche Studenten in Bologna (1289–1562)*, [Berlin], 1899). There is no matriculation record for Wiser at Padua either (see *Acta Graduum Academicorum Gymnasii Patavini, ab anno 1435 ad annum 1450*, ed. J. Brotto (Padua, 1970) and *Acta Graduum Academicorum Gymnasii Patavini, ab anno 1451 ad annum 1460*, ed. M. P. Ghezzo (Padua, 1990), Fonti per la Storia Università di Padova, 4 and 11). The possibility raised by Spilsted ('The Paleography and Repertory', p. 174, n. 9) that Wiser is the 'Johannes Organista de Monaco' who matriculated at the University of Vienna in 1454/55 (*Die Matrikel der Universität Wien . . .*, ed. Szaivert and Gall, i, p. 31, no. 47) cannot be ruled out, and it certainly acquires added interest in the light of the present proposal that work on Trent 90*C* may have been drawing to a close at around this time (the date of matriculation was 2 November 1454, not the summer semester of 1455 as given by Spilsted). While there is no reason why Wiser could not have travelled from Munich to Trent via Vienna (although this would leave unanswered the question of if and how he completed his degree), it should be pointed out that my own watermark searches of dated Viennese manuscripts of the 1450s have so far revealed no trace of any of the Trent 90/93 papers.

[105] Gozzi, *Il manoscritto Trento, Museo Provinciale d'Arte, cod. 1377 (Tr 90)* (above, n. 22), p. 11, n. 22, cites a payment of 13 March to 'Viser pro scriptura procuratorii'. Prior to this the latest known reference to Wiser is in a chapter document of 12 April 1497 (TAC, Instrumenta Capitularia XIII, fol. 135^{v}; cited in G. Boni, 'Origini e memorie della chiesa plebana di Tione', *Studi Trentini di Scienze Storiche*, 19 (1938) [part 3], p. 253).

[106] *Dictionnaire de droit canonique*, ed. R. Naz, 7 vols. (Paris, 1935–65), 'Ordination Sacrée', vi, col. 1126.

[107] The document of 30 July 1455 citing Wiser as succentor (TAC, Instrumenta Capitularia IX, fol. 284^{r-v}) refers to him simply as 'Johannes Wissar', suggesting he had not yet been ordained a priest, whereas in the document of 3 March 1458 (*ibid.*, fol. 333^{r-v}), in which he is first cited as 'magister scolarium', and in all subsequent archival references, his name is accompanied by the title 'dominus'. As master of a church school he would have needed to be ordained.

was drawn up before 30 July 1455; it seems he had fallen seriously ill (at one point he was even mistaken for dead) and was making the necessary provision.[108] The period during which he is most likely to have made his will – the first half of 1455 or the late months of 1454 – was also, as we have seen, the very period when Wiser is most likely to have completed his work on Trent 90*C* and travelled to Trent to take up his new appointment. While it may be merely fortuitous that he did so at the time of Lupi's apparent decline, it may equally be that something more than coincidence was at work here.

Wiser must have quickly become acquainted with Lupi once he arrived in Trent (assuming that they did not know each other previously). Whatever the state of Lupi's health in the middle of 1455, he evidently recovered well enough to be able to continue with at least some of his duties, which apparently included those of cathedral organist, until his death in 1467.[109] Organist and succentor must have worked together closely on a regular basis; when Wiser was installed as a cathedral altarist in 1459, it was Lupi who was named as collator of the benefice, a task normally entrusted to a friend or close acquaintance. There is even evidence to suggest that at some level they collaborated, since the two groups of manuscripts for which they were respectively responsible are scribally connected.[110] Moreover it appears that Lupi must have altered his original bequest of his music books to the parish church of his native town of Bolzano, since there is no record of the bequest having been executed or of the codices having belonged to this church. An encounter between the two men – one ailing, his career as a musical scribe over, the other young, energetic and at the outset of his – could have provided precisely the impulse for such a change of mind, and prompted Lupi to bequeath his music books to his younger colleague. But it could also be that

[108] For full details of Lupi's biography, see Wright, 'On the Origins' (above, n. 9), pp. 255–60.

[109] The only references to Lupi's appointment as organist date from the early 1450s, but since it was customary for this post and that of altarist of San Maxentia in Trent Cathedral to be held concurrently, and since Lupi is known to have occupied the latter post from at least 1447 until his death, it seems reasonable to suppose that he remained organist for the rest of his life (Wright, 'On the Origins', p. 257). The likelihood that he did so is confirmed by the fact that no successor to him was appointed until 1467 (Gozzi and Curti, 'Musica e musicisti', p. 92).

[110] See Wright, *The Related Parts* (above, n. 56), pp. 83–6.

Lupi's apparent demise itself prompted the search for a suitable figure to 'carry the torch'. Although there is no evidence that Lupi was active as a music copyist beyond the early 1440s, his lengthy tenure of the post of cathedral organist suggests that he remained a significant and influential musical figure in the locality. It could well be that a need was felt to replace his skills in some shape or form, and that the post of succentor was even created specifically in response to this need.[111]

The idea that parts of Trent 90 and Trent 93 may be of Bavarian origin finds support in an important study by Nicole Schwindt, who claims to have discovered traces of Bavarian dialect in the two German songs located in Trent 93-2 (and copied by Wiser's assistant, scribe X, on the same paper that opens Trent 90), and has identified both these pieces and the first of the two German songs in Trent 90, entered just a few folios after the conclusion of Trent 90*C*, as works belonging to the south German/Bavarian tradition of song writing.[112] And the fact, noted by Schwindt, that the only concordances to any of these three works occur in sources with Bavarian/south German connections[113] may not be without signif-

[111] The first known reference to the post of succentor in the cathedral chapter acts is that associated with Wiser. However, Lupi's will, which probably dates from just a few months earlier, contains a bequest to an unnamed holder of this office (Wright, 'On the Origins', p. 270, ll. 138–9). This could be a reference to Wiser, or to the occupant of a post in the parish of Caldaro, where Lupi was rector. One of the wealthiest and most important parishes of the diocese, Caldaro appears to have had its own school and *rector scolarum* (TAC, Capsa 26, no. 23–1).

[112] Schwindt, 'Die weltlichen deutschen Lieder' (above, n. 32), pp. 46–54. The two songs in Trent 93-2 are *Dein trew dy ist noch wol* (fol. 368r) and *Der summer gar leiplichen* (fol. 369v), and the first of the Trent 90 songs is *Mein hertz in staten trewen* (fol. 294v). To these observations one might add the fact that the work that immediately follows Trent 90*C*, *Parle qui par la vudra*, with the contrafact 'Nesciens mater virgo virum' (fol. 282v), is otherwise known only from a Bavarian source, albeit a much later one, namely the collection of songs and Gregorian chant assembled and copied by Johannes Greis, schoolmaster at the Benedictine Abbey of Benediktbeuern, in 1495 (MBS, Cgm 5023). The song appears in this source with the contrafact 'O salutaris refectio'. A thematic index of the polyphonic pieces is given in *Handschriften mit mehrstimmiger Musik des 14., 15. und 16. Jahrhunderts*, ed. K. von Fischer and M. Lütolf (Répertoire International des Sources Musicales, B IV 3–4; Munich and Duisberg, 1972), B IV 3, pp. 360–72. According to Lorenz Welker (private communication), the dialect features identified by Schwindt as Bavarian are also to be found in the Tyrol.

[113] Schwindt, 'Die weltlichen deutschen Lieder', p. 46. *Der summer gar leiplichen* has concordances with the Lochamer Liederbuch (Staatsbibliothek zu Berlin, Preußischer Kulturbesitz, MS 40613), which was copied in or near Nuremberg during the 1450s, and the Buxheim Orgelbuch (MBS, Cim. 352b), which, while unlikely as formerly believed to emanate from Munich, contains a repertoire with strong connections with this region. (On the origin of this manuscript see Lorenz Welker's forthcoming article 'Das

icance in the present context. While the number of mid-fifteenth-century polyphonic sources previously known or suspected as being of south Bavarian origin may be small, it is still larger than for other parts of central Europe and furnishes ample evidence of polyphonic practice in the region.[114] The fact that it includes no vocal sources of sacred polyphony should not, however, stand in the way of acceptance of the idea that Trent 90 and at least part of Trent 93 may be Bavarian in origin. Had the Trent Codices not survived, what grounds could there ever have been for claiming the city of Trent as an important centre for polyphonic music? Or to put the question another way: 'Since nobody would have suspected the existence of the Trent collection before it was discovered, how many other centres of polyphonic musical practice around Europe might be forgotten today?'[115]

Strohm's theory of the origins of Wiser's collection, which is partly a reformulation of the old Austrian position, remains an attractive one. The idea that the initiation of what was to become the most important musical collection of the fifteenth century was the result of a 'comprehensive re-orientation' within the church at Trent seems distinctly plausible. And one can see the appeal of such an idea to a scholar who has engaged as fully as Strohm has done with issues concerning the relationship between central European musical sources and the institutions for which they were created (not to mention the extent to which he has furthered our understanding of these issues). But the absence of firmer supporting evidence makes Strohm's theory hard to sustain. So far there is no real basis for believing that Hinderbach's appointment as provost had the far-reaching effects that Strohm claims: there is no evidence that he was present in Trent either before or during his time as provost, or that at this point in his career he would

Buxheimer Orgelbuch: Provenienz und Überlieferungsgeschichtliche Einordnung', which the author kindly allowed me see in advance of its publication.) *Mein hertz in staten trewen* has a concordance with the Schedel Liederbuch (MBS, Cgm 810), which, though largely copied in Leipzig, has additions possibly made during 1462–3 when its compiler, Hartmann Schedel, was in Augsburg and at his home in Nuremberg.

[114] Of the various fifteenth-century fragments brought to light by Martin Staehelin, at least two are of Bavarian origin. See M. Staehelin, 'Münchner Fragmente mit mehrstimmiger Musik des späten Mittelalters', in *Nachrichten der Akademie der Wissenschaften in Göttingen* I, Phil.-hist. Klasse, Jg. 1988, no. 6 (Göttingen, 1988), pp. 167–90: MBS, Clm 29775, nos. 2 and 6.

[115] Strohm, 'European Cathedral Music', p. 15.

have been in a position to influence decisions there; any connection of him at this stage with either Wiser or Prenner remains entirely speculative.[116] There is, however, evidence, as we have seen, to suggest that Wiser embarked on Trent 90 before Strohm's critical year of 1455, that he did so not in Trent but in southern Bavaria (probably Munich), and that it may have been more as a result of his own natural career aspirations than as a consequence of any grander designs that his great collection came into being.

University of Nottingham

[116] Strohm, *The Rise of European Music*, p. 511, goes as far as to describe Wiser as 'his [that is, Hinderbach's] schoolmaster'. It is, of course, quite possible that Hinderbach, whom Wiser was to serve as a chaplain during the 1470s, was at some level influential on the later development of the collection.

APPENDIX 1

Trent Watermark Equivalents Organised by Type

Note: watermark types are listed in order of their first appearance in Trent 93 and Trent 90. Full details of each source are given in Appendix 2.

Cross (Trent 93-1) *1450–3* Figure 1
ITL, U. I 1350: Innsbruck, 21 January 1450: A
MBH, AR 395: [Landshut, L. Bavaria] 1453: B
MBH, KAA 228: Munich, 17 December 1450: A
MBH, KAA 228: Munich, 25 March or 15 August 1451: A
MBH, KU 27910: Straubing (L. Bavaria), 2 April 1452: B
MS, Kamm. 1/60: [Munich] 1451: A + B
TAS, APV, s.t., Capsa 27.l: Termeno (S. Tyrol) 10 January 1453: A

Bull's head 1 (Trent 93-1) *1450–1, 1454 [or 1452?]* Figure 2
ITL, U. I 3719: Innsbruck, 14 December 1450: A2
ITL, U. I 6223/5: Innsbruck, 10 December 1450: A2
ITL, U. I 6225/24: Innsbruck, 11 June 1451: A2
ITL, U. I 6484/1: Innsbruck, 22 November 1450: A1(?)
ITL, U. I 6484/3: Innsbruck, 20 December 1450: A2(?)
ITL, U. I 6484/4: Innsbruck, 20 December 1450: A2
ITL, U. II 350: Innsbruck, 19 July 1451: A2
MBH, KAA 1949: Starnberg (U. Bavaria), 4 July 1454 [or 1452?]: A2 (later state?)

Cross-on-mounts (Trent 93-1) *1450–3* Figure 3
ITL, U. I 6228/3: Bolzano (S. Tyrol), 19 September 1451: A1
ITL, U. I 6229/25: Innsbruck, 28 November 1451: A1
MBH, AR 395: [Landshut, L. Bavaria], 30 March 1453: A1
MBH, KAA 228: Kötzting (Oberpfalz, Bavaria), 24 September 1451: A1
MBH, KAA 1574: Regensburg (Oberpfalz, Bavaria), 27 June 1450, A2
MBS, Cgm 396: Bavaria 1452: A1 + A2
TAS, APV, s.t., Capsa misc. no. 9: (S. Tyrol/Trentino) 14 November 1451: A2

Bull's head 2 (Trent 93-2, Trent 90) *1452, 1454, 1455* Figure 4
IU, Cod. 45: Stams (N. Tyrol), completed 14 June 1455: A^2 + B^2
MBH, AR 270: Ingolstadt (U. Bavaria) 1452: A^1 + B^1
MBH, KAA 1: Rauhenlechsberg (U. Bavaria), 17 October 1454: A^1

Bull's head 3 (Trent 93-2, Trent 90) *1454* Figure 5
ITL, U. I 3139: [N. Tyrol], mid-fifteenth century: A
MBS, Cgm 379: Augsburg (Schwabia) 1454: A + B

Tower (Trent 90) *1453–4* Figure 6
MBH, AR 395: [Landshut, L. Bavaria] 1453: A*a*? + B*a*
MBH, KU 9753: [Munich?], 6 July 1454: A*a*
MBH, KU 27592: [Munich?], 23 October 1454: A*a*
MBH, KU 35960: [?Schaunberg, U. Austria], 17 April 1454: A*a*
MBS, Cgm 351: [Tegernsee, U. Bavaria], btw. 1440 and 1460: A*b* + B*a/b*
MBS, Cgm 519: Augsburg (Schwabia), completed 26 December 1454: A*b* + B*a* + B*b*
MBS, Cgm 549: Schäftlarn (U. Bavaria) 1454: A*c* + B*a*
MBS, Cgm 572: Augsburg? (Schwabia), btw. 1440 and 1460: A*b* + B*b*
MBS, Cgm 1114: Augsburg (Schwabia), 4 October 1453 – 5 January 1454: A*b* + B*a*

Crayfish (Trent 90) *1453–5* Figures 7 and 8
ITL, Hs. 175: Liechtenberg (N. Tyrol) 1453: $B1^{1}$
ITL, P 1348/2: Bolzano (S. Tyrol), 18 April 1453: $B1^{1}$
ITL, U. II 8396: [Imst, N. Tyrol], 21 July 1455: $B1^{4}$
MBH, AR 270: Ingolstadt (U. Bavaria) 1453: $B2^{1}$
MBH, AR 395: [Landshut, L. Bavaria] 1453: $B2^{1}$
MBH, AR 396: [Landshut, L. Bavaria] 1454: $B1^{3}$ + $B2^{3}$ (+ $B2^{2}$)
MBH, KU 9750: [in or near Landsberg, U. Bavaria], 12 June 1454: $B2^{5}$
MBH, KU 15064: [Riedenburg, L. Bavaria], 17 September 1455: $B1^{4}$
MBH, KU 18489: [Munich?], 19 September 1454: $B1^{2}$
MBH, KU 29241: [U. Bavaria], 10 April 1455: $B2^{5}$
MBS, Cgm 351: [Tegernsee, U. Bavaria], btw. 1440 and 1460: $B1^{1}$
MBS, Cgm 605: Munich, btw. 30 September and December 1454: $B1^{4}$ + $B2^{4}$
MBS, Cgm 641: Polling? (U. Bavaria), btw. 1440 and 1460: $B1^{4}$ + $B2^{4}$
MBS, Cgm 667: Tegernsee? (U. Bavaria), completed 15 March 1455: $B1^{3}$ + $B2^{3}$
MBS, Cgm 688: Bavaria, second half of fifteenth century: $B1^{4}$ + $B2^{4}$
MBS, Cgm 778: Tegernsee (U. Bavaria), early 1454: $B1^{2}$ + $B2^{1}$
MBS, Cgm 781: [Tegernsee, U. Bavaria], 1455: $B1^{3}$ + $B2^{3}$
MBS, Cgm 2153: Bavaria [Munich?], completed 30 October 1454: $B1^{3}$ + $B2^{3}$
MS, Kamm. 1/63: [Munich] 1454: $B1^{1}$
MS, Kamm. 1/64: [Munich] 1455: $B1^{4}$ + $B2^{5}$

Bull's head 4 (Trent 90) *1454–5* Figures 9 and 10
ITL, P 1080: [Bressanone region, S. Tyrol], 9 April 1455: B1*a*
MBS, Cgm 605: Munich btw. *c.* September and December 1454: B1*a* + B2*b* + others
MBS, Cgm 775: Bavaria: Munich? 1454: B2*b*?
MBS, Cgm 2153: Bavaria [Munich?] 1454: B1*b* + B1*c* + B2*a* + B2*b* + B2*c*

Bull's head 5 (Trent 90) *1454, 1455?, 1456, (1457)* Figure 11
ITL, U. II 1679: [Völs, N. Tyrol], 17 March 1456: B
MBH, AR 270: Ingolstadt (U. Bavaria) 1454: A + B
MBH, AR 313: [Ingolstadt, U. Bavaria] 1454/(?55): A + B
MBS, Cgm 351: [Tegernsee, U. Bavaria], btw. 1440 and 1460: A + B
MBS, Cgm 379: Augsburg (Schwabia) 1454: A? + B?
MBS, Cgm 521: Munich? 1456: A + B
MBS, Cgm 744: Rebdorf (nr. Eichstätt, Mittelfranken, Bavaria), btw. 1440 and 1460: A variant + B + B variant
MBS, Cgm 795: Rebdorf (nr. Eichstätt, Mittelfranken, Bavaria), btw. 1440 and 1460: A + B
TAS, APV, s.l. 26.28: Trent, 5 February 1454: A (variant state)

Bull's head 6 (Trent 90) *1454–6* Figure 12
ITL, Hs. 175: Liechtenberg (N. Tyrol) 1454: A + B^1
ITL, Urbar 166/1: Schnals (S. Tyrol) 1455: B^1
ITL, U. I 5982/2: [Innsbruck?], 8 April 1456 or shortly after: A
ITL, U. I 5984/2: Innsbruck, 19 April 1456: B^1
ITL, U. I 5985/4: Innsbruck, 29 April 1456: A
ITL, U. I 8518: (S. Tyrol/Trentino), 17 June 1456 or after: B^2
ITL, U. I 8522: (S. Tyrol/Trentino), 30 June 1456 or after: B^2
IU, Cod. 45: Stams (N. Tyrol) 1455: A + B^1
MBS, Cgm 744: Rebdorf (nr. Eichstätt, Mittelfranken, Bavaria), btw. 1440 and 1460: A + B^1

Crescents (Trent 90, Trent 88) *1456* Figure 13
TAS, APV, s.l. Capsa 22.6: Trent, mid fifteenth century: A + B
TAS, APV, s.l. Capsa 26.28: Trent/Volsana? (Trentino), 25 May 1456: A
TAS, APV, s.t. Capsa 53.xx: Castel Telvana (Trentino), 28 October 1456: A

APPENDIX 2

Archival Documents and Manuscript Books Containing Paper Related to that of Trent 93 and Trent 90

This appendix lists all newly discovered sources of the papers used in Trent 93 and Trent 90.[1] In the vast majority of cases the watermarks contained in these sources are identical to those of the musical codices, but in a small number of cases they are so nearly identical as to suggest a common origin. In each case only the most pertinent information about a source is given. For manuscript books, information about such matters as provenance, date, structure and scribes has been extrapolated from published catalogues. An indication is always given of whether a mark should be viewed from the recto or the verso of a leaf.

Innsbruck: Tiroler Landesarchiv (ITL)

Handschriften (Hss.)

ITL, Hs. 175. Comprises seven oblong-format account books from Liechtenberg (N. Tyrol): one, apparently of 1453,[2] contains Crayfish B1^{1}; another, of 1454, contains BH6-A and BH6-B^{1}.

Parteibriefe (P)

ITL, P 1080. Legal document (with seal) of 9 April 1455, [Bressanone region, S. Tyrol]; single leaf containing BH4-B1*a* (verso). See Figure 9b.

ITL, P 1348, [no. 2]. *Mandatum* (concept, without seal) of 18 April 1453, Bolzano (S. Tyrol); single leaf containing Crayfish B1^{1} (recto). See Figure 7b.

Urbare

ITL, Urbar 166/1. 1455, Schnals (S. Tyrol); 6 fols., unnumbered; uses BH6-B^{1}.

Urkundenreihe I (U. I)

ITL, U. I 1350. Legal document (with seal) of 21 January 1450, Innsbruck; single leaf containing Cross A (recto).

ITL, U. I 3139. Mid-fifteenth-century copy of a letter dated 15 January 1450, Innsbruck; bifolium containing BH3-A (fol. 1^{r}).

[1] A small number of these documents were subsequently found among examples of the Piccard Archive and are listed below in Appendix 3.

[2] Headed 'Raittung von liechtenberg von dem lij Jarnucz', this book appears to have been copied in 1453 (fol. 6^{v}).

ITL, U. I 3719. Receipt (with seal) of 14 December 1450, Innsbruck; single leaf containing incomplete BH1-A2 (verso). See Figure 2c.

ITL, U. I 5982, no. 2. Contemporary copy of a *mandatum* dated 8 April 1456, Innsbruck; unfoliated bifolium containing BH6-A ([fol. 2^v]).[3]

ITL, U. I 5984, no. 2. Letter (with seal) of 19 April 1456, Innsbruck; single leaf containing BH6-B^1 (verso). See Figure 12d.

ITL, U. I 5985, no. 4. Letter (with seal) of 29 April 1456, Innsbruck; single leaf containing BH6-A (recto). See Figure 12b.

ITL, U. I 6223, no. 5. Receipt (with seal) of 10 December 1450, Innsbruck; single leaf containing incomplete BH1-A2 (recto).

ITL, U. I 6225, no. 24. Receipt (with seal) of 11 June 1451, Innsbruck; single leaf containing BH1-A2, partly obscured by seal (verso); document is on same paper and appears to be in same hand as ITL, U. II 350, written the following month (see below).

ITL, U. I 6228, no. 3. Receipt (with seal) of 19 September 1451, Bolzano (S. Tyrol); single leaf containing incomplete Cross-on-mounts A1 (verso).

ITL, U. I 6229, no. 25. Receipt (with seal) of 28 November 1451, Innsbruck; single leaf containing incomplete and partly obscured version of Cross-on-mounts A1 (verso).

ITL, U. I 6484, no. 1. Receipt (with seal) of 22 November 1450, Innsbruck; single leaf containing remains of what appears to be BH1-A1 (recto).

ITL, U. I 6484, no. 3. Receipt (with seal) of 20 December 1450, Innsbruck; single leaf containing remains of what appears to be BH1-A2 (verso).

ITL, U. I 6484, no. 4. Receipt (with seal) of 20 December 1450, Innsbruck; single leaf containing BH1-A2 (recto).

ITL, U. I 8518. Contemporary copy (S. Tyrol/Trentino) of contract dated 17 June 1456, [Trentino]; bifolium containing BH6-B^2 (fol. 2^v).

ITL, U. I 8522. Contemporary copy (S. Tyrol/Trentino) of a letter dated 30 June 1456, Trent; bifolium containing BH6-B^2 (fol. 2^r).

Urkundenreihe II (U. II)

ITL, U. II 350. Letter (with seal) of 19 July 1451, Innsbruck; single leaf containing BH1-A2 (recto); document is on same paper and appears to be in same hand as U. I 6225/24, written the previous month (see above).

ITL, U. II 1679. Contract of 17 March 1456, [Völs, N. Tyrol]; single leaf containing BH5-B (verso).

ITL, U. II 8396. Legal document (with seal) of 21 July 1455, [Imst, N. Tyrol]; single leaf containing Crayfish B1^4 (verso).

[3] The copy bears the date 'Anno lvj' in a fifteenth-century hand.

Innsbruck: Universitätsbibliothek (IU)

IU, Cod. 45. Hugo de Prato Florido. 326 fols. (folio size); Stams (N. Tyrol), completed 14 June 1455 (fol. 323va). Structure: VII $^{13(14)}$ + 26 VI $^{324(326)}$; single scribe.

The last two papers used in the manuscript are BH2 and BH6 respectively. BH2 is used in fols. 224–5 and 233–66, but in distinctly later states than those found in any of the other known sources of this paper (A^{2}: 263^{v}, B^{2}: 251^{r}), and BH6 is used for the remainder of the manuscript (fols. 267–325; A: 324^{r}, B^{1}: 318^{v}).

Munich: Bayerisches Hauptstaatsarchiv (MBH)

Herzogtum Bayern: Ämterrechnungen bis 1506 (AR)
MBH, AR 270. Ingolstadt (U. Bavaria) 1447–55. 462 fols., arranged in eleven gatherings, only some of which are relevant. Each gathering covers one or two years of payments, sometimes with the later year entered first, suggesting that it was in this year rather than the earlier one that the gathering in question was inscribed. The relevant gatherings are as follows:

Gatherings VI (196–242) and VII (243–8): entries from 1451 and 1452, but not in sequence; almost certainly inscribed 1452; BH2 paper used throughout (e.g. A^{1}: 226^{v}, B^{1}: 217^{r}, with possible variant states). See Figures 4b and 4d.

Gathering VIII (249–302):[4] apparently copied in 1453, with most entries dated that year, alongside retrospective payments for 1452; has an insert ([262]/282*a*) dated '1453' containing the remains of Crayfish B2^{1} (282*a*^{r}, clearly in same hand as surrounding material). See Figure 8a.

Gathering X (351–406): apparently copied in 1454, most entries dating from that year, alongside retrospective payments for 1453; uses BH5 (e.g. A: 382^{v}, B: 406^{v}) in all but two sheets.

MBH, AR 313. [Ingolstadt, U. Bavaria] 1454 (1454/?55). '1454 Rechnung im Oberland' on front cover. Eleven folio-size leaves folded vertically and foliated 1–22. Most entries dated 1454, but a few later additions dated 1455 (fols. 15, 16, 19). All but one of the watermarked leaves contain BH5 (A: 1^{r}, 8^{v}, 19^{r}; B: 9^{r}). See Figures 11b and 11d.

[4] Strictly speaking this comprises three gatherings, one of which (249–57 and their conjugate folios, 294–302) encloses two others (258–85 and 286–93).

MBH, AR 395. [Landshut, L. Bavaria] 1453. On front cover: 'Aller Ambtleut Rechnung*en* meins genadigen herrenn herzog ludwigs etc lannde Indem Ranntmaister ambt zu lannczhuet Bey Fridreichen Tobelhaym Ranntmaister Anno Quinquagesimo Tercio etc'. 132 fols. arranged in two gatherings, I (4–62) and II (63–132), which are both preceded by and include a number of inserts, most of which are loose and unbound. All dates contained in the body of the book give the year 1453, although a number of the inserts, the nature of whose relationship to the book is often unclear, bear a date of 1454 (see fols. 3, 32, 46, 61, 89, 114, 115). Relevant watermarks are found in three of these inserts:

fol. 2: receipt (with seal) dated 9 March[5] 1453; contains Cross-on-mounts A1 (recto). See Figure 3b.

fol. 44: dated 1453 and in same hand as surrounding contents; contains Cross B (recto).

fol. 122: Crayfish B2[1] (recto; n.d., but clearly contemporary with surrounding material, all of which dates from 1453).

Gathering II has variety of marks including the Tower, found in two adjacent sheets: fols. 78/116: 78^{r} (B*a*) and 79/112: 112^{v} (A*a*?). See Figure 6e.

MBH, AR 396. [Landshut, L. Bavaria] 1454. On the cover: 'Aller Ambtlaute Rechnungmems genadign Herrn Herzog Ludwigs etc lannde Inndem Ranntmaisterambte zu landzhuet bey Fridrichen Tobelhaimer Ranntmaister vom liiij Jare'. 102 fols. arranged in two gatherings, I (1–48) and II (49–102); Crayfish paper (B1^{3} and B2^{3}) is used in all but two sheets of gathering I, and in just one sheet (49^{r}: B2^{2}) of gathering II. See Figures 8b and 8d.

Kurbayern: Äußeres Archiv (KAA)

MBH, KAA 1, fol. 20. Concept of 17 October 1454, Rauhenlechsberg (nr. Apfeldorf, U. Bavaria); contains BH2-A^{1} (recto).

MBH, KAA 228, fol. 175. Concept of 17 December 1450, Munich; contains Cross A (verso).

MBH, KAA 228, fols. 187–8. Concept dated 26 March or 20 August[6] 1451, Munich; contains Cross A (187^{r}).

MBH, KAA 228, fol. 239. Letter (with seal) dated 18 September 1451, Kötzting (nr. Cham, Oberpfalz, Bavaria); contains lower portion of Cross-on-mounts A1 (recto).

[5] 'Freitag vor dem Suntag als mon singet letare in der heiligen vasten', here taken to mean the Friday before Laetare Sunday (11 March).

[6] The date, 'freytag nach unsere liebenfrauen tag', could refer to either the Annunciation (25 March) or the Assumption (15 August).

MBH, KAA 1574, fol. 68. Report of 27 June 1450, Regensburg (Oberpfalz, Bavaria); contains Cross-on-mounts A2 (recto).

MBH, KAA 1949, fol. 40. Letter (with seal) of 4 July 1454 [1452?],[7] Starnberg (U. Bavaria); contains BH1-A2 (recto; later state?).

Kurbayern: Urkunden (KU)

MBH, KU 9750. Receipt (with seal) of 12 June 1454, [in or near Landsberg, U. Bavaria]; single leaf containing incomplete Crayfish $B2^5$ (verso).

MBH, KU 9753. Receipt (with seal) of 5 July 1454, [Munich?]; single leaf containing incomplete Tower A*a* (verso). See Figure 6b.

MBH, KU 15064. Legal document (with seal) of 17 September 1455, [Riedenburg, L. Bavaria]; single leaf containing Crayfish $B1^4$, partly obscured (recto).

MBH, KU 18489. Receipt (with seal) of 19 September 1454, [Munich?]; single leaf containing incomplete Crayfish $B1^2$, partly obscured (recto). See Figure 7d.

MBH, KU 27592. Receipt (with seal) of 23 October 1454, [Munich?]; single leaf containing Tower A*a* (recto).

MBH, KU 27910. Receipt (with seal) of 2 April 1452, Straubing (L. Bavaria); single leaf containing Cross B, partly obscured (verso).

MBH, KU 29241. Receipt (with seal) of 10 April 1455, [U. Bavaria]; single leaf containing incomplete Crayfish $B2^5$ (verso).

MBH, KU 35960. Letter (with seal) of 17 April 1454, [?Schaunberg, U. Austria]; single leaf containing Tower A*a* (verso).

Munich: Bayerische Staatsbibliothek (MBS)

MBS, Cgm 351. Heinrich von Langenstein • Evangelistar • Sprüche • Gebete • Meisterlieder. III + 278 fols. (quarto size); [Tegernsee], Bavaria; Part I: btw. 1440 and 1460; Part II: btw. 1420 and 1440.

Two independent parts bound together at the end of the fifteenth century, of which only Part I (2 + 173 + 1) is relevant. New foliation.

Structure of Part I: $(VI\text{-}2)^{10}$ + 6 VI^{82} + IV^{90} + 4 VI^{138} + II^{142} + VI^{154} + V^{164} + $(V\text{-}I)^{173}$.

Nine sections: 1. 1^r–87^v; 2. 87^v–88^r; 3. 91^r–142^v; 4. 143^r–153^v; 5. 153^v–154^r; 6. 155^r–156^r; 7. 156^r–169^r; 8. 169^v–172^v; 9. 173^{r-v}.

Tower paper is used at the end of section 1 (for most of the gather-

[7] Dated 'Sand Ulrichs tag Anno etc. liiij^{do}'. The use of the incorrect superscript form ('do' rather than 'to') may indicate that the scribe meant to date this document 1452 rather than 1454.

ing comprising fols. 83–90) and in section 6 and the opening of section 7 (together occupying one gathering comprising fols. 155–64). A*b* ($83^{r}/90^{v}$) is combined with a mark that may be either B*a* or B*b* ($84^{r}/89^{v}$, $156^{r}/163^{v}$, $158^{r}/161^{v}$): because this is a quarto-size volume and part of a mark is always buried in the 'gutter', it is difficult to be completely certain.

BH5 paper is used alongside Tower paper in section 1 (one sheet: 86/87), and throughout much or most of the section comprising fols. 91–142 (A: $119^{r}/122^{v}$, B: $118^{v}/123^{r}$). A pair of marks closely related to BH5 is found throughout fols. 1–58 and 165–73, and then interspersed with the BH5 pair in fols. 91–142.

Sheets of Crayfish $B1^{1}$ paper are used for sections 4 and 5, contained in a single gathering comprising fols. 143–54 ($144^{r}/153^{v}$, $146^{r}/151^{v}$, $148^{r}/149^{v}$).

MBS, Cgm 379. Augsburger Liederbuch. 225 fols. (quarto-size); Augsburg (Schwabia), *c.*1454, with later additions. At the end of one of the book's numerous sections (fol. 147^{v}) is a completion date of 11 July 1454; at the head of fol. 166^{r} is the date '1454' in the same hand as the contents.

Structure: $(VI\text{-}1)^{11} + 8\ VI^{107} + V^{117} + 9\ VI^{226}$.

New foliation 1–226, skipping from 221 to 223.

BH3, one of three papers used, is employed throughout gatherings II–XI (12–141; A: $14^{r}/21^{v}$; B: $110^{r}/115^{v}$), each of which is in the hand of the main scribe of the manuscript. For most of the rest of the manuscript a paper is used containing marks almost identical to BH5 (A: $170^{v}/173^{r}$, B: $146^{r}/149^{v}$); these represent either different states of the Trent marks or sibling marks. See Figures 5b and 5d.

MBS, Cgm 396. Belial • Ps.-Bernhard de Clairvaux. 110 fols. (quarto size); Bavaria 1452.

Structure: $2\ VI^{24} + (VI\text{-}2)^{35} + VI^{47} + (VI\text{-}1)^{59} + 2\ VI^{83} + VII^{97} + (VI\text{-}2)^{107} + III^{113}$.

New foliation 1–113, skipping from 4 to 6, 32 to 34, 56 to 58; single hand throughout.

Cross-on-mounts paper used in fols. 84–107, combining A1 (e.g. $96^{r}/85^{v}$) and A2 (e.g. $98^{r}/107^{v}$).

MBS, Cgm 519. 'Gemahelschaft Christi' u.a. I + 276 fols. (folio size); Augsburg (Schwabia) 1454 (completed 26 December); apparently written for the monastery of St Ulrich and St Afra.

Structure: $(VI + 1)^{12} + 22\ VI^{275}$; single hand throughout.

New foliation 1–275; does not include blank folio between 178 and 179.

Tower paper is used in a single sheet ($159^{v}/164^{r}$) and four consecutive gatherings (168–215), all of which occur in the first and longest section of the manuscript. A*b* (e.g. 171^{v}) is combined with B*a* (e.g. 183^{r}) and B*b* (e.g. 173^{v}).

The presence at front and rear of the volume of parchment fragments thought to belong to the same manuscript that serviced MBS, Cgm 572 (see below) strengthens the possibility that the two manuscripts share the same provenance and approximate date.

MBS, Cgm 521. Historienbibel • 'König von Reussen' • 'Der Heiligen Leben'. I + 302 fols. (folio-size); Bavaria (Munich?); completed 2 February 1457 (fol. 297^{v}).

Structure: 12 VI^{143} + $(VI\text{-}1)^{149e}$ + 10 VI^{269} + 2 VII^{297}; single hand throughout.

New foliation 1–297, does not include five blank folios between 149 and 150.

Four sections: 1. 1ra–146vb; 2. 146vb–149va; 3. $149^{va–vb}$; 4. 150va–297vb.

BH5 is used throughout fols. 36–143, and in the gathering comprising fols. 144–149*e* (A: 47^{r}; B: 149d^{v}) alongside a paper marked with a decorated tower.

Given the completion date of the manuscript, and the location of the BH5 paper in the first half of the book, it is clear that this paper cannot have been used any later than 1456.

MBS, Cgm 549. Oberbayerisches Landrecht • Wasserburger Stadtrecht. 88 fols. (folio size); Bavaria: Schäftlarn (at least section 1) 1454.

Structure: 6 VI^{72} + $(VI\text{-}2)^{82}$ + $(VI\text{-}8)^{86}$ + $(VI\text{-}10)^{88}$.

At the end of the first of the three sections of the manuscript (55^{r}) is a deleted colophon with the date 1 April 1454 and the name 'Scheftlarn' just legible.

Gatherings I and II (1–24) use Tower paper; the marks are difficult to read because of the dense script: the identity of Tower B*a* (mark and mould) is clear (e.g. 19^{v}), whereas Tower A (3^{r}) appears to be almost but not quite identical to both A*a* and A*b* – hence its designation 'A*c*'.

MBS, Cgm 572. Herzog Ernst, lat. und dt. Prosa. 72 fols. (folio-size); Schwabia: Augsburg?, btw. 1440 and 1460.

Structure: 6 VI^{71}.

Tower paper is used in gathering II (13–24), combining A*b* (e.g. 23^{r}) and B*b* (e.g. 24^{r}); the ensuing change in paper is accompanied by a change of hand. See Figures 6c and 6f.

The presence at front and rear of the volume of parchment fragments thought to belong to the same manuscript that serviced MBS, Cgm 519 (see above) strengthens the possibility that the two manuscripts share the same provenance and approximate date.

MBS, Cgm 605. Otto von Passau • Tauler • Johann von Neumarkt u Martin von Amberg. 212 fols. (folio-size); Munich 1454.

Structure: 17 VI^{203} + (VI-4)^{211}.

Old foliation *I–CXXX*, jumps from 76 to 78, duplicates 84; new continuation 131–211, duplicating 198.

Five sections: 1. 1ra–132vb; 2. 132vb–138ra; 3. 138va–207vb; 4. 207vb–208rb; 5. 208rb–209vb.

Entire manuscript copied by a single scribe (Georg Werder), who indicates that the first section had been completed by 30 September 1454 (132^{v}), and that the remainder of the manuscript was completed the same year (209^{v}).

Crayfish paper is used in fols. 174–209, with a combination of $B1^{4}$ (e.g. 185^{v}) and $B2^{4}$ (e.g. 175^{v}).

BH4 is used in fols. 91–170 and 210 as follows:

B2*b*: 91^{v}, 99^{v}, 101^{r}, 103^{v}, 108^{r}, 117^{v}, 132^{v}, 139^{r}, 142^{r}, 143^{r}, 151^{v}, 154^{r}, 156^{r}, 164^{r}, 165^{r}, 166^{v}, 169^{r}, 210^{v}. See Figure 10c.

B1*a* (= Trent 90): 116^{v}, 119^{v}

B1 variant: 100^{r}, 115^{r}, 136^{v}, 137^{v}, 146^{v}, 148^{v}, 157^{v}, 158^{v}

B variant 1: 98^{v}, 118^{v}, 127^{r}, 129^{r}, 131^{v}, 170^{r}

B variant 2: 128^{v}, 130^{r}.

All the Crayfish paper and most of the BH4 paper must have been inscribed between 30 September and the end of December 1454.

MBS, Cgm 641. Vocabularius Ex quo u.a. • Alanus ab Insulis: Distinctiones. II + 313 fols. (folio size); Bavaria: Polling?; Part I. btw. 1440 and 1460, Part II btw. 1400 and 1450. Two different parts bound together between 1440 and 1460; only Part I (I–183) is relevant.

Structure of Part I: (VII-2)^{14} + 8 VI^{110} + V^{120} + 5 VI^{179} + (V-6)^{183}.

New foliation 1–313, duplicates 166.

Crayfish paper used throughout Part I, combining $B1^{4}$ (e.g. 120^{r}) with $B2^{4}$ (e.g. 101^{r}; a sub-state of this mark is found in fol. 116^{v}). See Figure 8e.

MBS, Cgm 667. Vocabularius Ex quo. 156 fols. (quarto-size); Tegernsee? (U. Bavaria) 1455. Explicit (156^{v}) indicates that the volume was completed 15 March 1455.[8]

[8] The entry for this manuscript in the published catalogue gives the year as 1454. In response to my querying of this interpretation Dr Dietrich Kudorfer of the Bayerisches Staatsbibliothek kindly confirmed 1455 as the correct reading.

Structure: 13 VI^{156}.

Uses a variety of papers, including the Crayfish, which is found in the final gathering (XIII: 145–56) but with the marks split between conjoint folios. States B1^{3} (147^{r}/154^{v} and 149^{v}/152^{r}) and B2^{3} (145^{r}/156^{v}) occur together here.

MBS, Cgm 688. Antonius Rampegolus • Glossare • Gesta Romanorum • Evangelistar • Antonius Azaro de Parma • u.a. I + 251 fols. (quarto size); Bavaria; seven different parts, of which only Part V (192–213*a*), dated second half of fifteenth century, is relevant.

Structure of Part V: VI^{198e} + V^{208} + (V-4)^{213a}.

Factitious manuscript. New foliation 1–243; omits one folio between 66 and 67, counts 76 twice, does not include empty folios (five between 198 and 199, one between 213 and 214).

Part V comprises three gatherings (192–198*e*, 199–208, 209–213*a*), the first and third of which use Crayfish paper, combining B1^{4} (193^{r}/[198*d*^{v}],197^{v}/198^{r}) with B2^{4} (195^{v}/[198*b*^{r}], 211^{v}/213*a*^{v}: the lower part of the mark is obscured by script).[9]

MBS, Cgm 744. Gebete, z. T. Umkreis Johann von Neumarkt • Lektionar • Katechetische Texte • Johannes von Indersdorf • Heinrich von Langenstein. 262 fols. (quarto size); Bavaria: Rebdorf (nr. Eichstätt, Mittelfranken); Parts I, III 1480–1500, Part II btw. 1440 and 1460.

The manuscript was bound together from three different sections. The new foliation skips from 111 to 113, omits one folio between 159 and 160 and does not include empty folios (one between 94 and 95, three between 104 and 105).

Only Part II (105–64) is relevant; structure: 5 VI.

BH5 is used in the first two gatherings of Part II (105–17 and 118–29; B: 106^{v}/116^{r}, 109^{v}/113^{r}; B variant: 108^{v}/114^{r}; A variant: 121^{v}/126^{r}).

BH6 is used in the third gathering (130–41; A: 130^{v}/141^{r}, 133^{v}/138^{r}; B^{1}: 134^{v}/137^{r}). A generically related variant of the Tower B mark occurs in 123^{v}/124^{r}.

MBS, Cgm 775. Johannes von Indersdorf • Spruchsammlung von Eigenbesitz • Büchlein von der geistlichen Gemahelschaft. I + 270 fols. (quarto size); Bavaria: Munich? 1454.

Structure: V^{9} + 14 VI^{171e} + (III+4)^{181} + 5 VI^{241} + (VI-1)^{252} + (VI+1)^{265}.

New foliation 1–265, omitting five empty folios between 171 and 172.

[9] Folios 209 and 213a are artificially conjoined, but since 213a contains the upper part of the mark and 209 the lower part it seems likely that they were originally conjugate leaves.

Four sections: 1. 1^{r}–160^{v}; 2. 160^{v}–165^{r}; 3. 165^{r}–171^{v}; 4. 172^{r}–263^{r}.

Section 4 contains two leaves of BH4, one (173^{r}) with what appears to be the upper half of B2*b*, the other ([$264a^{v}$]) with what appears to be the lower half; each leaf lacks its conjugate, but it does not appear that they were ever conjoined with each other.

MBS, Cgm 778. Mystische Texte, u. a. Meister Eckhart • Acht Traktate des 'Tegernseer Anonymus' • Johannes von Indersdorf • Albrecht Lesch • Cato. 157 fols. (quarto-size); Bavaria, Part I Tegernsee, Parts I–II btw. 1440 and 1460, Part III *c.*1400.

Three different parts bound together, of which only Part I is relevant. New foliation 1–151, not including one empty folio between 99 and 100, another between 121 and 122, and two between 53 and 54 and 140 and 141.

Structure of Part I (1–121^{a}): $I^{2} + 2\ VI^{26} + VIII^{42} + 6\ VI^{111} + (VI\text{-}1)^{121a}$; copied by six hands working contemporaneously.

Total of twenty-two sections, of which nos. 4 (40^{v}–52^{r}) and 5 (52^{v}–53^{v}), both in the same hand, coincide with the relevant paper.

A note on fol. 74^{v} ('han ich dir mit churczen worten yn der benanten czedel geschriben und dir zwm newen jar geschikt anno Xpi 1454') suggests Part I was begun early in 1454.

Crayfish paper used for gathering comprising fols. 43–[53*a*] ($B1^{2}$: $45^{v}/52^{r}$; $B2^{1}$: $47^{v}/50^{r}$, $48^{r}/49^{v}$).

MBS, Cgm 781. Buch von geistlicher Armut. 194 fols. (quarto-size); Bavaria: [Tegernsee], 1455. On fol. 1^{r}, written in a script closely contemporary with the manuscript itself, is the following note: 'Das puchlein ist des closter Tegernsee'.

New foliation 1–193, not counting two empty folios between 1 and 2; skips from 166 to 168.

Structure: $I^{1a} + 4\ VI^{48} + V^{58} + 11\ VI^{191} + (VI\text{-}10)^{193}$; single hand.

Tegernsee shelf-mark on front and rear covers.

Crayfish found in ten consecutive gatherings (71–191); marks are buried in the binding and difficult to read, but appear to be $B1^{3}$ (e.g. $169^{r}/178^{v}$, but with possible evidence of a more advanced state in $173^{v}/174^{r}$) and $B2^{3}$ (e.g. $183^{v}/188^{r}$).

MBS, Cgm 795. Passionen • Heinrich von St. Gallen • Ps.-Bonaventura • Johannes Gerson • Drittordensregel • u.a. 164 fols. (quarto size); Rebdorf (Mittelfranken, Bavaria), Part I end of fifteenth century or beginning of sixteenth; Part II btw. 1440 and 1460.

Two different parts bound together. New foliation 1–148, skipping blank folios, including two between 134 and 135.

Only Part II is relevant, comprising a single gathering (135–48) of BH5 (A: $140^{r}/143^{v}$, B: $135^{v}/148^{r}$, $137^{r}/146^{v}$, $138^{r}/145^{v}$) inscribed essentially by a single copyist.

MBS, Cgm 1114. Belial. 76 fols. (folio-size); Augsburg (Schwabia) 1453–4.
New foliation 1–76.

Structure: 6 VI^{72} + $(\text{III-2})^{76}$. Copied by one scribe, Georg Mülich, apparently btw. 4 October 1453 (3ra) and 5 January 1454 (75va).

Tower paper used in gatherings III–VII (25–76): A*b* (e.g. 57^{r}) and B*a* (e.g. 33^{r} = Trent 90).

MBS, Cgm 2153. Münchener Stadtrecht. III + 47 fols. (folio size), Bavaria [Munich?] 1454.

New folio numbering Ia, I–II, pagination 1–93.

Structure: $(\text{VI-1})^{18}$ + 3 VI^{90} + 2. Copied by one scribe, Andreas Rackendorffer, and completed 30 October 1454; uses two papers, BH4 and Crayfish.

Crayfish combines B1^{3} (e.g. 93) and B2^{3} (e.g. p. 73). See Figures 7e and 8c.

With BH4 the situation is complex, since there is more than one version of each twin:

B1*b*: II^{r}, 4, 5, 32, 36. See Figure 9c.
B1*c*: 22
B2*a*: 24 (= Trent 90). See Figure 10b.
B2*b*: 2, 34, 18 (later state)
B2*c*: 20.

Munich: Stadtarchiv (MS)

MS, Kammerrechnungen 1/60. Munich, city accounts; [Munich] 1451; 108 fols.; Cross paper (A: e.g. 67^{r}, + B: e.g. 55^{r}) used throughout. See Figures 1b and 1d.

MS, Kammerrechnungen 1/63. Munich, city accounts; [Munich] 1454, with later additions from 1455; 121 fols.; volume includes a loose, inserted and unnumbered sheet of Crayfish B1^{1} folded vertically; dated 1454, it apparently forms part of the main contents of the manuscript. See Figure 7c.

MS, Kammerrechnungen 1/64. Munich, city accounts; [Munich] 1455, with later additions from 1456; I + 115 fols.; Crayfish paper ($B1^{4}$: e.g. 115^{v}, + $B2^{5}$: e.g. 110^{v}) used throughout. See Figures 7f and 8f.

Trent: Archivio di Stato, Archivio Principesco-Vescovile (TAS, APV)

Sezione Latina (s.l.)

TAS, APV, s.l., Capsa 22.6. Investiture book, 342 fols; uses a large variety of papers; apparently copied in Trent; bears dates ranging from 1447 to 1464; it is clear from the relationship between the dates of individual gatherings and the papers on which they are inscribed that this must be wholly or partly a retrospective collection. One gathering, that comprising fols. 183–94, bears dates from 1447 to 1450, yet uses Crescents paper (A: 186^{v}; B: 187^{v}, 188^{v}, 192^{r}, 193^{r}, 194^{r}), a paper otherwise known only from two documents of 1456. See Figure 13d.

TAS, APV, s.l., Capsa 26.28. Eight loose, unnumbered sheets, each containing a single document. Among these are: (i) a receipt (with seal) of 5 February 1454, Trent, containing BH5-A (verso; variant state); (ii) a receipt (with seal) of 25 May 1456, Trent/Volsana? (Trentino), containing Crescents A (verso).

Sezione Tedesca (s.t.)

TAS, APV, s.t., Capsa 27.l. Receipt (with seal) of 10 January 1453, Termeno (= Tramin, S. Tyrol); contains Cross A (recto).

TAS, APV, s.t., Capsa 53.xx. Inventory (with seal) of Castel Telvana, nr. Trent (Trentino), dated 28 October 1456; unfoliated bifolium containing Crescents A ([fol. 1^{r}]). See Figure 13b.

TAS, APV, s.t., Capsa misc. no. 9. Letter (with seal) of 14 November 1451 (S. Tyrol/Trentino); large sheet containing Cross-on-mounts A2 (verso). See Figure 3d.

APPENDIX 3

Trent 93 and Trent 90 Watermark Data

This appendix presents a synopsis of published and unpublished data for each watermark or pair of watermarks contained in Trent 93 and Trent 90, listing these in order of first appearance in the two musical codices. Each entry falls into two parts:

1. A description of the watermark type; the measurements of each mark to the nearest half-millimetre (height then width, these dimensions referring to the most distant opposite points unless otherwise indicated); the position of each mark's attendant chain-lines (referred to by counting from left to right); the archival equivalent cited by Saunders (with reference to Piccard) and the degree of actual identity involved.
2. A list of all examples in the Piccard Archive (see above, n. 41) that have been found to be either the same as ('=') or bearing a close similarity to ('≈') the Trent mark(s) in question. The details accompanying each drawing (archival details, place and date) are those provided by Piccard.

Key to abbreviations:

FA Nst	Neuenstein, Hohenlohe-Zentralarchiv
HStA	Hauptstaatsarchiv Stuttgart
HStAMÜ	Hauptstaatsarchiv Munich (= MBH)
mLF°	mould-side, left folio (designated 'A')
mRF°	mould-side, right folio (designated 'B')
SAA	Stadtarchiv Augsburg
SAF	Stadtarchiv Frankfurt am Main
SAGÖ	Stadtarchiv Göttingen
SA, MÜ	Stadtarchiv Munich (= MS)
SAN	Stadtarchiv Nördlingen
StAJ	Staatsarchiv Innsbruck (= ITL)
StAK	Stadtarchiv Königsberg

Cross (Trent 93-1)   Figure 1

Small cross on a base.

A: 33.5 × 24.5 [3, 4]   B: 33.5 × 25 [3, 4]

Only one mark is reproduced in Saunders (Figure 17, p. 245 = A), which is equated (p. 203) with Piccard Findbuch XI, Kreuz II 463, where it is given in reverse. This is a good match, as is II 464 for Cross B. (For details of the actual source of these marks, see Appendix 2, s.v. 'MS, Kammerrechnungen 1/60'.)

Piccard Archive: Fach 12/12
FA Nst Li A 23: Meissen (nr. Dresden) 1451 ≈ A
SA, MÜ Kammerrechnungen: Munich 1451 = A (see Appendix 2, s.v. MS)
SAN Missive: Munich 1450 ≈ B
StAK O.B.A.: Neuhaus (= Gurjevsk, Russia), May 1451 ≈ A in reverse

Bull's head 1 (Trent 93-1) Figure 2

Bull's head without eyes, surmounted by a five-petal flower on a single stem.
Both members of the pair appear in mLF° and are therefore designated 'A1' and 'A2'.
A1: 118 × 34.5 [3, 4] A2: 116 × 35.5 [3, 4]
Only one mark is reproduced in Saunders (Figure 18, p. 246 = A1), which is equated (p. 203) with Piccard Findbuch II, Ochsenkopf XII 67–8. XII 67 is only vaguely related, XII 68 much more strongly, lying especially close to A2.

Piccard Archive: Ochsenkopf Fach 6/1 XII 67–8
StAJ Lehnbücher, Liber fragm. II, 213: Innsbruck 1450 ≈ A1 in reverse
StAJ Lehnbücher, Liber fragm. II, 222: Innsbruck 1450 ?= A2 in reverse
StAK O.B.A.: Elbing (= Elblag, Poland), January 1452 ?= A1
StAK O.B.A.: Königsberg (= Kaliningrad, Russia), August 1452 = A2
StAK O.B.A.: Thorn (Toruń, Poland), August 1451 ?= A2 in reverse

Cross-on-mounts (Trent 93-1) Figure 3

Three mounts surmounted by a cross on a two-line stem.
Both members of the pair appear in mLF° and are therefore designated 'A1' and 'A2'.
A1: 105.5/106 × 34 [3, 4] A2: 105.5/106 × 30 [3, 4]
Saunders's Figure 19 (p. 247 = A2) is equated (p. 203) with unpublished German marks from 1451 (Lauingen) and 1452 (Königsberg), which presumably correspond to examples listed below.

Piccard Archive: Fach 13/12
SAGÖ Kämmereiregister: Göttingen (Lower Saxony) 1452/53 ≈ A1
SAN Missive: Lauingen (Schwabia, Bavaria) 1451 ≈ A2 in reverse
SAN Missive, Wemding (Schwabia, Bavaria) 1454 = A1
StAK O.B.A.: Königsberg (= Kaliningrad, Russia), March 1452 ≈ A2
StAK O.B.A.: Löbau (nr. Dresden), September 1452 ≈ A2
StAK O.B.A.: Marienburg (= Malbork, Poland), April 1455 = A1

Bull's head 2 (Trent 93-2, Trent 90) Figure 4

Bull's head with eyes, surmounted by a seven-petal flower on a single stem forking into a double stem.
A: 104 × 36 [3, 4] B: 100 × 35 [3, 4]
Saunders's Figure 20 (p. 248 = A) is equated (p. 203) with Piccard Findbuch II, Ochsenkopf XIII 39 (Neustadt a.d. Aisch 1454; not 1453–4 as given in Saunders), to which it approximates quite closely. Saunders's Figure 23 (p. 251 = B in reverse) is equated (p. 203) with Findbuch II, Ochsenkopf XIII 37 (Ilgenburg 1455), to which it is quite close.

Piccard Archive: Fach 6/8 XIII 37–9
Seventeen examples ranging from 1451 to 1455, with most concentrated in the years 1452–4; unusually large number of examples, which are so closely related to each other as to suggest that they are representations of the same mark.
FA Nst GA 50, 7: Öhringen (Baden-Württemberg) 1454 = B
FA NSt GA 78 235 and 236: 1454 = B
FA Nst Li.A.23: Öhringen (Baden-Württemberg) 1454 = A, B in reverse
SA Ulm 1109: Nürnberg (Bavaria), March 1452 = ?A, ?B in reverse
StAJ Lehenbücher, Liber fragm II 256: Innsbruck 1452 = A in reverse
StAJ Sigmundiana. IX, 62: Brixen (= Bressanone, S. Tyrol) 1454 = A
StAJ Sigmundiana. VIII, 20: Innsbruck 1452 = B in reverse
StAK O.B.A.: Danzig (= Gdańsk), May 1455 = B in reverse
StAK O.B.A.: Elbing (= Elblag, Poland), March 1455 = A
StAK O.B.A.: Königsberg (= Kaliningrad, Russia) 1452 = B in reverse
StAK O.B.A.: Marienburg (= Malbork, Poland), January 1453 = A
StAK O.B.A.: Rawe (? = Rawa Mazowiecka, Poland), April 1453 = B in reverse

Bull's head 3 (Trent 93-2, Trent 90) Figure 5

Bull's head with eyes, surmounted by a six-petal flower on a single stem.
A: 91 × 33 [4, 5] B: 92.5 × 34 [2, 3]
Saunders's Figure 21 (p. 249 = B) is equated (p. 203) with Piccard Findbuch II, Ochsenkopf XII 255 (1452–6); the match, while the best among the published examples, is not particularly close. Saunders's Figure 22 (p. 250 = A, apparently in reverse) is equated (p. 203) with Piccard Findbuch II, Ochsenkopf XII 254 and 257, neither of which provides a convincing match. Piccard groups 254–7 together and gives a date range of 1452–6 for those variants whose dimensions correspond most closely to the BH3 marks.

Piccard Archive: Fach 6/3 XII 254–7
Twenty examples, drawn from a wide geographical and chronological spectrum (1451–71). Of these, just eight show some meaningful correspondence to the Trent marks, though none could be considered equivalent or near-equivalent. Those documents whose location is known come from Augsburg (one: 1451), Gdańsk (one: 1452), Nördlingen (three: 1452, 1453) and Öttingen (one: 1454).

Tower (Trent 90) Figure 6

Tower with three merlons. The Trent 90 twins are designated 'A*a*' and 'B*a*' in order to distinguish them from a closely related pair, 'A*b*' and 'B*b*'.
A*a*: 54 × 32 [4, 5] B*a*: 53 × 31 [3, 4]
Saunders's Figure 24 (p. 252 = B*a* in reverse) is convincingly equated (p. 203) with Piccard Findbuch III, Turm II 326 (Sterzing 1454, 1455; also given in reverse). Saunders's Figure 25 (p. 253 = A*a*) is apparently equated (p. 203) with Piccard II 327 (Erding, Munich; 1457, 1458), which it only loosely resembles.

Piccard Archive: Fach 8/8 II 171–762
HStA WR 2551: 1453: ?= B in reverse
HStAMÜ Kurbaiern U28869: Erding (U. Bavaria) 1457; only loosely similar to A; bears the number 327
SAF r.s.i. 5048/7: [Munich] 1458; only loosely similar to A*a*; bears the number 327
StAK O.B.A.: Sterzing (= Vipiteno, S. Tyrol), January 1455 = B*a* in reverse; bears the number 326.

Crayfish (Trent 90) Figures 7 and 8

This mark is not a scorpion, as Saunders and others have suggested, but a Crayfish with a letter 'S' appended; the height and width here refer to the body of the fish. Both members of this pair, if viewed with the 'S' at the bottom, appear in mRF° and are therefore designated 'B1' and 'B2'.
B1: 42 × 13.5 [3, 4] B2: 42 × 13.5 [3, 4]
Saunders's Figure 26 (p. 254 = B1 in reverse) is equated (p. 203) with an unpublished example (provenance unspecified) from the Archivio di Stato, Brescia (1453).[10]

Piccard Archive
While there is as yet no published Findbuch that covers this type of mark, there are a number of Crayfish marks in the archive, currently in the process of being sorted. Four of these belong to the same type as the Trent marks:
SA MÜ Kammerrechnungen, Munich 1455 = $B1^4$ (in reverse) + $B2^5$ (see Appendix 2, s.v. MS)
SAN U7488, 1: Nördlingen (Schwabia, Bavaria) 1455 ≈ $B1^4$ in reverse
SAN Missive: Nördlingen (Schwabia, Bavaria) 1455 = $B2^5$ in reverse

Bull's head 4 (Trent 90) Figures 9 and 10

Bull's head with eyes, surmounted by a five-petal flower on a single stem. Both members of the pair appear in mRF°; they are designated 'B1*a*' and 'B2*a*' in order to distinguish them from closely related variants of the same type.
B1*a*: 116 × 33 [2, 3] B2*a*: 121 × 31 [3, 4]
Saunders's Figure 27 (p. 255) is equated (p. 203) with Piccard Findbuch II, Ochsenkopf XII 177 (1454–6); while this certainly provides a close match for the mark shown as Figure 27 (B1*a* in reverse), it provides an even closer match for its twin mark (B2*a* in reverse), with which it is all but identical.

Piccard Archive, Fach 6/2 XII 177–8
Just five examples are given, only three of which may be considered related:
SAN Missive: Wimpfen (Baden-Württemberg) 1455 ≈ B2*a* in reverse
SAN Missive: Nördlingen (Schwabia, Bavaria) 1455: ≈ B1*a*

[10] This could be the example reproduced in Mazzoldi, *Filigrane di cartiere bresciane* (see n. 58 above).

StAJ Sigmundiana XIII, 70: Brixen (= Bressanone, S. Tyrol) 1454 = B2*a* in reverse; this must be the example published as Piccard Findbuch II, Ochsenkopf XII 177.

Bull's head 5 (Trent 90) Figure 11

Bull's head with eyes, surmounted by a seven-petal flower on a two-line stem.
A: 110.5 × 34.5 [centred on chain-line 4]
B: 109 × 34.5 [centred on chain-line 3]
Saunders's Figure 28 (p. 256 = B in reverse) and Figure 29 (p. 257 = A) are equated (p. 203) with Piccard Findbuch II, Ochsenkopf XIII 246–7 (1452–9). 246 is a poor match for A or B, 247 a reasonably close match for A.

Piccard Archive: Fach 6/9: XIII 246–7
Nineteen examples in all, ranging from 1452 to 1462, most (and the most closely related) of them dating from 1454–5:
SAA Baumeisterrechnungen: Augsburg (Schwabia, Bavaria) 1454 = A + B
SAN Missive: Agram (= Zagreb) 1455 ≈ B in reverse
SAN Missive: Pappenheim (Mittelfranken, Bavaria) 1459 ≈ A
SAN Vollmachten: Eichstätt (Mittelfranken, Bavaria) 1455 ≈ A

Bull's head 6 (Trent 90) Figure 12

Bull's head with eyes, surmounted by a six-petal flower on a single stem.
A: 94 × 34.5 [4, 5] B: 95.5 × 33 [3, 4]
Saunders's Figure 30 (p. 258 = B in reverse) and Figure 31 (p. 259 = A) are equated (p. 203) with Piccard Findbuch II, Ochsenkopf XII 253 (1454–8), which approximates closely to A in reverse.

Piccard Archive: Fach 6/3 XII 253
SAN U7505,1: n.p., 1455: = A in reverse
StAJ MS 175: Liechtenberg (nr. Innsbruck) 1454 = A + B (see Appendix 2, s.v. ITL, Hs. 175)
StAJ U. I 5984: Innsbruck 19 April 1456: = B (see Appendix 2, s.v. ITL)
StAJ U. I 5982: Innsbruck 8 April 1456: = A (see Appendix 2, s.v. ITL)
There are several examples from Böblingen (one: 1456), Bressanone (two: 1458) and St Raphaelsberg (three: 1458) that provide loose approximations.

Crescents (Trent 90)   Figure 13

Two crescents surmounted by a star on a single stem.
A: 33 × 28 [3, 4]   B: 33 × 29 [3, 4]
Apparently no published examples.
Saunders's Figure 32 (p. 260 = B in reverse) is equated (p. 203) with TAS, APV, s.l., Capsa 26.28 (see Appendix 2); this document in fact uses Crescents A rather than B.

Early Music History (2003) Volume 22.
Printed in the United Kingdom

INSTRUCTIONS FOR CONTRIBUTORS

EDITORIAL POLICY

Early Music History is devoted to the study of music from the early Middle Ages to the end of the seventeenth century. The journal demands the highest standards of scholarship from its contributors, all of whom are leading academics in their fields. *Early Music History* gives preference to studies pursuing interdisciplinary approaches and to those developing new methodological ideas. The scope is exceptionally broad and includes manuscript studies, textual criticism, iconography, studies of the relationship between words and music, and the relationship between music and society.

1. SUBMISSIONS

All contributions and editorial correspondence should be sent to: The Editor, Dr Iain Fenlon, *Early Music History*, King's College, Cambridge CB2 1ST, UK. The Editor can also be contacted via email at iaf1000@cus.cam.ac.uk.

Submission of an article is taken to imply that it has not previously been published, and has not been submitted for publication elsewhere. Upon acceptance of a paper, the author will be asked to assign copyright (on certain conditions) to Cambridge University Press.

Contributors are responsible for obtaining permission to reproduce any material in which they do not own copyright, to be used in both print and electronic media, and for ensuring that the appropriate acknowledgements are included in their manuscript.

2. MANUSCRIPT PREPARATION

All contributions should be in English and must be double spaced throughout, including footnotes, bibliographies, annotated lists of manuscripts, appendixes, tables and displayed quotations. In the event of the manuscript being accepted for publication the author will be asked to submit the text on computer disk (Apple Macintosh or IBM compatible PC) as well as in hard copy, giving details of the wordprocessing software used (Microsoft Word or WordPerfect). However, the publisher reserves the right to typeset material by conventional means if an author's disk proves unsatisfactory.

Typescripts submitted for consideration will not normally be returned unless specifically requested.

Artwork for graphs, diagrams and music examples should be, wherever possible, submitted in a form suitable for direct reproduction, bearing in mind the maximum dimensions of the printed version: 17.5 × 11 cm (7″ × 4.5″). Photographs should be in the form of glossy black and white prints, measuring about 20.3 × 15.2 cm (8″ × 6″).

All illustrations should be on separate sheets from the text of the article and should be clearly identified with the contributor's name and the figure/example number. Their approximate position in the text should be indicated by a marginal note in the typescript. Captions should be separately typed, double spaced.

Tables should also be supplied in separate sheets, with the title typed above the body of the table.

3. TEXT CONVENTIONS

Spelling

English spelling, idiom and terminology should be used, e.g. bar (not measure), note (not tone), quaver (not eighth note). Where there is an option, '-ise' endings should be preferred to '-ize'.

Punctuation

English punctuation practice should be followed: (1) single quotation marks, except for 'a "quote" within a quote'; (2) punctuation outside quotation marks, unless a complete sentence is quoted; (3) no comma before 'and' in a series; (4) footnote indicators follow punctuation; (5) square brackets [ ] only for interpolation in quoted matter; (6) no stop after contractions that include the last letter of a word, e.g. Dr, St, edn (but vol. and vols.).

Bibliographical references

Authors' and editors' forenames should not be given, only initials: where possible, editors should be given for Festschriften, conference proceedings, symposia, etc. In titles, all important words in English should be capitalised; all other languages should follow prose-style capitalisation, except for journal and series titles which should follow English capitalisation. Titles of series should be included, in roman, where relevant. Journal and series volume numbers should be given in arabic, volumes of a set in roman ('vol.' will not be used). Places and dates of publication should be included. Dissertation titles should be given in roman and enclosed in quotation marks. Page numbers should be preceded by 'p.' or 'pp.' in all contexts. The first citation of bibliographical reference should include all details; subsequent citations may use the author's surname, short title and relevant page numbers only. *Ibid.* may be used, but not *op. cit.* or *loc. cit.*

Abbreviations

Abbreviations for manuscript citations, libraries, periodicals, series, etc. should not be used without explanation; after the first full citation an abbreviation may be used throughout text and notes. Standard abbreviations may be used without explanation. In the text, 'Example', 'Figure' and 'bars' should be used (not 'Ex.', 'Fig.', 'bb.'). In references to manuscripts, 'fols.' should be used (not 'ff.') and 'v' (verso) and 'r' (recto) should be typed superscript. The word for 'saint' should be spelled out or abbreviated according to language, e.g. San Andrea, S. Maria, SS. Pietro e Paolo, St Paul, St Agnes, St Denis, Ste Clothilde.

Note names

Flats, sharps and naturals should be indicated by the conventional signs, not words. Note names should be roman and capitalised where general, e.g. C major, but should be italic and follow the Helmholtz code where specific ($C_{,,}$ $C_{,}$ C c c' $c''$$c'''$; c' = middle C). A simpler system may be used in discussions of repertories (e.g. chant) where different conventions are followed.

Quotations

A quotation of no more than 60 words of prose or one line of verse should be continuous within the text and enclosed in single quotation marks. Longer quotations should be displayed and quotation marks should not be used. For quotations from foreign languages, an English translation must be given in addition to the foreign-language original.

Numbers

Numbers below 100 should be spelled out, except page, bar, folio numbers etc., sums of money and specific quantities, e.g. 20 ducats, 45 mm. Pairs of numbers should be elided as follows: 190–1, 198–9, 198–201, 212–13. Dates should be given in the following forms: 10 January 1983, the 1980s, sixteenth century (16th century in tables and lists), sixteenth-century polyphony.

Capitalisation

Incipits in all languages (motets, songs, etc.), and titles except in English, should be capitalised as in running prose; titles in English should have all important words capitalised, e.g. *The Pavin of Delight*. Most offices should have a lower-case initial except in official titles, e.g. 'the Lord Chancellor entered the cathedral', 'the Bishop of Salford entered the cathedral' (but 'the bishop entered the cathedral'). Names of institutions should have full (not prose-style) capitalisation, e.g. Liceo Musicale.

Italics

Titles and incipits of musical works in italic, but not genre titles or sections of the Mass/English Service, e.g. Kyrie, Magnificat. Italics for foreign words should be kept to a minimum; in general they should be used only for unusual words or if a word might be mistaken for English if not italicised. Titles of manuscripts should be roman in quotes, e.g. 'Rules How to Compose'. Names of institutions should be roman.

4. PROOFS

Typographical or factual errors only may be changed at proof stage. The publisher reserves the right to charge authors for correction of non-typographical errors.

5. OFFPRINTS

Contributors of articles and review essays receive 25 free offprints and one copy of the volume. Extra copies may be purchased from the publisher if ordered at proof stage.